POSTCARDS FROM AUSCHWITZ

Postcards from Auschwitz

Holocaust Tourism and the
Meaning of Remembrance

Daniel P. Reynolds

NEW YORK UNIVERSITY PRESS

New York

NEW YORK UNIVERSITY PRESS
New York
www.nyupress.org

References to Internet websites (URLs) were accurate at the time of writing. Neither the author nor New York University Press is responsible for URLs that may have expired or changed since the manuscript was prepared.

Library of Congress Cataloging-in-Publication Data
Names: Reynolds, Daniel P., author.
Title: Postcards from Auschwitz : Holocaust tourism and the meaning of remembrance / Daniel P. Reynolds.
Description: New York : New York University Press, [2018] |
Includes bibliographical references and index.
Identifiers: LCCN 2017038142 | ISBN 9781479860432 (cl : alk. paper)
Subjects: LCSH: Holocaust, Jewish (1939–1945)—Historiography. |
Concentration camps—Europe. | Holocaust memorials. |
Heritage tourism—Social aspects. | Dark tourism—Social aspects. |
Collective memory.
Classification: LCC D804.348 R49 2018 | DDC 940.53/18—dc23
LC record available at https://lccn.loc.gov/2017038142

New York University Press books are printed on acid-free paper, and their binding materials are chosen for strength and durability. We strive to use environmentally responsible suppliers and materials to the greatest extent possible in publishing our books.

Manufactured in the United States of America
10 9 8 7 6 5 4 3 2 1
Also available as an ebook

CONTENTS

PREFACE AND ACKNOWLEDGMENTS

The first concentration camp memorial I ever visited was Breendonk, just north of Brussels, Belgium, where my family lived for several years while my father, a U.S. Army officer, was stationed at NATO headquarters. The occasion was a field trip consisting of about fifty high schoolers and was part of our curriculum on World War II. Breendonk, built in 1909, had been a Belgian fort; in 1940 the SS took it over during the Nazi occupation of Belgium. Built entirely of concrete, the camp was remarkably well preserved—and perhaps the most frightening, cruelest place I had ever seen. The visit impressed the reality of brutality upon me in a way that exceeded my teenage imagination's efforts to comprehend the Third Reich's mass murders through history textbooks or the recently aired television miniseries, *Holocaust*. Our tour was led by a former prisoner who stressed quite emphatically that the camp held captive not only Jews (though Jews did constitute half of the camp's inmates) but also political prisoners such as himself. I remember being struck by the remark, not only because it departed from my exclusive association of concentration camps with Jewish victims but also, perhaps more important, because I thought I detected resentment toward the Nazis' most numerous victims. Whether I understood the guide's sentiments correctly or not, it had never occurred to me that victims might not be united in their suffering, and this impression troubled my idealistic assumption that something positive and harmonious could emerge from the calamity of Nazi terror.

Over the last decade, well after my only prior experience of a concentration camp site, I have toured other camp memorials in Germany, Austria, the Czech Republic, Poland, and France. Yet, at least superficially, the circumstances of these recent tours have not been so different from that of the high school field trip. The thirty intervening years have allowed for deeper preparation, greater agency in my participation, and a richer educational context, but one constant throughout the visits has been a sense of dislocation, experienced as uncertainty about the right way to be—or even whether to be—at these sites. Is speaking at such places appropriate? Photography? I have felt compelled to consider my relationship to a space deemed sacred and to ask whether tourism is an intrusion of the profane. Often it has been the other tourists who have prompted introspection, either by the way the visit visibly affected them or by the behavior of some I found disruptive: people laughing, posing for pictures, or otherwise showing less deference than I assumed appropriate, leaving me to wonder if or how I should respond. In the end, I have always left these tours with the desire to learn more about what I have seen and even to return. This book is an effort to account for that dynamic of dislocation and increased curiosity in my experiences as a tourist.

I am grateful to many people and agencies for their support of this project and their continued encouragement. The research for this book was supported by a grant from the National Endowment for the Humanities, whose advocacy for scholarship in many fields outside the sciences is a vital national resource. I would also like to acknowledge Grinnell College's sustained support of my research through travel grants and time to complete the work. I am grateful to Jennifer Hammer, Dorothea Halliday, and Amy Klopfenstein at New York University Press for their encouragement and feedback and for ushering the book through the publication process. I have many colleagues at Grinnell College to thank, especially David Cook-Martin, Karla Erickson, and Astrid Henry, who offered their critical acumen and their valuable time to support this work at many stages. I am also grateful to my colleagues Jenny Anger, Todd Armstrong, and David Harrison, who took an interest in the work and who each organized and participated in some of the travels and conversations that shaped it. Valerie Benoist also read portions of the project and offered her helpful insight. I'd also like to thank Carolyn Dean, Torben Jorgensen, Thomas Pegelow Kaplan, Desmond Wee, and Stephan Sonnenburg for valuable feedback and opportunities to further develop the research. I thank Konstanty Gebert for enriching my thinking about Polish efforts to remember the Holocaust. Hanna Červinková and Juliet Golden at the University of Lower Silesia organized an especially valuable trip to the Auschwitz-Birkenau Memorial and Museum in 2016. I am grateful to Ian Stout and Luc Janssen for their editorial contributions and to my students, both past and present, who have sharpened my thinking about the subject of this book.

Locally, I am grateful to Mark Finkelstein of the Jewish Federation of Greater Des Moines, Rabbi David Kaufmann, Stephen Gaies at the University of Northern Iowa's Center for Holocaust and Genocide Education, and Elke Heckner at the University of Iowa for opportunities to share this work.

I would especially like to acknowledge Pamela Lalonde and Pepe Avila, who provided needed companionship, conversation, and considerable car mileage to join me on trips to some of Europe's most haunting and remote memorials. Thank you!

Finally, I would like to thank my family: my parents, Patricia and Regis, my sisters, Julie and Jennifer, and my spouse, Garrett, all of whom have been travel companions at various times to the sites explored here but, more important, who have been a constant source of support. This book is dedicated to them.

Introduction

The Auschwitz-Birkenau Memorial and Museum saw record attendance in 2016, receiving more than two million visitors from all over the world. There have been so many tourists to Auschwitz since its establishment as a memorial in 1947 that the concrete steps in the former barracks, now the main exhibition halls, have been worn smooth and concave from heavy foot traffic. Since 1999, when the memorial museum launched its website, the number of tourists to Auschwitz has climbed dramatically.[1] Accommodating such numbers presents enormous logistical challenges for crowd control, for scheduling, and for the provision of personally guided tours in seventeen different languages each day. In the face of such massive demand, how does the memorial provide its visitors with a meaningful experience that amounts to more than macabre voyeurism or crass consumerism? Despite the challenges in managing a site that was never intended to host crowds of tourists, the memorial's mission to remember and prevent future barbarism attracts more people today than ever before. The museum's director, Dr. Piotr M. A. Cywiński, explains the global lure and core message of Auschwitz in the present: "In an era of such rapid changes in culture and civilization, we must again recognize the limits beyond which the madness of organized hatred and blindness may again escape out of any control."[2] It is tempting to read Dr. Cywiński's comment as self-referential, as if the description of controlled madness applies as much to Auschwitz tourism as to the events the museum commemorates and documents.

The first impressions at the Auschwitz-Birkenau Memorial and Museum can indeed be chaotic, with long lines at the ticket windows, tour guides frantically rounding up their groups, a cacophony of languages, a parking lot full of buses entering and exiting. Tourists ostensibly come to learn about the perils of "organized hatred and blindness" that generated the Holocaust; they are challenged to put the values of tolerance into practice as they share limited space with one another. Sightseers vie for elbow room to take photos of confiscated luggage, canisters of poison, prisoner uniforms, crematoria furnaces, and other reminders that more than 1.1 million people were murdered here between 1940 and 1945. They fill the museum bookstores, they stand in line to pay for refreshments and use the restrooms, and they crowd the post office window to mail postcards of the memorial to their friends and family back home. What remains to be seen is whether these visitors take any lessons with them after they leave.

It is this image of buying postcards at Auschwitz that I choose to represent the phenomenon at the heart of this book, "Holocaust tourism." Sightseeing connected to the genocide of European Jews and the murder of millions of other victims will inevitably strike some as a cringeworthy, inauthentic, and commercialized practice that has no place in connection to a history as inviolable as the Holocaust.[3] After all, the problem of understanding Nazi crimes through earnest scholarship or committed art is vexed enough without entering the profane realm of tourism.[4] At first glance, postcards are emblematic of the tackier side of tourism, often depicting clichéd scenic views in garishly enhanced colors, so to discover their presence at the most notorious site of Nazi mass murder seems somewhere between distasteful and obscene. Postcards reflect the presumed superficiality of tourism, a momentary and forgettable act of sharing an image.[5] But postcards have a flip side, literally and figuratively, making them a good metaphor for tourism as a practice that allows for more sophistication than meets the eye. A postcard invites travelers to inscribe their own commentary on the back, to direct the postcard image to a particular audience and to accompany it with a commentary that may undercut the representation of the place the card is meant to promote. Postcards have the capacity to reveal more than the tourism industry authorizes, and they offer a medium for tourists to exercise a degree of critical agency (if they so choose). In contrast to the medium's cliché, postcards from Auschwitz usually exhibit muted tones and portray somber images, indicating a different mode of tourism that promotes reflection, even unease, over enjoyment. Tourists who send a postcard from a place of atrocity are likely to be more self-conscious about what they inscribe on the back, since their own text exposes them to critique by their readers. What could one say on the back of a postcard that could possibly be commensurate with the history of Auschwitz?

As valid as misgivings about postcards from Auschwitz and the phenomenon they represent may be, Holocaust tourism continues to flourish. The recurrence of genocide around the world should make us skeptical that such tourism has done anything to prevent the kind of insanity and violence that, more than seventy years ago, murdered six million European Jews; yet visitors to Holocaust memorials typically express appreciation for the opportunity to learn important lessons about humanity and its capacity for violence. And they do so at a growing number of Holocaust memorial sites in places as far away from the original event as Sydney and Shanghai.[6] Tourists in Washington, DC, wait in long lines to secure limited passes to the United States Holocaust Memorial Museum in similar numbers, with 1.62 million visitors in 2016.[7] Since its completion in 2005, the number of visitors to the information center of Berlin's Memorial to the Murdered Jews of Europe has steadily increased from 360,000 to a record of 475,000 in 2015—a number that does not include the many visitors to the outdoor memorial who do not enter the information center.[8] These numbers are part of a larger picture about tourism of all kinds, which UNESCO characterizes as the world's largest industry and one that is expected to continue to grow globally.[9] Our highly visual global culture seems increasingly obsessed with seeing that which most of us, thankfully, will never endure. It is the job of scholars to offer an account of tourism's motivations and complexities, to take seriously its modalities of signification, to acknowledge both its appeal and its peril, and to put forth the questions that prompt deeper reflection.

At present, there has been little effort to take tourism's role in Holocaust remembrance seriously and attempt to understand not only its popularity but also its possible value. The two terms—"Holocaust" and "tourism"—have only recently been brought together, usually in a context in which the writer can disavow the phenomenon.[10] Indeed, the study of tourism of any kind, let alone Holocaust tourism, is something of a marginal field of inquiry within the academy. Those who research tourism have struggled to have their inquiry taken seriously, combatting well-established attitudes within the realm of scholarship against that which is seen as commercial or frivolous. In contrast, the Holocaust occupies an overwhelming position in Western thought, having defined the trajectory of research in the humanities, social sciences, and even the natural sciences like no other event since 1945. Unlike the study of tourism, the study of the Holocaust has become so firmly established in the academy that some approaches have achieved the status of doctrine, for better or worse. In focusing on Holocaust tourism, this book questions the attitudes and beliefs that inform the study of both the Holocaust and tourism, asking if they are still adequate to address the continued prevalence of the Holocaust in the Western imagination or to acknowledge the new realities of tourism as the world's largest industry.

I enter this discussion as something of an outsider, trained in the field of German studies with a focus on literature. While the Holocaust occupies a central place in German studies, it is a field in its own right that draws on research from numerous other disciplines in the humanities and social sciences. But it is safe to say that tourism has been, at best, a marginal topic in both German studies and Holocaust studies. To undertake an analysis of Holocaust-themed tourism, I have turned to work undertaken largely by anthropologists, whose questions about travelers have helped me immensely in framing my approach. Holocaust tourism is an unwieldy topic that challenges the boundaries of disciplinary knowledge while simultaneously challenging the boundaries of comfortable discourse. The topic fuses two realms of experience—that of the Holocaust as an unparalleled historical event, and that of tourism as a popular mode of intercultural encounter—that are generally kept separate. This book argues that anyone interested in understanding Holocaust tourism engages by necessity in a broadly interdisciplinary inquiry. It draws upon the numerous inquiries into both the Holocaust and tourism that, despite their abundance, have remained largely disconnected from one another. In connecting them, I also rely on personal experiences and observations shared by many Holocaust tourists, as well as my own. The goal here is not to "correct" either disciplinary or non-academic accounts of the Holocaust or tourism but, rather, to engage in a conversation about both the pragmatics and the ethics of Holocaust tourism, to identify problems, and to acknowledge possibilities for contributing to public memory.

The task of theorizing Holocaust tourism is daunting, not least because of the seemingly incommensurate loci of the Holocaust and of tourism in the imagination. The disciplinary developments of Holocaust studies and tourism studies have generated insights and methodologies that have made sense within certain disciplinary confines. Holocaust tourism, however, challenges both fields by exposing the lacunae between the academic theory and an emerging form of practice that neither field has been particularly eager to address.

"Tourism" and "Holocaust": Disciplinary Responses

While the Holocaust has had a prominent role in defining intellectual life in the West since World War II, tourism has received more limited scrutiny within academia, having been marginalized until recently even by those fields where it now flourishes. The more limited interest in tourism studies no doubt relates to the cultural bias against tourism as a lowbrow form of cultural experience.[11] Unflattering stereotypes abound both inside and outside academia, portraying tourists as uncritical consumers who exploit people marketed as Others from exotic places.[12] The difference between the Holocaust and tourism in terms of their perceived importance presents an awkward situation for the student of Holocaust tourism. After all, what could differ more from tourism and its presumed triviality than the Holocaust, around which a complex array of philosophical, ethical, historical, and aesthetic approaches have evolved in response to a cataclysm so profound as to challenge the very foundations of knowledge? Consequently, if tourism is regarded chiefly as a problem, then Holocaust tourism must be a particularly odious form of the activity, grafting the hopelessly banal onto the utterly momentous.

But in regarding tourism, including Holocaust tourism, as a problem to be overcome rather than a practice to be understood, scholars preempt any analysis of this growing phenomenon. In order to address seriously the legitimate concerns one may have about the ethical value of tourism, one must first be willing to acknowledge that tourism is tremendously diverse, encompassing a vast range of motivations, topics, locales, and ideologies. Only by allowing for that variability can one hope to understand how—or if—one can distinguish visits to a death camp from visits to any historical museum, ancient ruin, or medieval cathedral. As we will see, casting a visit to Auschwitz as the ethical equivalent of a trip to Disney World flattens both kinds of travel into meaningless diversions, denying the potential for even a modicum of value in either instance.[13]

A dismissive stance toward tourism prevents more meaningful analysis in more than one way. First, it suggests that destinations themselves have no intrinsic qualities that resist tourism's presumed superficiality. Second, it regards tourism as an undifferentiated practice based primarily on consumerism and entertainment rather than education or personal enrichment. But tourism is not simply an empty form into which one pours arbitrary content, nor are tourists itinerant automatons passively swallowing the latest marketing schemes from the travel industry—at least, not in all cases. Rather, tourism is a multifarious form of cultural encounter whose aims may or may not include entertainment and shopping, education about history, practice of a second language, appreciation of art and architecture, visits to sites of trauma, or pilgrimages to sacred places. Tourism has rarely been a matter of simple diversion.

The recent field of tourism studies arose in the social sciences in the 1960s and 1970s, particularly in the fields of political science, economics, sociology, and most prominently, anthropology.[14] Whether focused on tourism to sites of pleasure (e.g., so-called 3S tourism—"sea, sand, and sun") or to sites of disaster (as in what the business scholars Malcolm Foley and J. John Lennon have called "dark tourism," which could include Holocaust tourism),[15] their point of departure emphasizes the gathering and interpretation of data through empirical methodologies and neutral terminology. Tourism studies defines tourism, differentiates among its various modes, and explains its significance to those who participate in it and are affected by it.[16] It documents the flows of people and currency, catalogs the rationales for different kinds of travel, and categorizes the experiences shared by tourists. In these studies, tourism emerges as a differentiated field that encompasses the vacationer, the business traveler, the shopper, the sunbather, and the adventurer as well as the student, the researcher, and the pilgrim.

The wealth of information about types of tourism forms the basis for important ethical and ideological considerations, such as tourism's role in the exhaustion or preservation of natural and human resources or the ways in which the tourist's experience of foreign culture is authentic or staged.[17] Feminist scholars address the gender politics of tourism, focusing, for example, on the intercultural collision of values about gender roles or the economic impacts of tourism on an indigenous population's distribution of wealth along gender lines.[18] A related area of tourism study explores the link between the exotic and the erotic, focusing on tourism's potential for sexual exploitation of indigenous cultures, most obviously captured by the study of sex tourism.[19] Marxist anthropologists portray tourism's role in the spread of globalized capital, whereby locations become tourist markets and the labor of performance commodifies indigenous culture for the traveling consumer.[20] An emerging area of tourism study takes up the question of tourism's sustainability, concerning itself not only with the economic and cultural preservation of the sites tourists "consume" but also with the ecological impacts of tourism on the natural environment.[21]

Historians have also contributed crucial insights into the evolution of touristic practices, reminding us that tourism is both older and more varied than its most popular current manifestations. The origins of tourism in its modern form are a topic of some debate, but many argue that tourism has its origins in religious pilgrimage.[22] In that sense, Boccaccio's *Decameron* or Chaucer's *Canterbury Tales* can be regarded as early portrayals of a strain within tourism that continues to this day. (The distinction between the tourist and the pilgrim is a recurring motif in the study of Holocaust tourism and points to the risk of overly essentializing these two identities.) Tourism also has roots in commerce, as the development of trade routes produced tales of distant lands and cultures, luring others to embark on their own adventures. The word "tour" became more commonly employed in seventeenth-century Europe to refer to an organized form of travel to a "canon" of sites. This was the Grand Tour, the purpose of which was to educate the wealthy sons of aristocrats in the languages and arts of neighboring countries.[23] Of course, both the pilgrimage and the Grand Tour participated in tourism's commercial and entertainment aspects, necessitating lodgings, meals, and the usual diversions along the way. With the emergence of the middle class, particularly since the industrial era, and the development of mass forms of transit and communication, tourism began to display some of its more modern manifestations as a mass phenomenon—and gave rise to the inevitable complaints about the entry of the masses into a previously elite arena. With the development of tourism as a mass phenomenon, the more commercial aspects of tourism have tended to eclipse the social capital attributed to previous eras, but that should not imply the erasure of tourism's educational value. The multiplicity of historical roles played by the tourist—pilgrim, trader, or student—has important implications for Holocaust tourism, where the tendency to distinguish between the pilgrim and the tourist can be problematic. Tourism resists stable forms of identity; indeed, some forms of tourism may bring about a profound destabilization of identity. That is especially the case with Holocaust tourism.

If historians have reminded us of the fluidity of touristic practices over time, anthropology has documented the ways in which tourism continues to evolve and to present new challenges. Anthropologists began to take up the study of tourism in earnest in the 1960s, and by the 1980s one could identify a fairly coherent field of tourism studies within anthropology. While economists and political scientists had certainly contributed empirical analyses of the phenomenon, the emergence of tourism studies in anthropology happened to coincide with the field's "linguistic turn," that is, its receptivity to postcolonial theory and to poststructuralist theories of language. So when anthropologists began pursuing tourism studies, they did so with a critical awareness of the limitations of empirical methodology.[24] Emerging from their self-critical turn in the wake of postcolonial critique, anthropologists sought to understand their own position as visitors to other cultures and their own production of the foreign and the exotic as discursive formations.[25] In other words, anthropologists began to appreciate the ways in which social science did not simply observe phenomena but also participated in and even produced them through social-scientific discourse. Anthropology's investigation of culture based on otherness, it turned out, helped to produce the very otherness it sought to explicate. As the anthropologist Dennison Nash explains, this insight has led some within anthropology to shun tourism studies. "To be accused of exploitation is a very black mark indeed for anthropologists. So in the anthropological community the study of tourism could be construed as an invitation to guilt by association with things that anthropological work definitely is not supposed to be: the pursuit of pleasure; superficial observation; and the exploitation of peoples."[26] But, Nash and his colleagues argue, the study of tourism actually provides an opportunity for anthropologists to reflect both on the ways in which anthropology is itself complicit in the packaging and selling of the Other and on the ways in which tourism, so easily maligned, is itself a more complicated practice than meets the eye.

The thrust of anthropological approaches to tourism is the encounter between two cultures, that of the tourist and that of the native. Tourism is one of the ways in which intercultural contact is managed, negotiating what is available from the native for display or performance and what is desired by the tourist for consumption. While the aim of social-scientific inquiries into tourism is to offer an empirically based account of its various forms and practices, the research often leans toward stressing the troublesome aspects of tourism, informed by the anthropologist's ideological commitments—hence the abundance of Marxist, postcolonialist, environmentalist, and feminist approaches to tourism. The result is a dominant portrayal of tourists as the "exploiters or unwitting representatives of exploiting forces such as international hotel chains, airlines or other national or international agencies which have become involved with native populations."[27] By the same token, the native is regarded either as vulnerable to exploitation, susceptible to cultural contamination, or complicit in the less sincere aspects of the tourist industry.[28]

Such accounts are critical and point to real problems in tourism, but they do not exhaust the range of touristic practice that occurs in the world today, nor do they claim to. Indeed, anthropology regards the study of tourism as a wide-open field in its early stages of development. Nor should we assume that a field as large as tourism can be exhausted by anthropological inquiry. For one thing, anthropology is predicated on the intercultural encounter between the foreign and the native or between the present and the distant past. But not all modes of tourism emphasize cultural difference. The visitor to historical museums, for example, may be in search of some affirmation or deepening of an already-embraced cultural identity. Similarly, the heritage tourist may be in search of some knowledge about one's own ancestors so as to better comprehend one's current position at home. Meanwhile, the eco-tourist travels with a critical awareness of tourism's impact on the environment; in an effort to reduce the harmful effects of poorly managed resource exploitation, the eco-tourist attempts to minimize or even eliminate the harmful environmental and social effects typically associated with mass tourism. While such types of tourism can be evidence themselves of a kind of unequal cultural dynamic (e.g., the unequal distribution of economic resources required to engage in heritage tourism or ecotourism), there are motivations at work in the individual tourist's journey that resist a reduction to intercultural encounter between natives and foreigners.

As we shall explore in the chapters ahead, Holocaust tourism is another mode of tourism that cannot be contained so easily by the familiar paradigm of the foreign and the native. In the context of the Holocaust, one must question if the notion of culture has any real meaning at all, unless we want to speak of an encounter with the disappearance of culture. When one enters the grounds of a former concentration camp or visits streets once located inside a Jewish ghetto, one is confronted with absence: the absence of those who made the place one of significance for the tourist. We confront the inherent paradox in the phrase "Nazi culture,"[29] where the traces and relics we seek once aimed for the fulfillment of a racist fantasy of Aryan superiority by erasing a culture marginalized as Other. Instead of culture understood as the signifying practices of life, we come upon the death of culture. In the vacuum created in such places, we erect a substitute—a culture of memorialization. Or of amnesia. Different locations manage the dialectics of absence and presence in different ways, and that variety will be one of the recurring topics in the chapters that follow. The point here is that Holocaust tourism complicates the anthropological understanding of tourism as the encounter between foreign and native cultures by seeking something more radical than cultural difference—cultural destruction.[30]

There are other reasons not to cede the cultural analysis of Holocaust tourism, or of any other kind of tourism, solely to anthropology.[31] As a social science, anthropology regards tourism as interconnected with other modes of making sense of the world and sees its diverse manifestations as instances of a larger phenomenon subsumed under the name of "culture."[32] Touristic encounters in turn enter into some relation, whether affirmative or critical, to other forms of cultural expression back home. As one manifestation of culture among many, tourism provides a lens through which the ethnographer locates particular beliefs and values that mediate the encounter of the traveler with a new location. While the practices and beliefs of the tourist may become the subject of theoretical (e.g., feminist, Marxist, poststructuralist, ecological, economic) analysis, the anthropological fieldwork of tourism studies is premised on the close observation of touristic behavior disentangled from the personal biases of the anthropologist. The anthropologist's approach to tourism necessarily embraces a form of cultural relativism, in which one culturally positioned subject (the anthropologist or ethnographer) documents the signifying practices of another culturally positioned subject (the tourist), preferably in its own terms.[33]

Here again, Holocaust tourism presents challenges to anthropological assumptions. Given the Holocaust's positioning within Western thought as a limit case of morality, an exemplar of ultimate evil, the anthropological commitment to observation must stumble in the face of the moral imperatives that the Holocaust demands. Observation of atrocity unaccompanied by an expression of moral condemnation risks the appearance of indifference, complicity, or approval. In the case of Holocaust tourism, the object of study is not just any kind of travel but, rather, travel to sites where Western humanistic and scientific values (of which modern anthropology is one manifestation) utterly collapsed.[34] The rationality that shapes anthropology (and all modern science since the Enlightenment) itself becomes suspect in its encounter with the Holocaust. After all, barbarity reasserted itself under the Nazi regime with unparalleled destruction, despite the advances of the Enlightenment's promise toward emancipation from ignorance and its humanist principles of reason and equality.[35] Can there be reliable, accurate, or adequate representations of the event that do not reinstantiate the instrumental logic that enabled the Holocaust in the first place?[36] This epistemological problem, first articulated in 1944 by the philosophers Max Horkheimer and Theodor Adorno in *Dialektik der Aufklärung* (Dialectic of the Enlightenment), and further developed by Adorno in subsequent works, has proven generative of an immense body of scholarship.[37] The anthropology of tourism certainly affords a window onto one way of confronting the genocide, but like any window, it cannot uncover what lies outside of its frame. The questions arising from Holocaust tourism exceed any anthropological inquiry into touristic practices and cultural transfers between the foreign and the native.[38]

Anthropology is hardly unique in its limitations; if anything, the field models an exemplary openness to influences from both scientific and humanistic disciplines beyond its walls. But even a hybrid of scientific observation and interpretive semiotics cannot hope to offer anything like an exhaustive account of the Holocaust. Any effort to comprehend or portray the Holocaust through disciplinary knowledge confronts problems that exceed disciplinary expertise.[39] Put simply, the Holocaust is too vast, too immense an event to contain within traditional disciplinary approaches.

Take the example of Holocaust testimony, which alone "not only refers to statements elicited from survivors by courts of law or simply for the historical record, as well as to the chronicles, diaries, journals and reports produced during the war and written memoirs and oral history produced after it, but also frequently encompasses other modes of expression to which survivors have had recourse, such as the short story, the novel, and lyric poetry."[40] As the literary scholar Thomas Trezise makes clear in his work on the reception of Holocaust testimony, if the act of bearing witness to the Holocaust exceeds any single genre's representational strategies, then efforts to listen to and respond to such acts of witnessing must also draw on many kinds of understanding. Even if the object of study for anthropologists is Holocaust *tourism* and not the Holocaust itself, the underlying event that motivates such tourism will demand a historical and a moral reckoning that cannot be kept at bay by a desire to police disciplinary boundaries. Indeed, in understanding cultural practices as interconnected, anthropology itself acknowledges that Holocaust tourism must be understood alongside many other forms of Holocaust memorialization, which in turn will inevitably call on multiple forms of knowledge. To understand Holocaust tourism, one has to engage with debates in philosophy, historiography, theology, literary analysis, art history, and many others that have asked, What is to be remembered? How is it to be remembered? and What lessons may one learn or not learn from the event?

Tourism and the Representation of the Holocaust

While no single account can claim to provide complete knowledge of the event, one must nevertheless approach the Holocaust from somewhere, and how one approaches the Holocaust is simultaneously an epistemological and an ethical choice. The question of how to represent the Holocaust—through which disciplinary tools, which media, and which institutional structures—unavoidably engages with an ethics of representation. Take again the example of survivor testimony. How does one weigh testimony and take into account the fragile, sometimes unreliable nature of human memory? How does one portray the victims' suffering without turning it into a spectacle? Holocaust museums and memorial sites must address these questions and others as they curate their exhibits and manage flows of tourists, who in turn are seeking a personal encounter with testimony in a place that avers authenticity. As a highly (but not exclusively) visual practice, the representation of testimony at such places, whether through documents and photos or through videotaped interviews, always negotiates the boundaries between knowledge seeking and voyeurism.[41]

As with written accounts of the Holocaust, sites of remembrance make choices about the specific stories they want to tell, which beginnings and endings to emphasize. Since there is no shortage of stories to relate, Holocaust representations, including those encountered in tourism, produce many "emplotments," each different in some way from the next.[42] Did the Shoah start with the Wannsee Conference of 1942, or the Nuremberg Laws of 1934? Perhaps its beginnings must be sought even earlier, in the anti-Semitic propaganda of the NSDAP (the National-Socialist German Workers Party, i.e., the Nazis) that was already on display for all to see in the 1920s. As for its end, many survivors of the Holocaust still bear with them a trauma that extends their experience of victimization into the present. The traumatic experiences of victims impose ethical obligations on those who listen to and represent testimony.[43] One major challenge for Holocaust studies has been to recover historical knowledge from traumatic memory, since trauma implies a rupture—an inability or, at least, a difficulty—in rendering experience into a coherent narrative. The translation of individual trauma into collective memory is further complicated by the fact that not all individuals process trauma in the same way.[44] What's more, the category of trauma may account for some memories of the Holocaust but not all, so the nature of Holocaust memory cannot be reduced to the traumatic without obscuring non-traumatic memories that recall the event. Finally, recent theories see collective trauma as transgenerational, suggesting that the Holocaust has not finished shaping lived experience.

The variety of accounts of the Holocaust is also reflective of the vast geography in which the event unfolded, requiring immense levels of bureaucratic coordination, the active participation of thousands of perpetrators, and the passivity or quiet approval of millions of by-standers. Tourism, as an engagement with space, confronts the Holocaust's physical immensity and its many variations of scale, location, and execution, as well as the differences in how its traces and artifacts are preserved from one place to another. While the earliest Holocaust memorials were the remains of liberated camps in Europe, the history of Holocaust memory has evolved from a strictly European experience to a global one.[45] Since the end of the Cold War, many of the camps that previously lay on the other side of the Iron Curtain now have become part of a much more freely moving and thriving tourism industry. One result of the freer flow of tourism after 1990 is that sites previously administered under a more narrowly national or ideological perspective now partake in an increasingly international, even global, network of remembrance. To cite one example, the cooperation among the Auschwitz-Birkenau Memorial and Museum, the United States Holocaust Memorial Museum, and Yad Vashem in Jerusalem illustrates that Holocaust memorialization is indeed an example of what the sociologists Daniel Levy and Natan Sznaider call "cosmopolitan memory," a term they use to describe the interplay between local values and narratives and distant ones that are increasingly linked by modern technologies of travel and communication. Local and global practices around Holocaust memorialization and education are now thoroughly intertwined, often leading to debates about the local versus the global ownership of Holocaust memory.

Tourists who travel to multiple sites of Holocaust memorialization develop that network of cosmopolitan memory by comparing one act of remembrance with another. Tourism ensures that those who administer Holocaust memorials appeal to an increasingly sophisticated, diverse touring public that brings a wide range of experiences and knowledge to the sites it visits. The variations that tourists encounter from site to site reflect both the different histories of these sites, the ideologies of the regimes that inherited the task of preserving them, and the different resources available for administering those sites. For example, remote extermination camps such as Sobibór and Bełżec in eastern Poland reflect, among other things, the administrative reach of Heinrich Himmler's SS on the heels of German military victories in the East, the determination to carry out killings in secrecy, and the grim logic of systematized murder from arrival to cremation. They also reflect the limited resources in postwar Poland for preserving them and the ideological hindrances to remembrance of Jewish suffering. Meanwhile, a site like the House of the Wannsee Conference reminds the tourist of the so-called desk perpetrators, the bureaucrats who coordinated the "resettling" of Europe's Jews from distant administrative centers, and its postwar history also displays the shifting value placed on confronting the Nazi past in postwar Germany. The disparities in the ways in which these sites are administered today points to the different memorial cultures that have evolved over the course of the last seventy years in Poland and Germany.

The variety among Holocaust memorial sites also raises the very politically charged issue of whom to include among its victims, since the persecution of other groups, such as the Roma people or the mentally and physically disabled, were no less abhorrent than the murder of Jews.[46] Sites of Holocaust tourism respond to this challenge in a number of different ways, with important and often controversial implications for the role of Holocaust memory in different contexts. Indeed, the acknowledgment of the Holocaust as the destruction of European Jewry was slow to emerge as the dominant narrative at many of the camp memorials, where narratives of liberation, martyrdom, or political persecution first took precedent. For an example that we will explore further in the following chapter, the earliest remembrances at Auschwitz emphasized Polish victimization and made little reference to the distinct fate of the Jews, the vast majority of whom were deported there for immediate extermination. Tourism has provided a platform from which to witness those transformations.

Tourism depends on the willingness of travelers to help create the experience they are seeking and even to hold sites accountable for their management. Tourists exercise considerable agency over how much they will contemplate, what they will or will not see, which routes they will take, whether they will pose questions of their guides, or even how compliant they will be with guidelines. Agency is a prerequisite for the educational function many Holocaust memorials and museums serve, which includes unearthing and preserving sites of perpetration, housing invaluable archival resources, and providing educational programming. This point also serves to remind us that tourism and education have always shared a link and that the distinction between the tourist and the researcher or student is at best a matter of degree, not kind. Still, non-specialized visits to Holocaust memorials remain suspicious to many, since tourism is identified with mass culture, and the bias in the academy against mass culture has deep roots.[47] The premise of this volume is not that mass culture is problem free; rather, it is that Holocaust tourism is a multifarious practice that, like other cultural phenomena, includes its good and bad actors and that its ubiquity demands thoughtful reflection by scholars. In an era of globalization, tourism is becoming an increasingly common way to make sense of a world whose expanse is becoming ever more accessible.

The prevalent skepticism against mass or popular culture has done nothing to halt the production of popular portrayals of the murder of two-thirds of Europe's Jews. New films, novels, histories, memoirs, and even forged testimonials appear year after year, reaching a diverse global audience and also eliciting a common critical response. Whatever the most recent Holocaust-themed novel or film may be, criticisms of it as voyeuristic or exploitative, as inadequate or inaccurate, are practically assured.[48] Among the voices in debates about the inability of mainstream culture to address the Shoah appropriately, none has been more influential than that of the recently deceased Elie Wiesel. A survivor of Auschwitz and a Nobel Prize–winning author, Wiesel has been one of the most powerful voices to situate the Holocaust in Western thought as an event whose horror lies beyond our ability to understand yet commands future generations to remember.[49] A refrain in Wiesel's writing and speaking is that the Holocaust can never be fully comprehended by those who did not experience it, that it must forever remain a mystery to those who were not there. So what is the best way to portray an event that cannot be fully understood? In his own writing, Wiesel reflects on this challenge by insisting that his works do not fit neatly into generic categories. Discussing his own book, *A Beggar in Jerusalem*, Wiesel contends that it "is neither novel nor anti-novel, neither fiction nor autobiography; neither poem nor prose—it is all this together."[50] Wiesel's motivation for negating any specific generic claim for his work is a response to the epistemological challenge presented by Auschwitz, suggesting that whatever the genre or medium, each effort to convey the Holocaust will necessarily prove inadequate, at best offering only a partial account.

Wiesel's skepticism about the adequacy of forms of representation to portray the Holocaust extends to popular culture more generally. In his critique of the 1978 NBC miniseries *Holocaust* in the *New York Times*, he makes abundantly clear his mistrust of television as a sufficiently dignified or sophisticated medium for portraying the profundity of the Holocaust:

> Untrue, offensive, cheap: as a TV production, the film is an insult to those who perished and to those who survived. In spite of its name, the "docu-drama" is not about what some of us remember as the Holocaust.
>
> Am I too harsh? Too sensitive, perhaps? But then, the film is not sensitive enough. It tries to show what cannot even be imagined. It transforms an ontological event into soap-opera.[51]

While no portrayal could ever adequately represent an event that "cannot even be imagined," Wiesel implies there are some media that should be disallowed a priori on the basis of their apparent shallowness. With the television miniseries as emblematic, Wiesel's critique sees in contemporary mass culture an inability to deal with philosophical problems in any depth. Instead, he concludes, the mass cultural medium of television turns history into entertainment.[52] (Wiesel was to take this skepticism into his work for the United States Holocaust Memorial Museum, where he was insistent on a presentation of the Holocaust that would resist the public's desire for a redemptive narrative that invited universal identification with the victims.)

The case of the miniseries *Holocaust* proves illustrative of the danger in discounting mass cultural productions too easily. Panned by Wiesel and others as melodrama (a critique that was certainly justifiable, but hardly exhaustive), the broadcast in fact marked a pivotal moment in the United States and elsewhere in bringing the Holocaust to the forefront of cultural consciousness. Nowhere was this truer than in the Federal Republic of Germany, where the miniseries was the most widely viewed television event on record up to that time and which, as the German film scholar Anton Kaes has written, "broke through thirty years of silence and left an indelible mark on German discussion of the Holocaust."[53] This discussion included both media and politicians and may have affected voting patterns among the members of the Bundestag.[54] In an article from 1980 on the broadcast, the German studies scholar Mark Cory suggests that the miniseries had an impact beyond the living room: "Visitor attendance at Dachau is up sixty percent since the broadcast in Germany, . . . Paraguay has been persuaded to revoke the citizenship of Josef Mengele, and . . . the Federal Republic of Germany has abolished the statute of limitations on war crimes scheduled to halt new prosecutions of atrocities after December, 1979."[55] The link Cory points out between tourism to Dachau and the television broadcast is especially telling and suggests that the television show may have initiated a deeper search for truth about the Holocaust and that visits to locations depicted in the television show, however inaccurately, figure as one element in that search for a more authentic encounter with history. Perhaps audiences appreciated the limits of the miniseries as a genre while grasping the import of the event it so imperfectly portrayed, thus begetting a deeper search for more authentic portrayals that might be found on site.

In fact, popular culture has supplied numerous examples of works that have had an enormous impact on Holocaust remembrance for many decades. A well-known case, one that long predates NBC's television broadcast, also points to a definite link between representations in mainstream culture and tourism. Anne Frank's diary, and the play based on it, had already achieved international renown in the 1950s, and they continue to be featured as a regular part of school curricula in many countries.[56] There have been numerous film versions of Anne's story, shown on television and in cinemas. The broad appeal of Anne Frank's diary has much to do with the author's undaunted optimism, which tends to eclipse the gruesome fate that awaited the young woman at Bergen-Belsen in 1945 (she died of starvation and disease under the murderous conditions the Nazis fostered in the camps). Because of the sense of faith in humanity that the diary expresses, some scholars question the centrality of her diary as an appropriate vehicle for Holocaust remembrance, since it fails to confront the death that awaited millions of victims like her. The Holocaust scholar Lawrence L. Langer writes of Anne Frank and her diary's legacy, "She is in no way to blame for not knowing about what she could not have known about. But readers are much to blame for accepting and promoting the idea that her Diary is a major Holocaust text and has anything of great consequence to tell us about the atrocities that culminated in the murder of European Jewry."[57] Furthermore, Frank edited her diary for eventual publication as a book, so it is both a document of her experience as well as an aestheticized text. In short, its status as a source of information about the Holocaust is problematic, even if one concedes that Frank and her family were hardly the only Jews to hide from their persecutors and that these stories depict an aspect of the Holocaust experience that merits attention. But as a catalyst for engagement with the Holocaust, there have been few works that have made such an indelible mark on their readers.

The link between Anne Frank's story and Holocaust tourism is striking: Lines of tourists queue up to see the house in Amsterdam where the young girl hid with her family, making it one of the city's most heavily visited destinations.[58] In what ways do visitors to the house encounter similar questions we might ask about the book, the play, and the films? Do visits to the house distort the reality of the Holocaust by focusing, not on violence and death, but on a doomed effort to survive? Does the museum portray the Holocaust accurately or in a morally responsible way? Does it educate, entertain, or do both? Clearly there are as many responses to these questions as there are tourists at the Anne Frank House. There is good reason to be suspicious of the insights gained by some visitors, but surely some of those who see the exhibit are capable of critical reflection on the Holocaust and its memorialization. Furthermore, whether through reading her diary or touring her house, Anne Frank's story can be a point of entry into learning about the Holocaust that does not end when the last page is turned or the museum's exit is reached.

Holocaust Tourism: A Phenomenological Approach

As the examples of the miniseries *Holocaust* and the Anne Frank House show, the collective remembrance of the Holocaust depends at least in part on representations in mainstream culture, and tourism has a close connection to other forms of popular culture in literature, film, and television. Holocaust tourism raises many of the same questions about what can be known about the calamity, and how we can know it, that other genres do, but it also adds other considerations about places of memory. In turn, what we discover about tourism to sites of Holocaust remembrance can inform how we consider reading texts or viewing films. A common feature of many essays on the ethics of Holocaust representation is that the perspectives of readers and viewers are usually secondary to considerations of aesthetic form. Most critics of Holocaust-related cultural productions foreground matters of genre or medium when analyzing a book, a memorial, or a film, exploring their signifying structures and codes as if they were determinative of their meaning independent of the audience with which they engage. Just as texts need readers to generate meaning, tourism is not possible without tourists. Of course, form matters, and this book pays attention to formal aspects of tourism: how museums are arranged, how tour guides shape the experiences of visitors to camp memorials, how displays use text and image, and so on. But the perspective of tourists remains central to the inquiry, which, relying on a term first articulated by the social anthropologist Eric Cohen and further developed by other scholars since, I am characterizing as a phenomenological approach to Holocaust tourism.[59] By that I mean that it is an account of the ways in which tourists interpret sensory stimuli to produce knowledge and negotiate their identities in relation to the surrounding place.[60] That includes a consideration of how tourists encounter visual displays of artifacts, photos, and documents; how their hearing is addressed both intentionally through audio recordings, lectures, or guides communicating through headphones, as well as through ambient sources, including other tourists; or how tourists' bodies navigate configurations of space. Tourism, though heavily visual, relies on a full array of sensory experience in imparting both rational and more affective impressions to travelers. In the case of Holocaust tourism, I address how tourists process their encounters with places of remembrance, including their affective and sensory qualities, in order to construct a coherent narrative of the Holocaust and to situate themselves in relation to the event and its memory.

In applying this approach, I place more emphasis on exploring the possibilities for knowledge than on a quantitative or statistically verifiable ethnographic account of Holocaust tourists. Such work would be a welcome contribution to the study of Holocaust tourism, but it must build on an awareness of the full range of available responses that tourists have to Holocaust sites if it is to ask the right questions.[61] Furthermore, it will have to confront the reality that tourists to Holocaust sites come from such a variety of backgrounds and experiences that any effort to make definitive claims about the phenomenon will face enormous challenges in identifying broad trends shared among different visitors. This book identifies an observed range of subjectivities available to travelers: not just as consumers, but also as witnesses, pilgrims, mourners, commemorators, students, and educators. By linking the questions about knowledge and representation that drive Holocaust studies with theoretical and empirical insights from tourism studies, this book aims to offer a rich account of those who undertake travel to these destinations and what they recall, including my own experiences and those of other travelers, who often share their responses in print and online media. It also draws on conversations with tour guides, reports by agencies that manage such sites, and tourist literature. It identifies tourist responses to sites that go beyond a description of the business of tourism, although I pay attention to the role of market forces in shaping accessibility to sites of remembrance. In addressing the possibilities for knowledge and acknowledging a range of responses, I hope to counter a prevailing tendency in many common responses to tourism at Holocaust museums and memorials, namely that it is appalling that a market for this kind of travel exists. This tendency, which finds expression in both general and more academic critiques of tourism, has played an especially important role in one particular branch of tourism studies concerned with "dark tourism."

As noted above, the term "dark tourism" was coined by J. John Lennon and Malcolm Foley, British researchers of tourism and management. Lennon and Foley define "dark tourism" as travel to places of death and disaster, including Auschwitz, Hiroshima, Robben Island, and the Sixth Floor Museum in Dallas, which is dedicated to the assassination of President John F. Kennedy. Such places draw tourists because of the heavy circulation within media accounts of the calamities that took place there. Indeed, for Lennon and Foley it is the mediatized nature of these places (or, rather, of the events they have come to represent) that links them together, lending them an allure within mainstream culture that they might not otherwise possess. (We see here an echo of the concern for mainstream culture that runs from Horkheimer and Adorno through to Wiesel.) These aspects of dark tourism theory certainly reinforce the connection between Holocaust tourism and other forms of popular culture. But for Lennon and Foley the association is rather negative, raising questions of poor taste on the part of travelers whom they regard as "invariably curious about suffering, horror and death," which become "established commodities" within the tourism industry.[62] While Lennon and Foley allow that some tourists may have more noble motivations than others, their typical dark tourist is the traveler seduced by media images into spending money on an inauthentic experience.[63] Ultimately, dark tourists appear as postmodern travelers who disregard the distinction between the original event and its subsequent representations.

Like many other critiques of tourism, the dark tourism model focuses on tourism as commodification. Evoking familiar concerns about mass culture, dark tourism sees those who purchase tourism's commodities as submitting to the dominant logic of capitalism—the logic that Adorno and Horkheimer saw as enabling the establishment of extermination camps. A certain superficiality adheres to the rather obvious and not very insightful observation that tourism involves commodification. It is as if, by establishing a fact that few would legitimately dispute, one has adequately dispensed with an age-old phenomenon that continues to diversify and draw ever more people into its networks.

Despite the admonitions about the dangers of commodifying history as aesthetic object, we cannot ignore the impact of tourism in disseminating awareness of the genocide. Nor did Adorno ever imagine that his negative critique of mainstream culture would obviate all engagement with a calamity that has so often been called "unthinkable." Too negative a view of mainstream culture bears a defeatist, even elitist element that cannot imagine resistance or critical reflection as a widespread practice within humanity. And to insist on the incomprehensibility of the Holocaust on the basis of its horror is to invite resignation in the face of atrocity.[64]

Instead, horror can motivate comprehension. Even Adorno advocates for a moment beyond or apart from rational thought, for an *affective* moment that is productive. Specifically, he insists that we recoil in the face of Auschwitz. When we learn of the gas chambers and the mass executions in forests and the deaths from starvation and disease, we should respond in horror, but that horror, in turn, should lead us to engage in deep thought about the structures and systems in any society that produce violence. However we engage with the Holocaust, there is a place for affect in our pursuit of knowledge. To dismiss tourism as an inauthentic fascination with the macabre is to ignore the ways in which affect becomes the grounds upon which a critical rationality can build.[65]

Of course, we can maintain a distinction between genuine affect and the kind of sentiment fostered in mass entertainment that Adorno and others would dismiss as kitsch. Holocaust tourism comprises a range of efforts that span the sincere to the sensationalized. And yes, there are "dark tourists" who are drawn to the macabre—but they don't necessarily leave the destination with the same morbid curiosity that might initially have drawn them. And even some who conceive of their travel as pilgrimage may, in fact, exhibit a superficial engagement with the site they visit. The point is, tourists are capable of varied and even contradictory behaviors and insights during the same journey. Travel to museums, memorials, and other locales related to the murder of six million European Jews can be both problematic and productive. Holocaust memorial sites evoke affective responses through a variety of representational strategies, some more capable of engendering reflection than others. It is time to see in tourism a sincere effort on the part of many travelers and their hosts, if not all, to engage with a topic that is so ubiquitous in Western culture and that challenges many basic beliefs people have about themselves, about the nature of good and evil, and about the value of human life in all its diversity. In tourism, I locate an effort by many travelers to claim agency in relation to Holocaust memory. Holocaust tourists are searching for truth amid a sea of representations about the twentieth century's most notorious event. The knowledge that tourists seek is embodied in space, and that fact of embodiment is, I argue, central to the experience of Holocaust tourism. By going directly to sites of perpetration, they are looking for a sense of immediacy to history, even though their encounters are ultimately mediated through strategies of memorialization. When visiting museums in places that are remote from the site of perpetration (such as Yad Vashem in Jerusalem or the United States Holocaust Memorial Museum in Washington, DC), tourists are nonetheless exploring a spatial reality that is very distinct from that which surrounds the exhibition. The fact that tourists can never inhabit the Holocaust itself, only its traces and its representations, opens the door to questions about absence and presence, about the past and the present. The embodied encounter with the traces of mass murder also motivates reflection on the physical and the metaphysical and about the ephemeral materiality of one's own body, one's temporality, and the possibility—or impossibility—of finding transcendence or redemption in sites of extreme suffering. These are the stakes that are foregrounded in the subsequent chapters.

Organization of the Book

The organization of this book is both thematic and geographic. Part I, "Tourism at the Camp Memorials," takes up tourism to concentration camps, paying special attention to those that were specifically designated as extermination centers. The camps have epitomized the Nazi genocide in the public imagination, even though many victims of the Holocaust perished in ghettos from starvation and disease or faced death by mobile killing squads near their own villages.[66] Here we consider the experiences of memorial space that tourists encounter during their visits. Part II, "Urban Centers of Holocaust Memory," moves increasingly outward from the camps as the epicenters of mass murder. It examines how the Holocaust is represented to future generations, looking at four urban centers of Holocaust remembrance. The first two are Warsaw and Berlin, both sites of Holocaust perpetration, although in very different ways. The second two are Jerusalem and Washington, DC, where the Holocaust has been memorialized in museums and archives in two nations that each lay claim to the history of the Holocaust—again, in very different ways. By looking comparatively at four national capitals with different degrees of connection to the Holocaust, we can consider how these sites vary in their strategies for collective memory.

Ultimately, this book engages with a broad range of perspectives—historical and theoretical, documentary and fictional, academic and informal—to produce a more differentiated account of Holocaust tourism. The aim is not to generate a unified theory of tourism and Holocaust remembrance but, rather, to lay a foundation for a more nuanced, less disciplinarily bound approach to both. In attempting such a discussion here, I participate primarily as a humanist, albeit one who is hoping to learn from and contribute to the work of social scientists, historians, and a diverse audience of tourists. I draw on both my own experiences and those of other visitors to Holocaust memorial sites, not with the aim of quantifying particular responses, but to give some sense of the range of responses that Holocaust tourism can elicit. If the balance of the arguments here seems to emphasize the positive features of Holocaust tourism, that is because such arguments are much harder to find elsewhere, and by presenting them here, perhaps I can contribute to a more reflective, less reactive discussion. At the same time, the productive contributions made to Holocaust memorialization through tourism are inextricable from the commercial practices that accompany them and that point to the problematic ethics of travel and spectatorship. The arc of this book's argument ties the phenomenon of visits to Holocaust-related sites to other discussions about Holocaust understanding and representation. In doing so, it demands a serious look at tourism itself as a mode of representation and interpretation and thereby claims tourism as an object of study not only for anthropologists, sociologists, and economists but also for philosophers, literary critics, and art historians.

By bringing tourism into the realm of Holocaust studies, this book also represents an effort to move beyond some of the more dogmatic, doctrinal aspects of research into the Nazi genocide that have had the unfortunate consequence of preempting certain lines of inquiry, at least until recent years. Those doctrines, which we will explore in greater detail throughout the volume, include such notions as the impossibility of representing the Holocaust; the cautions against comparisons of the Holocaust with other genocides; and the insistence that the Holocaust offers no redemptive potential through aesthetic production, no ultimate meaning that can be salvaged from such senselessness. In many ways I embrace these doctrines and have certainly been stamped by them in my own development as a scholar, but at the same time I believe it is necessary to recognize their limits and, frankly, their shortcomings for generating Holocaust remembrance in an era after the survivors have gone.

Ultimately, Holocaust tourism represents the emergence of an evolving way of grasping human experience that can range from the simplistic to the sophisticated. By examining the phenomenon, perhaps it is not too crass to hope that Holocaust tourism can continue to confront the full range of human capabilities, from the brutal to the noble.

PART I

Tourism at the Camp Memorials

1

Listening to Auschwitz

A dozen SS men stood around, legs akimbo, with an indif-
ferent air. At a certain moment they moved among us, and in
a subdued tone of voice, with faces of stone, began to inter-
rogate us rapidly, one by one, in bad Italian. . . . And on the
basis of the reply they pointed in two different directions.

Everything was silent as an aquarium, or as in certain
dream sequences. We had expected something more apocalyptic: they seemed simple police agents. It was disconcerting and disarming.
—Primo Levi, *Survival in Auschwitz* (1996), describing his
arrival at Auschwitz in January 1944

It is a stunningly beautiful sunny day with a light refresh-
ing breeze. The mountains in the distance—which we came
through yesterday on the train—can be seen through a light
mist; just as the prisoners here could have seen them.
—Martin Gilbert, *Holocaust Journey* (1997), describing a
visit to Auschwitz-Birkenau in the summer of 1996

In June 2007, a group of colleagues and I traveled to some of the most
important Holocaust memorials in Europe, including the Auschwitz-
Birkenau Memorial and Museum. For most of us, myself included, it
would be our first trip to Poland, let alone to an extermination camp.
A few days before our tour of Auschwitz, we met in Warsaw with Konstanty Gebert, a prominent Polish journalist and a member of the local
Jewish community. Gebert was known for his antigovernment activism
during Communist Party rule, and since the end of Communism he
has worked persistently to improve relations between Poland's majority
Catholics and its estimated 20,000–30,000 Jews, about 5,000 of whom
live in the capital today.[1] While discussing his ongoing work with us,

Gebert ended our conversation with an unexpected admonition about our itinerary: "Don't go to Auschwitz," he told us. When we asked him to elaborate, he expressed dismay at the conversion of the most notorious death camp into a tourist destination. He shared with us his concern that many tourists were poorly prepared for the visit and thus unable to appreciate either the spiritual or historical import of a site that was, in essence, a massive cemetery. He referred also to the heavy traffic of noisy school groups and vacationing tourists arriving in caravans of buses that, in his view, brought irreverence to a place of immeasurable suffering. The presence of tourists in all their vulgarity was, for Gebert, inappropriate to the site's significance as a cemetery, a place that demanded piety and respect.

In an article describing an invitation to lead a group of Jewish tourists from the United Kingdom on a day trip to Auschwitz in 1999, the art historian Griselda Pollock anticipates Gebert's misgivings about tourism and describes her reasons for ultimately deciding not to go. Her explanation echoes Gebert's, but she frames it in more personal terms: "Many considerations constrained me: The short notice, the responsibility for 'education' for such a group of British Jewish visitors to these sites, the condition of travel. . . . Most of all, there was a conviction that I should never go to Auschwitz."[2] In a footnote, Pollock also notes her misgivings about being "taken around by Polish guides, with little special attention or sensitivity to the meaning the site has for visitors who are Jewish."[3] Pollock elaborates on her conviction to stay away:

> I am certainly too scared. At a personal level, the terror of being that close to that danger threatens me too unbearably. At a less unpredictable level, I am perplexed at the ethics of going to, visiting, touring a place whose all too real and still powerfully symbolic function was to be a horrific terminus, the end of a line, the factory of death, a place from which none was intended to return.[4]

Pollock's reasons for declining the invitation are abundantly clear. Her sense of fear at the proximity to terror identifies an anxiety shared to varying degrees by many who consider such travel, whether they go in the end or not. She articulates the heightened sense of threat faced by many Jewish travelers to the site, who arrive knowing that the place would have meant their own death at another time or that it was the place where friends or relatives were indeed murdered. But Pollock's understandable existential fears about the horror of Auschwitz are accompanied by other anxieties related to the appropriateness of tourism. By placing the word "education" in scare quotes, she doubts whether a day trip to the camp can truly deepen tourists' understanding about the Holocaust; by doing so, she reflects a common skepticism toward tourism as insufficiently intellectual. Above all, it is the notion that the tourist enters and leaves, almost casually, that Pollock finds incompatible with the meaning of that site, resulting in her ethical concerns about tourism to Auschwitz.

To be fair, Pollock does not condemn all travel to Auschwitz. She contrasts the day trip she declined with the experience of her son, who traveled to Auschwitz as "part of a planned educational tour of formerly Jewish Eastern European sites, organized for teenagers."[5] Acknowledging the preparation that informs these travels, Pollock suggests a spectrum between tourism and pilgrimage, with educational tours located at some "intermediary subject position" between the two.[6] Intertwined in her ethical considerations are two related yet different questions. Alongside the question of *whether* to go is the question of *who* should go. Implicit in Pollock's distinction between tourists and pilgrims is a presumed lack of preparation or inappropriate motivation on the part of the former in comparison to the latter. Her chief concern is that tourists, those unreflecting consumers of mass culture, lack the ability to appreciate the distinction between the site as it exists today and the historical event it commemorates. Pollock positions the "touristic" as the "default condition to which representation will recur unless a crucial distinction is made between *the place* that can be visited and left, and the problematic burned into Western European culture by what Paul Celan simply called 'that which happened', the event."[7] In other words, tourists conflate the place of Auschwitz as it currently exists with its operation as an extermination camp roughly seventy years ago; legitimate visitors, on the other hand, somehow appreciate that the current place is a representation of the past, not the past itself.[8] Her characterization consigns the tourist to the superficial endpoint of a spectrum whose other end is the deep historical and ethical awareness embodied by visitors with a legitimate reason for being there. Beyond the stereotypically diminished intellect Pollock ascribes to tourists, there is also a barely concealed exclusivity in her approach to the question of who should go to Auschwitz, whereby only those connected to the site through family history, group identity, or formalized education are ethical actors. All others who travel to Auschwitz are tourists, exemplifying the worst aspects of a superficial, consumerist approach to history. Pollock asks important questions, but her conclusions seem to be based on unflattering—and ultimately unsatisfying—assumptions about tourism, assumptions that are widely shared.

Shared, in fact, by our own group as we planned our trip to Poland. While my colleagues and I asked ourselves many of the same questions about seeing Auschwitz, we ultimately decided to go. Our itinerary had been planned months before Gebert's admonition, and we had spent considerable time reflecting on our reasons for going well before our meeting with him in Warsaw. Like Pollock's validation of her son's visit, we justified ours in the name of education. At some level our trip was based on the belief that there was something to be gained by being there, something perhaps to be learned and subsequently shared with our students and with those who read our work. We knew we wanted to see the place, but first we felt we had to legitimate our gaze.

Without knowing it, our search for a label other than "tourist" had repeated a trope that typifies many academic reflections on travel not only to Auschwitz but also to other places where tourists go. Characterized by the anthropologist David Brown in the formula "They are tourists, I am not," the distinction between legitimate travelers (scholars, students, pilgrims) and casual travelers exemplifies an almost ritualized exercise in self-justification that my group was reenacting.[9] By cleansing oneself of any affiliation with tourism, one legitimates travel by invoking more respectable terms. That is not to erase any distinctions between the anthropologist's extended immersion in a non-native culture, a historian's immersion in a distant archive, or a language student's immersion in a foreign tongue, on the one hand, and the (presumably typical) tourist's often-cursory encounter, on the other. Rather, it is to ask in greater specificity how they are different, but also how they are the same. What goes unacknowledged in the invocation of the "They are tourists, I am not" formula is that tourism can vary in lengths of stay, degrees of preparation, and impact on the traveler's life. Furthermore, given the growth

Figure 1.1. The gathering point for the tour at the Auschwitz-Birkenau Memorial and Museum, just outside the main entrance at Auschwitz I, July 2012. Tourists have already entered the terrain once occupied by the Nazi camp, as illustrated by enlarged aerial photos on large placards at the back left. A concession stand and bookstore are at the rear right. Photo by the author.

of tourism worldwide and the emergence of new forms of it, such as eco-tourism or service tourism, the reliance on stereotypical characterizations of tourists that deny the legitimacy of their travels appears increasingly simplistic.[10]

The remainder of this chapter explores in greater depth the "who" question as it relates to tourism at Auschwitz. If, as Pollock suggests, the ethics of Holocaust tourism asks travelers to consider their subject position, I would argue that dichotomies between the tourist and the pilgrim, the tourist and the educator, or other modulations of the "they are tourists, I am not" formula are inadequate to capture the motives, identities, and experiences of visitors to this site. Such formulations put tourism into an all-too-predictable binary relationship with other roles that are presumed to be more legitimate. I will argue instead for a concept of the tourist that is inclusive of numerous, fluid, and even contradictory subjectivities, ranging from the pilgrim and the researcher to the uninformed and the morbidly curious. To arrive at a more complex view of present-day tourism to Auschwitz, I explore how the site itself has developed over time. The aim is to demonstrate that the space of Auschwitz is itself fluid, meaning that it has developed over time and that it continues to respond to both the ethical imperatives of history and the political/economic exigencies of the tourist industry. This condition of flux is, I contend, apparent to tourists in a number of ways because the memorial openly acknowledges its ongoing evolution.

After summarizing the history of Auschwitz as a memorial, I shift into a discussion of the kinds of insights tourists can gain by visiting Auschwitz today. This approach relies in part on a phenomenology of tourism that emphasizes how sensory perception of the space can produce knowledge. As many scholars have acknowledged, tourism relies heavily on vision, but it would be a mistake to reduce the perceptions available to tourists to sight—smells, sounds, temperatures, and other non-visual sensory experiences shape the tourist's experience at Auschwitz as well, and not necessarily in expected ways.[11] By giving an account of the tourist's encounter with the memorial space of Auschwitz, I examine how tourists are invited to reflect on their relationship to the Holocaust, both in terms of the event experienced by those who were there from 1941 to 1945 and as a collective memory in the present. I frame this reflection in terms of bearing witness, asking how tourists to places like Auschwitz receive and process testimony from the past. Tourists do not arrive as blank slates but as socially and politically situated subjects with different degrees of historical knowledge who bring expectations to Auschwitz and other such memorials, hoping that they will acquire some new or deeper understanding of the murder of six million Jews. By hoping to access the space of an event that is temporally beyond reach, tourists search for an immediacy they may not find in literature, film, or other media. The degree to which expectations are fulfilled affects the nature of bearing witness through tourism.

Historically, tourists to Auschwitz have embodied multiple and even contradictory identities, both over time and across its terrain. This variety of tourist experiences belies the categorization in so much scholarship of visitors as either tourists or pilgrims (or some other term in a binary opposition). Instead of the stale tourist/pilgrim (or tourist/student, tourist/scholar, tourist/artist) dichotomy, which merely

recapitulates the "they are tourists, I am not" scheme, witnessing offers a framework that is especially relevant for Auschwitz and possibly
explanatory of its evolution as a memorial site. The focus on witnessing does not magically resolve the tension between the tourist and the
pilgrim; instead, it focuses on what the visitor perceives at Auschwitz
in relation to the suffering of prisoners, the brutality of perpetrators,
or the indifference of others. Since tourists arrive after the event being
memorialized, actual witnessing seems at first to be impossible. But if
we explore the concept somewhat further, thinking of witnessing as an
intersubjective, communicative mode of transferring knowledge, there
is some merit in characterizing tourism to Auschwitz as such.[12] The
claim of witnessing needs to overcome the inescapable temporal gap
that separates tourists from the perpetrators and victims. If tourists are
called to bear witness, what or who takes the place of the dead whose
testimony they seek? The history of the memorial may offer clues that
begin to answer that question.

Auschwitz as Memorial and Museum: The Postwar Era

Like other Nazi concentration and extermination camps, Auschwitz has
existed as a memorial and museum far longer than it functioned as a
center for torture and killing. Obviously the evacuation of the camp by
the Nazis and its liberation by the Red Army mark a definitive moment
in the site's history, the end of the Nazis' largest and, by the end, most
developed site of genocide and repression. The Red Army arrived to witness a camp that had been abandoned by the SS, who had attempted
to destroy the evidence of their crimes by blowing up the remaining
crematoria. But the destruction was far from complete, and many prisoners remained behind to bear witness to what had transpired there. The
story of the site since 1945 has been the effort to gather and preserve evidence of what took place there, to create a site for memorialization and
education, and to contextualize the Nazi crimes within competing and
shifting political narratives. At the same time, Auschwitz has undergone
a gradual transformation from a local to a global tourist destination.[13]

   That evolution was not clear from the outset, at least during the Cold
War. As the historian Tim Cole points out, Auschwitz was better known
on the Eastern side of the Iron Curtain than on the Western side for

decades after the war. Because different liberating armies reached different camps, Bergen-Belsen and Buchenwald were more familiar names to Great Britain and to the United States, respectively.[14] As the Holocaust became an ever-greater part of public discourse in the West, the name of Auschwitz became better known by the 1970s, so much so that by now it has become a "metonymy for the Holocaust as a whole"[15] in the East and West alike. The end of the Cold War meant easier access to the site for Western scholars, whose accounts of Auschwitz began to appear in the 1990s.[16] As these studies have shown, the archives at the Auschwitz-Birkenau Memorial and Museum serve as an important primary source of documentation about the Holocaust, but they also serve a secondary purpose: They offer an account of the management of the site as a tourist destination, not only conveying facts and figures but also revealing the geopolitical currents the site's managers have had to navigate over the years.[17] The development of tourism has in fact been a constant feature of the place's postwar history, a force both shaping and being shaped by the memory and remains of Auschwitz since 1945.

Before the arrival of the Red Army on January 27, 1945, the SS had already taken the majority of prisoners on a deadly forced march westward, but some 9,000 prisoners who were too sick or feeble to be evacuated were left behind. In the immediate aftermath of liberation, the camp served as a field hospital and displaced-persons camp for those who remained. Although Red Army and Polish volunteers worked to restore the health of those whom they could save, malnutrition and disease continued to claim many lives. Of the former prisoners who recovered, most were able to leave the camp by March or April 1945.

Meanwhile, as medics and volunteers tended the sick, investigators began to gather evidence of the crimes committed there. As early as November 1942, the Soviet Union had established the Extraordinary Soviet State Commission for the Investigation of the Crimes of the German-Fascist Aggressors, a body devoted to prosecuting and punishing perpetrators of Nazi war crimes. It was this body that had mandated the preservation of the camps liberated by the Red Army. Before reaching Polish territory, the Soviets had preserved evidence of the murders committed in Soviet and Baltic territories by the Einsatzgruppen, the SS units that liquidated Jewish populations as the German Wehrmacht advanced eastward. In July 1944, the Red Army discovered the Majdanek camp on the outskirts of Lublin, and within a month it had established a museum on the site to bear witness to the atrocities perpetrated there. Among the barracks and mass graves, Majdanek also held ample evidence of the use of gas chambers to murder Jews sent there for extermination.[18] Thus, by the time the Red Army reached Auschwitz six months later, it had already made clear its intention to preserve evidence of war crimes for posterity.[19] While the first official steps at establishing a museum at Auschwitz date to April 1946, slightly more than a year after the Red Army's arrival, the conceptual foundations for preserving the camp as testimony predate its liberation. In other words, the twin purposes of gathering forensic evidence and ensuring memorialization shared the goal of preserving the camp as a form of testimony, a top priority for liberators and survivors alike.[20] As a native communist government was groomed for leadership in Poland, Polish agencies began taking over this work in the camps situated within its borders, including all of the *Vernichtungslager*, or extermination camps (Auschwitz-Birkenau, Bełżec, Chełmno, Majdanek, Sobibór, and Treblinka). By April 1946, a little more than one year after liberation, the Polish Ministry of Culture and Art sent a committee of former prisoners to Auschwitz to begin work on the museum, led by the former prisoner Tadeusz Wąsowicz,[21] whom Nazis had imprisoned for membership in the Polish resistance and who was to become the museum's first director.

While the camp's liberators needed to preserve evidence for prosecution and punishment of war criminals, the camp's preservation as a site of commemoration was also always a long-term goal—albeit one with multiple and even contradictory agendas. In the case of Auschwitz and Majdanek, forensics and memorialization were both facilitated by the relatively intact state of the camps, which had been in operation just before liberation, leaving the Nazis insufficient time to destroy the evidence of mass killing. Despite their relatively intact state, there were immediate obstacles to ensuring preservation of the camps. The widespread deprivation across war-ravaged Poland meant that resources were scarce, and some of the physical structures of both camps were dismantled to serve the needs of the living. The wood used to build the barracks was needed for construction elsewhere in Poland, and so in March 1946 the District Liquidation Bureau, the Polish agency charged with the management of buildings and inventory that came into Polish possession after the war, oversaw the dismantling of the barracks at Birkenau.[22] Tourists today can see the results of such scarcity at Birkenau and Majdanek, where the vast majority of wooden barracks are gone. At Birkenau, only brick chimneys remain where the majority of barracks once stood. The exceptions are a few wooden barracks at both memorials—some of them reconstructed—and the first barracks built from brick at Birkenau in what was to become the *Frauenlager*, or women's camp. Along with the salvaged building materials went other "articles of everyday use" found at the camp, distributed across Poland to families who had lost everything in the war.[23] These included utensils, pots and pans, tools, fabrics—whatever was salvageable and practical.

The primary mission of the Extraordinary Soviet State Commission for the Investigation of the Crimes of the German-Fascist Aggressors was the preservation of a past that could be used to bring about the swift punishment of the Nazi perpetrators. Trials of accused perpetrators were important for establishing the legitimacy of communism in Eastern Europe as the vanquisher of fascism.[24] Of course, this narrative necessitated officially mandated amnesia about the pact between Stalin and Hitler to devour Poland, which had lasted until Germany launched Operation Barbarossa against the Soviet Union in June 1941. Given Poland's victimization at the hands of both Hitler and Stalin, the pro-Soviet agenda did not coincide comfortably with the postwar aspirations of Poles for a liberated and independent state. The competing interests of the Soviet liberators and the Polish survivors of Auschwitz led to tension over whose story would be told—and whose story would be suppressed.[25] Soviet oversight of Poland's new communist government, by no means an expression of Poland's popular will, ensured the dominance of Polish-Soviet brotherhood in official discourse.[26] But Polish national identity could not be so easily suppressed, and Stalin's imposition of communism reinforced Poland's sense of victimization at the hands of both Germany and the Soviet Union.[27]

Polish and Soviet tensions had an immediate impact on the organization of the Auschwitz-Birkenau Memorial and Museum as its staff pondered which messages visitors would receive. Would the site commemorate Polish resistance to Hitler in heroic terms? Would it acknowledge the other national, ethnic, and religious groups of victims who perished there? Would it commemorate Polish martyrdom or celebrate liberation by Stalin's Red Army? How would murdered Red Army prisoners of war, the first group to be gassed at Auschwitz with Zyklon B, be commemorated? However these questions were to be answered, it was clear from the outset that the emphasis would not be on Jewish suffering. Nor would the site emphasize the suffering of other groups such as the Sinti and Roma (Gypsies), homosexuals, Jehovah's Witnesses, and so-called asocials (the indigent, prostitutes, and other social outcasts).[28] While brief mention was made of these victims, their suffering was to be subsumed into a triumphant master narrative of communist-led liberation.

Since the guiding ideology for any postwar memorial at Auschwitz had to advance a pro-Soviet narrative, the museum's displays had to conform to a worldview that saw history in terms of class, not religion, race, or ethnicity. The fact that the vast majority of Auschwitz's victims were Jews, or that Gypsies were also selected on the basis of alleged biological difference, was not acknowledged. Instead of emphasizing the racism inherent in Nazi ideology toward its victims, under Soviet influence the museum portrayed the victims, perpetrators, and resisters in terms of a class-based ideology that sought to overcome ethnic and religious identities. The Second World War (the Great Patriotic War, in the Soviet Union's parlance) was cast as a war between the capitalist/imperialist ambitions of Hitler's fascism on the one hand and the international liberation of workers and peasants through Stalin's communism on the other. The Soviet view blurred the victims' identities into an international collective united in having suffered under Hitler's capitalist-imperialist aggression.[29]

Despite the unavoidable submission to Soviet-guided propaganda, the reality of Auschwitz's location in Poland, its management by Polish authorities, and its outreach to Polish visitors assured that Polish suffering would dominate the museum's displays. The first incarnation of Auschwitz as a memorial highlighted the (mostly Catholic) Polish political prisoners interned and murdered there. The prevalence to this day of the word "martyr" at the memorial subsumes the diverse identities of the camp's victims into a Polish Catholic perspective whereby the camp is interpreted as a site of national persecution cast in distinctly Christian terms. (I shall return to the use of the term "martyr" momentarily.) While Auschwitz's victims included some 150,000 Catholic Poles, more than 1 million Jews, 23,000 Sinti and Roma, 15,000 Soviet soldiers, and thousands of other minorities were killed there.[30] The imperatives of Stalinist ideology and Polish Catholic nationalism converged to de-emphasize the fact that Jews formed the vast majority of the camp's victims.

The researcher Andrew Charlesworth makes the case that the relatively preserved state of Auschwitz I (the original section of the Auschwitz camp system, also called the *Stammlager*) facilitated its prioritization of Polish over Jewish suffering. He suggests that the District Liquidation Bureau's permission to dismantle numerous buildings in Auschwitz II (Birkenau), where the majority of Jewish victims had been murdered, allowed officials to sidestep the unique disaster of Jewish suffering. The emphasis on Auschwitz, Charlesworth points out, served a more sinister purpose of actively ignoring Jewish suffering:

> [Of these] six death camps whose primary function was the extermination of European Jewry, . . . Chełmno, Bełżec, Sobibór, and Treblinka could be deemed inappropriate in that they had been destroyed by the Nazis, leaving little or no trace remaining. This was also very convenient for those who wished to ignore the specificity of Jewish suffering, as these were wholly death camps for Jewish extermination. This left Auschwitz and Majdanek.[31]

Charlesworth's implication, namely that tacit anti-Semitism motivated the choice of Auschwitz as a central memorial to Polish victims, is hard to evaluate. While the history of anti-Semitism and the plight of Jews in postwar Poland certainly legitimate this suspicion, there were less cynical considerations to take into account as well, particularly in light of the state of ruin that characterized postwar Poland. As Charlesworth acknowledges, Auschwitz was the most extensive, the most recently operating, and the most intact of the Nazi camps in Poland. That fact alone could be sufficient to explain why Auschwitz was chosen as a memorial facility over other sites. Moreover, the solid brick buildings of the Auschwitz I *Stammlager* were a premium in a war-ravaged country where standing structures were in short supply, quite in contrast to the readily dismantled or burned wooden barracks found at Auschwitz II (Birkenau) or Majdanek. Furthermore, the fact remains that both

Jewish and non-Jewish Poles were murdered at Auschwitz, albeit by different methods and in different numbers. Finally, it is important to resist the temptation to reduce either Soviet-sponsored socialism or Polish nationalism to anti-Semitism, even if both were capable of patently anti-Semitic policies and attitudes.

Despite the emphasis on Soviet communist and Polish nationalist ideologies (and the inherent tensions between them), over time it proved impossible to ignore the anti-Semitism behind the Nazis' murderous logic. A gradual and much belated shift occurred in the portrayal of fascism, from describing it as a rogue form of capitalism (the Soviet view) to acknowledging the racism inherent in Hitler's fantasy of German superiority. Today, tourists to Auschwitz are informed explicitly about the genocidal logic of the camp and the system of extermination that evolved there for the purpose of ridding Europe of its Jewish population. Given the inhospitable climate in Stalinist Eastern Europe for acknowledging the victimization of Jews, Roma, or any other group defined as an ethnicity, one must wonder how and when that shift in narrative came about and how tourism has been a witness to that shift.

Even before the war's end, knowledge about the Holocaust had spread internationally among occupying forces and displaced populations, both of which were on the move. The American and British experience of liberating concentration camps such as Bergen-Belsen, Buchenwald, and Dachau, though technically not extermination camps like Birkenau, made indelible impressions on those troops and the journalists who accompanied them.[32] While these camps within the German Reich were not originally established for the sole purpose of murdering Jews, they became the destination of forced marches from the extermination camps as the Nazis moved their prisoners westward away from the advancing Red Army. Of those who survived the death marches, many died in horrible conditions of disease and starvation in the camps liberated by the Western allies.[33] In short, the shocking encounters with Nazi camps was an experience shared by Soviet, American, and British allies.

Likewise, the Jewish diaspora ensured that knowledge of the Holocaust would spread beyond the borders of Nazi-occupied Europe. Wartime experiences and continued anti-Semitism in Eastern Europe after 1945 led large numbers of Jews who had survived the Holocaust to migrate to new countries, especially to the United States, Canada, and the British Mandate of Palestine.[34] As accounts of the genocide spread internationally among Jewish communities, the local administration at Auschwitz found it impossible to ignore the growing global awareness of what had taken place there, even if that pressure met with considerable ideological resistance from the state. By the late 1960s, the emphasis at Auschwitz on Polish victimization began to make way for a more forthright acknowledgment that the vast majority of victims at Auschwitz were murdered for no other reason than being Jewish. What is remarkable is that this transition took place at a time when the Communist Party in Poland was becoming increasingly and overtly anti-Semitic. Tourism, particularly in the mode of service tourism and commemorative visits, had begun to relocate the responsibility for Auschwitz memorialization in a more deliberately international context, with groups from other countries demanding a role in shaping remembrance and preservation at the memorial, as we will see below. Tourism thereby played an important role in furthering the process of acknowledging the Jewish victims at Auschwitz, even at a time when the political climate in Poland would seem to have been unfavorable.[35]

Throughout the Cold War, alternating periods of tension and thaw between East and West had a direct impact on tourism, severely restricting travel across the Iron Curtain at some times while easing restrictions at others. But tourism also exerted pressure of its own to allow access to travelers. Besides the fact that tourism was one of the few ways in which citizens from East and West could get to know one another, the considerable amount of wealth generated by the tourism industry was crucial to the struggling economies of postwar Europe. That was particularly true for the Soviet-dominated East, whose currency had little purchasing power internationally. The fact that tourism brought in the West's hard currency to the economically struggling Soviet Bloc ensured that the doors could never stay closed for long. And whenever those doors opened, tourism between East and West represented an exchange not only of currency but also of cultural values, despite the strident rhetoric of postwar propaganda.[36]

Tourists always bring expectations, and the tourism industry has to work to respond and accommodate those expectations while in turn making demands of its own on tourists. The dynamics of tourism as a market, as a circulation not only of goods and services but also of cultural expectations and performances, applies as much to Auschwitz as to any other tourist destination. The dramatic transformations that have taken place at the Auschwitz memorial site are a powerful reminder that tourism cannot be reduced to the passive consumption of displays decided by others. Rather, tourism both responds to and helps influence policies that govern the memorial sites. Whatever other geopolitical factors have shaped access to Auschwitz—and they are considerable—tourism has also played a decisive role, and indeed, one could argue that tourism offered a highly visible stage where geopolitical tensions could find expression. In the years following World War II, tourism became one of the most public arenas in which communist and Polish nationalist narratives at Auschwitz could be challenged by an international public, the grounds on which struggle over access to the site was waged, and the measure by which the gradual opening of Auschwitz to the international community was achieved.[37]

The Evolution of Tourism to Auschwitz: The Cold War and Beyond

The earliest tourists to Auschwitz were composed of school groups from Poland, whose visit to the site was a mandatory part of the curriculum.[38] These school groups saw Auschwitz I, the *Stammlager*, where the Nazis kept Polish figures whom they regarded as ideological enemies, including Polish Communists and many members of the Catholic Church. The first crematorium was built in Auschwitz I, and an adjacent room that had been designed as a morgue was converted into a gas chamber, even though Auschwitz I was not established originally as a center for extermination on a massive scale. At the *Stammlager* was the infamous Block 11, where the torture and executions of prisoners, including Father Maximilian Kolbe, were carried out. Other prisoners killed at Auschwitz I included 600 Soviet prisoners of war who were murdered in 1941, gassed in experiments using Zyklon B that led to the use of that chemical as the principal method for mass murder at Birkenau. Since the Polish state after the war exercised a monopoly on school curricula, the intact remains of Auschwitz I provided a powerful teaching moment that could be used to reinforce a sense of Poland's indebtedness to their Soviet liberators and point to sacrifices made by the Red Army

Figure 1.2. The crematorium at Auschwitz I, August 2007, with the entrance to the gas chamber that was originally a morgue. The gas chamber was reconstructed to include shower heads to depict the destroyed gas chambers of Birkenau. Photo by the author.

to defeat Germany. At the same time, Polish schools reinforced a sense of Polish national solidarity by emphasizing the martyrdom of such figures as Father Kolbe.

Meanwhile, Auschwitz II (Birkenau) remained beyond the earliest guided tours. Visitors could cover the two kilometers to the site on their own, with no guide to accompany them. With limited resources for managing such an expansive site and few suitable structures in which to install exhibitions, Birkenau remained largely a ruin; the story of Birkenau was instead told at Auschwitz I. The collections of hair, the suitcases and the personal effects of the new arrivals, much of which had been warehoused at Birkenau, were brought to the *Stammlager* after the war to be shown to tourists. The museum faced an overwhelming task of managing a camp complex that included over forty subcamps, of which Birkenau was the most notorious. Given the infamy of Birkenau as an extermination camp, clearly some arrangement would have to be made to emphasize Birkenau in the geography of tourism to Auschwitz, even if the site did not so easily conform to the ideology of the immediate postwar era.

As early as 1957, the museum announced an international competition to erect a monument at Birkenau that would serve as a focal point for memorialization there.[39] The monument was not erected until 1967, and even there, the Jewish and Gypsy identities of those gassed on arrival was blurred into the undifferentiated and incorrect number of "four million [*sic*] people [who] suffered and died here at the hands of the Nazi murderers between the years 1940 and 1945."[40] As James E. Young, a pioneer scholar in the field of Holocaust memorialization, explains, "The figure of 4 million was as wrong as it was round, arrived at by a combination of [camp commandant Rudolf Höss's] self-aggrandizing exaggerations, Polish perceptions of their great losses, and the Soviet occupiers' desire to create socialist martyrs."[41]

While the Iron Curtain ensured that most visitors to the camp memorial would come from Poland and other Warsaw Pact nations, a gradual process of stabilization in relations with the West during the Cold War brought about the steady increase in tourism to the Auschwitz-Birkenau Memorial and Museum from other parts of the globe.[42] These groups ranged from church groups from East and West Germany, who began traveling to the site in 1966 as a gesture of atonement,[43] to the Israeli-sponsored March of the Living, which has been gathering Jewish participants from around the globe since 1988 to travel to Poland and Israel as a way of identifying with a collective Jewish trauma and its redemption in a Jewish state.[44] Meanwhile, school groups and socialist youth organizations from across the Eastern Bloc countries continued to visit the camp as a way of forging solidarity among one another, united in their suffering under fascism, their liberation by the Soviet Union, and their shared project of realizing socialism.

Among the tour groups traveling to Auschwitz from abroad, one of the oldest comes from both sides of a divided Germany. Since the 1960s, the ecumenical Christian organization Aktion Sühnezeichen, or Action Reconciliation, has organized travel by volunteers for service abroad as an effort to acknowledge and make restitution for crimes committed by Germany during the Third Reich. While the organization extended into both East and West Germany, the Cold War made collaboration between both branches extremely difficult. Still, both branches played active roles in the maintenance of Auschwitz and other camps in Poland as sites of remembrance. Among the activities of Aktion Sühnezeichen was the unearthing of Crematorium II and Crematorium III in Birkenau, meant as a way to acknowledge Germany's perpetration of genocide.[45] Aktion Sühnezeichen presented a case of "volunteer tourism," a term that has emerged in more recent years to describe service-oriented travel. For Aktion Sühnezeichen, the purpose of these trips was conceived as a form of penance, a religiously inflected modality of the German discourse of *Aufarbeitung der Vergangenheit* (working through the past).[46] The presence of Aktion Sühnezeichen in Auschwitz, and its status as an alternative to compulsory military service in West Germany, merged two discourses of reconciliation in West Germany. The first, a specifically Christian discourse of atonement, sought reconciliation through confession and good works. The other, the political discourse of the Federal Republic, sought to overcome the divisions of the Cold War that had its clearest manifestation in a Germany divided into two states.[47] These two discourses were not mutually exclusive; indeed, they informed and enhanced one another.

While Christian-based service tourism was allowed to make inroads into the landscape of Holocaust memory in Poland, Jewish organizations faced a less hospitable climate. With the establishment of the state of Israel in 1948, the early Cold War years made some accommodation to Jewish remembrance possible. But the period of tolerance toward anything perceived as Jewish nationalism on Eastern European soil was fated to run afoul of the prevailing Stalinist narrative for the postwar era. In Poland, many Jews wished to preserve some sense of a separate ethnic identity that they saw as compatible with socialism, and thus enabled their participation in the Polish government and party offices. That comity came to an abrupt halt in 1968, when Poland purged Jews from the government. The image of Polish anti-Semitism made an unwelcome return to the world stage and positioned Jewish commemorators at Auschwitz in an oppositional relationship to the Polish state. Poland had put itself in the awkward position of suppressing the Jewish remnant within its borders while still having to maintain some openness to Jewish interests in the Auschwitz memorial from abroad.

The fusion of political and religious interests is apparent in another prominent tour group that has been traveling to Auschwitz since 1988. The March of the Living brings Jewish teens from all over the world to Poland and to Israel "to learn the lessons of the Holocaust and to lead the Jewish people into the future vowing '*Never Again*'" (original emphasis). Each year its participants go "to Poland on Yom Hashoah, Holocaust Memorial Day, to march from Auschwitz to Birkenau, the largest concentration camp complex built during World War II," after which they travel "to Israel to observe Yom HaZikaron, Israel Memorial Day, and Yom Ha'Atzmaut, Israel Independence Day."[48] Clearly tied to a narrative of national and religious identity, the mission of the March of the Living is "both universal (fighting indifference, racism and injustice) and particular (opposing anti-Semitism, and strengthening Jewish identity and connection to Israel)."[49] It positions the march at Auschwitz as a cornerstone in the establishment of a Jewish future.

The religious studies scholar Oren Baruch Stier characterizes the March of the Living as a form of "memory tourism," relying on the familiar notion of tourism as pilgrimage suggested in different studies by the anthopologists Dean MacCannell and Nelson Graburn, in which travelers engage in a ritualized commemoration of history. But, as Stier also points out, there is an undeniably secular dimension to this ritual that incorporates what some see as troubling images of nationalism.[50] Participating youths frequently wave or drape themselves in the Israeli flag at Auschwitz and elsewhere on the March in a gesture of national pride that underscores the March's emphasis on the resurgence of the Jewish people despite all attempts to eradicate them. But the contrast between the visit to Auschwitz, framed as the European past, and the subsequent journey to Israel, framed as the land of rebirth, casts a harsh light on Poland. As the anthropologist Jack Kugelmass has described, Jewish youth may experience unwelcome reactions from some Poles they encounter, which they are likely to attribute to anti-Semitism.[51] For the young American Jews participating in the March of the Living whom Kugelmass describes, the scant knowledge they have of Eastern Europe as an ancestral home comes into direct contact with Eastern Europe as a living place, and what visitors experience as hostility means that "the mythic becomes tangible."[52] History may become more real to these travelers, but at the same time the present-day experience of Poland gets read through a particular historical narrative that ignores the perspective of present-day Poles, who may understandably resent being equated with the perpetrators and bystanders of the Holocaust. This is the argument by the Israeli anthropologist Jackie Feldman, who points out that the participating youths' negative perceptions of Poles goes relatively unchallenged because of the minimal contact that the participants have with the local population.[53] But Feldman also concedes that some participants may reexamine their impressions as they acquire other travel experiences that challenge such simplistic associations.[54]

Whatever one may feel about the ritual of commemoration at Auschwitz for specific political purposes, it has been a feature of the site since its liberation. Jonathan Huener explains that the grounds have

> always functioned as a stage for public commemorative ritual and political tourism. Its monuments, structures, and open spaces have attracted pilgrims, politicians, and activists participating in any variety of politically charged demonstrations. Polish nationalist commemorative ceremonies on the anniversary of the liberation, rallies organized to condemn American imperialism, Roman Catholic services at the site on All Saints' eve [sic], or penitential German pilgrimages to the site—such are the ways that Auschwitz has been used throughout the postwar decades.[55]

However problematic the use of Auschwitz as a "stage for public commemorative ritual and political tourism," the fact that such commemoration has taken place since the establishment of a memorial reinforces the notion that tourism is not merely incidental to geopolitical shifts but part and parcel of it. The fact that these acts of commemoration remain controversial suggests that tourism becomes not the cause of historical or contemporary geopolitical tensions but, rather, one arena in which these issues are addressed, debated, and perhaps even resolved.

A closer look at the relationship between the Catholic Church and the Auschwitz Memorial illustrates the point. In recent years, controversies have erupted over Catholic commemoration at Auschwitz in deeply Catholic Poland and anti-Semitic utterances by many Polish Catholic clergy, including Cardinal Józef Glemp and Bishop Tadeusz Pieronek.[56] The use of crosses to commemorate the murder of notable Catholics at Auschwitz, such as the Carmelite nun Edith Stein or the Franciscan friar Maximilian Kolbe, have been a source of ongoing tension. Stein was born into an observant Jewish home in Poland but converted to Christianity in 1922. Pope John Paul II raised her to sainthood in 1998, but Jewish groups argue that she was murdered because she was regarded by the Nazis as a member of the Jewish race, not because she was a devout Catholic. The infamous hunger cell in Block 11 where Maximilian Kolbe starved to death is also presented to the tourist as a site of Catholic martyrdom. Kolbe was arrested by the Gestapo for assisting refugees hiding from the Nazis and subsequently sent to Auschwitz, where he was murdered along with nine other inmates as collective retribution for three escapees from the camp. The controversies around the canonization of Catholic martyrs during John Paul's papacy led to an international outcry on behalf of Jewish victims and survivors, whose own suffering had been historically obscured by a Polish narrative of national martyrdom. Perhaps in response to these outcries, some in the Vatican recognized the need to respect the diverse religions of the camps' victims and to acknowledge the genocide perpetrated against Jews. The shift in the Vatican's public approach to Auschwitz was marked by John Paul's 1993 order to disband a Carmelite convent that had established itself on the camp's grounds in 1984 in a structure that had once been used to warehouse Zyklon B.

The list of controversies is long and seemingly inexhaustible, suggesting that the complexity of commemoration at the camp is unavoidable. But they also testify to the uneasy evolution from a monument chiefly to Polish "martyrdom" to an appropriate recognition of the Holocaust of Europe's Jews. At present, the commemorative activities at the camp seek to accommodate both of these narratives equally. The camp faces a difficult choice: to allow the victims to commemorate their own suffering in ways that are meaningful to them, even at the risk of historical distortion, or to foreground the perspective of Nazi ideology to explain why different groups, but especially Jews, were sent there. As the camp has evolved, it appears that the memorial has increasingly acknowledged the perpetrator's perspective, educating the touring public about the ideology that led to genocide and mass murder. This has led James E. Young to worry that the camp may provide an unwitting victory to Nazi ideology, since the artifacts on display "force us to recall the victims as the Germans have remembered them to us: in the collected debris of a destroyed civilization."[57] That is, tourism recollects the Nazis' intentions at the expense of the lives of their victims. Young is, of course, correct in a sense—Auschwitz is perceived as the embodiment of the Nazi genocide. But in fairness, the camp memorial makes an effort to remind the visitor that each victim had a biography, a family, a hometown. The Auschwitz-Birkenau Memorial and Museum includes several national exhibitions, each in a block at the *Stammlager*, each with a different way of telling stories about the victims deported from their lands.

While I would not wish to ignore Young's concern about memory as the camps preserve it, I would point out that tourism to Auschwitz has proven perfectly capable of accommodating different ideologies that do not resign themselves to a view of Auschwitz as the last word on the victims. The history of tour groups to Auschwitz and the tensions over the site's message remind us that memorialization is a process, that the apparent fixity of place can often give the illusion that history itself is somehow static, rather than a process of continual discovery. Indeed, Young himself acknowledges the ability of memorials to adapt.[58] The fact that different tourists at different times have encountered different incarnations of the Auschwitz-Birkenau Memorial and Museum should remind us that tourism is a fluid enterprise, an evolving encounter with places and events that respond to changing contexts. The danger in tourism is that the visitor may not be informed of these changes and may entertain the illusion that the place is unchanged since the event it commemorates. The museum staff therefore has an obligation to inform its visitors not only about the development of Auschwitz from a concentration camp to an extermination camp but also about its continual development as a memorial.

The examples of tourism to Auschwitz presented thus far—Polish-sponsored tourism as a place of national suffering, German service tourism as a form of atonement, or Israeli efforts to instill a sense of unity in the Jewish diaspora centered around the Jewish state—suggest that the motivations for travel to the site are various and sometimes incongruous with one another. But they share a common belief that being there matters, that one's presence leads to increased historical insight, deeper intercultural understanding, or better knowledge of one's own place in the world.[59] Anthropological studies of tourism explore these beliefs and lead to portrayals of all kinds of tourism as pilgrimage, as modern-day ritual, as a search for transcendence.[60] But such labels also raise serious questions, if for no other reason than because the solemnity they grant travelers may be unwarranted. The idea that modern-day tourism's motivations can be reduced to a single root impulse universal to all humans is an anthropological fantasy that offers no help in accounting for the disparities among travelers and their experiences. While many visitors cast the journey to Auschwitz as a spiritual experience, others see it as a sense of civic duty, while others may go along because of group pressure. Some visitors articulate all of these motivations, moving fluidly from one to another as they negotiate their pathways. Vacationers in Poland, for example, often visit Auschwitz as a day's excursion from nearby Kraków, to which they will return and resume some more obviously pleasurable mode of tourism after a day they regard as pilgrimage. School groups travel to Auschwitz because they have to—it is an assigned field trip, and students may actually resist the experience of tourism assigned to them. Politicians, dignitaries, and even soccer teams pay their respects at the site on certain occasions. To see Auschwitz—or to be seen seeing Auschwitz—has become such a staple of contemporary travel in Eastern Europe that one is just as likely to comment on its omission as on its inclusion.[61] The point is that tourism, including Holocaust tourism, accommodates both lofty and more mundane motivations.

The separation of visitors to Auschwitz into tourists versus pilgrims, tourists versus dignitaries, tourists versus scholars, or other variations of "they are tourists, I am not" is a well-rehearsed strategy for assigning legitimacy to some forms of travel by denying it to others.[62] The tourist always becomes the signifier of the shallow, superficial, or consumerist term in a binary that is all too often self-serving. But solemnity and frivolity, abstinence and indulgence, frugality and consumerism often travel as pairs. For example, the presence of a bookstore at a holy site invites the pilgrim's participation in some form of commercial tourism; by the same token, a non-believer's participation in a group tour that includes a holy site may produce an attitude of reverence or deeply personal response to a foreign tradition or faith.[63] One need only recall the blend of piety and ribaldry in Chaucer's *Canterbury Tales* to recover an image of pilgrimage that is open to playful diversion.[64]

What is required to demonstrate that one is a serious pilgrim, not a frivolous tourist? Take the case of Adolek "Adam" Kohn, an Auschwitz survivor, whose return to Auschwitz along with his family demonstrates the difficulty in equating pilgrimage with seriousness or decorum. Kohn appears at Auschwitz, Dachau, Theresienstadt, and other sites in a video, still available on *YouTube*, filmed by his daughter Jane Korman in 2009.

In the clip, Kohn appears with four of his grandchildren dancing to Glo-ria Gaynor's disco hit, "I Will Survive." No doubt the video was intended as an expression of triumph of a family that has lived for three genera-tions despite everything. For Kohn's daughter and grandchildren, the trip was a visit to sites in Poland and the Czech Republic that had been part of their family's history—what many might call a pilgrimage.[65] The video went viral on the Internet and drew strong criticism from view-ers, including some from the survivor community, who understandably objected to the idea of anyone dancing on the victims' graves.

If tourism is inclusive of solemnity and profanity—and for many, Kor-man's video was an illustration of the latter—is it always the wrong side of the coin? If by "profanity" we mean the worldly, as opposed to the sacred, then the tendency in tourism studies to elevate the everyday into an ersatz form of the sacred may undervalue what is precisely not pil-grimage in Holocaust tourism. The anthropologist Malcolm Crick makes the important observation that "there is a problem, however, in elevating notions of play or sacred quest into a general explanatory framework."[66] His statement is a warning to avoid overstating the case for tourism, but I also take from his remarks the need to take the non-religious, non-transcendental aspects of Holocaust tourism seriously. Since the col-lapse of the Iron Curtain, the number of visitors to Auschwitz has rapidly grown to over two million per year.[67] Most are not survivors like Kohn, or perpetrators, or their descendants. Most are travelers curious about a site whose meaning they perceive as primarily historical.

One of the more critical accounts of tourism to Auschwitz comes from the historian Tim Cole. Like Pollock, Cole rightly situates travel to Auschwitz within the context of broader cultural representations of the Holocaust, reminding us that tourism is not hermetically sealed off from other forms representation, such as cinema, literature, or history books. He discusses the problematics of Holocaust remembrance in our media-saturated era and effectively points to the ease with which popular culture can misrepresent history while commercializing it—a familiar approach to Holocaust remembrance within mass culture.[68] Cole ultimately consigns tourism to the unethical body of practices, alongside Hollywood films or sensational novels, that distort Holocaust memory in an effort to profit from it. In his book *Selling the Holocaust*, he provides numerous examples of questionable tourism related to the

Holocaust. For example, he describes the phenomenon of "Schindler Tourism," in which travelers to Kraków visit the neighborhoods depicted in Steven Spielberg's famous film, allegedly without appreciating the distinction between Hollywood and history. In particular, he deplores the Schindler tour for reinforcing the film's oversimplification of the Holocaust into "a story of 'good versus evil'" that displaces attention from the Jewish victims to the heroism of an atypical German "savior."[69] Another tourist destination that Cole finds problematic is the highly visited Anne Frank House in Amsterdam, which also perpetuates the myth of a young teen's optimism in the face of disaster, as foregrounded in her diary. The attention to Anne Frank, whose diary Cole characterizes as "*the* canonical 'Holocaust' text," tends to lead its many readers to celebrate her perseverance while in hiding at the expense of confronting her terrible demise in Belsen after her deportation.[70] These criticisms derive from familiar critiques by the scholars Lawrence Langer, Alvin Rosenfeld, and others, but Cole applies them to tourism without exploring the ways in which tourism is distinct from the arts.

Having consigned several popular examples of Holocaust remembrance to the status of sellouts, Cole goes on to paint travelers to Auschwitz as duped consumers of a distorted history. While he reserves legitimacy for those he calls pilgrims (including himself), he portrays others as visiting a Holocaust theme park, which he dubs "Auschwitz-land":[71]

> Walking through "Auschwitz-land" we do not see an authentic past preserved carefully for the present. We don't experience the past as it really was, but experience a mediated past which has been carefully created for our viewing. . . . At "Auschwitz-land" we perhaps unwittingly enter a "Holocaust theme-park" rather than a "Holocaust concentration camp".
>
> We visit a contrived tourist attraction, which offers that which a culture saturated with the myth of the "Holocaust" expects to see. "Auschwitz-land" both plays a part in creating and perpetuating that myth, and depends upon the myth for its continued popularity. A tour round "Auschwitz-land" is about the consumption of a familiar landscape.[72]

Cole certainly has company in his concerns for the perception of Auschwitz as a "theme park," but his formulation of what he calls the

"Holocaust myth," which leads him to put the word "Holocaust" into quotations marks, is ill advised.[73] To be fair, Cole does not mean to imply the irreality of the genocide, as some might presume; rather, he points to the ubiquity of its literary and filmic representations. And if by "contrived" he means the lengths to which the Auschwitz-Birkenau Memorial and Museum has gone to preserve and even to restore certain structures, then he is correct in some superficial sense, although the camp hardly presents itself as a Holocaust reenactment à la Plimoth Plantation or Sturbridge Village.[74] If the Auschwitz-Birkenau Memorial and Museum is not a functioning concentration camp any more, why must it be a theme park? Cole's characterization of tourism to Auschwitz presents tourists as so unsophisticated that they cannot distinguish between a carefully managed monument and a simulated killing center.[75]

As Holocaust remembrance passes through a critical juncture—the inevitable passing of eyewitnesses to the disaster—it disperses into every corner of cultural representation. The emergence of Holocaust tourism is symptomatic of that dispersal. The diffusion of Holocaust memory into popular forms of remembrance, of which tourism is only one part, exceeds any simple pilgrim/tourist or concentration camp/theme park binary that seeks to contrast Holocaust tourism with prescribed modes of religious, scholarly, or aesthetically exclusive forms of remembrance. Admittedly, it is hardly surprising that Auschwitz should elicit the "They are tourists, I am not" response with such frequency and intensity. The ethical implications involved in "consuming" such a site loom large, and there are certainly tourists to Auschwitz whose engagement is superficial, even inappropriate. There are others, though, for whom a tour to Auschwitz is the catalyst for deeper reflection about the Holocaust.

Tourism makes reflection possible, but does not guarantee it. One must admit that some tourists will leave Auschwitz with little new insight or interest in further reflection. But the narrative that dominates the accounts by visitors to this site is that of a powerful or disturbing personal experience. Even visitors who complain about the noise or distractions of other tourists insist on the significance of their personal experience.[76] Tourists articulate a sense of responsibility to what they have observed and frequently exhort others to follow in their footsteps. Some define their insights more precisely than others, but they share a common theme of having seen something important and having learned from it. The question for the remainder of this chapter is whether their experiences constitute acts of witnessing.

The Tourist and Testimony

Tourism's heavy reliance on visuality alone might tempt us to think of tourists as "eyewitnesses," at least after the fact. Much as the liberating forces observed evidence of what had taken place prior to their arrival, tourists come to Auschwitz to view the traces of genocide in its most industrialized incarnation, although the scenes they encounter are vastly different. For tourism to enable a kind of witnessing, however, it must amount to more than a simple act of viewing displays that have been curated by museum staff for the last seventy years. Even if Auschwitz were unchanged from the moment of its liberation in 1945, seeing the remains of destruction would not suffice to grant tourists the designation of "witness."

"Witnessing" names a communicative act that translates a moment of experience into an utterance that, in turn, is heard by another.[77] At stake in the exchange is the veracity of the experience—the witness testifies in order to have an experience of reality confirmed. One becomes fully a witness only when one's report to a listener has been received and acknowledged. Witnessing is, in short, intersubjective.[78] For tourism to Auschwitz to embody witnessing, there needs to be the double articulation of something enunciated and something heard. The idea that the Auschwitz memorial complex conveys testimony about the Holocaust to interested tourists may appear to be a straightforward claim. One can compare a memoir written by a survivor with the evidence of the genocide presented through displays, documents, and narrations by tour guides, acknowledging their similarities in communicating a past experience. But often tourists are called upon to bear witness and produce testimony themselves, and the idea that such testimony can be of value may appear more dubious. As we will see, there is nothing simple about either claim.

To take up the first issue—how tourism to Auschwitz encounters the testimony of eyewitnesses (beyond the excerpts from such testimony that are on display)—it is useful to compare the artifacts, photographs, or even the landscape itself as forms of testimony that, though non-linguistic, engage in a form of communication with their viewers.[79] To ponder the nature of witnessing in this larger sense, the reception of written survivor testimony may indicate ways of thinking, not only about written or spoken eyewitness accounts, but also about such non-linguistic components of tourism that, nevertheless, say something about the past.

Survivor testimony is a thriving genre; indeed, Elie Wiesel has even claimed testimony as the genre of our age.[80] Whether read as books at home or encountered as videotaped interviews in museums, accounts by survivors, perpetrators, and other eyewitnesses promise their readers some degree of immediacy or affective connection to the disaster that dispassionate histories cannot.[81] Given the fallibility of human memory, historians are suspicious of the ability of testimony to enrich our factual knowledge about the Nazi genocide. Testimonial accounts nevertheless engage their readers on both a visceral and a metaphysical level, involving them emotionally and intellectually in profoundly troubling considerations about humanity and violence. Tourism draws on the power of such testimony to heighten the sense of immediacy that being there promises.[82] Survivor testimonies ask their audiences to listen carefully, to hear not only the account of the past but also the urgency and the struggle inherent in the survivor's struggle to render the account in words.[83] Readers are the audience that survivors require if their testimony is to be received, thus fulfilling the task of bearing witness.

But the intersubjectivity demanded of witnessing emerges as a critical problem in the reception of survivor testimony, some of which draws rather pessimistic conclusions about the adequacy of language to communicate a survivor's traumatic experiences. If such pessimism has a common origin, it may lie in the survivor accounts themselves. Whether they are Elie Wiesel's *Night*, Primo Levi's *Survival in Auschwitz* (also published as *If This Is a Man*), or any other testament to the ordeal of the Holocaust, survivor accounts typically express the need to remember, and, at the same time, they lament the hurdles to transmitting memories through language. In survivor testimony, witnessing is framed as obligation and impossibility, a Sisyphean task that can never be achieved adequately. We see this predicament in the preface to Levi's *Survival in Auschwitz*, where the author identifies a gap between his need to speak and his ability to provide a complete account:

I recognize, and ask indulgence for, the structural defects of the book. Its origins go back, not indeed in practice, but as an idea, an intention, to the days in the Lager. The need to tell our story to "the rest," to make "the rest" participate in it, had taken on for us, before our liberation and after, the character of an immediate and violent impulse, to the point of competing with our other elementary needs. The book has been written to satisfy this need: first and foremost, therefore, as an interior liberation. Hence its fragmentary character: the chapters have been written not in logical succession, but in order of urgency.[84]

Levi makes plain for his reader the therapeutic necessity of convincing "the rest"—which comes to encompass future generations as much as contemporaries who did not experience the camp—even at the expense of a logical progression. The fragmentary account cannot claim even to render Levi's own experiences exhaustively, suggesting that the experience of Auschwitz itself resists any logically ordered or complete representation; instead, Levi's need to bear witness appears as a "violent impulse."

Like Primo Levi, Elie Wiesel names a painful gap between the experience of the camp and its representation in testimony. Addressing the urgency to bear witness, Wiesel speaks of writing his testimony itself as a form of trauma, wondering if he composed *Night* "so as *not* to go mad or, on the contrary, to *go* mad in order to understand the nature of madness, the immense, terrifying madness that had erupted in history and in the conscience of mankind."[85] Wiesel goes on to identify language as the chief barrier to providing a full account:

Convinced that this period in history would be judged one day, I knew that I must bear witness. I also knew that, while I had many things to say, I did not have the words to say them. Painfully aware of my limitations, I watched helplessly as language became an obstacle. It became clear that it would be necessary to invent a new language. . . . I would conjure up other verbs, other images, other silent cries. It still was not right. But what exactly was "it"? "It" was something elusive, darkly shrouded for fear of being usurped, profaned. All the dictionary had to offer seemed meager, pale, lifeless.[86]

Wiesel bemoans the inadequacy of language to convey what he and others experienced, and in doing so he negates his own testimony's capacity to convey his experiences to others:

> Deep down, the witness knew then, as he does now, that his testimony would not be received. After all, it deals with an event that sprang from the darkest zone of man. Only those who experienced Auschwitz know what it was. Others will never know.[87]

For Wiesel, the obligation to bear witness becomes itself a kind of trauma because it seems doomed to fail. Wiesel registers this double traumatization not only through expressions of helplessness but in the very representation of his own consciousness as split. To underscore the impossibility of transferring knowledge through testimony, Wiesel portrays a disjuncture between the narrator of this passage and the younger self who wrote *Night*, referring to himself not as "I" but in the third person (something Wiesel does with some regularity in his prose). And yet that double traumatization mirrors the double articulation of bearing witness—Wiesel must become his own listener, since only one who has experienced what he did can receive his message.[88]

The prevalence of trauma as a category for approaching Holocaust survivor testimony suggests that tourism, to the extent it relays the experiences of camp prisoners, must overcome the same inadequacies of communication. Trauma theorists posit a breach between the survivors' experience, one the one hand, and their ability to convey that experience coherently to those who were not there, on the other. This breach is often expressed in terms of the Holocaust's unspeakability or its incomprehensibility. Dori Laub, a psychoanalyst and himself a Holocaust survivor, likens the Holocaust testimonial's survivor/reader relationship to patient/analyst relationship in trauma therapy. In laying out a psychoanalytic framework for thinking about survivor testimony, Laub describes a communicative structure involving a wounded speaker and a sympathetic listener. The project of remembering is fraught, and so the patient and therapist must work together to confront a past that seems to elude comprehension even by those who experienced it.[89] In fact, Laub advances the incomprehensibility theory one step further, arguing that the Holocaust was an event without witnesses, an alarming notion he introduces as a "theoretical perspective" meant to explain the unique aspect of the trauma experienced by the Nazis' victims. Laub claims that "what made a Holocaust out of the event is the unique way in which, during its historical occurrence, *the event produced no witnesses*. Not only, in effect, did the Nazis try to exterminate the physical witnesses of their crime; but the inherently incomprehensible and deceptive psychological structure of the event precluded its own witnessing, even by its very victims."[90] The unfamiliarity of the event was so radical, in others words, that the ability of the human mind to observe and remember was hopelessly compromised.

In response to the trope of incomprehensibility that accompanies so much thought about survivor testimony, the work of the Judaic and literary studies scholar Gary Weissman offers a useful intervention. Countering Wiesel's contention that only those who experienced the Holocaust directly can understand it, Weissman suggests that "perhaps just the opposite is the case; perhaps because it is a historical concept comprising myriad events which no one person experienced directly, the Holocaust can only be understood historically."[91] That is, if it is the case that the Holocaust lies beyond the witness's ability to relate testimony in a comprehensive and coherent manner, then it is up to the listener to put that testimony into a historical, explanatory context that reaches beyond the experiences of the individual survivor. Weissman distinguishes between the Holocaust as the individual experiences of all those caught up in it and the Holocaust as an event with discernible components that can be learned as a set of facts: "The Holocaust and a survivor's Holocaust experience constitute related but distinct objects of knowledge. It is one thing to understand the antecedent conditions of the Holocaust . . . and quite another to understand 'what it was like' to live and die at Auschwitz-Birkenau or in the Warsaw ghetto."[92] The trope of incomprehensibility encountered in so much survivor testimony and its reception makes the mistake of conflating these two objects of knowledge. To know the experience of another person as though one experienced it oneself may be impossible no matter how harmless the event. But as Weissman points out, it is perhaps that cognitive distance that creates an opportunity for a different kind of knowledge, one that he calls "historical."

Weissman's reminder that receiving testimony does not require a direct transfer of experience is useful in getting past the debilitating trope of incomprehensibility. Understandably, survivors express anguish about being heard and understood, but that neither silences their expression nor bars their audience from listening and drawing conclusions about the event. The absence of a direct transfer of experience is not a failure to communicate. While written survivor accounts may arouse the empathy of their readers and speak to a yearning to experience secondhand that which the survivor has endured (hence the term "fantasies of witnessing"), Weissman also rightly comments that "no degree of power or monumentality can transform one person's lived memories into another's."[93] Indeed, it is the awareness that the survivors are passing that produces a hunger to claim as personal memory that which must become something else when the survivors are gone.[94] That something else is collective memory, which, in a strict sense, is not memory at all, but remembrance. The hunger for experiencing from a safe distance what victims and survivors endured makes such experience impossible a priori, but Weissman does not conclude that testimony therefore loses its purpose. The "fantasy of witnessing"—the mistaken belief that there is a way to comprehend the survivor's experience in its fullness—still enables the compassionate reception of another's testimony within a historical framework.

Weissman's admonition not to confuse the reception of witness testimony with experiencing trauma also helps explain the phenomenon of Holocaust tourism, which may be motivated by similar "fantasies of witnessing." In fact, he opens his volume with an account of a son who accompanies his father, a survivor, to the Mauthausen camp memorial in Austria, where the latter was interned. Hoping to know somehow more directly what his father experienced by visiting the site, he is instead disappointed by the normality of the place. He does not encounter abject horror; "instead, he felt distanced from the actuality of what had occurred decades ago in the places where he stood. In response to this feeling, Michael's desire to experience what Mauthausen had been for his father in 1944 gave way to a more basic effort to feel, to experience something, whatever would enable him to overcome his sense of estrangement from the Holocaust past."[95] (Perhaps Michael's estrangement is not so different from the experience of some prisoners, as Weissman suggests. Primo Levi's description of his arrival at Auschwitz recounts a sense of surprise that he is not immediately confronted by the "apocalyptic," instead encountering a semblance, however brief, of the familiar.) Tourists like Michael hope through proximity to find a sense of immediacy that they cannot find by reading survivor testimony, even if they are the children of survivors.[96] But the inability to experience the horror begets something equally important to the transmission of testimony, and that is an act of imagination—in Michael's case, about what it must have been like for those who suffered. "Finally it was hearing stories of how prisoners suffered and died in the quarry, told at the very scene of the crime, that enabled him to come closest to something of the missing horror, however fleetingly."[97] (We will explore in the following chapters the ways in which Holocaust tourism invites its participants to engage in a more difficult act of imagination—identification with the perpetrators.)

Weissman's distinction between historical knowledge and experiential knowledge reminds us that we should not discount knowledge that is "merely factual"; instead, we should acknowledge the role such knowledge plays in the act of testifying to experience. Surely the job of Holocaust museums and memorials is to ensure that historical knowledge, too, is transmitted on behalf of the victims. In court cases, where testimony has its primary locus, the jury's task is not to take on the identity of the victim, to endure the victim's experiences, but to find truth. Courtrooms are frequent sites where traumatic experience is articulated, but that does not negate the assumption that one can get at a sense of truth through testimony in combination with other forms of evidence. Let us remember that the origins of the camp memorials stem also from this same sense of bearing witness for evidentiary purposes.

If a tour to Auschwitz enables witnessing, understood as the tourist's reception today of testimony from those who were there in the past, it must, at the very minimum, involve a communicative act between an absent speaker and a present listener. The most obvious way in which Holocaust museums and memorials present testimony comes in the form of displayed quotations or videotaped interviews from survivors, which are often running on continual loops as tourists move from one display to the next. Survivor accounts are also well represented in most Holocaust museum bookstores. Sometimes, though very rarely now, survivors themselves give guided tours through memorials.[98] But the primary voice that tourists hear at Auschwitz is that of their tour guide, who is usually a credentialed, university-trained educator from Poland, who recounts the experiences of the deportees to the visitors, often trying to humanize the victims by giving narrative accounts of specific individuals or groups. For example, the guide may stop at the photo of a prisoner and tell what we know about his or her fate. When the tour reaches Birkenau, the guide may describe the calamity that befell the Hungarian Jews, who were deported to Auschwitz and murdered in the summer of 1944, and for whose arrival the rail spur through the middle of the extermination camp was built. This last example is often the focus of guided tours at Auschwitz because the only known case of a transport photographed from arrival to selection to the march to the crematoria depicts an arrival of Hungarian Jews. The photos, taken by the SS and recovered by a prisoner after the camp was evacuated, allow the Auschwitz-Birkenau Memorial and Museum to illustrate the process of mass murder by placing photos at the spot where they were taken. (These images will be discussed at greater length in the next chapter.)

Of course, that SS photographer did not accompany the doomed into the gas chamber, so it is fair to ask if the examples of testimony presented overrepresent the survivors and perpetrators at the expense of the more than 1.1 million people who were murdered at Auschwitz. Perhaps the closest the memorial site comes to representing the voices of the murdered is to incorporate testimony recovered by members of the *Sonderkommando*, who were forced to carry out the killings. *Sonderkommandos* were routinely exterminated after a few months and replaced, since there were to be no eyewitnesses to the gas chambers. Several prisoners wrote detailed descriptions of what they witnessed and buried them in containers on the camp's grounds, some of which have been recovered. A resistance group at Auschwitz smuggled a camera to a *Sonderkommando* unit, and a few photographs have been recovered. Some of the few *Sonderkommando* survivors have recounted the last words they heard from the doomed, as documented in Claude Lanzmann's film *Shoah*. But the fact remains that the vast majority of victims were murdered in anonymity, unable to leave testimony in written words. Herein lies the importance of such artifacts as the piles of suitcases, eyeglasses, shoes, and even human hair that are on display in Auschwitz I, all of which function as visual testimony of the deportees' fate.

It is this concern for bearing witness for the dead who could not testify that informs the philosopher Giorgio Agamben's insistence on the "sayability" of Auschwitz, even for those who have been silenced.[99] Agamben cites Primo Levi and Elie Wiesel on the problem of the survivor who inherits the burden of speaking for the millions who were murdered.[100] Although survivors did not share the terminus of the gas chambers, they can—must—relate facts about the killing.[101] Agamben's aim is not to deny the chasm between the dead and the survivors; like Weissman, he recognizes a distinction between that which a subject experiences in its affective entirety and that which a subject can put into words, which must always be a partial account. He elaborates: "The aporia of Auschwitz is, indeed, the very aporia of historical knowledge; a non-coincidence between facts and truth, between verification and comprehension."[102] That space between experience and testimony is not a void; rather, it is a place for productive potential that calls forth witnessing. Rejecting Laub's notion of an "event with no witnesses," Agamben insists that ethics post-Auschwitz *require* witnessing, the inadequacies of language notwithstanding. While Agamben's gesture toward a "new ethics" has invited criticism from some, his notion of witnessing as a way to bridge silence and speech recalls what has always been a fundamental attribute of witnessing.[103] Testimony, the expression of the personal memory of the camps, is predicated upon that very distinction between experience and its translation into reported facts, a point made very clearly by Weissman.

Tourists may come to Auschwitz with the explicit expectation of a more experiential kind of knowledge (akin to Weissman's notion of a "fantasy of witnessing"), and some no doubt leave with a mistaken belief that they know "what it was like." But many others will reflect the experience of Michael, who accompanied his father to Mauthausen, and realize that they can never truly experience the ordeal of a site that is now guided by a trusted staff member, perhaps in the comforting presence of friends or family. Still, there is a knowledge of space that tourists acquire that may indulge a desire to bear witness, much like the one Martin Gilbert conveys in his description of Birkenau at the outset of this chapter. Like Gilbert, one experiences the geography, the landscape, the relation of one locus to another, and one's own status within a given space, which in turn produces knowledge that can be accounted for in phenomenological terms. The conditions under which tourists encounter that landscape can vary radically and impart different affective dimensions to the experience of a tour. For example, my first visit to Auschwitz occurred on a beautiful, sunny day, and I was not prepared to experience the tree-lined lanes among solid brick structures as superficially pretty. In some ways, that incongruity of expectation and experience made the knowledge of the crimes committed there that much more horrible. In addition to the setting, I found myself as attuned to other tourists as I was to the site itself, which introduced a disconcerting sense of doubling in my perception: I observed the memorial, while also observing how others observed the memorial. Some of the other tourists were teenagers on school trips, a few of whom talked loudly, giggled, or, in the case of one pair, took advantage of their perceived freedom from adult supervision to kiss. Needless to say, such experiences are incongruous with expectations of utter solemnity. I would suggest that such unexpected encounters, rather than undermine the value of tourism to Auschwitz, actually intensify it. Ranging from the minor distraction to disturbing behavior, such disruptions prompt visitors to ask what is appropriate and what is inappropriate at a site whose very existence is obscene to begin with. They place the tourist in a bind between standing by or expressing disapproval, wondering whether one has any right to dictate behavior to others when the traces of brutal coercion— guard towers, once-electrified fences, gallows, and crematoria—are never far away. The comparison is both overblown and, at the same time, all that the reflective tourist has. There is nothing about the experience of visiting Auschwitz, including the most coercive practices common to tourism (queuing up, waiting, moving at a dictated pace, obeying certain prohibitions), that can ever amount to the brutality endured by prisoners, and yet the expectation of respect for the memory of the dead places tourists in a relationship of obedience to authority.

It is this awareness of the camp as authoritarian space that makes Agamben's work most relevant to tourism. If there is anything truly new in his notion of witnessing, it is the way he links his understanding of the communicative nature of witnessing with an account of the spatial dynamics of power. His focus on the camps as "spaces of exception"—a term he borrows from the political theorist Carl Schmitt—and his reliance on the philosopher Michel Foucault's theories of biopolitics and surveillance allow Agamben to show how discourses of community determine who belongs and who does not and how these discourses are realized in spatial configurations that include and exclude, that reveal and conceal.[104] Discourses of exclusion are made manifest in the concentration camp, where those deemed outside the lawful community are relocated to a space that lies beyond the protection of the law.[105] By linking the spatial or visual with the discursive, Agamben reintroduces the juridical sense of witnessing, which relates observation and testimony, what I am insisting on as the intersubjective quality of bearing witness.[106] We should not forget the ways in which witnesses to the Holocaust continue to provide testimony in a juridical setting to this very day. Beginning with the early trials of the Allies in 1945, through the Nuremberg trials and the Eichmann trial in Jerusalem, to the recent cases against former SS guards in Germany charged as accessories to murder, witnessing continues to fulfill a desire for justice to redress the Nazis' crimes.[107] Indeed, the juridical sense of witnessing and the desire to comprehend the space in which abuses of power unfold coincide. It is no trivial matter that the judges in the first independent efforts to prosecute camp personnel in West Germany, the Frankfurt trials of 1963–1965, traveled to Auschwitz to tour the grounds for themselves before reaching their verdicts.[108]

Agamben's awareness of power as unfolding not simply in discourse (ideology, law) but also in perceptible space has clear implications for tourism's capacity to bear witness. Tourists temporarily inhabit structures and places imbued with cultural significance and arranged in ways to communicate particular messages: An art museum may showcase a national heritage, a historical movement, or the evolution of a particular artist; journeys into the wilderness promise to take the tourist away from civilization into pristine nature; and beach resorts encourage travelers to break free from their routines (and to spend money in the local economy). In the case of tourism to Auschwitz, travelers encounter a space conceived for the exercise of power by one group of human beings over others. The guided tour directs the visitor's gaze to the spatial configurations of a violent authority that excluded individuals from the human community by including them in a space designed to dehumanize them.[109] At the same time, the way in which tourism directs the gaze, and the ways in which tourists may or may not comply, offer a pale reflection of that interplay of power, discourse, and space.

By emphasizing spatiality, the tourist to Auschwitz becomes a witness by encountering the scene of a crime and confronting its arrangements of space.[110] This experience of space includes an understanding of the relationship of the camp to nearby surroundings—at Auschwitz, the camp's adjacency to a center of population is startling. One is forced to accept the simultaneity of brutality and everyday life side by side. Did the locals know? Did they intervene? This encounter with Auschwitz as a physical space where people still live and work may confound, shock, even disappoint the tourist who expected something more overtly extraordinary or terrifying. In this way, tourism encounters Agamben's "aporia of Auschwitz"—that is, of the incommensurability between experience and facts. Tourism requires the visitor to do the work of witnessing to seek whatever comprehension is available, even if that comprehension can never be considered complete. The museum and memorial are physical manifestations of the facts, not the reenactment of imprisonment and extermination, and as such they impart a form of historical understanding combined with an experience of sharing the space with one's contemporaries.

The doubling of perception mentioned above, the duality of listening to the past and to the present, is not only an unavoidable aspect of historical tourism, it is also one of its most important mechanisms by which tourism enables reflection. While the primary communication between the site and the visitor conveys testimony from the past, there is a continual act of communication focused on the present. From the moment the tourist arrives at the Auschwitz-Birkenau Memorial and Museum, the museum complex begins to speak not only about the extermination but also about the manner of tourism that is expected. Along with the usual indicators guiding the visitor to the ticket windows and restrooms, there are signs that announce the site's expectations of decorum from its visitors. One may not smoke on the grounds, one must dress properly, and most important, one must behave "appropriately" (a vague notion, to be sure, and not always heeded).[111] The first conscious communication the tourist has with Auschwitz comes in the form of directives: where to go and how to behave. These initial messages set the parameters for the communicative experience of the tour, establishing a code shared by the speaker and the listener that stems not only from a basic notion of respect for the victims who perished but also from a belief that tourists are there to bear witness.

These directives help regulate an encounter that can be quite chaotic. The reception hall, which was built by the SS as the "intake" facility, is often crowded, and the lines to purchase tickets and to wait for the tour to commence become tangled.[112] Numerous guides conduct simultaneous tours, with many languages competing for the attention of their respective groups. The guide first takes an assigned group, which can range in size from five to thirty members, out of the reception area to the infamous entry of the prisoner's camp, marked with the motto "Arbeit macht frei" in wrought iron. For larger groups, the guide speaks into a microphone that plays on headsets distributed to the group's members. The group is led through several of the "blocks"—the two-story brick buildings that once served as prisoners' barracks, administrative offices, interrogation and punishment cells, and the "hospital" where many were killed by lethal phenol injections into the heart. The museum has converted these buildings into a series of themed exhibition spaces: One block explains the evolution of the camp from a deserted Polish army base into the Nazis' largest center for extermination. Another depicts the living conditions of prisoners in the camp. A third focuses on forensic evidence of genocide, including physical traces of victims (ranging from piles of eyeglasses and prosthetics to the hair shaved from women's heads). Tourists are exhorted not to use flashes in these interior spaces. There are five blocks that house the permanent exhibition, all told.[113] The amount of information conveyed to the tourist is vast, with the guide's narrative accompanied by explanatory signs and contemporary documents, photographs, maps, and artifacts on display. Among these are maps that show the evolution of particular spaces, including photos that reveal the condition of the camp upon liberation, so tourists can observe what has been rebuilt. Crematorium I, with its reconstructed gas chamber and furnaces, is typically the last stop at the *Stammlager*.

After the tour of the Auschwitz I *Stammlager*, which typically lasts about ninety minutes, the group travels to Auschwitz II (Birkenau), located about two kilometers to the northwest. The contrast between the two sites is stunning. While the tour begins in the fairly compact area of

Auschwitz I, often under crowded conditions, it recommences at the vast expanse of Birkenau. Many visitors express shock at Birkenau's enormity, which encompasses an area of approximately 350 acres, dwarfing the 50 acres of Auschwitz I. Fences and guard towers extend out to the northern and western horizons. The guide usually takes the group from the so-called Gate of Death, which sits on the eastern boundary of the camp, along the rail spur that bisects Birkenau. To the south of the track, one sees the smaller but relatively intact *Frauenlager* (women's camp) and, to the north, mostly ruins of the wooden barracks that were dismantled after the war for building materials. A row of wooden barracks has been reconstructed near the Gate of Death, showing visitors the three-tiered bunks on which prisoners were forced to sleep as many as twelve to a platform only three meters wide. The group walks along the rail spur to the so-called *Judenrampe*, built for the arrival of the Hungarian Jews in 1944, where the guide explains the selection process. Finally, the guide brings the group to the ruins of the gas chambers at Crematorium II and Crematorium III, adjacent to a memorial erected in 1967.

Figure 1.3. Part of the men's camp in Birkenau, with the chimneys marking the spot of former barracks, August 2007. An intact barracks stands beyond the barbed wire fence to the left of the frame. Photo by the author.

At the end of three and a half hours, the group has experienced the space of the camp and heard many stories about the prisoners and their killers. Their mobility through the space where these accounts are set allows tourists to establish a historically informed relationship to a very real and present place. Given the dual awareness of spatial proximity and unbridgeable temporal distance that tour groups encounter, in what sense have they borne witness to the Holocaust? Surely the forensic sense of listening to the testimony, however mediated through the museum, applies to tourism at Auschwitz, which seeks to convert the experience of touring the space into historical knowledge. The degree of success of this kind of witnessing depends on the authenticity of the memorial space.[114] That requires that the museum acknowledge any changes to the place, thereby allowing visitors to appreciate what has been altered, restored, or neglected. The tourist encounters not only the evidence of the Final Solution but also the absence of evidence—its loss through destruction or attrition, or its replacement through (openly acknowledged) reconstructions, or its not having yet been retrieved. Tourism presents its participants with speech and silence, with presence and absence, and calls upon the tourist to bridge that gap. Tourism presents the visitor with the challenge of understanding the relationship between trauma and its representation, between experienced event and spoken testimony. Rather than be satisfied with the idea that the Holocaust is beyond comprehension, Holocaust tourism—indeed, the Holocaust itself—demands room to acknowledge that there is a referent, an event that discourse points back to even if it cannot perfectly portray it. The point here is not to overcome silence and absence; rather, it is to point out the ways in which they are the very objects of witnessing the Holocaust.

If we insist on bearing witness to testimony as parallel with an analyst's listening to a traumatized survivor in the context of therapy, then the contribution of tourism has to be qualified. While psychoanalytic theory may help elucidate survivor testimony, tourists do not engage in great depth with individual experiences. Instead, tourism at Auschwitz is a collective enterprise, presenting multitudes of victims and experienced with crowds of other tourists. The time will come when there are no living survivors, so it is only collectively and transgenerationally that we can still speak of tourism as listening to traumatic memory. In the context of a collective trauma (a term I use with caution so as not to equate individual experience with collective memory), tourism plays a salutary role inasmuch as the very presence of visitors affirms the reality of the past and thus resists the damaging voices of Holocaust denial. Tourism may function as a kind of collective therapy that answers a sense of collective trauma, an inheritance from the past that demands reckoning.

Over the history of Auschwitz as a tourist destination, the camp has come to represent the Holocaust on an international scale, reflecting the diverse ethnic and national origins of the victims and perpetrators. The stories of the Holocaust have dispersed along with the survivors around the globe, and tourism at Auschwitz involves speakers and listeners from many parts of the world. Tourists themselves travel to Auschwitz with their own stories about the genocide and its impact on their family or community, sharing this knowledge with other travelers and tour guides, who in turn become the mediums through which these stories are passed on further. As both primary and secondary witnesses, tourists encounter not only the direct evidence of the past but also its preservation and presentation in the present. They see the spatial remains of the Holocaust at the same time that they see its memorialization. Furthermore, they encounter one another. Tourism bears witness in a general sense to the memory of the Holocaust and, more specifically, to itself and its participants as stewards of that memory. While not all visitors may embody this realization, the tour to Auschwitz imposes an ethical imperative on visitors to remember, to acknowledge the crimes of the past and also the obligations that the past hands down to the future. The mirror that tourism holds up to visitors in the form of other visitors is a reminder of that commitment.

At the end of the tour, when visitors share their photos and impressions with friends or colleagues, tourism recirculates testimony about the crimes of the Final Solution heard on site. Tourists convey their travel experiences in words and in images, posting on travel sites or social media, writing in journals, or sharing photos and postcards. It is that ability to witness Holocaust remembrance through images that I wish to explore further in the next chapter.

2

Picturing the Camps

As photographs give people an imaginary possession of a past that is unreal, they also help people to take possession of space in which they are insecure. Thus, photography develops in tandem with one of the most characteristic of modern activities: tourism. . . . It seems positively unnatural to travel for pleasure without taking a camera along.
—Susan Sontag, *On Photography* (1973)[1]

Tourists can be conspicuous for many reasons, but nothing marks them more plainly than their cameras. The stereotypical tourist is a lens-wielding traveler on a mission to record anything that appears exotic, historical, or typical of the locale. Most of us who travel with a camera have probably found ourselves fulfilling this cliché, more or less self-consciously, taking pictures of buildings or monuments that have already been photographed a thousand times by other photographers, often with far greater skill than we possess. As the writer Susan Sontag observes, photography and tourism are so mutually enabling that they are hard to imagine without each other.

Picture taking plays a ritualistic role in tourism, so much so that the choice *not* to photograph something can be as deliberate as the choice to do so.[2] Photography is one of the ways the traveler fulfills the journey's promise of making new memories; it provides a purpose to travel and offers the sightseer a familiar, portable identity. In the midst of an unfamiliar location, photography is a reassuring activity, easing the tourist's insecurity by helping to incorporate the disorienting experience of unfamiliar places into the practice of everyday life.[3] While exotic pictures may reinforce the distinction between home and abroad, the act of pointing the camera, framing the image, and pressing the shutter button is a constant that bridges the experience of travel and home life—a fact made more evident today with the ubiquity of handheld devices with digital cameras. Photography lets tourists extend the travel experience beyond the period of the tour, easing the transition from a time of adventure to the routine of home and work. Whether through the assembly of photo albums, the editing of digital pictures, the slideshow before a captive audience, or self-produced videos, photographic practices posttravel permit a sense of mastery over unfamiliar places, promoting tourism's gaze well beyond the actual time of the journey and giving tourists the pleasure of virtual travel.[4] Sontag's claim that photography provides the illusion of possession over an "unreal past" (in reference to the idealized representation of family photos) suggests that tourists seek that same sense of possession over place.

If tourists are capable of being sophisticated makers of meaning, as more recent scholarship in tourism studies increasingly contends, then surely photography is one of the means by which they do so. The fun of taking pictures as souvenirs need not obscure the more earnest characterization of tourists as storytellers, documentarists, and ethnographers; as the literary theorist Jonathan Culler has said, "Tourists are the agents of semiotics: all over the world they are engaged in reading cities, landscapes and cultures as sign systems."[5] Tourists are making sense of their travels and, in the process, of their own place in the world.

That is not to say that photography is innocent of its involvement in many problematic touristic behaviors. Think, for example, of the habit some travelers have of spending more time looking through a camera than directly at their surroundings; perhaps they (or we) do so out of a sense of insecurity about what to notice or out of fear of missing something "important." More troubling, tourists with cameras can be culturally insensitive guests who reduce their hosts to exemplars of the exotic.[6] No doubt photography is complicit in tourism's pursuit of superficial pleasure, which its critics cite as evidence of tourism's inherent frivolity.[7]

The sociologist John Urry has highlighted the ways in which the pleasure gained in tourism is deeply visual. For Urry, vision becomes a primary axis along which tourism, the invitation to gaze upon other people and other places without inhibition, rewards travelers with pleasure. In the most recent edition of his canonical book, *The Tourist Gaze*, Urry, together with the cultural geographer Jonas Larsen, characterizes the centrality of vision in tourism as follows:

Gazes organize the encounters of visitors with the "other", providing some sense of competence, pleasure, and structure to those experiences. The gaze demarcates an array of pleasurable qualities to be generated within particular times and spaces. It is the gaze that orders and regulates the relationship between the various sensuous experiences while away, identifying what is visually out-of-ordinary, what are relevant differences and what is "other."[8]

Urry, like Sontag, identifies seeing with pleasure, though he defines pleasure very broadly to include the intellectual gratification of competence, of having structured experiences; in other words, not simply as an emotional or libidinal response. At the same time, by including the contact between self and other as one form of visual pleasure that can accompany "various sensuous experiences," Urry also acknowledges the possibility of libidinal—that is, voyeuristic—enjoyment in the tourist gaze, implicating vision as a means by which to exercise power over the other.[9]

However conceptualized, Urry's and Sontag's understanding of the tourist gaze as an exploitative pleasure is difficult to reconcile with the concept of Holocaust tourism as a kind of witnessing that I introduced in the previous chapter. Witnessing locates the tourist within ethical territory, and if pleasure is derived from the act of bearing witness, it should be the pleasure derived from fulfilling a moral obligation, not from getting libidinal satisfaction. The uncertain morality of the gaze reminds us that tourism, to the extent it is a visual practice, is inextricably bound up with an ethical problem that situates our own pleasure in close proximity to our regard for others. Photography is one way the tourist enters this ethically challenged terrain, linking entertainment with obligation to others. Tourists take pictures not only for fun but also to find a sense of proximity to the other, to make real what has been presented as extraordinary.[10]

To complicate further the reduction of vision in tourism to a form of pleasure, remember that the camera can prove a physical burden, one more object for the tourist to tote around. Cameras expose tourists, thus enhancing the sense of dislocation and conspicuousness one might feel in unfamiliar places. Cameras can get tourists who do not observe restrictions or local customs into trouble, risking embarrassment at the least or even fines and expulsion from a site. If tourism is a kind of labor expended to comprehend one's world, then cameras, like journals and postcards, are the implements used to carry out that work. Cameras, by their very presence, admonish their owners to play the role of tourist, to record new experiences, and to see with an attentive eye. Picture taking can be fun at times, but it can also feel like a chore. In other words, tourist photography participates in a complex web of visuality that links pleasure not just with obligation, routine, and power but also with perception, contemplation, and insight. Pleasure and resentment can surface together when the tourist becomes the photographer, and the attempt to resolve their apparent paradox may lead to reflection.

Furthermore, the reduction of the tourist gaze to pleasure poses special problems for travelers who visit Holocaust sites. The potential for pleasure points to an abiding concern within Holocaust studies about the ethics of representation. In the context of Holocaust tourism, the possibility of deriving pleasure from the tourist gaze suggests some superficial benefit gained from the suffering of millions of victims. Tourism raises the same problem that routinely arises in connection with fictional or filmic accounts of the Holocaust. If we experience pleasure in reading survivor accounts, viewing films like *Schindler's List* or *The Pawnbroker*, or visiting Holocaust memorials and museums, then we may be violating one of the chief taboos of Holocaust remembrance, namely that we must not instrumentalize the suffering of victims for any purpose that gives that suffering redemptive value.[11] Perhaps so, but in contrast, one might ask if the improvement in a reader's, film viewer's, or tourist's appreciation of history and humanity's capacity for barbarism ever really constitutes a redemption of the victims' suffering, let alone one that we must abjure. I would hesitate to condemn the acquisition of knowledge on the grounds that it amounts to an improper redemption of needless suffering or that it is a self-serving effort to derive pleasure through intellectual satisfaction, neither of which strikes me as capable of redeeming an event so monstrous as the Holocaust.[12] Still, a moral burden lies with those who engage with representations of the Holocaust, whether as producers or consumers, to demonstrate that there is an ethical value in them that exceeds the category of pleasure.

To be more than a form of voyeurism, the gaze within Holocaust tourism must play an ethical function by demonstrating a capacity to acknowledge, or even to construct, the tension between entertainment and solemnity, between personal pleasure and responsibility toward others. If some form of pleasure, however cerebral, is unavoidable, then the question should be whether it is accompanied by other responses, such as a sense of obligation or even ethical action. Photography, I contend in this chapter, plays a pivotal role in negotiating the distinction in the tourist gaze between visual pleasure and ethical practice. As the international relations and cultural studies scholar Debbie Lisle has observed at the National September 11 Memorial and Museum, situated at Ground Zero in Manhattan, New York—a site whose tourism she compares with Auschwitz's presentation of atrocity—visitors exhibit a "potent mixture of titillation and shame . . . that suggests a reflexivity not often ascribed to tourists."[13] The tension between these two aspects of the tourist gaze is worth considering more deeply to see how reflexivity can result in reflection.

In exploring photography's ambiguous role in Holocaust tourism, this chapter explores travel to other extermination camps beyond Auschwitz: Chełmno, Sobibór, Bełżec, Treblinka, and Majdanek, all of which were located on territory liberated by the Red Army. There is a logic to this order—I begin with Chełmno in part because it was the first killing center but also because its placement at two different, though proximate, locations helps illustrate the variation in photography that I want to highlight. I then move on to Sobibór, which is the least developed of the camp memorials, hidden in a forest and situated on the Polish frontier to Ukraine and Belarus. Then I turn to Bełżec, which for most of its postwar history was in a similar state to Sobibór but now has been transformed into a monumental installation. Treblinka, the next site I discuss, strikes a fascinating balance between the monumental and the modest, between being hidden and being revealed. It is also a site that makes important use of historical photos in a way that lets me consider tourist photography in relation to pictures taken by perpetrators. Finally, Majdanek returns to a site that is relatively intact, and because of that it has a particular history in the use of photography to document the camps. While the chapter's organization revolves around the remaining extermination camps, it will also attend to some the concentration camps liberated by the western Allies, such as Bergen-Belsen, Buchenwald, and Dachau. Some of these camp memorials are comparatively hard to reach and are underdeveloped compared to the Auschwitz-Birkenau Memorial and Museum. The variety of camp memorial sites corresponds to different strategies for picture taking by tourists that are directly related to a memorial's setting, its scale, and its presentation of historical information. By the same token, these diverse memorial sites make use of historical photography in distinct ways, affecting both tourists' experience of the memorial as well as their relationship to photography and its role in the Holocaust.

By discussing the camp memorials and the practices of photography that these more remote sites invite, this chapter elaborates on the investigation of Holocaust tourism as a form of witnessing, which I introduced in the previous chapter. Photography's plasticity as a medium and its adaptability to different spaces equips the tourist with a common "language" for making meaningful experiences out of often very disparate places. For example, tourists may find memorials that present themselves as expansive vistas to convey the immensity of the disaster, or they may find secluded clearings in forests that narrow the range of viewpoints. In terms of iconography and information, tourists may encounter remembrances of Polish or Catholic martyrdom rather than Jewish suffering, read inscriptions that offer inaccurate counts of the dead and interned, or find very little information translated into a language they can understand. Photography helps mediate that range of memorials. Some sites appear well maintained, others neglected. At Chełmno, Bełżec, Sobibór, and Treblinka, there is simply less to see in the way of buildings or infrastructure from their time as killing centers compared to Auschwitz and Majdanek. For as intact and preserved as Auschwitz may be, tourism to the other camps reveals the Nazis' success at erasing the evidence of their crimes. By using a camera, tourists create a body of images that form the foundations of a narrative account of their travels and, at the same time, a narrative account of the Holocaust that documents those acts of erasure.[14]

Photography in Holocaust tourism involves not only pictures taken by tourists but also tourists' encounters with photography produced by others and curated by memorial staff. Tourists encounter many photographs displayed on walls or in vitrines, on informational signs, and in books and postcards for sale in information centers. As many critics have commented, tourists may see the same images repeated from one site to the next.[15] That shared-image repertoire in turn influences the photos taken by the tourists themselves and informs tourists' understandings of themselves as witnesses. Historical photos of the Holocaust have long been assumed a key instrument in the task of bearing witness to Nazi atrocity, but more than seventy years have passed since the liberation of the camps, and so the nature of bearing witness, as discussed in the previous chapter, has by necessity changed.[16] Given the degree to which the Nazis were able to dismantle some sites, one has to ask what photography specifically can hope to witness in places of erasure, where the instruments of brutality have vanished into a forest or been plowed into the green earth. The almost compulsory use of the camera in tourism faces a unique challenge at such places, asking tourists to ponder the relationship between what one can see in the present and what one can remember from the past.

As in the other chapters, the images I have included here are my own photographs, shot either with a (now ancient) Fuji FinePix A350 digital camera with no wide-angle capacity or an iPhone 5. In other words, these are amateur photos taken with basic equipment that make no claim to be especially professional or artistic or especially awful. I, like most travelers, have never had any formal training in photography. When traveling, I tend use the camera primarily as a mental prosthesis to help me remember what I have seen.[17] As such, I tend to focus more on the place (buildings, landscape, monuments) than on people, although other tourists inevitably appear in the frame. I took many of the photos with this book in mind, so their role here is also intended to be illustrative; that is, they complement the textual account of the places I analyze. I use captions to name the place or object presented, to provide the date I took the photo, and when appropriate, to acknowledge the import of a scene that led me to photograph it in the first place. My estimation of my own pictures as typical of tourist photography is not intended to hide the variation from one tourist's talents or interests to another's—it goes without saying that there is immense variation in the quality, frequency, or subject matter of pictures taken by tourists. But a perusal of tourist photography on social media or shared on public websites such as Flickr, TripAdvisor, Facebook, or VirtualTourist provide a ready means to ensure that I do not generalize too much from my own practice. By focusing first on amateur shots, I hope to illustrate the questions that tourists attempt to ponder with the aid of a camera lens. As these images will show, my pictures and those of many other tourists reflect the ways in which the tourist gaze has been shaped by images already in circulation.

Photographing the Ordinary: Chełmno

No tourist can photograph the Holocaust. That obvious fact bears mentioning because it serves to remind us that tourism is not—and never can be—an immersion into the experience it commemorates. Tourists never experience the Holocaust in any direct sense, only its spatial traces, mediated through the work of representation. Among such traces are historical photos from the era that seem to infuse the site with a spectral quality, as if the past might intrude into the present. Marianne Hirsch, a professor of English and comparative literature at Columbia University, writes that historical photos "function as ghostly revenants from an irretrievably lost past world."[18] Susan Sontag points out how photos attest to the reality of an event that is no longer there, seeming even more real than the place experienced in the present: "Photography is the reality; the real object is often experienced as a letdown."[19] While photos may be seen as indexical of the real, they also confirm that the reality they document belongs to the past, and therein lies their potency. The historical photographer has seen what we cannot. Taken together, Hirsch and Sontag let us say that historical photos certify both the reality and the irretrievability of the past event.

The contrast between historical photos of the extermination camps and their present-day condition is striking. Instead of terror and brutality, tourists navigate the space with the implicit assurance of their physical safety. When Sontag insists that the contrast between historical photos and present reality is a "letdown," she implies a voyeuristic desire to look upon horror directly that is denied in Holocaust tourism.[20] But the contrast between historical image and immediate reality, while possibly letting the tourist down, also urges the tourist to face the finality of the Nazi genocide. The irreversible extermination of millions of human beings produced an absence that is palpable. Tourists encounter the absence of victims' bodies, which were burned to ash, and even the structures built to murder and incinerate them have been removed. Tourists may visit extermination camps to see the mechanisms of erasure, only to find that those mechanisms themselves are largely invisible. While former *shtetlekh* (plural of *shtetl*) and historically Jewish neighborhoods in Berlin or Kraków may recall places of Jewish lives, the camps recollect the final stage of their obliteration. To explore the relationship between erasure and photography in more concrete terms, consider the case of tourism to the first camp to be established as an extermination facility: Chełmno.

A rural hamlet located 50 km northwest of Łódź on the Ner River, Chełmno lies in a part of Poland annexed into the Third Reich as the Warthegau, today the Wielkopolska and Łódź districts of central and western Poland. After expelling all the local inhabitants, the German occupiers renamed the village Kulmhof. The SS established a camp that operated from 1941 through 1944 and whose purpose was to murder the Jews and Roma of this region, including the Jews of the Łódź Ghetto, the second-highest concentration of Jewish life in Poland after that of Warsaw. Led by officers who had gained experience with killing through the T4 euthanasia program inside Germany, Chełmno's staff murdered more than 150,000 victims.[21] (T4 refers to the address of Tiergartenstrasse 4 in Berlin, the headquarters of the Nazis' program for killing those with physical and mental disabilities in pursuit of a eugenic fantasy to strengthen the Aryan race.)

Today the physical structures of the killing complex are nearly completely gone, having been destroyed by the Nazis before the Red Army's arrival into Nazi-occupied Poland. The hamlet is remote, and road signs pointing tourists to the camp are sparse, so it helps to have done one's research with maps before attempting to drive there.[22] Once one enters Chełmno by road, one comes upon the camp memorial almost unexpectedly, situated next to the prominent village church. A driveway leads past a villager's house into a clearing. Surrounded by trees and fences, the area is dotted with a few buildings, one of which is the small main office of the camp museum.[23] Beyond the office lies the exposed foundation of a manor house that stood until its destruction by the SS in 1943. It was this manor house upon which that the SS centered the killing operations in Chełmno. When deportations of Jews from the Warthegau began in December 1941, together with thousands of Roma and Sinti from nearby Łódź, inhabitants were transported to Chełmno and marched to the manor house, which the SS presented as

Figure 2.1. Chełmno killing site as it appeared in 2010, with the museum office at left, and the granary used to store arrivals' belongings at right (now an exhibition space). The manor house lay between the two structures in front of the trees. More than 150,000 died here by asphyxiation. Photo by the author.

a disinfection facility prior to further transfer to a labor camp. After undressing, the arrivals were led through a passageway into the back of specially designed vans, where up to seventy people at a time were forcibly loaded into the cargo holds before the doors were shut.[24] The ignition was started, and the exhaust fed back into the cargo holds of the vans. After about ten to twenty minutes, most or all victims were dead. Their bodies were driven to the nearby Rzuchów forest, where the members of a prisoner labor detail cremated them.[25]

Unlike the looming presence of the iconic Gate of Death that straddles the rail spur leading into Birkenau, there is nothing at Chełmno that dominates the scene in such a monumental fashion, nothing that presents itself so prominently as a reminder of what took place there, despite the magnitude of destruction. Chełmno is almost subterranean, a barely unearthed archeological site. What is left for the tourist to photograph that attests to the crimes of 1941–1943, the camp's first period of operation? The location appears decidedly humble, certainly not imposing or intimidating to an unsuspecting passerby. The exposed foundation of the manor house is visible, outlined by a handrail with some modestly produced signs explaining the site in Polish and English. More recently, a group of signs has been placed between the manor house's foundation and the nearby granary, which served as the storage facility for the victims' confiscated belongings and which today includes an exhibition space of those objects.[26] Throughout the site, visitors have added their own memorials, laying stones on top of engraved monuments and placing candles around an area where bodies were burned.

Tourists might believe that the village grounds are the extent of the Chełmno memorial, since no directional signs indicate the existence of the much larger memorial area about 5 km to the northwest in the Rzuchów forest, where the victims' bodies were cremated. In March 1944, a year after the SS had blown up the manor house with the last remaining prisoners inside, a new killing operation was established in the Rzuchów forest, with buildings erected to fill the function of the former manor house—to receive deportees and funnel them into gas vans. This second phase of Chełmno, during which the Nazis liquidated the Łódź Ghetto, lasted from June until July 1944, with prisoners remaining until January 1945 with the task of dismantling the camp to hide evidence from the approaching Soviet forces.[27]

There are no buildings from the camp that remain intact in the Rzuchów forest today. Instead, a large monument dominates the site, preceded by two smaller memorials that mark the entryway. The first is a large boulder engraved with a menorah and bearing a plaque proclaiming the site a Polish national cemetery; the second is a distinctly Christian memorial in the form of a hollowed-out cross and an altar. They point the way to the main monument in the background, a massive polyhedron that rests on much smaller, almost hidden pillars, such that the suspended cenotaph seems ready to collapse with all its weight on the site. Paths lead to a second clearing a few hundred meters away, where the shapes of structures that once constituted the camp are outlined in stone. This area designates the Jewish victims of the camps, with gravestones and monuments adorned with Stars of David, menorahs, or Hebrew characters. Many of these memorials have been privately donated by families and communities, and they remember particular victims with moving inscriptions.

Figure 2.2. Chełmno memorial at the cremation site in the Rzuchów forest, June 2016. Here prisoners were forced to carry out the mass cremations of deportees, and a second phase of extermination took place here in the summer of 1944. Photo by the author.

The two distinct settings of Chełmno encapsulate the variety of spaces and photographic responses that camp memorials present to tourists. Looking at Chełmno through the lens of the camera, one's attention is drawn to a difference in scale between the two locations. The small killing center, which hides in plain sight, now almost as it did then, does not lend itself to panoramic images. There is no distant vantage point to capture the enclosed area, defying one of tourism's common photographic impulses. Rather, the various elements of the site—the manor house's foundation, signs and plaques, engraved stones, personal memorials—require the tourist to come close to read and record the inscriptions on memorials. If the tourist's desire is to capture an iconic image that exposes the place's past atrocity, the utter ordinariness of Chełmno Village thwarts such intentions. The first impression one might have from a tourist's photo is that there is nothing to see—no gas chambers, no guard towers or barbed-wire fences, no replicas of the gas vans, not even the building that funneled victims to their deaths. Large signs installed in 2015 attempt to address this absence by displaying photographic images from the camp's history, acknowledging the lack of apparent structures of atrocity.

The Rzuchów forest memorial, in contrast, is a vast area. Incorporating the memorial into a discordantly peaceful landscape, the memorial terrain of the Rzuchów forest positions the photographer-tourist much differently then the village museum does, and it addresses the tourist in the familiar photographic idiom of outdoor landmarks. While the village site, though small, is difficult to grasp in any single shot, the large forest site provides several focal points for the camera's lens from multiple angles at some distance, as if to answer tourists' desire to take a picture that corresponds to the scale of horrors that transpired there. Situated firmly within a natural environment, the large-scale monument and the widely dispersed memorials linked by extensive pathways, all located in a forest clearing, shift the scale to something approaching landscape portraiture.[28]

The different photographic strategies elicited by the two locations at Chełmno highlight the important role the camera plays in constructing the tourist gaze at camp memorials. Typically, the camera is the means by which tourists frame an object as unusual or exotic. While the first impression one has of Chełmno Village with the naked eye suggests nothing unusual, a photograph from the location bestows an aura of importance that tourists seek: It was photographed, so it must show *something*. Photographs have a "revelatory character": They present their image as if uncovering that which has been hidden or overlooked.[29] The sense of exposing a place for scrutiny through photography is one of the ways tourism attempts to answer the demand of travelers for new experiences.[30] Furthermore, if a photograph can reveal something, then it may enable the tourist to step into the role of witness.

Before accepting the proposition that photography enables the tourist to witness in any meaningful sense, it is worth asking what a photo of Chełmno, at either location, actually reveals. One can document the terrain on which the manor house stood and gas vans waited, but it is precisely their absence that a picture records. The new image necessarily differs from the historical event to which it is intended to refer. Of course, all photographs are images that differ in fundamental ways from their referents, but the lure of tourist photography as a form of documentation rests upon the reading of the photo as an emanation of the real. Here, the reality is that of a razed death camp, some of its traces still in place and marked by commemorative displays. While tourist photos certainly bear witness to the status of Chełmno as a memorial, it is by no means clear how they can bear witness to the Holocaust itself. While a guided tour, signs and images, or the physical traces of the camp call upon the tourist to receive the forensic testimony the site has to offer, the present-day tourist photo adds another layer of mediation; indeed, tourist photography is a mediation in response to a mediation. The single tourist snapshot cannot independently convey the rich discursive context of the tour—guides, pamphlets, signs, conversations with other visitors—except to capture a sense of place where this information is contained.

Returning to Sontag's claim about the revelatory character of photography, perhaps the kind of tourist photography that one undertakes at camp memorials today is really a *performance* of revelation, stemming from a desire to bear witness as investigated in Gary Weissman's *Fantasies of Witnessing*. Photography performs revelation at Chełmno in its ability to recast the camp memorial as hidden in plain sight. A picture at Chełmno village insists that the site is not empty, that it really is a place of significance despite the sparse image. By taking a picture at Chełmno, the tourist calls for a second look to find more than first meets the eye. The sense of revelation promised by the tourist photograph is, in some uncomfortable ways, a fabrication, but it also exposes the way in which the site itself has already been imbued with meaning prior to the tourist's arrival. A tourist's photograph adds a new image onto an already existing image repertoire, and it engages tourism in a hermeneutic circle of interpretation and revision to reconcile the historical location of the camp with the present-day memorial.[31] In visually mapping the present onto an already much charted past, tourists are neither autonomous generators of significance nor empty vessels ready to be filled by the tourism industry.[32]

Following the anthropologist Edward Bruner's notion of tourism as performance, we can see in tourist photography the performance of revelation. Photography's performative aspects suggest that itinerants engage with the medium both as an aesthetic form of expression and as a means to document the real. Regardless of the falseness of such a dichotomy, the practice of reading photographs one way or the other—or both at the same time—speaks to an abiding tension within the medium's reception as either art or document.[33] The notion that photography provides a means of bearing witness tends to favor the equation of the photograph with the real. But to take a picture is also to create an aesthetic object, and seeing photography as subjective, aesthetic production tends to come at the expense of its value as objective documentation. But the insistence on a binary, either/or relationship between representation and reality tends to obscure what is a dynamic, mutually constitutive relationship.[34] What counts here is the creation of an image that establishes a relationship between the photographer and the place together with its history. When tourists create a photographic record of what they see, they draw upon a wealth of aesthetic strategies to elicit an intended response, made even more possible in today's age of digital editing.[35] One might expect that the ability to stylize images to comport with a preconceived notion of what the Holocaust should look like would tempt some tourists to sensationalize a site like Chełmno Village—to convert its ordinariness into a more familiar sign of horror, for example, by depleting the image of color or holding the lens at a jarring angle. But in contrast to both grainy, black-and-white historical photos and those with a pronounced artistic intent, most publicly available tourist photos show that visitors use the camera to document Chełmno in the here and now, in color, rather than to sensationalize or otherwise transform it.[36] Whatever the intentions, photographs that record the tourist's presence at Chełmno can render meaningful, provocative images precisely because they accentuate the location of the Holocaust in familiar, seemingly ordinary places.

Regardless of the aesthetics of any particular image, taking pictures at a site like Chełmno can never be value neutral, for the qualities that make a "good" photo include both aesthetic and moral considerations.[37] The encounter with the utter ordinariness of Chełmno Village challenges the photographer to create images that convey the place's notorious history. Photography prompts a reflection about what separates day-to-day life from the brutality of genocide, what links a cataclysmic past with a familiar present that bears little resemblance to the atrocity images from Bergen-Belsen that Sontag recollects.[38] Given the importance Sontag places on the shock value of those first Holocaust images, tourist photography at the camp memorials must seem inadequate to the task of conveying the horror of the Holocaust; if they shock us, it is by their refusal to conform to our expectations. Recall, though, that Sontag describes the initial shock of the Bergen-Belsen photos as fleeting. "At the time of the first photographs of the Nazi camps, there was nothing banal about these images. After thirty years, a saturation point may have been reached. In these last decades, 'concerned' photography has done at least as much to deaden conscience as to arouse it."[39]

Sontag is one of the first in a long line of critics who have questioned the value of atrocity photos, from which tourist photography at the camp memorials substantially differs. In her line of argument, the more accustomed we become to seeing violence, the less it affects us.[40] But are violent images the only kind that can shock viewers, and is shock the requisite precursor to ethical thinking and action? If there is a shock available from the tourist's snapshot of Chełmno village, it is the shock of the ordinary. Chełmno surely challenges the mainstream perception of the Holocaust as a monstrous, monolithic operation of global dimensions, presenting instead a seemingly insignificant settlement in the middle of nowhere. As a memorial site, Chełmno offers testimony to the diffuse nature of the Nazi genocide and its occurrence at the most nondescript of locations—certainly a disturbing recognition if not a shocking one. Perhaps brutality's shock is more intense, if not as long lasting. As Sontag comes to believe in her later book about photography, *Regarding the Pain of Others*, shock may characterize an image's first impression on a viewer and provide a necessary impulse for action, but shock is not the ultimate goal.[41] Nor is habituation the inevitable result of repeated exposure to shocking images, as some critics claim.[42] Nor is shock always necessarily related to images of atrocity. At Chełmno, shock comes, not so much from seeing horror, but from realizing that horror can transpire seemingly anywhere.[43]

Photography, Landscape, and Imagination: The Operation Reinhard Camp Memorials

Chełmno is not alone in presenting a subdued scene that defies the expectation of horror that one typically associates with images of mass extermination. The Operation Reinhard camps—Sobibór, Bełżec, and Treblinka—are also eerily bucolic, located near quiet villages accessible only by winding country roads. These three extermination camps operated from 1942 to 1943 and served the sole purpose of murdering all the Jews within the General Government (the remaining stump of Polish territory not officially annexed into the German Reich, which included Kraków, Warsaw, and Lublin).[44] Drawing on the practices of Chełmno and the T4 euthanasia program carried out in the Reich, all three camps asphyxiated their victims in gas chambers filled with carbon monoxide piped in from combustion engines. The Operation Reinhard camps were similar in design—a more or less rectangular area hidden by trees and lined with barbed-wire fences, with an enclosed section within the camp designated for the extermination of deportees, segregated from the prisoner barracks and the SS facilities. Upon arrival at the edge of the camp, Jews were hastily unloaded from trains that had pulled up to this interior enclosure. To maintain order, camp personnel told prisoners they were to get showers and their clothes were to be disinfected before they could travel further to a labor camp. Men were then separated from women and children, and while the men disrobed, women and children were sent into a building where their hair was shorn. While prisoners from the work detail cut the women's hair, the men were marched into the "tube" or "sluice," a fenced-in path that led directly to the gas chamber. After the men were murdered and their bodies removed, the women and children were chased through the tube, forced into the gas chambers, and were gassed. In all, about 1.5 million Jews, and thousands of Sinti and Roma, were murdered between 1942 and 1943 as part of Operation Reinhard. In 1943, the remaining prisoners whose forced labor had maintained the camps knew that they would be murdered, so at Sobibór and Treblinka they staged desperate revolts. In each case, some prisoners escaped, though most were caught and executed.[45] With Operation Reinhard largely completed, the camps were thoroughly demolished in 1943, and debris was either removed or turned under the earth.

Today, only the altered terrain remains as a witness to the murders. Bełżec is on the outskirts of the village of the same name, between a stand of pines to the north and railroad tracks to the south; Sobibór and Treblinka, like the Rzuchów section of the Chełmno memorial, are surrounded by forest. The Operation Reinhard camps, like Chełmno, confront the tourist today with what has been erased, although they do so in strikingly different ways. While Sobibór is notable for the extent to which the landscape stands alone as a silent witness to what lies underneath, Bełżec and Treblinka present large memorial installations that convey a sense of the camp's surface area and layout while memorializing the victims in the figurative language of monuments.

Sobibór

Sobibór lies in a wooded area several kilometers away from the village of the same name, remote and almost forgotten, and reachable only by car. After driving through miles of woods, one reaches the roadside entrance to the memorial in a small settlement of a few houses alongside an overgrown railway track. A pathway leading into the woods is marked by a large plaque and informational signs that explain Sobibór's history. As one walks into the forest, a path veers off from the main walkway, marking the tube that funneled prisoners to the gas chambers. Also called by the camp guards the *Himmelfahrtstrasse* ("road to ascension"), the path is lined with engraved stones commemorating individuals who perished at Sobibór. At the end of the main walkway stands a large mausoleum, a mound of ashes from roughly 200,000 people who died there.[46] Weeds sometimes grow out of mausoleum, testimony to the relative obscurity of Sobibór relative to other camp memorials. Instead of the uniformity of a pine forest in a well-maintained clearing, as at the Rzuchów forest in Chełmno, the Sobibór forest is a mixture of deciduous and evergreen trees growing on sandy soil, with spotty vegetation on the ground and brush, moss, and shrubs mingling among the trees. Since 2007, excavation work has been undertaken at Sobibór to reveal foundations of the gas chamber and other past structures that had been buried, but these efforts have been stalled in bureaucratic wrangling, with areas that were once accessible to tourists now sealed off.[47] At my last visit in 2016, a statue of a mourning female figure that once stood at the center of the memorial space had been temporarily removed to a maintenance building near the memorial's entrance, and the mausoleum sat about 100 meters behind a cordoned-off area.[48]

Sobibór presents itself in perplexing ways to the photographer. In his book on photography and trauma, the comparatist Ulrich Baer analyzes a photo taken by the German artist Dirk Reinartz depicting the sylvan terrain of Sobibór. The image, appearing in a volume of

Figure 2.3. Mausoleum at Sobibór in June 2016, containing the ashes of nearly 200,000 victims. This was the rough location of the gas chambers and cremation areas, which prisoners entered via the cynically named *Himmelfahrtstrasse*, or "road to heaven." Plans for a memorial wall that would wrap around the mausoleum are currently on hold amid concerns for the archeological integrity of the site. Photo by the author.

photos the artist created of former camps, shows no traces that mark the Sobibór memorial as anything other than natural space. Baer focuses on this photo precisely because of the way it highlights the production of landscape photography as a genre for considering traumatic memory. Most tourists take pictures of the memorial structures, but much like Chełmno's Rzuchów forest, the incorporation of structures into tourists' photographic images often retains the scale and logic of landscape photography—a panoramic scene with some interplay between foreground and background, ultimately a projection of an imagined relationship between the human and the natural.[49] While Baer's attention to landscape photography develops a romantic relationship to nature predicated on the absence of human structures, the fusion of memorial objects and natural scenery in tourist photos of Sobibór blurs the line between the natural and the constructed. Tourist pictures at Sobibór explore the relationship between humanity and nature within the framework of the Holocaust, which itself has so often been cast as the horrific outcome of Western culture's effort to overcome nature through technology. The image of vegetation among the memorial's scattered objects invokes nature as transcending the span of a human lifetime, reclaiming a space that was temporally disrupted by the extermination camp and now cohabiting the space with memorial objects.

A photograph of Sobibór refuses to offer us the content of an atrocity photo; it instead shows us the efforts to remove evidence from the scene. As documents of erasure, photos confirm the difficulty in acquiring knowledge about the Holocaust through a visual examination of its more forgotten places, recapitulating the idea that, as a collective trauma, the murder of six million Jews challenges our understanding of history and our relationship to it. Left with the aesthetic strategies of landscape photography, the presentation of a scene of disquieting beauty stands in stark contrast to the atrocity of the gassings that took place there.[50] Taking a picture may be a way to work through the difficulty of reconciling the place one encounters today with historical images of atrocity, fixing the historically defined place in a moment of our own lived time. While the tourist may hope to experience a sense of immediacy to places of the Holocaust by being there, the camera at Sobibór confirms the impossibility of accessing the past save through mediated experience. The tourist photo at camp memorials can become a way to remind us that we are always belated witnesses.[51]

While pictures of Sobibór are belated acts of witnessing the Holocaust, tourists are not too late to be primary witnesses to the condition of the memorial installation.[52] Current pictures showing a forest overtaking a memorial takes on a political dimension when one considers how Holocaust memory remains a point of contention in Polish national discourse today. Some in Poland still see Holocaust memorialization as an effort to impugn their country as a perpetrator nation, in opposition to the preferred nationalist narrative of Poland as a victim of Nazi aggression and Soviet perfidy. The present resurgence of nationalist politics in Poland (and increasingly throughout the West) leaves little space for the kind of ambiguity that acknowledges the complicity of some Poles in Judeocide while acknowledging the resistance of others.

Perhaps public awareness of Sobibór's current condition will dislodge the logjam over the site's development, but the proposed memorial itself gives plenty of cause for concern. Plans announced in 2011 by the Polish Ministry of Cultural and Natural Heritage called for a 5 million dollar visitor center and monument in the form of a mile-long wall that would trace the path taken by deportees as they marched toward the gas chambers. The plans for the new monument have many worried that the new structure will disturb archeological finds yet to discovered. After all, it was only in 2014 that archeologists discovered the foundations of the gas chamber, which had been thought to have been completely destroyed. There is also worry that the proposed memorial will disturb human remains. Given the possibilities for reflection I see in engaging with the site as it currently exists, I worry that the placement of the new memorial and visitor's center on the grounds of the camp's ruins will draw attention from the outdoors into an interior space that never existed at the camp and will certainly interrupt the possibility for the kind of landscape photos that I, along with Baer, find so meaningful. A looming wall of concrete will bisect the memorial from the flora, a striking departure from the death camp's incorporation of nature as camouflage to hide mass murder from view and therefore, in my mind, obscuring one of the most important aspects of extermination that tourism can encounter. The most impactful memorial for Sobibór in my mind would be one that preserves the sense of haunting that still suffuses the place, that welcomes tourists to reflect on their relationship to history through the medium of landscape photography, all of which is still possible now, even with the signs of stalled maintenance everywhere. It would be better for the visitor's center to be located on the periphery of the memorial grounds, not upon it.

Bełżec

An indication of what Sobibór might become awaits visitors today at the Bełżec memorial. Located between Lublin and Lviv, the camp is where approximately 500,000 victims were murdered between March and December 1942. Only two people are known to have escaped Bełżec and survived the war.[53] After closing the death camp, the SS built a farmhouse for a Ukrainian camp guard, who in turn managed the land as a farm to provide a false alibi for his benefactors. (The same ruse was deployed by the Nazis at Sobibór and Treblinka to hide evidence of atrocity.)[54] The landscape at Bełżec remained much as it was in 1943 until twenty years later, when the most modest of memorials was placed there.[55] The first memorial installed at Bełżec in 1963 consisted of a minor excavation of the grounds and a decidedly humble monument. Prior to the construction of a new memorial complex in 2002, visitors to Bełżec would walk into a birch forest up a hillside along an old railroad track, where they would find the modest concrete memorial, and if they looked closely at the grounds, evidence of what transpired there: bones, ashes, shell casings, pieces of clothing or personal effects.[56] One visitor to the site in 2000, Rabbi Shaul Rosenblatt, wrote:

> Auschwitz/Birkenau is a major tourist attraction. Treblinka has a heart-wrenching memorial. But at Bełżec, there are only bones. It's a quiet spot, in a pretty forest. And if you spent a few years there, you might just be able to pick them all up. But what touched me most deeply about Bełżec, and continues to do so, was its loneliness. It is a forgotten camp. So few people visit. The first tragedy is that so many died here. But the more immediate tragedy is that nobody really seems to care.[57]

Rosenblatt movingly documented the neglected state of the site that had become a memorial to humanity's willingness to forget. While Rosenblatt conveyed the powerful impression the Bełżec memorial left on him, the relative dearth of memorialization led him to worry about remembrance in the absence of adequate monuments.

Today, as if in response to Rosenblatt's account, Bełżec is a very different place. Now it features a new museum and a massive memorial dedicated in 2004.[58] The entire area of the camp has been covered with an installation of stylized rubble, with a large monument at the northeastern end where the gas chamber would have stood. There are no barracks, no burial pits, no crematoria; the lonely forest that once grew over this site has been cleared back to the northern edge of the site. Visitors walk between two fields of mangled concrete and steel along a path that simulates the *Schlauch* ("sluice" or "tube"), the camouflaged passageway that led to the gas chamber. At the southern corner of the memorial sits the museum, a discrete underground facility that does not disturb the view of the memorial. A pyre of stacked railroad tracks in the western corner serves as a reminder of the cremation of corpses on top of these makeshift grates. As the tourist enters the memorial site,

Figure 2.4. Bełżec memorial, June 2010. Since 2004, a field of jagged stone and metal enclose a representation of the "tube," once a fenced pathway camouflaged with branches to hide the prisoners from view as they were forced into the gas chambers at the other end. Only a few people are known to have escaped Bełżec—all other arrivals, some 500,000, died here. Photo by the author.

these structures are situated effectively behind the viewer, and when the camera points at the central monument, they lie outside the frame.[59]

The new memorial, while impressive in its claim to permanence, has displaced the desolation that once stood here and that Rosenblatt conveys so somberly, and it ultimately conceals more than it reveals. The possibilities for visitors to explore the terrain, to discover the evidence of mass graves, and to feel the collective amnesia that hovered over the place have been obliterated. True, the former memorial's modesty was not necessarily by design—a combination of scarce resources and insufficient local interest had consigned it to obscurity. It is also the case that some visitors would disturb and even remove objects they discovered, an intolerable violation of the site's integrity as a resting place for the victims. To address these problems, the new monument has literally paved over the grounds, marking it with a massive gravestone, and keeping tourists on a prescribed path. The museum provides ample information and fills an important educational role that was sorely missing, but the surrounding memorial is so monumental as to risk displacing visitors' efforts to imagine the place as it was during the camp's operation. Concrete and steel speak of a massive, industrial-scale operation, but what is so troubling about places like Bełżec, Sobibór, and Treblinka was their intentional impermanence. They were built of largely flimsy wooden structures that were to be destroyed after the mass murders.

It is hard to imagine a starker contrast to Sobibór or to Chełmno village. Tourist photography's revelatory impulse seems no match for the totalizing scene that now confronts the tourist at Bełżec. Forgetfulness and shame have given way to the desire to remember—but should we not also remember forgetfulness?[60] For surely the neglect and desire to forget is part of the historical response to the Nazi genocide that Rosenblatt and others found so moving, even if they longed for something else. One feels that a certain final and static statement on memory has been substituted for the once-melancholic scene where nature marked the passage of time. While the memorial insists that the will to forget has been overcome, continual acts of Holocaust denial and anti-Semitism in Poland and beyond should caution us to doubt the triumph of memorialization over forgetfulness.

Despite the more prescribed experience of the site demanded by the new memorial, tourists still find strategies for making their own sense of the place, and the camera is one tool that allows tourists to engage critically with the Bełżec memorial site. By generating a repertoire of tourist photography that is readily accessible on Flickr, Google, Yahoo, and other familiar sites that allow image searches, tourists document the changes in memorialization and preserve a record of remembrance and neglect. The tourist repertoire includes photos by visitors prior to 2002 that depict the desolation and humility of a remote, possibly forgotten memorial—except that the photo proves that someone did pay attention. As documentation of the memorial's earlier condition, photographs taken by amateurs at Bełżec can challenge the authority of the current monument by recalling what preceded it and by placing it into an "unauthorized" context of evolving collective memory. Tourist photos of Bełżec before 2002, although in the minority of available images, have themselves become historical documents by virtue of depicting what is no longer there, and in that important sense they enter into an intimate relationship with the historical photos of the camp that are on display in Bełżec's subterranean museum. Through photography as a collective enterprise, stored images reveal layers of memory that lie upon the site. Tourist photography has become an archive of public memory, and collectively photography's revelatory power is confirmed, not by looking at one image in time, but by looking at many images over time. Thanks to the new memorial's seeming permanence, the once-overgrown site no longer yields so readily to nature as the marker of time, in contrast to Sobibór, but the growing archive of tourist photographs can reassert the temporality of all memory. Tourism includes the capacity, however unintentional, to document gradual changes at the new Bełżec memorial, like updated signage, the annual spread of rust from metal engravings on concrete, and the wear and tear of weather and foot traffic, thereby troubling the sense of permanence the current memorial evokes. Photography at Bełżec's memorial, both past and present, may restore a sense of haunting to Bełżec that the current monument has, regrettably, displaced.

The memorials at Bełżec and Sobibór, currently two very different places, remind us that the camera's ability to document the Holocaust is circumscribed by decisions others have made about what can or should be seen—including the perpetrators who buried the evidence of their crimes. Like Bełżec, the proposed new memorial at Sobibór will necessarily add another prescribed view to which tourists will doubtless respond with aesthetic strategies of their own when they reach for the camera. Many photos will fall short of the aesthetic criteria for serious, original art and will reinforce Pierre Bourdieu's assessment of the medium as impossibly "middlebrow." Indeed, the complaint about most tourist photography is precisely this: that it does not produce original works of art so much as reproduce those marketed by others.[61] A more generous interpretation of tourist photos might instead see them in a critical relationship to that which they observe, as affirmations, as refutations, or as thoughtful reflections on the aesthetic strategies of Holocaust memorials.

Treblinka

As a memorial site, Treblinka incorporates all the possibilities for tourist engagement through photography seen at Chełmno, Bełżec, and

Sobibór, a reflection in part of its scale and its location. As an extermination camp, Treblinka was the place where approximately 800,000 people were murdered, making it the second most lethal Nazi installation after Birkenau. The camp was located several kilometers from the village of the same name, about eighty-two kilometers northeast of Warsaw. As in Sobibór, a prisoner revolt in took place in 1943, during which approximately 100 prisoners—about half the number from the Sobibór uprising—managed to escape and avoid recapture.[62] Afterward, the SS closed and razed the camp.[63] Much like the commemorative installations at Chełmno's Rzuchów forest, the memorial at Treblinka is situated in a forest clearing dominated by a large cenotaph, roughly at the point were the gas chambers stood, surrounded by a lapidarium denoting the many communities that were deported there. In contrast to Bełżec, which presents a massive field of concrete and rebar, the variety of stone monuments at Treblinka recalls the diversity and vitality of Jewish culture that the Holocaust destroyed. Leading to that lapidarium, wooden planks simulate the rail ties of the spur that brought transports into the camp. Because nothing remains of the camp's former structures, not even the pathway taken to the gas chambers, visitors have to rely on signs that explain the layout of the camp. Among these signs are large photos of the camp from the time of its operation, taken by the camp's sadistic second-in-command, Kurt Franz, for a souvenir album he called *Schöne Zeiten* (Happy times). Through their encounters with these photographic images, tourists to Treblinka today look at the scene through the lens of the perpetrator's camera as well as through their own. That apparent similarity becomes an important aspect for understanding the tourist gaze, but in ways that far exceed the presumed identification with the perpetrator gaze that some critics have suggested. To understand the similarities and differences, it helps to dwell for a moment on photographs such as those taken by Franz.

Franz kept his album in his home in Wuppertal, West Germany, after the war, where it was discovered during a search in 1959. The album ultimately became a damning document in the trials of Treblinka personnel in the 1960s, and in 1965 Franz was sentenced to life in prison for his crimes. He was released in 1993 for health reasons and died five years later.[64] Franz's photos do not show prisoners at Treblinka; instead, they capture a sentimentalized view of the camp as a bucolic assignment

Figure 2.5. The Treblinka cenotaph, June 2011, located at the site of the gas chamber where 800,000 prisoners were asphyxiated with carbon monoxide. Treblinka was the most lethal killing center after Birkenau. The plaque intones "Never Again." Photo by the author.

for an SS officer, complete with a small zoo on the camp grounds. Aside from the smiling uniformed SS men it depicts, Franz's perverse war souvenir exposes important components of Treblinka's true nature. There is the excavator used at Treblinka to dig mass graves and later to unearth the bodies for cremation on large pyres. And there is a series of photos of Franz's St. Bernard, which he trained to attack prisoners on command.

The *Happy Times* album is not the only album of photo souvenirs taken by Nazi perpetrators. The Germanist Daniel H. Magilow documents a number of such albums and explores the relationship between the perpetrator's gaze and their function, whether intended or not, as bearers of witness.[65] A better-known example is the set of photos taken by two SS officers working in the *Erkennungsdienst* (identification service) unit at Auschwitz-Birkenau. These photos, some 200 in total, document the arrival and selection of Hungarian Jews, among the last deportations to Auschwitz. In a stunning turn of fate, the album was discovered by a survivor of that very same transport, Lili Jacob, who found the volume in evacuated SS barracks in the Dora-Mittelbau camp, where she had been transferred for the remaining weeks of the war.[66] Jacob eventually donated the photo album to Yad Vashem in Jerusalem, although she had allowed copies of photos to be made in preceding years and shared them with the Auschwitz-Birkenau Memorial and Museum.[67] We know these images today as *The Auschwitz Album*.

Both *The Auschwitz Album* and *Happy Times* contain images that have been reproduced in many documentations of the Holocaust; however, placement of those images at the spots where they were taken in Birkenau and Treblinka, respectively, negotiates a direct link between the place where tourists stand in the present and the Holocaust whose historic traces tourists seek. By placing these pictures at their very points of origin, the images help visitors ponder how the memorial differs from the death camp it commemorates. These photographs are particularly valuable at Treblinka, where they substitute for the missing physical structures that would otherwise orient the tourist within the vanished camp's geography. But in gazing upon these images, tourists find themselves relying on the eye of the perpetrator to understand where they are.

The invitation to see through the perpetrator's eyes at Treblinka, Auschwitz, and the numerous sites where perpetrator photography forms part of the exhibit has suggested for some critics that the tourist gaze becomes in some sense complicit with the act of destruction through the common reliance on the camera.[68] Images by perpetrators include the intake photographs of new arrivals not selected for immediate death, records of the infamous medical experiments conducted on inmates, executions, and pictures of camp personnel—SS men in uniform smiling in posed shots or administrators in front of their office barracks, perhaps sent back home to family members.[69] Prisoners were often photographed or filmed for propaganda purposes by the Reich, perpetuating the lie that the camps were transit destinations on the way to resettlement. The documentary *Der Führer schenkt den Juden eine Stadt* (The Führer gives the Jews a city; 1944) is perhaps be most notorious instance, depicting life in the Theresienstadt Ghetto north of Prague as an urban idyll, when the reality was a grim confined area of disease and starvation used as a center for deportation to Auschwitz.

It is certainly tempting to draw a parallel between the tourist gaze at Treblinka or other camp memorials with that of the Nazi perpetrators who used the lens as an instrument of control. This uncomfortable commonality of the camera may lead some tourists to reflect about the ways in which their own device has the capacity to objectify others, to lend itself as a means of surveillance and domination of the worst sort. In *On Photography*, Sontag goes so far as to argue that "the act of photographing is . . . a way of at least tacitly, often explicitly, encouraging whatever is going on to keep on happening."[70] By such logic, even the photos taken by camp liberators and accompanying journalists become complicit after the fact. Any hope the tourist might have of identifying with the more redeeming gaze of the liberator is undermined by the suspicion of endorsement. But the claim that viewers of atrocity photos endorse the ideology of the perpetrator is too simplistic. The anthropologist Cornelia Brink takes up this question in her book, *Ikonen der Vernichtung* (Icons of annihilation), where she contrasts the critical evaluation of perpetrator images with the pedagogical intentions of memorial sites that put them on display.[71] Brink shows that there is nothing intrinsic in the medium of photography that insists on such easy identifications; rather, photography raises questions about subjectivity, whether taking pictures or viewing them. In the particular case of perpetrator images of victims, Brink points out that every photo has a double nature. She takes issue with critics who tend to insist that the viewer of the photograph identifies either with the photographer or the victim, arguing persuasively that both positions insist on a straightforward identificatory approach to understanding how we view photographs. Instead, Brink describes a tug-of-war between these options.[72] With Brink, I would argue that there is no position of untarnished innocence from which one can view atrocity, as much as one might feel anguish for the victim.

And yet precisely this tug-of-war of identification with the photographee/victim or the photographer/perpetrator is one of the ways in which tourism engages viewers in ethical reflection. Rather than concluding that photography is complicit, we should acknowledge that the medium is morally ambiguous. Perpetrator images on display at Treblinka, Auschwitz, and elsewhere can make tourists aware of the moral ambiguity of their own gaze.

There are aspects inherent in the medium of photography that further complicate any notion of tourist photos at sites of Holocaust perpetration as mimicking the gaze of the perpetrator.[73] While the cultural philosopher Walter Benjamin's attention to photography as "mechanically reproducible" denied the genre the kind of aura that could be associated with an original work of art (e.g., a masterpiece painting), something of the auratic is restored, I would claim, when reproduced historical photos are encountered at the place where they originated. The place itself is the ultimate original, even if it is altered by the passage of time. Moreover, while photographic images may be reproduced, there remains the singularity of each occasion in which a photographic image is viewed. To view the image of an excavator at Treblinka on the very grounds where it exhumed bodies for cremation engages tourists with that particular space in much more profound way than is possible for a distant viewer of the same photo, however momentarily. Furthermore, the reproduction of photographs of atrocity is in fact part of what makes the Holocaust so abhorrent, highlighting the routinized process of murder millions of times over. Tourists' own photographs can only relate to perpetrator photography in an ironic sense, that is, from a position of commentary on the perpetration of atrocity.

I can best illustrate this notion of a critical or ironic distance between tourist photos and perpetrator photos by pointing to a particular subgenre of tourist photography: photographs of photographs. One could think of such photography as a kind of quotation, an act of repetition that also preserves something of the context from which the quote originates. Photographs of historical photographs arise by design and by accident: The ubiquity of photos at Holocaust memorial sites means that historical photos can be hard to keep outside the tourist's frame. But such photographs may also be intentional, ways of recording information that can be consulted later. The tourist's intentions may be more abstract and conceptual, as in a picture that frames a historical photograph in such a way as to juxtapose the past and the present, highlighting either continuity or rupture in time. When tourists enter Auschwitz, for example, they stand first beside the mess hall in the same spot where an orchestra played while prisoners went to or returned from work details. In front of the former mess hall is a photo of the orchestra playing at the spot where the tourist now stands. The tourist who takes a picture of same spot, framing the historical image within their own, creates a temporal bridge that links the spot where the tourist stands with photographer who took the historical image. Similarly at Treblinka, photos from Kurt Franz's *Schöne Zeiten* appear at the spots where they appear to have been taken so the tourist can compare then and now and again frame the past within the present, in a sense claiming a connection to that past. Tourists do not bear direct witness to the event of the past; rather, they place themselves in a temporal relation to history in a way that is grounded in place and experience. History becomes more real through such images.

Figure 2.6. The lapidarium that surrounds the central memorial at Treblinka, June 2011. In the foreground, a photo from the SS officer Kurt Franz's photo album, *Happy Times*, showing equipment used to exhume bodies for subsequent cremation. Photo by the author.

But there may be more at work in such framings. When tourists take pictures that include historical photos, the camera performs two functions. First, it helps bridge the temporal distance that separates the tourist from the suffering that took place seventy years ago. The historical image on site has a way of bleeding into the present moment when viewed on site, inviting the viewer to consider the connections between then and now. Second, it may even amount to an effort by the tourist to overcome identification with the perpetrator by containing the prior image within a frame of one's own making. There is a contradiction between these two notions: The first suggests a removal of a (temporal) barrier, while the second reinserts (a psychological) one. Marianne Hirsch argues that photographs make images present to viewers while at the same time they insert a "screen" between the viewers and images; that screening effect may be enough to stop the bleeding of an image onto the present, but the strategy of framing that image within a tourist's own picture suggests that the screen may be insufficient, at least when viewed at the same location.[74] The juxtaposition of the black-and-white image within a tourist's color frame gives the illusion that history itself is somehow contained. Additionally, by "capturing" the historical photograph in a picture of one's own, a tourist's engagement with a historical photo on site can be deferred for some later time after the tour has taken place. Such efforts to gain mastery over perpetrator images may also explain the purchase by tourists of books and postcards that reproduce these images within the confines of familiar media.

One could reasonably argue that the purchase of such items signals the kind of endorsement of their contents that worries Sontag when she claims that viewing atrocity photos is a tacit encouragement of atrocity itself. But when applied to Holocaust tourism, such a dismissal of atrocity photos as mere commodity proves reductive. If the perpetrator photograph itself objectifies victims, then the purchase of the photograph in another medium only underscores an existing problem. If, however, the photograph is regarded as a form of testimony that can inform viewers, the circulation of the photograph in the tourist market helps fulfill that task. By purchasing a reproduction of *The Auschwitz Album*, for example, tourists help fulfill the intentions of Lili Jacob to remember her community and its terrible fate. Purchasing a book featuring Franz's photos of Treblinka, by extension, affirms the evidentiary nature of these photos that were used to prosecute Franz and others. (Franz's album itself is not replicated as a commodity; rather, the images circulate in a critical context in numerous publications.)[75] The albums of personal photos taken by perpetrators were meant to be private, and by converting them into publicly shared documents, tourism participates in thwarting the intended secrecy of these images.[76] Both *Happy Times* and *The Auschwitz Album* enable a kind of secondary witnessing that fulfills testimony's need for an addressee, quite contrary to the intentions of the perpetrator/photographer and much more in line with the intentions of Allied photojournalists who took images of camps and survivors upon liberation.

Liberator Photography and Majdanek

By the end of 1943, Bełżec, Sobibór, and Treblinka had been dismantled, burned, and buried, meant by those who conceived them to remain a secret lost to history. But as Operation Reinhard concluded, Auschwitz-Birkenau and Majdanek entered their deadliest periods. With the Red Army on the offensive, the Nazis seemed intent on fulfilling the task of annihilating Europe's Jews, even as it became clear that Germany faced military defeat. At Majdanek, Jews were exterminated in gas chambers using both carbon monoxide and, later, Zyklon B, sometimes upon arrival and sometimes after being registered for labor. Of the approximately 80,000–100,000 prisoners who perished at Majdanek between 1942 and 1944, about 60,000–70,000 were Jews.[77] The majority of these, some 43,000 Jews, died as part of Aktion Erntefest, or Operation Harvest Festival, the roundup and murder of the remaining Jews in the Lublin region of the General Government, most already interned at the Majdanek, Trawniki, and Poniatowa camps. Many of these were Jews whose labor was coerced for Operation Reinhard, but after the uprisings at Sobibór and Treblinka, the SS perceived them as a potential threat, so they were rounded up and shot in trenches in November 1943.[78]

Eight months later, Majdanek became the first extermination camp to be liberated by the Red Army. The SS did not have time to dismantle the camp before retreating, and so, like Birkenau, there are some intact barracks on display today (not all are reconstructed facsimiles—some have the original signage on them), although most of the barracks have vanished. Also like Birkenau, the camp occupies a vast area surrounded by guard towers. Quite unlike Birkenau, Majdanek is located on edge of a major center of population in the eastern outskirts of Lublin. At the time of its operations, the smoke rising from its crematoria would have been visible to many thousands living in the city and in neighboring villages. Today the intact gas chamber/crematorium at the extreme southern edge of the camp stands next to a large mausoleum, a concrete dome suspended over an immense mound of human ashes. The mausoleum is situated at the opposite end of a road that originates at the northern entry point of the camp. A large stone monument dominates this entry and presents a concrete and granite gate suggestive of struggling human bodies or of let- ters of the alphabet struggling to be decoded.[79] Where the memorial at Birkenau seems something of an afterthought, located at the end of the guided tour near the crematoria ruins, the gate monument at Majdanek marks both the beginning and the ending of any tour to the camp.

Figure 2.7. Majdanek, with the gateway memorial in the foreground. The distant mausoleum and crematorium chimney are framed by its base in the background. Inset: a display in one of the barracks containing victims' shoes. On August 12, 2010, just a month after these photos were taken, arsonists set fire to this barracks and destroyed it. Photo by the author.

Majdanek occupies a unique role in the history of photography that documents the Holocaust, and tourists, whether consciously or not, stand in relation to a journalistic tradition of photography as a means to bear witness. In her thorough study of the journalists who toured the camps upon their liberation, the media and communications scholar Barbie Zelizer explains the evolution of photojournalism as a means for documenting atrocity. In Zelizer's account, Majdanek became instantly notorious—and instantly forgotten. "The Russians were curiously uneven in their attempts to make public releases on Bełżec, Sobibór, and Treblinka. And they did little to publicize Auschwitz's liberation until after the liberation of the western camps. Yet to Majdanek they invited a select group of Western correspondents to tour the camp. This made Majdanek the one camp that drew Western attention."[80] Despite that initial attention, Zelizer documents the deep mistrust between the Western and Soviet presses. For the former, "it was easier to regard the information trickling out as Russian propaganda."[81] Still Majdanek played an influential role on western journalists by offering a kind of "dress-rehearsal for recording the unbelievable."[82] When the western Allies finally liberated Buchenwald, Dachau, and Bergen-Belsen in Germany, some members of the press had already become familiar with the difficulties in reporting on atrocity in both word and image: "The Western coverage of Majdanek was important because it established a standard by which reporters and photographers could later bear witness to Nazi atrocity, that is, take responsibility for what they saw."[83]

What Zelizer has characterized as "images of witnessing" are important for understanding the relationship between the tourist lens and the act of bearing witness.[84] First of all, they established the importance of photographs as documentary proof of what had taken place prior to liberation. While intent on recording evidence of atrocity, the photographers who accompanied the liberators knew they had come too late, a sentiment frequently expressed by reporters in their articles.[85] All that remained to document were countless dead bodies and a small numbers of survivors, often skeletal in appearance because of the horrible sanitary conditions, hunger, and ensuing disease that ravaged them. The first journalists who accompanied liberating troops had to search for a convincing idiom to document atrocity, in spite of—or because of—coming too late. One such idiom was the description of camp topography, which became "word tours" to help readers imagine what the journalists were seeing.[86] These first word tours, accompanied by photos, allowed readers and viewers to visualize the machinery of atrocity on a large scale and spoke to the exceptional nature of the camps as spaces that lay outside the realm of experience for those who liberated them. Because these places were unprecedented in the minds of the liberators, journalists impressed upon their readers the importance of seeing the camps in order to believe them, and photography offered a means by which they could do so.[87]

Obviously, the scenes of deprivation that greeted the liberators and the first journalists at the camps have been replaced by sanitized memorial spaces that make tourism possible in the first place. Despite the important differences, tourists still tend to mimic the early journalistic accounts of camp topography. In spaces like Majdanek or Birkenau, the rows of barracks (most absent, but their footprints still visible) along an open field or hill slope call for a panoramic shot that transmits the vast expanse of the camp to the viewer. The alignment of Majdanek's monuments, on an axis from the entry gate to the distant mausoleum and crematorium, allow the tourist's camera to record images on a large scale. By creating an image of the terrain, tourists, like the journalists who preceded them, create a kind of map of atrocity.

Also like the first journalists, tourists may find themselves drawn to their cameras as a kind of compensatory response to horror. At the barracks and crematorium at Majdanek, tourists can view exhibits that highlight details of the camp's deadly operations, often confronting what Zelizer calls the "accoutrements of atrocity"—canisters of poison, the furnaces of the crematorium, sites of execution.[88] One barracks is filled entirely with shoes, a display that shares the vernacular of Holocaust exhibits at Auschwitz and at the United States Holocaust Memorial Museum, where piles of shoes have become a synecdoche for the human beings who have perished en masse. Such displays are often controversial, both praised and condemned for their overwhelming depiction of nameless multitudes of victims. Tourists show many different responses to such exhibits: Some are moved to tears; some shake their heads; some simply move on, unsure how to respond to what is an impossible problem: imagining each individual to whom such personal effects once belonged. Reaching for the camera is a frequent response, an effort to reassert some sense of perspective or agency in the face of overwhelming brutality. The attempt to comprehend the masses of dead, at Majdanek or at any other Holocaust site, is no doubt one of the greatest challenges that history leaves to those who live in the wake of genocide. If the mind simply shuts down in the face of such enormity, perhaps the camera becomes a way to postpone the engagement, to save the image for another time and place when contemplation may be more possible.

Conclusion: Repetition, Agency, and Tourism's Self-Reflexivity

Tourist photos often repeat iconic images already in circulation, those that are published in tourist brochures, guidebooks, posters, and websites, evidence of what Urry calls a "ritual of quotation."[89] But the act of photographic quotation is not mere repetition; rather, it is always an act of recontextualization that expresses the tourist's agency. By more or less consciously creating one's own version of familiar scenes, tourists take photos as a way of laying claim to a genealogy of iconic images already in existence. For example, the most iconic images at Auschwitz are undoubtedly the gates of the *Stammlager*, with the infamous slogan "Arbeit macht frei" in wrought iron, and the Gate of Death that arches over the rail spur leading into Birkenau. Even if tourists arrive unfamiliar with these emblematic scenes, they will reencounter their reproductions on postcards, book covers, and tourist brochures, all of which signal the iconic status of the site to the tourist. At the Operation Reinhard camps, where the camp structures were destroyed, the postwar mausoleums and monuments offer themselves as landmarks that also may be encountered in tourist literature on site. The compulsion to repeat these images is a testament to their power, an effort to capture for oneself what has been witnessed by others, to capture the auratic quality of the real thing. The resulting picture is the tourist's admittance into a community of witnessing where the goal is not to be the first or to be the most original but, rather, to affirm what others have acknowledged. That includes the images that derived from early photojournalism at places like Majdanek, but it also links tourism to other representations of the Holocaust.[90]

Whether one sees in tourist photography at the camps a kind of obsession with the same images already in circulation, evidence of an unresolved collective trauma, or simply an attempt to interact with a scene that is saturated with significance, one should also consider the repetitive nature of tourist photography in general, a phenomenon that is not unique to Holocaust tourism.[91] Repetition is commonplace at tourist sites one would not normally associate with trauma; tourists take more or less the same pictures of Mount Rushmore, the Eiffel Tower, or Mount Fuji that one encounters in numerous other media. While trauma theory may elucidate one aspect of the reception of Holocaust photography and tourists' relation to it, the context of tourism points to other motives for repetition, including self-reflection and the exercise of agency, that help tourists define their own relationship to distant times and far-away places. Taking a picture of an iconic site is a way to claim some degree of ownership over its representation or at least to participate in the community of those who affirm a particular, already-established representation. It becomes one of the ways tourists engage with their place in history and geography.

Suggesting that tourists reflect on their relationship to history and to geography may seem like a tall order for critics of tourism. But self-consciousness among tourists is hardly uncommon; indeed, it is what so frequently leads travelers to disavow any resemblance to negative stereotypes of tourists (remember David Brown's phrase, "They are tourists, I am not.") Through repetition and the multiplication of the gaze, the camera offers one more way for tourists to disavow any association with tourism, or at least with its crasser components. Tourist photography includes two uniquely touristic motifs: pictures of pictures, and pictures of other tourists. In both cases, tourists produce photos that incorporate the gazes of people looking back.

The social psychologist Alex Gillespie has coined the term "the reverse gaze" to describe the self-awareness that pictures stimulate in tourists when the eyes of those photographed stare back. "The reverse gaze refers to the gaze of the photographee on the photographer as perceived by the photographer."[92] The importance of this returned gaze is that it "can play an important role in constituting the emerging self of the tourist photographer."[93] In particular, the reverse gaze has the capacity to expose "a discrepancy between Self's image of Self and Self's image of how Other perceives Self."[94] That is to say, the reverse gaze has the power to engender self-awareness in the tourist photographer precisely as a tourist, an identity many tourists avidly seek to disavow.

Despite the absence of the Holocaust victims, the reverse gaze in Holocaust tourism remains possible in two ways: by photographing historical photographs of people now long dead, and by photographing fellow tourists who are very much present. Regarding the former, the historical photos that fill most exhibits, including the famous and oft-recirculated images, contain the frightened faces of those persecuted, often photographed by their tormenters. In such images, the stare back at the camera may awaken a disquieting sense of complicity in the viewer, engaging the tourist in the reflection on their own subjectivity that we discussed in connection to perpetrator photography in general but now intensified through the gaze caught on film. As bearers of the same instrument of surveillance, tourists may feel urged to confront similarities or affirm differences between their act of photography and those of the perpetrators. Similarly, liberator photos depicting victims may raise questions in the mind of the tourist about one's relationship to the spectacle of atrocity. Photos of skeletal bodies, both living and dead, are a reminder that liberation came too late for too many, and the suffering that marked the appearance of survivors denies such images any triumphalist quality that one may seek in the act of liberation. There is no use of the camera or any other touristic medium that can undo the suffering documented at camp memorials. Through such images, the tourist is reminded that spectatorship, whether through photojournalism or tourism, is not enough to undo the violence it encounters.

The second kind of reverse gaze occurs when tourists turn their cameras on one another, producing a mirror image of their own subjectivity that may aid or confound the urge to disavow any association with other tourists. When tourists photograph one another, whether by accident or design, they construct a frame around an established practice of photography, generating a metadiscourse that opens tourists to the possibility of self-reflection. Tourists pose for and orchestrate such photos of one another all the time, even at concentration camp sites. Most of the time, the gazes of friends and family are innocuous; sometimes, however, unknown tourists wander into the frame and look back, perhaps with disapproval at the attention one calls to oneself when arranging such photos. Indeed, tourist photography can easily violate the sense of decorum that a site commands, and tourists can be critical of those among them who fail to exhibit respect for the site. The presence of tourist groups holding selfie-sticks as they pass under the words "Arbeit macht frei" at Auschwitz is unsettling, to say the least.

There are important restrictions on photography at the camp memorials, prescribing certain behaviors that are dictated by a code of ethics about proper ways to show respect and bear witness, as well as by the necessities of preserving artifacts. When those restrictions are violated, the reverse gaze is a common result. At Auschwitz, for example, flash photos are prohibited at the indoor exhibits out of concern for preservation of artifacts from harmful flash bulbs. The display of human hair, which the Nazis harvested from victims for a number of purposes, is perhaps chief among these artifacts threatened by flash bulbs (but not uniformly prohibited to flashless photography).[95] The only place where photography, even without a flash, was expressly prohibited during my visits was the gas chamber at the *Stammlager*, where tour guides admonished their groups to refrain from taking pictures out of a sense of decency owed toward the victims. The result is an uneven invocation of respect toward victims, one that extends to a facsimile of the gas chamber then in use, but not to personal belongings of victims. Of course, not all visitors observe the rules. Occasionally, one sees a flash go off in the crowd despite the explicit instructions forbidding it. Because they validate misgivings about tourism as a proper vehicle for remembrance, tourists who violate strictures on taking pictures may be greeted by censure from other tourists eager to distance themselves from the offender. Such violations are typically greeted by stares, frowns, or verbal disapproval by guides and other tourists eager to preserve the legitimacy of their presence. Disapproving gazes from compliant tourists to those who err are commonplace in tourism, but their opprobrium feels even more intense when tourism accesses places where dignity was denied to victims.[96] At a place loaded with so much significance, the weight of the returned gaze can be intensely embarrassing or shaming.

But even if one obeys all the rules, can one really show reverence for a site and simultaneously take a picture of it? The answer depends, of course, on whether one considers photography a profane or reverent act.

As museums, the camps today make extensive use of photography, so it is hard to argue that their dependence on photography maintains a reverence that tourist photography violates. There is certainly no opportunity to reobjectify the victims at the camp memorials today, since there are not even marked graves identifying the dead. The concerns raised by Susan Sontag in *On Photography*—that taking pictures of atrocity is equivalent with encouraging it—seem less applicable in a context of belated witnessing, where the event is temporally distant.

Moreover, it is a position that Sontag herself came to abandon. In her final work on the topic of photography, *Regarding the Pain of Others*, Sontag returns to the kind of images that first shocked her when she beheld the liberated camps. She focuses primarily on the work of photojournalists, whom she calls "those professional, specialized tourists."[97] Recalling her earlier belief that the shock of photographs of violence and murder is short-lived, Sontag reconsiders: "Yet there are cases where repeated exposure to what shocks, saddens, appalls does not use up a full-hearted response. Habituation is not automatic."[98] Ultimately, the moral responsibility to look at such photos and think about them, to resist the tendency toward numbness, rests with the viewer: "People don't become inured to what they are shown—if that's the right way to describe what happens—because of the *quantity* of images dumped on them. It is passivity that dulls feeling."[99] In other words, the sense that there is nothing one can do when faced with images of brutality may lead to sympathy but not necessarily to action. Reflection, memory *work*, is an effort to think beyond the passivity of viewership and instead to consider one's own relationship to violence and ultimately to change behaviors that contribute to it.

That work of reflection reminds us that photography is not limited to the moment of taking a picture. Tourists return home, and they face choices about the pictures they bring back: which ones to keep, how to show them, and to whom. Even if tourists never share their photos with others, the images they carry ask questions and demand explanations—where was this, what does it show, why was it photographed? While taking pictures at the camps offers a form of evidence of our having been there, they also ask us, "Now what?" The images travel, and so do the ethical imperatives they connote. By showing what has been, photos serve as a reminder that the tour is over but that the need for reflection carries on.

Holocaust tourists who visit camps have an intermediate journey to undertake before they return home. As we saw, the Nazis chose locations for the extermination camps that, for the most part, were far from major centers of population (Majdanek is an exception that, like Auschwitz, was originally designated for forced labor, not for the immediate extermination of deportees). To reach these sites, tourists usually embark from a nearby city, often Warsaw or Kraków, sites that are also very important landmarks of Polish national heritage, and it is to such cities they return upon completing their tour. To return to a modern metropolis buzzing with life after a day spent at factories of death makes for one of Holocaust tourism's more disorienting experiences, and different travelers make the transition from one space to another with different degrees of ease or difficulty. For those who are so minded, their interest in comprehending the Holocaust will also inform the ways in which they consume those cities as tourist destinations. Many large cities memorialize lost Jewish life by preserving and restoring abandoned synagogues or commemorating homes and neighborhoods where Jews once thrived. Some cities explain how the architects of the Holocaust established ghettos and centers of deportation where the local Jewish population was already concentrated. Other urban memorials call attention to documented acts of bravery or betrayal by one's non-Jewish countrymen and countrywomen. While for many tourists the camps represent a distillation of the Holocaust into a space that is singularly conceived for its destructive purposes, cities present a far more complicated way of perceiving the Holocaust as death unfolding in the midst of life. Sites of perpetration coexist with signs of Jewish life, both before and after the Holocaust in some cases, and they coexist with rapidly transforming urban cultures that are anchors of both local and national identity, as well as centers of migration in an era of globalization. It is the remembrance of the Holocaust in four national capitals—all places of intense intercultural contact, economic transformation, and modernization that welcome the future while preserving their history—that the next chapters explore.

PART II

Urban Centers of Holocaust Memory

3

Warsaw

We passed a miserable replica of a park—a little square of
completely clear ground in which a half-dozen nearly lifeless
trees and a patch of grass had somehow managed to survive.
It was fearfully crowded. Mothers huddled close together
on benches nursing withered infants. Children, every bone
in their skeletons showing through their taut skins, played in
heaps and swarms.

"They play before they die," I heard my companion on the
left say, his voice breaking with emotion.

Without thinking—the words escaping even before the
thought had crystallized—I said:

"But these children are not playing—they only make believe it is play."

—Jan Karski (2010), recalling the Warsaw Ghetto

If major cities are places that balance aspirations for the future with the
preservation of their past, then Warsaw presents an outlier. The final
months of World War II nearly wiped the Polish capital from the face of
the earth, so that the end of the war left little of the city's historical structures to preserve. The razing of Warsaw occurred as the advancing Red
Army reached the Vistula River opposite the city's edges in August 1944.
Believing their liberation was at hand, the Polish resistance rose up in
arms against the Nazi occupation, counting on Stalin's promise of support to defeat a mutual enemy. Instead, in yet another betrayal of Poland
by the Soviet Union (the first being the 1939 Molotov-Ribbentrop non-
aggression pact that divided Poland between Nazi Germany and the
Soviet Union), Stalin's forces sat and waited for the Nazis to defeat the
Warsaw Uprising. After two months the fighting was over, and in retali-
ation for its armed resistance, the Nazis razed Warsaw. By January 1945,
Poland's largest city had been turned into a vast field of rubble and ashes.

Only then did the Red Army enter what was left of the city and expel the German forces. Nearly 200,000 citizens of Warsaw had perished during the Nazis' systematic destruction of the city. Before the uprising, hundreds of thousands of Warsaw's residents had either already fled the city, been forcibly deported, or been murdered, so that by war's end, fewer than 200,000 inhabitants remained in the ruins of a city that had counted roughly 1.3 million residents at the war's outbreak.[1]

Of those prewar inhabitants, about 350,000 Varsovians, over one-quarter of the city's population, were Jews. Most of them lived in the Muranów, Nowolipki, and Mirów neighborhoods to the northwest and due west of the city center, all of which the Nazis enclosed in a sealed ghetto in November 1940.[2] In 1939, Poland was home to the largest Jewish population in all of Europe, some 3,000,000 in number, with more than a tenth of them living in Warsaw. In fact, Jewish roots in Poland are ancient and precede even some of the Slavic migrations to the territory.[3] Starting in the Middle Ages, Poland had provided Jews with a hospitable haven in Europe, with laws granting some degree of autonomy and extending protection by the state from the anti-Semitic violence that raged elsewhere on the continent.[4] In return, Jewish culture could thrive and foster unique traditions while also contributing to Poland's economic and cultural development. Poland was the birthplace of Hasidic Judaism, which emerged in the nineteenth century, and it was one of the centers of Reform Judaism. Jewish synagogues developed a unique architectural style in Poland found nowhere else.[5] The rise of the *shtetl*, the town or village in which Jews and Christians lived side by side, sometimes with Jews in the majority, also shaped the development of Poland as a multi-ethnic, multi-religious nation.[6] And Jewish neighborhoods in large cities like Warsaw, Kraków, Lublin, and elsewhere contributed to the vitality of urban life and were an important factor in local economies. Of course, there was also a history of persecution in the form of anti-Semitic laws and attitudes among non-Jewish Poles, culminating sometimes in pogroms, but by the nineteenth century Poland was a far more attractive place to live than Tsarist Russia, despite the poverty in which many lived.[7]

In Warsaw, where there had been a Jewish presence since the fourteenth century, Jews constituted the largest minority group after mass migrations from Russia, Ukraine, and Lithuania during the mid- to late nineteenth century. In their neighborhoods they established Jewish schools and religious institutions, but many Jews assimilated into Polish society, often through conversion.[8] The emergence of secular culture also offered an avenue for assimilation, and Jews became important members of the professional and educated classes. Assimilation was not without controversy among Jews who defined themselves less in terms of a religious identity and, increasingly, as a distinct ethnicity. Some, like Emmanuel Ringelblum, strove to define Jews in Poland as a distinct culture, embracing Yiddish as their language.[9] At the same time, they felt an allegiance to Poland as the state in which they could pursue their aspirations.[10] Everything changed in 1939 when the Nazis occupied Poland.

After isolating the Jews from the rest of Warsaw into a walled-off ghetto in late 1940, the German occupation systematically swelled the confined population by deporting Jews from elsewhere in Poland to Warsaw while simultaneously reducing the ghetto to an ever-decreasing area. The ensuing scarcity of food, medicine, and adequate shelter produced the inevitable and intended starvation and outbreaks of disease, claiming many lives. Those who remained were destined for deportation—that is, extermination at Treblinka—under Operation Reinhard. By 1943, the remaining Jews knew the truth about the extermination camps, and rather than die in the gas chambers, many chose armed resistance in what became known as the Warsaw Ghetto Uprising, occurring a full year prior to the Warsaw Uprising near the war's end.[11] Led by a coalition of organized resistance groups, the Ghetto Uprising lasted nearly a month from April to May 1943 and claimed about 100 German casualties.[12] Although ultimately vanquished, the Ghetto Uprising provided a powerful symbol of resistance against the Nazi oppressors, but it also laid bare the fractured nature of Polish resistance, which failed had to organize sufficient aid for the rebellion. By the time the Red Army had finally expelled the Nazis in 1945, only some 11,500 Jews from Warsaw had survived, about 3 percent of the prewar population.[13] "No Jews or Jewish dwellings remained in the Warsaw ghetto."[14]

The tale of two uprisings in Warsaw is indicative of the multiplicity of memories that confront tourism to the city today. The challenge for Holocaust tourism is to locate the traces of the history of the murder of its Jews among the other histories with which it is so closely intertwined. In a sense, Warsaw confounds any expectation that one can devote one's attention to the Holocaust in the same way one can at the extermination camps. Except for a few small segments of the ghetto wall, most evidence of the Holocaust comes from the vestiges of Jewish life that it eradicated. The Holocaust is visible to those with an eye for what is invisible, noticing the evidence of a population that has largely disappeared. Warsaw presents other histories that overlap with the Holocaust, and tourism becomes a way of making sense of the relationship between what is present and what is absent, what is future and what is past. A walk through the city will produce different meanings of the city, depending on the narrative that accompanies the tour.[15] The same pathway can tell a story of the Holocaust, of Jewish and Polish history prior to 1939, and of the resurgence of Warsaw after the war. In this chapter, I explore how tourism navigates among these overlapping memories and what it can contribute to Holocaust remembrance.

While the story of Jewish Warsaw's destruction overlaps with the story of Polish Warsaw's devastation and subsequent rebirth, the divergent endings of these two narratives suggest a cleft that is hard to bridge. To address the different strains of World War II–era memory in Warsaw, tourism relies on a long-abiding discourse that distinguishes between "Jews" and "Poles," a discourse I maintain with some hesitation in this chapter. The Polish/Jewish dichotomy obscures any sense that Poland was a multi-ethnic, multi-religious state for much of its history. This parlance is not original to tourism, for it continues to infuse most popular and academic discourse about Polish-Jewish relations. Nor is it unique to Poland—Germany still struggles with the correct designation for its Jewish citizens (German Jews? Jewish Germans? Jews in Germany?).[16] Tourism is a stage on which Poland, like other nations, reflects publicly on its own identity through its representations of the past and its aspirations for the future. As a representational medium, tourism reveals the subjective qualities of those who claim the right to represent the Polish experience and exposes received notions about who does and who does not constitute the nation. The persistent distinction between Jews and Poles throughout the country, with both identified as victim groups, is one of the discoveries relayed through Holocaust tourism in Poland. The fact that Jews and Poles lived among one another in such large numbers before 1940 also makes Warsaw a unique site for understanding how the Holocaust transpired. There is no doubt that both Jews and Poles suffered and died by the millions, yet despite that similarity, the differences between the experiences of the two groups are significant. In the case of Warsaw, tourism struggles, not always successfully, to present the city as a place with a coherent past.

Adding yet another complication to the task of Holocaust memory, modern-day Warsaw is a largely Catholic city in a deeply Catholic country. One wonders how an arguably less multi-cultural, less multi-religious nation can carry out the task of acknowledging the genocide of its Jewish former compatriots, whom it sees not so much as fellow Poles but as a distinct group of Others living in Poland.[17] Was the Holocaust something that happened *to* Poland or something that happened *in* Poland? In the context of tourism, these questions play out in the city's geography, shaping experiences of proximity and distance, inclusion and exclusion, accessibility and remoteness. Tourism puts the spaces of the city in relation to one another along some hierarchy of relevance to a specific interest. In the case of Warsaw, Holocaust tourism generates a map of the city that is related, but not identical, to other tourist maps of the city, for example, that of tourism dedicated to World War II more broadly or to the Communist era more specifically. Increasingly, the itinerary of Holocaust tourism in Warsaw has begun to share space with another tourist itinerary of the city, namely the exploration of the city's Jewish heritage. The relationships among these popular topics of tourism to Warsaw are complicated and suggest that Holocaust tourism cannot be disentangled from other, often happier narratives. While tourism is an evolving enterprise, my chief concern at the moment about Holocaust tourism in Warsaw is that the predominance of these other narratives may diminish the degree to which tourists understand how the Holocaust so profoundly curtailed any Jewish future for Poland. Warsaw is still figuring out how best to accommodate its distinct yet interconnected stories.

In other words, a tension lies between Warsaw's bold aspirations for tomorrow and its weighty traumas of yesterday, and that tension stems from differences in fates shared by the city's residents: On the one hand, visitors witness the miraculous survival of Polish Warsaw after its nearly total destruction only seventy years earlier. On the other hand, visitors encounter the near-total annihilation of its Jewish life in a city where it once thrived. Given the city's current aura of optimism and economic growth, the question of how these two different outcomes fit into

Warsaw's dreams for the future is a challenge to tourism. This is not to blame Warsaw for its own complicated history; rather, I point out that, as the national capital, Warsaw faces unique challenges, among which is the unenviable task of commemorating Poland's divergent histories. Like any national capital, it relies on the often-reductive idiom of monuments and memorials, which tend to advance simplicity over complexity. How can a memorial mourn the murder of Polish Jews without addressing the fact that some Poles participated in the killing? Should memorials celebrate Poles who rescued Jews without acknowledging the continued presence of anti-Semitism in Poland? Is it possible to represent the suffering of non-Jewish Poles who were imprisoned, tortured, and killed by the Nazis without appearing to be insensitive to the disproportionate suffering of Jews in Poland? Can tourist sites address resistance without addressing collaboration or name victims without naming perpetrators? These are some of the questions that greet efforts to recognize Warsaw's past, whether in the form of memorials, museums, commemorations, or representations in the arts. When put in the context of tourism, with its often fleeting or superficial approach to historical complexity, these questions also illustrate the potential for confusion or misunderstanding about the Holocaust and its place in Polish history and identity.

Such complexities do not deter travelers to Poland's capital. Each year, over two and a half million travelers from around the world help fuel Warsaw's reemergence as a European capital.[18] Today, nearly seventy years after its destruction, the city of 1.7 million residents is thriving: Its streets are teeming with cars, trams, and pedestrians, and towering glass buildings rise around a once-leveled historical center, itself restored to its colorful, ornate grandeur shortly after the war. Indeed, tourism has been both a source and a beneficiary of Warsaw's economic boom.[19] Those historically minded tourists who come to see how the city remembers its past encounter a work in progress: a growing array of different, event discordant memorials, sharing the space of the city with feudal castles, communist-era concrete-slab constructions, and present-day skyscrapers. They encounter the city's rich classical and folk traditions, its castles, its riverfront, and its parks. Many tourists make pilgrimages to see the home city of Karol Wojtyła, who as Pope John Paul II is revered by believers who see him as a saint and by patriots who celebrate his advocacy for the Solidarity movement. Many others still are drawn to Warsaw by family ties, having relatives who still live there, who fled the city in difficult times, or whose graves occupy the city's cemeteries. Heritage tourists include Jewish travelers for whom Warsaw signifies the lost hometown of their forebears.

While Warsaw is not exclusively synonymous with the Holocaust in the way that Auschwitz and Treblinka are, it nevertheless makes an important contribution to understanding the Holocaust through tourism. Its inclusion on many itineraries to Holocaust memorials reflects not only its unique place in the unfolding of the Nazi genocide but also its pragmatic, logistical positioning within present-day tourism. Sitting in the geographic center of the country, Warsaw is a hub for car, rail, and air travel, and so it is a logical starting point for travelers visiting sites in the city and elsewhere in the country. The towns around Warsaw include former *shtetlekh* whose Jewish citizens were rounded up and deported to the ghettos in Warsaw or Łódź or shot by German forces and buried in mass graves the victims had to dig themselves.[20] The killing centers of Treblinka and Chełmno are the nearest camp memorials from Warsaw, ranging from about two to four hours by car. Within the city, tourists can visit memorials to the Ghetto Uprising, see the place where Jews were forced to gather before their deportation, and see reminders of the life that thrived before the Holocaust and struggled to endure throughout the existence of the ghetto. The next pages survey the terrain of Holocaust tourism in present-day Warsaw, as experienced on many walks through the former ghetto, whose traces are present but very faint.

Touring the Remnants of the Ghetto

If there is a dearth of physical markers of the former Jewish ghetto, the Nazis are principally to blame. With the completion of Operation Reinhard, the need for walls to enclose Jews no longer pertained. During the Ghetto Uprising the Nazis leveled the remaining structures within the ghetto's area. As a result, a tour of the traces of the Holocaust in Warsaw necessarily finds a sparse array of ruins and postwar memorials. They can barely convey the sense of isolation and deprivation that residents of the ghetto had to endure, which Jan Karski, a member of the Polish resistance and later a professor of international relations at Georgetown University, captured so painfully when he wrote about his experiences infiltrating the ghetto (quoted above as the epigraph to this chapter).[21] Although a Catholic himself, Karski rejected the anti-Semitism he encountered among many of his fellow Poles and saw the Jewish plight under the Nazis as a Polish matter. He managed to reach London and, eventually, Washington, DC, where he met with Franklin Roosevelt. Despite hearing the account of Nazi brutality contained in Karski's detailed report, Roosevelt failed to offer the relief to Poland's Jews that Karski hoped for.[22]

Today one must search among numerous postwar apartment blocks to find the few traces of the ghetto to which Karski bore witness. Only three sections of the roughly ten-foot-high ghetto wall remain, ranging in length from about 20 to 100 meters. Two of them are actual fragments of the wall constructed in 1940, located at 55 Sienna Street and 62 Złota Street; the third is the first floor of a row of buildings at 11 Waliców Street, many of whose windows had been bricked up to seal the ghetto off from the rest of Warsaw, and were still visible in that state when I last visited in 2016. These ghetto wall fragments blend easily into the background, with small plaques declaring their historical status. Of the three, the fragment in Złota Street is probably the best preserved, thanks in no small part to the efforts of Mieczysław Jędruszczak, a resident in an apartment at that location who worked tirelessly to preserve the fragment of the wall adjacent to his home. I was fortunate to be with a tour group in front of the wall fragment in 2007 when Jędruszczak came from his apartment to the gate of his front yard to speak with us, asking the group to sign his visitor's book and, through our tour guide as interpreter, recounting his labors to honor Warsaw's murdered Jews. Perhaps he was aware that he offered one of the few possible encounters tourists might have with an eyewitness to Warsaw at the time of the Nazi occupation. Although Jędruszczak died in 2016 at the age of ninety-five, his legacy constitutes one of the most important physical reminders of the ghetto.[23]

The wall fragments at Złota and Sienna streets are in spaces between apartment buildings, and they give a vague sense of enclosure. One can see the buildings on the other side of the wall, a reminder that the city was visible but inaccessible to the ghetto's inhabitants. Maps help to visualize the expanse to which the wall fragments allude, but walking tours are perhaps the most meaningful way to comprehend the breadth of the ghetto, which included apartment blocks, market squares, schools,

Figure 3.1. The fragment of the Warsaw Ghetto wall that remains preserved at 62 Złota Street, thanks to the efforts of Mieczysław Jędruszczak, seen in the inset greeting our tour group in August 2007. Photo by the author.

hospitals, and synagogues. The most important sign of Judaism in Warsaw, the Great Synagogue, stood at what was the eastern edge of the ghetto. The Nazis destroyed it in 1943 after the Ghetto Uprising, its demolition the final act in the destruction of the ghetto itself. It was not rebuilt after the war, and so tourists must look elsewhere for the history Judaism in the city.

About half a mile's walk from the wall fragment at Sienna and Złota Streets toward the northeast stands Warsaw's only synagogue to have survived the Nazi occupation, the Nożyk Synagogue at Grzybowski Square. The location is also home to buildings that house offices of Jewish community organizations; next door is a kosher grocery, and around the corner is the Shalom Foundation, an organization that offers courses in Yiddish, hosts cultural exhibitions, and produces performances about Jewish culture in Poland for stage and television.[24] Concentrated on a small corner of the former ghetto, these signs of Jewish life today in Poland reveal a remnant that survives despite the odds, but they also serve as a reminder of the culture that has disappeared from much of the city.[25] The Nożyk Synagogue is a handsome yet modest structure that was restored after suffering damage under the occupation. It is impossible to spot from the street, sitting behind a brand-new glass-clad forty-four-story condominium tower. One wonders about the presence of the glass high-rise, an example of the forward-looking city with its Jewish heritage hidden in its backyard. It would be easy to conclude that the tower is an act of amnesia or disrespect, but perhaps it also lends privacy to the small buildings behind it and allows the community to persist in some semblance of calm.

A short distance away, on the eastern side of Grzybowski Square, stand several dilapidated brick buildings that are hard to overlook among the newly restored façades that surround them. Large photographic images have been fixed to the buildings' surfaces, showing images of Jewish life that once inhabited this area. The buildings stood out to me on my first visit to Warsaw in 2007, before the images had been mounted, because they seemed like a moment from 1945 frozen in time. With the images affixed to them, the buildings now enact the kind of reverse gaze discussed in the previous chapter, as if addressing themselves to the abundance of development all around them. There are plans to restore the buildings once their rightful owners have been identified and all the necessary permits obtained, but in my mind they would remain more impactful preserved in their present state, a reminder of the devastation that took place here. The buildings seem to affirm the claim of the Taube Center for the Renewal of Jewish Life in Poland, whose walking guide states that "Jewish memory has been all but obliterated and denied" in Grzybowski Square. Yet these buildings, appearing almost untouched since the war, serve as a powerful reminder of the Jewish life that once thrived there and of the wound inflicted on the city when that life was destroyed.[26] Plans to redevelop the buildings include the establishment of a Jewish community center, which ironically may put the interests of Holocaust-themed tourism at odds with the vital needs of the city's remnant community today.

About two-thirds of a mile or one kilometer to the north of Grzybowski Square is another site of importance both to Warsaw's Jewish heritage and the destruction wrought by the Nazis. At the address of Tłomackie 3/5, next to where the Great Synagogue once stood on the eastern edge of the ghetto, is the Jewish Historical Institute. The preservation of the building, lasting through the Nazi occupation and the postwar era into the present, is representative of an important achievement by some of its members during the ghetto period. The building was previously home to the Main Judaic Library of Warsaw and was completed in 1936, only three years before the German occupation of Poland. Emptied of its books by the Nazi invaders in 1939, the building became the headquarters of the Jewish Self-Help Society (the Aleynhilf), which played an instrumental role in maintaining whatever semblance of a civic life was possible within the ghetto.[27] It was here where the historian and community leader Emmanuel Ringelblum held secret meetings of the Oyneg Shabes, a group that dedicated itself to documenting the history of Jews in Poland. While begun before the war in the belief that it would improve Jewish-Polish relations, the group took upon itself the task of recording firsthand accounts of life in the ghetto and its ultimate destruction. The members of Oyneg Shabes worked by enlisting as many ghetto inhabitants as they could to record their daily experiences. Ringelblum, like many members of the organization, perished, but not before his team could gather numerous documents, seal them in metal boxes and large milk cans, and bury them in the ghetto in the hopes that they would be discovered after the war. Two of the three buried sites have been recovered, amounting to some 35,000 pages of preserved material and producing one of the most important eyewitness documentations of the Holocaust. Today the Jewish Historical Institute, established in 1947, continues the work begun by Ringelblum, including the indexing and preservation of this important archive. It also assists Jews from the diaspora who come to Warsaw to conduct genealogical research for traces of their ancestors in Poland.

Further to north of the Jewish Historical Institute, at the northern edge of the ghetto, is the memorial at the Umschlagplatz, or "transfer point," the German term designating the location where Jews were ordered to gather before boarding trains for deportation, to Treblinka in the case of Warsaw. The memorial is a rectangular space of about 1,200 square feet (115 square meters), enclosed on three sides by a stone wall engraved with Jewish and Polish first names to acknowledge the victims of deportation. It was dedicated in 1988 to mark the forty-fifth anniversary of the Warsaw Ghetto Uprising. The memorial is only a small part of the plaza where Jews gathered before being forced onto cattle cars bound for Treblinka. The adjacent building, now a neighborhood community center, lay on the other side of the wall that marked the northern boundary of the enclosed ghetto, and can be seen in some historical photos of the Umschlagplatz.

Just south of the Umschlagplatz is the best-known memorial to the Jewish ghetto in Warsaw, the Monument to the Heroes of the Warsaw Ghetto by the artist Nathan Rapoport. Until recently, this monument stood alone in a square surrounded by nondescript postwar apartment buildings, at one end of a city park lined with paths wandering among the lawn and trees. The park's relative emptiness was evocative of the ghetto as an enclosed, abandoned entity in the city, although the area of the square made up only a tiny part of the ghetto itself. The sense of enclosure that the lonely monument once conveyed was reminiscent of Giorgio Agamben's account of concentration camps as "inclusive exclusions," as outlined in chapter 1. Standing alone, Rapoport's monolith was

Figure 3.2. Nathan Rapoport's Monument to the Heroes of the Warsaw Ghetto as it stood, alone, in August 2007. Inset: a close-up of the memorial's two sides, one showing Mordecai Anielewicz and others in heroic form, and the other showing deportees walking to their deaths in shallow relief. Photos by the author.

the clear focal point in this large residential square, a somber but impressive monument that conveyed the heroism of the Ghetto Uprising and the calamity that befell the Jews of Warsaw.[28] Dedicated in 1948, Rapoport's lone monolith evoked a sense of isolation for visitors to the former ghetto, since the rest of the ghetto has been thoroughly reincorporated into the city.[29]

Official state functions at memorials are important performative dimensions of collective memory that often bind a site to a prevailing national narrative, itself subject to change over time as regimes come and go. Tourists provide local and international audiences for these performances, and the Ghetto Heroes memorial is no exception. As James E. Young has commented, the Ghetto Heroes monument, the first memorial erected in Warsaw after the war, and ultimately the only one erected by the Polish government to commemorate the Ghetto Uprising, was pressed into service to commemorate numerous other acts of Polish resistance.[30] Rapoport's memorial had touched a nerve in Poland because of the absence of a comparable memorial to the Warsaw City Uprising of 1944.[31] Indeed, as the only memorial site suitable for large-scale commemorations of acts of resistance, Rapoport's monument also hosted ceremonies at the anniversaries of the 1944 uprising. It became a site where foreign dignitaries laid wreaths, though not exclusively to the Ghetto Uprising that had inspired the monument. One notable visitor was Willy Brandt, the West German Social-Democratic chancellor who visited the memorial in 1970, laid a wreath at the site, and kneeled in a gesture of atonement. That event was memorialized in 2000 with the dedication of a plaque depicting Brandt's gesture, situated at the other end of the park from Rapoport's memorial and recalled in the plaza's new name, Willy Brandt Square. So Rapoport's memorial also has served to symbolize German acts of contrition alongside distinct acts of Polish of resistance. Through such ceremonies of officially sanctioned memory, a monument intended to commemorate a unique event within the Holocaust also functioned as a generic representation of suffering, resistance, and repentance for a generalized audience. As we will see shortly, new memorial installations may allow the memorial to return to its original purpose by unburdening it from some of its commemorative duties.

Sites of Polish Resistance

Tourism transpires in context, a fact that applies to sites of Holocaust remembrance as much as anywhere else. Even at places like the camps, Holocaust tourism is framed by the politics and economics of the day, the interests of travelers, and the current state of knowledge (and lore) about the Holocaust.[32] To understand the place of Holocaust tourism in Warsaw, one must explore the post–Cold War memorial landscape that has emerged over the last thirty years. Tourists encounter these memorials from World War II by accident and by design, and they read them in relation to one another.

Until 1989, there was only Rapoport's memorial to the 1943 Ghetto Uprising, with no memorials dedicated specifically to the city's fatal 1944 Uprising. The first of two new memorials to address that absence is the Memorial to the Fighters of the Warsaw Uprising at Krasiński Square in the city center, which was dedicated in 1989. This memorial depicts members of the Home Army, loyal to the Polish government in exile in London and long persecuted during the Soviet era in Poland because of their opposition to Communist Party rule. It depicts Home Army soldiers and civilians emerging from underground below a collapsing structure, situated in a plaza surrounded by a bronze colonnade. The location of the memorial marks the site of a manhole that was used by members of the resistance to escape from the Nazis during the uprising. Like the Ghetto Heroes monument by Nathan Rapoport, it speaks in a heroic vernacular and is comparable in scale. Outside the former ghetto walls, it sits at the point where the Old Town meets the new at a busy intersection. Thus situated, the memorial reinforces the master narrative that pervades Warsaw tourism in general and that seeps into Holocaust tourism, even if on its periphery—namely, that Warsaw suffered a tragic fall but has risen from the ashes in great triumph.

The second, more recent memorial to the city's 1944 rebellion is the Warsaw Rising Museum, opened in 2004. This institution presents an altogether different kind of memorial experience from the one in Krasiński Square. Located in the western parts of the city where the uprising was waged with great ferocity, the museum chronicles the experience of Warsaw and Poland during Nazi occupation leading up to the revolt, including a section dedicated to the 1943 Ghetto Uprising.

Interactive in nature, the museum is designed to replicate the dark, noisy, crumbling streets of the once-besieged city. Visitors can enter simulated bunkers, sewer tunnels, makeshift barricades, and clandestine meeting places. Videos of old newsreels punctuate the visit, as does extensive photodocumentation alongside such artifacts as weapons, uniforms, airplanes, cars and tanks, and a clandestine printing press. The sound of a beating heart permeates the museum, presumably the heart of Warsaw itself. Indeed, noise surrounds visitors throughout the exhibition space: gunfire, alarms, shells exploding, bombs falling. While such a facility has its appeal, particularly to younger audiences, it leaves little to the tourist's imagination. In particular, the insistence on an irrepressible city with a heart that won't stop beating makes it very difficult to comprehend the enormity of the losses inflicted on Warsaw by the Nazis. An article in the *Economist* summarizes the intentions and problems with this museum nicely:

> The museum has made strides in stoking the interest of Polish youth, too young to have grandparents who could spin first-hand uprising yarns, and so resigned to dull textbook fare. . . . [It] offers a narrative of the events in which the ingenious and doughty David, in the form of the resistance movement, is pitted against the Nazis' Goliath. And it paints the AK [Home Army] fighters and their commanders as irreproachable patriots to be revered, and presumably emulated.
>
> Critics allege that amid all this laudable educational activity one crucial fact has fallen through the cracks: unlike David, the Varsovians were ultimately defeated. They charge that too little attention has been paid to the price exacted from Warsaw and its population.[33]

To be sure, this critique of the museum could be applied to the tourist landscape of Warsaw more generally. The insistence on Polish national triumph flirts with amnesia about the irrecoverable losses suffered during World War II. While there is a compelling and admirable story of persistence against the odds to be told about Poland as a state, the almost total elimination of Poland's Jews cannot be seen in triumphal terms. The rhetoric of national resurgence to address Poland's survival stems at least in part from the relatively recent removal of the Soviet yoke that rested over Poland for forty-four years after the Nazi occupation; however, in recent years national pride has led to a traditionalist, antidemocratic trend that has been inflecting Polish politics. The Law and Justice Party, gaining majorities in Poland's parliament, the Sejm, in 2005 and again in 2015, has shown little patience for the kind of multi-religious, multi-cultural tolerance that membership in the European Union promotes. Indeed, the party's express affiliation with the Catholic Church also re-inforces the marginalization Poland's small remnant Jewish community, and anti-Semitic comments by some of the party's members have made matters worse.[34] In that political context, these most recent installations to Warsaw's memorial culture exist in some tension with the earlier memorials to the Holocaust. To be sure, Warsaw as the national capital bears the task of speaking both for itself as a city and for the Polish na-tion as a whole, but the traditionalist understanding of Polish national-ity refers more to ethnicity and religion rather than to citizenship and downplays the degree to which Warsaw was far more than a national capital before 1939. It was also home to the largest Jewish population in Europe. The current rhetoric of Polish national resistance to subjugation has not yet found a way to adequately acknowledge the fact that Jewish culture was as much a part of Poland's history as Slavic Christianity was.

Jewish Heritage Tourism

Thankfully, nostalgic nationalism is not the only public discourse on dis-play in Warsaw or in Poland's politics, even if the Law and Justice Party enjoys a slim majority in the Sejm. There are many in Poland who seek a more open confrontation with the complexities of Polish history instead of the mythologized versions of the past that have tended to prolifer-ate around World War II.[35] There is also a growing embrace of Poland's Jewish history, ranging from pseudo-klezmer bands playing for tourists in "Jewish" restaurants, to very sincere efforts to recover artifacts of lost Jewish life, and even to efforts to see Jewish life return to Poland.

At first glance, the loss of its once thriving Jewish community barely troubles the appearance of vitality and modernity that greets tourists in Warsaw. Most city tours include the ghetto and its memorials, but the extermination of 300,000 Jews tends to be subsumed into a big-ger narrative of the city's suffering at the hands of the Germans and its subsequent resurrection. Today, Warsaw's remnant Jewish population numbers somewhere between 2,000 and 5,000 members, far lower than the already decimated figure of 11,500 survivors at the end of the war, and less than 1 percent of its estimated prewar population.[36] The additional loss to the Warsaw community of several thousand members since the war's conclusion is due at least in part to postwar anti-Semitic outbreaks, including a notorious pogrom in the town of Kielce in 1946 and the purges of Jewish members from the Communist Party in 1968, all of which led the majority of remaining Jews in Poland to emigrate to safer shores. Until recently, visitors who wanted to find evidence of Jewish life in postwar Poland had to work hard to do so. That difficulty abated significantly with the opening in 2013 of POLIN Museum of the History of Polish Jews.[37] However, the deserved success of one very important new museum has had an ambiguous effect on tourism that tries to confront the destructiveness of the Holocaust—for better and for worse.

After several years of construction, POLIN opened its doors in the middle of the park that, for the last sixty-five years, has been home to the Ghetto Heroes monument. The museum focuses on the vitality of Jewish life that dates back 1,000 years in Poland, and it offers educational and cultural programming in addition to its permanent and temporary exhibits. Like the popular Jewish Museum in Berlin, the new Warsaw museum marks a growing awareness of the need to recall Jewish culture beyond its annihilation by the Nazis, to remember Jewish culture as a once-thriving, diverse, and ancient part of Polish history and culture. The final exhibition halls of the museum acknowledge the Holocaust and the absence it left behind, and they document the continuation of anti-Semitism in postwar Poland. But they also go on to document today's Jewish community and Warsaw's renascent interest in the Jewish traditions that once thrived there, manifested in an annual festival of Jewish culture that is attended by numerous Varsovians of all faiths.[38]

As important as the new museum is in commemorating the wealth of Jewish history in Poland, including the Holocaust and its aftermath, POLIN's placement in the middle of the square that once stood empty, save for the iconic Ghetto Heroes monument, has had a direct impact on the memorialization of the Holocaust from the perspective of tourism. Once a looming presence in the square, Rapoport's monument is now de-centered and dwarfed by the far larger museum. One could argue that the new museum is positioned in some kind of dialogue with the Ghetto Heroes monument, but the museum is disproportionately large by comparison, and it renders the monument, with its somewhat dated heroic idiom, as an anachronistic footnote. The plaza has become less a place for contemplation of the Ghetto Uprising, which had been encouraged by Rapoport's solemn, even forlorn monument. The tendency of tourism in Warsaw to eclipse the story of the Holocaust by foregrounding the story of Warsaw's resurgence has been compounded by the eclipsing—in a quite literal sense—of Rapoport's Ghetto Uprising monument by the POLIN museum, which places an appreciation of Jewish culture within the city's overall narrative of resurgence. Tourists will likely spend more time in the museum and make a brief stop at the monument, perhaps even conceiving of Rapoport's commemoration as an extension of the museum and therefore, in some sense, subordinate to it. Of course, if the museum had been located elsewhere, tourists might not come upon the monument at all. Furthermore, the museum and the monument together offer a fuller picture of what Poland has lost. POLIN's relationship to the Ghetto Heroes monument is unavoidably complicated, reflecting the nature of public memory of Jewish Warsaw in Poland today, and it rightly challenges the perception of Jewish history in Poland as beginning and ending with the Nazi extermination.

That problematic spatial relationship between the museum and the monument is reinforced by an outdoor sculpture depicting Jan Karski, the Polish resistance hero who managed to escape Poland after infiltrating the ghetto to witness firsthand the destruction of the Jews in Warsaw. After the war, Karski joined the faculty of Georgetown University, where his efforts on behalf of Warsaw's Jews were largely unknown until the release of director Claude Lanzmann's *Shoah* in 1985, in which Karski recounts what he witnessed in the ghetto. Because of his affiliation with the Home Army and the Polish government in exile, Karski's legacy was all but forgotten in his native Poland until the final decade of his life, when the post-Communist era ushered in a wave of public memory about previously taboo subjects. The Karski memorial in Warsaw depicts him sitting on a park bench between the Ghetto Heroes monument and POLIN, as if mediating between these two sites.[39] However, Karski looks away from the Ghetto Heroes monument, even though Rapoport's monolith more closely recalls Karski's own role in

Jewish Poland's ordeal under fascism. Facing the museum instead, Karski's likeness sits in contemplation of Jewish history that he, a devout Catholic, knew peripherally and with which he became most involved at its time of greatest duress.[40] It is as if even Karski's attention has been drawn away from the Holocaust; like Warsaw today, Karski seems intent on regarding the future, not the past, and the impressive new museum incorporating the memory of Jewish Warsaw into the city's fabric is one vision of that future that the Karski memorial reinforces.

The arrival of POLIN marks a fundamental shift in the Holocaust's placement at the center of Polish-Jewish relations since the end of World War II. The singularity of the Holocaust in the memorial landscape of Warsaw under Communism suited a government that was guided from Moscow and oriented against the "Hitlerite" aggressors whose heirs governed on the other side of the Iron Curtain. Furthermore, memorialization of the Holocaust could lend counterevidence to accusations of anti-Semitism on the part of the Polish Communist Party, despite the purges of Jews from the party in 1968.[41] In the Communist era it was easier to commemorate the destruction of Warsaw's Jews at the hands of the Germans than to commemorate the city's 1944 uprising, during which the Red Army offered no assistance. But it would be overly cynical to dismiss Holocaust memory in Warsaw during the Cold War as merely a matter of Communist Party propaganda. There were community-based efforts to memorialize the city's Jews, and the example of Mieczysław Jędruszczak is a case in point, a Jewish Pole who was imprisoned in the Soviet Union from 1944 to 1947 because of his association with the Home Army and who fought successfully to preserve the fragment of the ghetto wall near his home.[42] The continued efforts by Jewish survivors to unearth the Oyneg Shabes archives from the rubble of the city and to establish the Jewish Historical Institute demonstrate that Holocaust remembrance was not a top-down party agenda but, rather, a grassroots effort to remember, tolerated by a government that had its own agenda. In that light, it is no wonder that, after years of suppressing other memories from the past, the end of the Communist era should also witness the de-centering of the Holocaust from its place in Warsaw's memory landscape. The new emphasis on Jewish culture prior to the Holocaust reflects not so much amnesia about the Holocaust as an appreciation for what the Holocaust destroyed. One might be justifiably wary that the focus on Jewish culture may serve an exculpatory function among Poles who are uncomfortable with a more complicated understanding of Polish-Jewish history, but the POLIN museum does not shy away from the history of anti-Semitism in Poland from the Middle Ages into the present.

As tourists travel through the city, it becomes apparent that Jewish heritage tourism and Holocaust tourism are profoundly intertwined and that any effort to focus on one at the exclusion of the other will falter.[43] While it goes without saying that the Holocaust is a traumatic and unavoidable element of the Jewish experience in Europe, and therefore a substantial aspect of Jewish heritage tourism, it is also true that sites of Jewish heritage form a necessary part of Holocaust tourism in places like Warsaw, where the scattered traces of Jewish life that once flourished testify to its destruction. The case of the Jewish cemetery on Okopowa Street, first established in the early nineteenth century, is proof of the impossibility of insisting on a clear division between the two modes of tourism in Warsaw. While the marked graves predate the Holocaust, one can also see unmarked mass graves of victims who died at the hands of the Nazis; these graves are identifiable as indentations in the earth caused by the decomposition of bodies under the surface. The enormous cemetery stands as silent testimony to the expansive place Jewish culture once had in Warsaw and signifies both Jewish history and the Holocaust, depending on the attention of those who visit.

A challenge for Holocaust and Jewish heritage tourism is that some of its participants may incorporate inauthentic or even inaccurate information about Jewish Warsaw at the expense of a more sophisticated understanding of Polish-Jewish history. Some Polish tour guides still offer an account of the Holocaust that elides any mention of Polish collaboration while foregrounding stories of Poles who saved Jews.[44] More innocuously, but nonetheless misleading, some tours will include a meal at a restaurant featuring dishes labeled "Jewish" that are just as common to traditional Polish cuisine.[45] Popular cinema dictates the routes some tours take. Kraków offers tours to sites where Steven Spielberg's *Schindler's List* was filmed, while some Jewish-themed tours of Warsaw highlight the story of Władysław Szpilman, who was the subject Roman Polanski's film *The Pianist*—even though much of the film was shot across the river in the Praga neighborhood or at Berlin's Babelsberg Studios.[46] But in contrast to Kraków's Kazimierz neighborhood, Warsaw has been spared the flood of "Jewish restaurants," bands performing dubious versions of klezmer music, and the marketing of Judaica (menorahs, Torah pointers, mezuzot, etc.) in market squares, mostly sold by Poles to foreign tourists.[47]

One of the most jarring examples of Poland's memory of its Jews are carved wooden figurines, referred to as *Żydki* (little Jews), for sale at some tourist locales and often on display among the knickknacks in restaurants, cafes, and hotel reception areas. The figurines, along with paintings, usually depict Hasidic men in stereotypical ways, with exaggerated facial features, long black hair and beards, often holding a coin. Some are even sold with a fragment of a Torah scroll.[48] These "lucky Jews" suggest a strange mixture of anti-Semitic imagery and a kitschy nostalgia for a vanished culture. They are usually made by Catholic Poles who, according to the anthropologist Erica Lehrer, are not even aware that they can be read as anti-Semitic, evidence of the gap that still divides the majority of Poles from their now much less visible Jewish compatriots.[49]

Competing Memories

The nature of Holocaust tourism in Warsaw, as in other capital cities where states tend to focus their efforts at national collective memory, situates memorials to the murder of Jews alongside memorials to other significant historical events. While Jews in Warsaw suffered a unique and monstrous fate, their suffering occurred alongside the simultaneous torment and murder of non-Jewish Poles by the Nazis and their accomplices, including collaborators among the Poles. Unlike the isolated extermination camps erected by the Reich in remote locales of Polish territory, Warsaw's multi-ethnic and militarily strategic status dictated that the persecution of the city's Jews occur in the midst of a major population center. The deportation of Jews to the Warsaw Ghetto (and to the other major urban ghetto in Poland, Łódź) had to be coordinated with other aspects of Nazi occupation in Poland. Given limited resources in terms of military personnel and materiel, the SS coordinated their control over the ghetto with other military and administrative aspects of the Nazi occupation. Train schedules for the movement of troops and supplies were coordinated with train schedules for deportations. Ammunition and personnel had to be distributed among multiple objectives within Warsaw. The Nazis' isolation of the Ghetto led to strict enforcement of policies aimed at Poles, who were expressly forbidden entry into the ghetto and punished with execution if they aided Jews. The Holocaust, as it unfolded in Warsaw, was both separate from and part of the city's wartime experience. Tourism moves through the city in a way that highlights the tension between remembering and forgetting, between including and excluding this chapter of history.

The proximity of multiple memorials to distinct historical events is an urban feature Warsaw shares with other cities, including Berlin, Jerusalem, and Washington, DC, but it also tells tourists something about the specific history of Poland's capital. What tourism encounters is the presence of monuments to *simultaneous* events with vastly *different* outcomes within the urban population. If Holocaust tourism is an effort to identify and enter locales that have a direct relevance to the Nazi genocide, then the proximity of distinct memorial spaces means that Holocaust tourists must navigate urban memorial space in a highly selective way. Specifically, Holocaust tourism focuses very specifically on the northern part of the city, the former Jewish quarter and the site where the ghetto was eventually established. But that area of the ghetto is no longer the confined space walled in by the Nazis, and its borders are unclear. However successfully Holocaust tourism focuses on a particular zone of the city, it cannot dispel the awareness that simultaneous historical events haunt the same spaces. By touring Warsaw, it becomes apparent that the Holocaust itself is an event whose borders are hard to define in terms of its beginning and ending, the people it affected, and its geographical reach.

As is the case with tourism in general, the entangled map of Holocaust tourism and other tourist itineraries in Warsaw has both advantages and disadvantages. On the one hand, tourism to Holocaust memorials in Warsaw necessarily shows how the persecution of Jews was imbricated with war, occupation, collaboration, and resistance in the Nazi era. That is an aspect of the Holocaust that may be less apparent to tourists at the remote camp memorials and museums. But while the Holocaust in Warsaw appears firmly rooted within the context of Nazi occupation, the inverse is not true: The city's experience of Nazi occupation cannot be confined to the Holocaust, and therein lies the challenge for Holocaust tourism (and indeed, Holocaust memorialization) in Warsaw. The city's lack of geographical symmetry between the Holocaust specifically and Nazi occupation more generally has profound implications for the way modern-day Warsaw sees its past, especially its Jewish past. The difficulty in isolating the Holocaust from other dimensions of the Nazi occupation complicates the task of confronting the Holocaust as a unique occurrence in Poland, a task that befalls tourists, at least for the duration of their visit, and Varsovians in a more enduring way.

The problem of Holocaust memory in Warsaw, which tourism constantly reveals, lies in the perception that the Holocaust haunts the margins of the city's collective memory but does not occupy its center, neither geographically nor metaphorically. If there is an ongoing competition for memory in Warsaw between the murder of the city's Jews and the city's Poles, the story of Polish sacrifice has, at least until the opening of POLIN and the emergence of Jewish heritage tourism, appeared dominant.[50] The Krasiński Square memorial to the 1944 Warsaw Uprising sits centrally between the Old Town and modern Warsaw. The Old Town itself, painstakingly rebuilt after the war, serves as a memorial to destruction and rebirth, and tour guides rarely fail to frame it in that context. And everywhere in the city, tourists encounter the ubiquitous symbol used by the Polish resistance, an anchor shape consisting the letter P rising out of the letter W, usually assumed to signify Powstanie Warszawskie, or the Polish Uprising. The symbol shows up in museums, bookshops, posters, memorial plaques, and graffiti. Through the repetition of this symbol, the 1944 uprising fills the city's spaces regardless of other histories that draw tourists: the Old Town that recalls the city's feudal past; the postwar slab-construction apartment buildings that recall the Cold War, also conspicuous in the area of the former ghetto; and the new buildings that attest to Poland's future in the European Union. The iconic reminder of the uprising throughout the newly vibrant city thus reinforces the message that Warsaw has risen from the ashes, even in places where Jewish life was erased.

Most forms of popular tourism in Warsaw seem intent on offering a heroic story with a happy ending, a narrative that necessarily displaces

Figure 3.3. The ubiquitous symbol identified with the Warsaw Uprising of 1944, which can be seen throughout the city, including the former Jewish ghetto, June 2016. Photos by the author.

the Holocaust from the center of tourist narratives. The first paragraph on Warsaw in one popular guidebook is a typical case in point:

> Take a tour through Warsaw's pristine Old Town and Royal Castle and you'd think the city had enjoyed a comfortable existence the past 200 years. But at the end of WWII they, and nearly the entire metropolis, lay in rubble and ruin. The fact that Varsovians picked themselves up and rebuilt almost everything is reason enough to pay the country's capital a visit.[51]

There is no mention of those thousands of Jewish Varsovians who were liquidated because of their ethnic and religious identity and whose surviving remnant is too small to restore the community to its previous stature. Despite recent efforts to bolster the city's Jewish heritage, with POLIN chief among them, the fate of Warsaw's Jews cannot be rendered as a tale of triumphant return. The tale of annihilation has no place in this narrative of restoration, and so it is omitted.

The relative invisibility of Jewish Warsaw in comparison to Polish Warsaw in popular tourist literature means that the very important insight afforded by tourism to Warsaw—the complicated relationship between Warsaw's experience of the Holocaust and the war experience more generally—can be an obstacle to appreciating how, unlike the general population in the city, Jews were uniquely targeted as a people for annihilation. The simultaneity and spatial proximity of the Holocaust and World War II may lead tourism to err toward a generalized, shared war experience in Warsaw, thereby overlooking what was unique about the treatment of Jews, many of whom were not Varsovians, but for whom the city was a way station on the road to death. The danger of flattening out these differences is realized when guidebooks and popular guided tours of the city frame the Holocaust within an overarching story of Warsaw's victimization—a story whose upbeat ending belies the permanent losses inflicted by the Holocaust.

If tourists relied solely on guidebooks to inform their understanding of the city, then the unequal treatment of the city's two distinct uprisings in most guidebooks would lead tourists to comprehend the Holocaust as a secondary part of the Warsaw story. While most publications distinguish between the two events, the coverage is typically much greater for the 1944 Warsaw Uprising, while the 1943 Ghetto Uprising is mentioned in passing, often under the heading of "Jewish Warsaw." In one popular guidebook, the 1943 Ghetto Uprising receives a brief paragraph, while the 1944 Warsaw Uprising gets much lengthier attention in a highlighted textbox on the next page.[52] In another popular guidebook, the authors make the following misleading observation: "The city rebelled against the Germans twice, first in April 1943 . . . and the second in August 1944. . . . Both rebellions were ruthlessly crushed" (my ellipses mark spots where the book refers readers to further information on separate pages).[53] The phrasing here has already sewn the seeds of confusion. By naming "the city" as the agent of both uprisings, tourists get a history that is flattened, two-dimensional, and undifferentiated.[54] The Holocaust recedes into a general story of Warsaw, here equating the destruction of the city in 1944 with the genocidal intentions of the Nazis toward the Jews.

Tourists, thankfully, are not identical to one another, nor do they lack agency in constructing their experiences of place. Tourists bring different agendas with them, and those who are already informed about the Holocaust will not necessarily capitulate to the triumphalist narratives that agencies and guidebooks use to appeal to travelers. Still, that does not absolve those voices from within the tourism industry of their responsibility to continually revise their narratives, to find a better way to acknowledge the devastation of the Holocaust, and to complicate the story of Warsaw's rebirth as a fate enjoyed by some Varsovians more than others.

Absence is hard to make visible, and tourism remains a heavily visual medium. Loss has to be mapped and marked in order to be remembered through tourism. Warsaw does not hide its losses from tourists, but it struggles to find the right way to mark them. It is no surprise that, as the national capital, Warsaw greets tourism through the display of Polish pride, but for those who are ready to grapple with a history that is troubled and unresolved, one wishes for a more nuanced, self-critical account. The narratives of rebirth that pervade the tourist landscape in Warsaw, reinforced by Polish Catholicism and the Christian narrative of resurrection and redemption, are poor frameworks for facing the destruction of Jewish life.[55] And yet the emergence of an international market in Jewish-themed tourism, including Holocaust tourism, suggests the continued presence of countervailing tendencies in public memory. As the simultaneous popularity of such disparate entities as the POLIN museum and the Law and Justice Party suggests, the different strains of public memory in Poland are far from united. As the past fades, Warsaw's ability to evolve and adopt a more complex approach to its traumatic history will be measured in no small part by the way it presents the Holocaust to tourists. At the moment, tourists' demand for access to this past remains strong, but as time goes on, that, too, may fade.

4

Berlin

In the throes of a severe case of depression. I miss the old
Berlin of the Republic, the care-free, emancipated, civilized
air . . . . Day before yesterday Gillie [a former *Morning Post*
correspondent] took me to lunch at a pub in the lower part
of the Friedrichstrasse. Coming back he pointed out a building where a year ago for days on end, he said, you could hear
the yells of the Jews being tortured. I noticed a sign. It was
still the headquarters of some S.A. *Standarte*. Tess tried to
cheer me up by taking me to the Zoo yesterday.
—William L. Shirer, September 2, 1934, *Berlin Diary* (2005)

If the camp and ghetto memorials are where tourists grapple with the suffering endured by the victims of Nazism, then Berlin is the place where
tourists confront the fanaticism of the perpetrators. As the Third Reich's
seat of government, Berlin was the administrative hub of the Final Solution from its earliest conceptions. Berlin was also home to Germany's
largest Jewish population, some 170,000 of Germany's roughly 500,000
Jews in total, most of whom were expelled from the city in mass transports to the east.[1] Touring Holocaust sites in Berlin usually points to the
beginning of the ordeal awaiting Jewish Berliners, but it also calls attention to the administrative apparatus that authorized the violence that
ensnared millions of victims across Europe. As tourists wander through
the city's extensive and ever-evolving memory landscape, Berlin becomes
the place where the political philosopher Hannah Arendt's famous phrase
"the banality of evil" manifests itself in physical space.[2]

Like Warsaw, Berlin is intimately associated with World War II and
the Cold War in the minds of many visitors, and postwar tourism has developed numerous avenues for exploring the recent past: the Berlin Wall,
the Third Reich, East Germany, and Jewish Berlin are popular topics of
historically minded tourism today.[3] As in Warsaw, Holocaust tourism

in Berlin intersects with other topics of interest and is often part of a blended itinerary of interconnected histories.[4] Tourists with various interests inevitably survey multiple epochs, for in few places does the past feel as physically present as it does in Berlin, apparent in its architecture, its street names, and its memorials.[5] The twentieth century has molded the city into a unique expression of a tumultuous era, where seemingly endless cycles of construction, destruction, and reconstruction have made the city's absences as tangible as its presences.[6] Architectural statements from numerous eras and regimes stand side by side in such density as to suggest that history itself has chosen Berlin as its warehouse.[7] Even in the twenty-first century, as new buildings rise in once-abandoned zones, Berlin remains poised to historicize each new edifice as an exemplar of a particular era. The luminous spaces of Potsdamer Platz feel no less symbolic than the iconic Reichstag or the Brandenburg Gate.

In the last two decades, the Holocaust has become a focal point of governmental and private agencies guiding visitors through the city. That move toward a more deliberate emphasis on the fate of Berlin's Jews coincides with the development of what the cultural geographer Karen Till has called a "memory district" in the heart of Berlin.[8] Referring to the space of the city that used to be *Niemandsland*, the no-man's-land between the inner and outer Berlin Wall fortifications, this area extends north to south from the Reichstag and Brandenburg Gate to Potsdamer Platz, past the Memorial to the Murdered Jews of Europe, through the Topography of Terror, to the Jewish Museum of Berlin. If Warsaw has tended to locate Holocaust memory toward its margins, then Berlin seems intent on drawing the memory of the genocide into its center. The result is a tension between the more recent and massive centralized locales dedicated to the Nazi past and the older, scattered, and less monumental sites of memory throughout the city that remember specific moments of Nazi oppression. In this chapter, I discuss how this move toward centralization and monumentalism (despite the claims of the so-called countermonument) coincides with Germany's desire to prove to the world that it has learned from its past. Tourists are a ready-made audience for that message, although, as I will show, they add their own layers of meaning onto Berlin's sites of memory.

While the anomalies of Berlin have made it a tourist destination for many years, the fall of the Berlin Wall on November 9, 1989, resulted in a new tourist boom that still shows little sign of relenting.[9] In the early 1990s, tourists raced to the newly unified city to see what life looked like on the other side of the Iron Curtain, before the inevitable renovations that transformed the eastern districts into copies of the West. Berlin became an endless construction site, a sea of cranes as East and West Berlin were stitched back together—that alone had a powerful allure for tourists. Despite its rapid and stunning transformation, the city retains some of its Cold War vestiges: The architectural leftovers of the German Democratic Republic's concrete-slab architecture are still visible, as is the wide boulevard of Karl Marx Allee with its Stalinist pomp. But while the intensity of the city's east/west contrast has diminished, Berlin has managed to reinvent itself as both a living museum and a vibrant postmodern playground.[10] Tourists come to enjoy Berlin in such numbers that many Berliners worry about the city's quality of life for natives.[11] The city's multi-cultural composition, its lively arts scene, and its reputation for sexual tolerance stand in stark contrast to the legacy of fascism and authoritarianism. The presence of tourists, and their contributions to the local economy, coincide with—and perhaps even lend support to— Berlin's efforts to reclaim its prewar reputation as the lively bohemian metropolis whose disappearance the journalist William Shirer was already mourning in 1934. Holocaust tourism has found its place among these rapid developments in Berlin by becoming part of them, and it has to be understood in the context of Berlin's—really Germany's—transition from the front line of the Cold War to the center of twenty-first-century Europe. In transforming the landscape of Holocaust remembrance, tourists can explore whether Germany has relegated the genocide to an isolated chapter from its past or has incorporated it into its future.

Fifty-seven years separate the Weimar Republic admired by Shirer from what has become known as the Berlin Republic—that is, Germany since 1990. Since the absorption of the German Democratic Republic (GDR; East Germany) into the Federal Republic of Germany (West Germany), German politicians, intellectuals, artists, journalists, and ordinary citizens have addressed the nation's aspirations to return to a sense of normality, framing the Nazi and Cold War eras as an extended interruption. They express a desire to be accepted as equal members of the international community and to be regarded no longer as representatives of a pariah nation burdened by the guilt of its past. The discourse of *Normalität* describes the opportunities presumably afforded Germany since reunification; although this word tends to be used less conspicuously in more recent years, one can still find expressions of the desires it names.[12] In short, *Normalität* is the notion that a unified Germany has atoned for its Nazi past through forty years of postwar division and, having paid its dues, can again embrace practices other Western nations take for granted: expressions of national pride, participation in international military adventures, or the freedom to criticize other states' human rights abuses.[13] For critics of the discourse of *Normalität*, with political philosopher Jürgen Habermas foremost among them, the term seems to consign the Nazi past to the rubble heap of history, rather than encourage continued engagement with the past. The fear is that a Germany that strives to leave its past behind is at risk of forgetting the hard-won lessons of the last seventy years.

What does the idea of a "normal" Germany—that is, a Germany no longer encumbered by the burden of its past—mean for Berlin tourism in general and Holocaust tourism in particular? Or to put the question in reverse, what role does tourism play in helping Germany attain or perform normality? At first glance, it would seem that German *Normalität* is at odds with Berlin's eclecticism. Since part of the notion of *Normalität* relates to the way Germany sees itself in relation to its neighbors, allies, and competitors, it is, to use Daniel Levy and Natan Sznaider's phrase, a symptom of cosmopolitan memory, which explores the way local collective memory develops in a global framework.[14] Tourists are producers and bearers of cosmopolitan memory, if often in unconscious ways, for their flows to and from particular locales document the health of international relations, the appeal of the local economy, and foreign admiration for local culture. At the same time, tourists by nature are drawn to places that depart from their own "normal" experience—indeed, tourism even plays a role in confirming the uniqueness or exoticism of a particular destination.[15] With these characteristics of tourism in mind, I want to suggest that there is a certain tension between the German desire for *Normalität* and tourists' demand for the exotic or extraordinary. That tension materializes in the contrast between Berlin's older, more dispersed sites of memory and the newer, centralized memory district.

Berlin is the place where the German discourse of *Normalität* and tourism's search for the unusual collide. If there is anything that has made Germany other than normal, then it is its history, a word that almost euphemistically refers to the Holocaust, specifically, or to the years between 1933 and 1990, more broadly. Does the presence of foreign tourists in such large numbers every year in Germany, especially in Berlin, mean that *Normalität* remains elusive and that the hope of some Germans to overcome the past is a futile dream? [16] Or do tourists become Germany's alibis, strangers taking on the task of memory work while Germans go about their daily lives? In asking about the role of tourism in the expiation of German guilt, I caution that the variety of agendas motivating diverse tourists defies any simplistic conclusion about tourism's relationship to German history.

Berlin itself presents tourists with a variety of commemorative itineraries, even in the context of Holocaust memorialization. Holocaust tourism in Berlin has benefited immensely from what many have referred to as the "memory boom": the intensification of productions and consumption of Holocaust histories and representations since the 1980s, some of which predate the fall of the Berlin Wall.[17] The end of the Cold War, however, allowed the burgeoning interest in the past to coincide with booms in both tourism and construction in Berlin. The shift in Holocaust tourism in Germany's capital from what was previously a de-centered, neighborhood-oriented memorial landscape to the newly centralized "memory district," with new structures occupying Berlin's previously vacated middle, is the physical manifestation of that memory boom. Perhaps in an effort to resist the conformity implied by centralization, the new national memorials to the Holocaust and the Nazi era in central Berlin have often been characterized as "countermonuments": monuments that resist the interpretations of conventional monuments that usually authorize a singular, official, and often nationalistic understanding.[18] According to James E. Young, the countermonument has become the prevailing concept used to explicate Berlin's (and Germany's) newest Holocaust memorial sites, distinguished by their use of negative spaces (inaccessible voids, hollows, empty spaces) and the uncertainty of their meaning (through unconventional or abstract forms or the lack of inscriptions).[19] But over time, I contend, it has become apparent that the intentions of countermonuments may differ from their reception in tourism. After all, the countermonumental trend emerged roughly at the same time as the German discourse of *Normalität*. Through tourism, we can see how these new trends in Holocaust memorialization in Berlin's middle are far less innocent of German nationalist ambitions than others have suggested. If one considers tourism's relationship to these new memorials as a measure for Germany's self-presentation as "normal," then the connection of these memorials to German identity politics becomes even more suspect. But before getting to that discussion, it is important to put the emergence of modern-day Holocaust tourism into the historical context from which it, together with the desire for *Normalität*, emerged.

Touring the Anomaly of Berlin

Upon Germany's unconditional surrender in May 1945, the city's very ruins were to become its first postwar memorials, appropriately signifying the moral and military failures of the Third Reich. The broken façade of the Anhalter Bahnhof railway station, the crumbling Kaiser Willhelm Gedächtniskirche, the bullet-ridden museums on the River Spree, and, for a while, the charred and domeless Reichstag were to serve as reminders to residents and tourists alike of Germany's self-inflicted devastation. These ruins gave rise to the notion of what Germans call the *Mahnmal* as opposed to the *Denkmal*: both translate as "memorial," but the former signifies admonition, while the latter conveys commemoration.[20] New memorials would have to wait. In the case of Holocaust memorials, they would have to wait for several decades; meanwhile, Berlin was transformed into the Janus-faced capital of the Cold War, one metropolis with two diametrically opposed countenances.

Before the Nazis, Berlin had begun a legendary period of cultural and social innovation in the late nineteenth century that cemented its reputation as a diverse and lively metropolis. As Germany's first city to reach 1,000,000 residents,[21] Berlin experienced intense social upheaval that coincided with industrialization and German national unity. Technology reshaped transportation, communications, and the workplace, giving rise to the stratification of society into the bourgeoisie and the proletariat alongside the aristocracy. Women entered the workforce, forever changing family structures and gender norms. Berlin became famous for a sexual revolution that was both celebrated and prosecuted: Prostitution, homosexuality, and abortion were frequent targets for traditionalists, while simultaneously the emerging fields of sociology, psychoanalysis, and sexology worked to comprehend and de-criminalize "deviant" sexuality. The arts responded to all of these developments with bold modernist experiments and aesthetic revolutions: Expressionism, Dada, cabaret, jazz, and the Bauhaus all forged new modes of artistic expression to respond to new realities and to imagine new futures, and Berlin became an international center of modernist art. As the historian Brian Ladd has summarized,

> What came to Berlin in the late nineteenth and early twentieth centuries with startling speed was the bewildering set of changes that, for lack of a more precise formulation, we call modernity. It was a disorderly, disorienting, frightening era, but it was also exciting and liberating, and in light of what followed, it has come to be bathed in the light of nostalgia.[22]

Berlin became the city that William Shirer later remembered fondly and mourned, its reputation for artistic and social experiment having been firmly cemented by the time Hitler came to power. After twelve years of fascist dictatorship, it was this modernist legacy that Berlin tried to reclaim immediately after the war. West Berlin became a bohemian haven for young people from West Germany, while East Berlin drew poets, playwrights, and artists after the war who wanted to shape the face of socialism, whether that meant supporting or criticizing the East German state.

The establishment of the Federal Republic of Germany in May 1949, followed by the declaration of the German Democratic Republic the following October, left West Berlin an occupied city surrounded by the communist GDR, an island separated from the rest of the Federal Republic. Access to West Berlin was possible by air, rail, or car, the last two requiring passage on dedicated rail lines and patrolled highways. Until 1961, residents of Berlin could traverse the city's four sectors (American, British, French, and Soviet) with relative ease, having to pass checkpoints to inspect identification and work permits, but Berlin's subway system, its water mains, its telecommunications lines, and power its grid continued to link the city. But on August 13, 1961, Berliners awoke to find barbed wire and masonry separating them from family and friends on the other side. Over time, the Berlin Wall grew in sophistication and fortification, resulting in the infamous concrete barrier that eventually bisected the city and completely enclosed West Berlin. In many parts of the city there was an inner and an outer wall, and between them a no-man's land of mines, patrol units, guard dogs, automated guns, and guard towers.

Berlin's transformation into the Cold War's most tangible embodiment was deadly for many who tried to breach its inner border and intimidated others to stay put—but it got tourists on the move. That awareness of danger lent Berlin a special allure, and a guided tour across the Iron Curtain was an adventure into enemy territory from which tourists could safely return.[23] Detente and Willy Brandt's *Ostpolitik*, or "eastern policy," eventually allowed tourism to flow across the Berlin borders in the early 1970s and beyond.[24] Cold War–era tourists (of which I was one on several occasions during the 1980s) experienced the striking contrasts between the two sides of the city. In the West, Berlin seemed to display its bohemian side as proudly as it embraced opulent consumerism. Meanwhile, East Berlin's center developed into the jewel of the East German crown, a showcase for the successes of socialist engineering in the form of massive new apartment complexes and modern government buildings. But just behind the façade, East Berlin was dreary and gray; paint was in short supply, and historical façades that had been burned or bullet-ridden retained their scars. For Western tourists, that was all part of the adventure over the Wall, which many experienced as a form of time travel: Despite some impressive new edifices, East Berlin seemed to have been frozen in time in 1945, perhaps because it almost appeared as black-and-white in person as the historical photos or films that usually depicted the World War II era. West Berlin certainly had its frozen spots, the Reichstag and the Kaiser Wilhelm Gedächtniskirche most prominent among them, but they were surrounded by the colorful, sometimes tacky, and definitely modern bustle.

The odd sense that Berlin was a place for time travel had everything to do with the Germany's other-than-normal status after 1945. Division and occupation transformed Germany into the front line of the Cold War, with two German states playing opposite roles in the ideological conflicts and global proxy wars that defined the era. According to the West, the Federal Republic and West Berlin embodied a free Germany that had rejected its fascist past of oppression and genocide, while the

East was the totalitarian successor to Hitler; the East German Stasi were the descendants of the Gestapo or the SS, and East Germany itself was likened to a prison, a state-sized concentration camp or gulag. According to the East, however, it was West Germany that was the true heir of the Nazi party, demonstrated by the inclusion of former Nazi party members in the government, including Chancellor Kurt Georg Kiesinger and President Heinrich Lübke and members of Chancellor Konrad Adenauer's cabinet; East Germany, meanwhile, was oriented toward an antifascist future, unburdened by the crimes of the Third Reich because it had embraced Nazism's ideological archenemy, Communism. Tourists certainly got an earful from tour guides on either side, many of whom were themselves members of the occupying military forces. (In my first experience in East Berlin in 1981, a U.S. Air Force tour guide instructed our western tour group to smile and wave at a window in Alexanderplatz, where a camera was aimed at the square, telling us we were on "Commie Camera.") Tourists experienced Berlin as a place where the Cold War exceeded rhetoric and instead became very real, with armed front lines, soldiers, and fallen victims, some of whose names were commemorated along the Wall near the Reichstag.

Holocaust tourism to Berlin, which emerged only gradually and in step with the growing awareness of the Holocaust in both national and international public discourse, has to be understood within this context of tourism to Berlin as the capital of the Cold War, which showcased Germany's division as the wages of its past wrongs. Division, the mark of the country's anomalous status, was a strategic result of Cold War tensions, but it was also justifed as punishment for Germany's moral failure in embracing fascism and a preventive measure to deny Germany the ability to once again ignite war and perpetrate genocide in Europe. But the Holocaust was not articulated as the reason for German division in the beginning; rather, German division resulted from the ideological impasses that intensified between the Soviet Union and the West immediately after the war.

Tourism reveals how, over time, the Holocaust grew in public awareness and became increasingly incorporated into the justification for Germany's division after the fact. Tourists heard and saw far more about the Holocaust in their visits to the city in the 1980s than they did in the 1950s; however, the manner in which the Holocaust became the object of tourism was dependent on the prevailing ideological agendas on both sides of the Wall. The availability of sites where tourists could ground their understanding of the Holocaust in geography was determined in large part by the vicissitudes of the Cold War, including the changing economic fortunes of either side of Germany and the increasing willingness to acknowledge the Holocaust's victims rather than its liberators.

The Emergence of Holocaust Tourism in Berlin

The fact that Holocaust tourism emerged gradually in Berlin, usually on a smaller scale that addressed specific neighborhoods or individuals, is not surprising if we consider that Holocaust remembrance of any kind in Germany only materialized in public discourse in the 1960s. The question for this chapter is how tourism has participated in, and evolved with, the broader project of Holocaust remembrance, beginning when the city was divided physically and ideologically for forty years, a time when no pretense could be made that Germany's status was "normal." It is against that backdrop of confronting the Nazi past in a divided city that we can best understand the repositioning of Holocaust memory and tourism from Berlin's margins to the center, a move that coincides with the discourse of normality.

While awareness of the Holocaust was apparent in the immediate postwar era, it was not until the 1960s that the taboo against public discussion of the Nazi crimes began to fade with the first German trials of SS camp guards in the 1950s and 1960s.[25] But as the German film scholar Anton Kaes and others have pointed out, it was the broadcast in 1980 of the NBC miniseries *Holocaust*, the most widely watched program in the history of the Federal Republic of Germany, that marks the starting point for sustained public discourse about the Nazi past in Germany—at least in West Germany.[26] The vast majority of Holocaust memorials in both halves of divided Berlin were first dedicated in the 1980s, subsequent to the huge outpouring of interest in the Holocaust that the miniseries unleashed; the establishment of new memorials to the Nazis' victims has continued well into the present. The initial efforts in the 1980s to develop sites of Holocaust remembrance focused on existing locations dispersed throughout the city that had fallen into disrepair or neglect. Most of these sites, especially in East Berlin, predate the discourse of *Normalität* and the rise of the countermonument, and they help illustrate how the postwar establishment of a memory district is a departure from Berlin's dispersed, localized commemoration of the Holocaust.

East Berlin

While Jews lived throughout the city, the area in the middle of Berlin known as the Scheunenviertel, or "barn district," housed the largest concentration of newly arrived, poor Jewish families from Eastern Europe. They made up about 25 percent of Berlin's Jewish population before 1933. Located just north of Alexanderplatz in what became the Soviet sector of Berlin, the neighborhood had been converted from barns into urban slum housing to accommodate the influx of immigrants seeking work, especially the Jews from Russia, the so-called *Ostjuden*.[27] This neighborhood was also the seat of Berlin's largest synagogue and the home of the Reform Judaism movement. This meant the co-presence of a highly assimilated progressive Jewish community alongside newly arrived, largely orthodox Jews from the East.[28] Jewish life flourished in the city, and its vibrancy was depicted in Alfred Döblin's masterpiece novel, *Berlin Alexanderplatz*. Jewish Berliners were part of a mosaic of groups that constituted the modern metropolis, to include migrants from Italy, German colonies in Africa and the South Pacific, as well as peasants from the countryside who left agriculture for employment in Berlin's industrial factories. Modern Berlin overlapped with Jewish Berlin. The Nazis' attacks on modernism as degenerate were typically expressed in racialized terms: Modernism was "non-Aryan," the product of Jews and other "inferior" races.

The Holocaust virtually erased the presence of Jewish life in the heart of the city, leaving behind only a small remnant community. With the exception of a few locations in the Scheunenviertel, the East German government did not maintain sites of Holocaust perpetration or lost Jewish life as active memorial sites. In 1948, the Jewish community in the eastern half of Berlin placed a plaque to mark the site of the cemetery in the Große Hamburger Strasse that the Gestapo had destroyed in 1943; afterward, the commemoration of the Holocaust in the urban landscape of East Berlin ceased, while other agendas for commemoration were pursued. Predictably, memorials in the postwar years had two primary purposes: to celebrate the liberation of the eastern part of Germany by the Soviet Union, and to commemoriate Communists and resistance fighters who had opposed the Third Reich. As in Poland, the particularity of Jewish suffering was not paramount.

When Holocaust memorialization began its international boom cycle in the 1980s, the GDR took limited steps to restore some important sites of Berlin's Jewish past. Part of a larger effort to recover its pre-Nazi past, East Berlin's restorations in the era of Glasnost allowed for a nostalgic look back at the city's history, a break from the relentless future-oriented construction of "real existing socialism" that replaced so much of the city's bombed-out ruins. These restoration efforts coincided with Berlin's 750th anniversary in 1987, and they offered a chance for East Berlin to present itself as a flourishing, culturally rich alternative to its wealthier western counterpart. Tourism to commemorate once-vital Jewish neighborhoods was limited mainly to local residents and visitors from other Warsaw Pact countries. Western tourists had access to East Berlin under fairly reliable visa arrangements by the 1980s, but mass tourism from the West was still unthinkable. East German efforts to mark Berlin's Jewish life sewed the seeds for both Holocaust-focused tourism as well as Jewish heritage tourism, but both would have to wait for the fall of the Berlin Wall before they would thrive.

Meanwhile, sites of perpetration in the Soviet sector of the city had either been destroyed or repurposed. Chief among these perpetrator sites under East German control was the notorious concentration camp Sachsenhausen, situated in the neighboring village of Oranienburg to Berlin's north. Sachsenhausen was "the first camp to be built after 'Reichsführer SS' Heinrich Himmler was put in charge of the German police in July 1936."[29] Sachsenhausen initally held political foes of the NSDAP (the National-Socialist German Workers Party), especially communists but also defiant clergy, Jehovah's Witnesses, homosexuals, and other "asocials": prostitutes, criminals, and the indigent. Prior to the Wannsee Conference, Jews were sent to Sachsenhausen in growing numbers until the ghettos and extermination camps in the East were established. Soviet prisoners of war were held at Sachsenhausen as forced labor, many of whom were executed or died under extreme conditions. The gas vans that were eventually used at Chełmno in 1943 were first tested on Soviet prisoners of war in Sachsenhausen. Most prisoners were evacuated on forced marches from the camp as German defeat neared, but several thousand remained behind when the Red Army liberated the camp on April 22, 1945. Unlike Majdanek and Auschwitz, whose status as memorial sites was determined immediately upon liberation, Sachsenhausen continued to operate as a prison camp after the war, but run by the Soviet secret police to intern Nazi functionaries, collaborators, and Soviet deserters. The conditions remained deplorable and resulted in thousands of deaths. The prison camp was closed in 1950, one year after the founding of the GDR, and remained largely forgotten by all save the East German military, which used the facilities and grounds for training.

Only in 1961 was a museum established at Sachenhausen, which commemorated victims of fascism in predictably propagandistic terms. The museum commemorated not the extermination of Jews but, rather, the Nazi oppression of political opponents, most important of them, communists and resistance fighters. In other words, Germans in the GDR could visit the site and honor the "good Germans" who had rejected Hitler and thus identify as victims and heroes themselves. Over 100,000 people, mostly from the GDR, attended the museum's opening, and Sachsenhausen remained an important tourist destination for East German citizens.

Since reunification, the Memorial and Museum Sachsenhausen has been thoroughly redesigned. Rather than serve the commemorative needs of East German state doctrine, the memorial has been incorporated into unified Germany's more robust confrontation with the Nazi past, which, as I have suggested, plays a role in demonstrating the nation's moral restoration to the rest of the world. Today the camp memorial and museum is accessible by bus from the Oranienburg train station. The tour begins at an information center, where tourists see a diagram of the main camp area, view an introductory film, and begin their tour with an audio headset. The museum offers guided tours via advanced arrangement and has guides on site at the information center. From there tourists walk to the camp itself, where they encounter the triangular arrangement of buildings that ensured maximum surveillance of the prisoner barracks. Tourists enter through the main gate that, like Auschwitz, bears the motto "Arbeit macht frei." As tourists visit the exhibits in numbered barracks, the audio tour explains the function of each building during the Third Reich and also tells stories of the camp's

victims. As a whole, the walking tour emphasizes the camp's complicated evolution from a detention center for political foes to a deadly
concentration camp for the whole array of Nazism's enemies. Unlike the
exhibition in place during the GDR years, the site acknowledges very
clearly the racist ideology that led to the internment of Jews as well as
Sinti and Roma. As was the case with the camps located in Poland, the
Sachsenhausen museum in the GDR era limited itself to an ideological
emphasis on victims of fascist oppression, with no differentiation among
the victim groups by ethnicity, religion, or sexuality. Compared to the
extermination camps and ghettos in Poland, Sachsenhausen's place in
Holocaust history is less straightforward than what some visitors may
expect. Its original purpose was not the extermination of Jews, although
its role in Holocaust history became critical as the Final Solution was
enacted. In addition to gassings carried out at Sachsenhausen to test
their lethality, the personnel at the camp received important training
and experience that they used to deadly purpose elsewhere, among them
the future Auschwitz Kommandant Rudolf Höss.

It takes about an hour to reach the Sachsenhausen memorial from
the center of Berlin by public transportation. For tourists with less time
or willingness to venture beyond Berlin, there are sites of Gestapo and
SS perpetration in the city's eastern half, but the GDR did not promote
these places nearly as heavily as the Sachsenhausen camp. In the center
of the city were a few remaining fascist-era buildings that had housed
administrative entities of the Third Reich; they were used after the war
for GDR various ministries. Among these was a massive structure on
the Wilhelmstrasse, close to Potsdamer Platz, which had once been the
headquarters of Hermann Goering's Luftwaffe and civil aviation administration and which became the "House of Ministries" under the GDR.
No acknowledgment of the building's Nazi origins was made until after
reunification, when the federal government affixed a plaque to its side.
It now houses reunified Germany's Ministry of Finance.[30]

Rather than call attention to sites that marked Holocaust perpetrators, East Berlin eventually directed tourists to traces of Jewish life that
had been destroyed. Most promininent of these was the New Synagogue,
whose restored gilded onion dome is a dominant feature of the sky-
line in the center of Berlin today. The New Synagogue, in the heart of
the Scheunenviertel, was first established in 1866. A center of Reform

Judaism, it was the first Jewish congregation led by a female rabbi, Regina Jonas, who later died in Auschwitz-Birkenau. The synagogue is remarkable in that it survived Kristallnacht, but it was confiscated by the Wehrmacht in 1940. The Nazis desecrated its Torah and ransacked its historic treasures. The synagogue suffered heavy bomb damage by the Allies in 1943 and was left standing as a ruin for most of the postwar era. The GDR finally marked the site with a plaque in 1966 but only agreed to restore the golden dome in 1988; most of the restoration was not completed until 1995 under a reunified Berlin.[31]

Today the New Synagogue is the home of the Centrum Judaicum, which serves the interests of Berlin's growing Jewish population.[32] The building is accessible via guided tour, and tourists learn about the history of Berlin's Reform Jewish community and its present-day life. Tourists in Berlin who do not bother to take the guided visit offered by the Centrum Judaicum are prone to misperceptions about the buidling, assuming its interior has also been restored (it hasn't) or that the building's damage was inflicted by the Nazis (it wasn't). Its relationship to the Holocaust is, like Sachsenhausen's, more complicated, and tourists who make the effort to learn about the New Synagogue's history discover that the Nazis encountered unexpected resistance in their attempts to burn the building to the ground.[33]

Near the New Synagogue lies the oldest Jewish cemetery in Berlin in the Große Hamburger Strasse, wherein lay the remains of one of the most celebrated figures of the Enlightenment, Moses Mendelssohn. The Gestapo destroyed the cemetery in 1943, so that today there are almost no gravestones left. The Jewish community of Berlin placed a commemorative plaque at the gates of the cemetery, but no additional memorialization occurred until the 1980s, when a statuary group was placed at the cemetery gates depicting Jewish deportees. Farther east was the much larger Jewish cemetery of Weissensee, which was left relatively intact during the war despite some damage from air raids. The GDR designated the Weissensee cemetery as a cultural monument but only undertook significant efforts to restore it in the 1980s. In the case of both of these cemeteries, further restoration occured after reunification.

The New Synagogue and the Jewish cemeteries commemorate the Holocaust indirectly, testifying primarily to Jewish life in Berlin until its destruction. This fact, a feature shared with Warsaw, Kraków, and many other places where Jewish culture had roots, illustrates the way in which Holocaust tourism cannot be a discrete phenomenon in urban places; instead, tourists see the Holocaust in relation to other historical developments. There is a general sense in which anything Jewish in Berlin will evoke associations with the genocide without necessarily addressing Nazi ideology. As monuments to Berlin's Jewish history, they accentuate the vitality of Jewish culture that Berlin lost in the Holocaust and acknowledge Hitler's destructive intentions more obliquely than camp or ghetto memorials. As in Warsaw, Holocaust tourism in Berlin is entwined with Jewish heritage tourism; the two inform one another. Tourists who want to learn about the Holocaust will perceive the loss much more intensely if they encounter the signs of Jewish culture, its historical contributions to society, its vibrancy as a community, and Judaism's evolution as a religion in Europe.

But there is a sense in which Jewish heritage tourism also undermines the appreciation of loss. While Jewish heritage tourism in Berlin usually includes stops at sites of Holocaust memory, it also emphasizes Jewish Berlin as a living culture—which it undoubtedly also is.[34] The question is whether the tours do so in a way that suggests that the loss has been overcome. Next door to the New Synagogue, for example, is a kosher cafe where tourists can eat "Jewish" food—kosher dishes and Israeli cuisine—and tour guides inform Jewish travelers of kosher dining options in the city.[35] Adjacent to the Centrum Judaicum is a school for Jewish youth. Nearby is the building housing the Central Council of Jews in Germany, the leading advocacy organization for all of Germany's roughly 105,000 Jews today.[36] The *Jüdische Gemeinde* (the Jewish Community) in Berlin counts 11,000 members—significant, but still only about 5 percent of its size before 1933. As is the case in Warsaw, the presence of Jewish life in the city today is a welcome site that tempers the nihilism of the Nazis' intended extermination. At the same time it is important for tourists to understand that the losses inflicted by the Holocaust are too great to have been reversed. Guides from the Centrum Judaicum, in my experience, have been very frank about the challenges facing the Jewish community in Berlin, where it forms a small minority.

When undertaken with a critical approach, touring signs of Jewish life offers a way to explore the impact of the Holocaust on the present. Tourism ponders how such life today is still possible, despite the overwhelming efforts to end it, and whether there is more continuity or rupture in the experience of Jews living in Berlin. Jewish heritage tourism avoids the problem of presenting the Final Solution as a perverse accomplishment of the perpetrators by stressing Jewish life over Jewish death; however, if tours of "Jewish Berlin" de-emphasize the losses suffered in the past, there is a risk that some tourists will assume that the Holocaust has now receded safely into history and that all is "back to normal" between Germans and Jews. Such an impression would certainly lend support to the idea that Germany has become "normal," if by "normal" we mean that anti-Semitism has been placed squarely outside accepted public discourse. But that notion of normality is troubled by the presence of armed police officers in front of the New Synagogue and the nearby school, which testifies to the persistence of anti-Semitic threats still targeting Berlin's Jewish community, however unrepresentative they are of most Germans today. Although the state provides protection to the community in these instances, Jews in Germany can also feel like they are at odds with a German government that still struggles with accommodating different cultural norms. Controversies play out in politics and the media on matters ranging from the acceptability of traditional religious rituals (e.g., kosher slaughter, infant male circumcision) to international relations with Israel. Such controversies tend to garner a great deal of media attention both domestically and internationally, raising historical specters that trouble the fantasy of *Normalität*.[37]

West Berlin

Despite the different postwar conditions in the two halves of Berlin, the western half of Berlin also came late to commemorating the Holocaust in its expanses. The districts of Charlottenburg, Schöneberg, Wilmersdorf, Steglitz, and Zehlendorf in West Berlin, the historically wealthier half of the city, had been home to prosperous Jews who had assimilated into the bourgeoisie. When the Holocaust came, the traces of their lives were also destroyed—synagogues were burned, businesses vandalized and eventually stolen, homes expropriated, and Jews either fled into exile or, as was the case for the majority, were deported to the ghettos and, ultimately, the camps. Tourists in Berlin during the first decades after the war could certainly see traces of the Third Reich that had committed these atrocities. For example, one could visit the Olympic Stadium in Charlottenburg, an exemplar of fascist architecture and the place where Hitler played host to the games in 1936.[38] Tempelhof Airport, another example of fascist architecture, was still in use, but its significance as the focal point of the Berlin airlift in 1947 obscured its Nazi origins and instead foregrounded for its visitors the Western Allies' determination to stand firm against Soviet aggression. The Reichstag building, whose Empire architecture and parliamentary institutions were both despised by Hitler, stood just on the western side of the Wall, a burned ruin and a symbol of Germany's disastrous departure from democracy in 1933. But these sites made only general references to the Holocaust, embedded in a dominant narrative of Nazi dictatorship under which Germans also suffered. Tourists would have to search more creatively for sites that singled out the Holocaust for special attention, and until the 1980s they would find little in the way of official commemoration of the fate of the city's Jews. As the Federal Republic's willingness to acknowledge the historical responsibilities it inherited grew in the postwar era, the government invested in the restoration of some of the most important sites of Holocaust memory in the city.

West Berlin contained several gathering points for deportation where the city's Jews were ordered to appear for "resettlement" to the East. For many years, these sites went unmarked. One such site is in Levetzowstrasse near the angel-topped Victory Column, where a synagogue once stood; the building was badly damaged during air raids and was eventually demolished in the 1950s. From Levetzowstrasse, Jews would be taken by sealed trams to the Anhalter Bahnhof, whence they would be transported to ghettos and camps farther east. The memorial at Levetzowstrasse was installed in 1988, a year before the fall of the Berlin Wall. Similarly, at the Grunewald station further west in Berlin, another memorial documents the deportation of the city's Jews from the platform of Track 17. This site was first memorialized in 1991, shortly after reunification, in the form of a large cement block with hollowed out figures representing the deported. Later, a second memorial was installed at Track 17 in 1998 by the Deutsche Bahn, Germany's railway, in a gesture acknowledging its complicity in the deportations. This second memorial consists of placards at the edge of the platform with the dates and destinations of transports, along with the number of victims deported. These are quiet, local memorials that require effort on the part of tourists who want to see them. They are somewhat removed from the flow of tourist traffic, but tours dedicated to antifascist themes include them on their itineraries, and most tourbooks also mention the sites.

Perhaps the most significant and notorious site related to the Holocaust in West Berlin, if not the entire city, is the villa where the 1942 Wannsee Conference took place. Sitting on the shores of the bucolic Wannsee lake, far from the Zoo Station area that had become the symbolic center of West Berlin, it is on a street lined with luxurious villas, only a few doors from the home once inhabited by one of Berlin's most famous Jewish residents, the painter Max Liebermann. The house at Am Großen Wannsee 56–58 was purchased by the SS as a guest house in 1940 and was chosen for a conference organized by Reinhard Heydrich and Adolf Eichmann to finalize the implementation of the so-called *Endlösung der Judenfrage*, of the "final solution of the Jewish question." The conference, orginally scheduled for December 12, 1941, was delayed after Germany and the United States declared war against each other on December 11, and it took place on January 20, 1942. The Operation Reinhard camps opened later that year.

After the war, the villa was used by the West German Social Democratic Party (SPD) as an educational institute before it was sold to the Berlin district of Neukölln to be used as a school facility, which it remained in 1988.[39] In the intervening years, the former resistance fighter and Auschwitz survivor Josef Wulf worked to establish a documentation center at the Wannsee Villa dedicated to the Nazi murder of European Jews. Wulf died in 1974 before any such center was established at the villa. Finally, in 1992, after four years of planning, the villa was opened as a memorial and education center, devoted to the examing the Final Solution that had been declared there fifty years earlier.[40]

Today, the House of the Wannsee Conference holds an impressively informative permanent exhibition. Each room of the first floor documents a particular point on the road to the Final Solution: One focuses on the history of anti-Semitism, another the emergence of fascism in Germany, and the main conference room focuses on the meeting itself. The next rooms document the implementation of the Final Solution, and the exhibit concludes with observations by Jewish Berliners today. The site is free of charge, and larger groups can arrange for a tour guide who engages the group in discussion throughout the exhibit. It is a re-markably succinct and yet richly documented exhibit that takes an un-flinching look at the problems of racism, anti-Semitism, and politics that unfolded in Germany in the twentieth century. The contrast between the horrors the villa documents and its romantic lakeside setting are among the more jarring experiences that tourists take away, leaving them to ponder how plans for mass murder on an industrial scale could coincide with such a picturesque scene.

Another prominent site of Nazi perpetration in West Berlin lies just southeast of Potsdamer Platz in what was once a barren wasteland near the Wall. The Topography of Terror names the leveled terrain where the chief SS and Gestapo buildings once stood and where prisoners were routinely interrogated and tortured. When commercial developers made plans to build on the site in the early 1980s, Berliners keen on remember-ing the Nazi past began a program of grassroots education to preserve the traces they saw their city poised to forget. Their efforts eventually led to the excavation of Gestapo prison cells and the foundations of other buildings connected with Nazi terror.[41] After reunification the land was suddenly in the very center of the city and therefore even more profit-able for potential developers, leaving the Topography of Terror's future uncertain. Only in 1992 did Berlin agree to preserve the site as a perma-nent memorial, and after considerable delay caused by Berlin's troubled finances, a completed design by Ursula Wilms and Heinz W. Hallmann, which included a permanent documentation center, opened in 2010. As its name indicates, the Topography covers a large area in Berlin and shares in common both its centrality and its massiveness with two other postreunifciation Holocaust memorials in Berlin: the Jewish Museum and the Memorial to the Murdered Jews of Europe. Together, these recently built memorials form what Karen Till has called a "memory district" in Berlin's center. These facilities draw large numbers of tour-ists and ensure that Holocaust tourism is virtually a mandatory feature of any visit to the city. At the same time, this new memorial district may draw visitors's attention away from the many smaller-scale or more remote memorials scattered throughout the city. Furthermore, the To-pography of Terror is inclusive of all victims of the Nazi dictatorship, including German dissidents, and so Holocaust remembrance becomes intertwined with German suffering at the hands of fellow Germans.

The risk I see is that these new, centrally located, facilities monumentalize collective memory to promote a "normalized" German national identity that tourists affirm through their presence. As such, they differ profoundly from other countermonumental installations that began to appear in the city in the 1990s.

Post-1989

The House of the Wannsee Conference and the Topography of Terror in the city's western half and the New Synagogue in the former East were initiated as memorials in the 1980s prior to reunification, but they were not fully realized until after 1990. The collapse of the Berlin Wall on November 9, 1989, inaugurated a new era of memorialization in Germany as the tensions of the Cold War retreated and the earlier past seemed to reemerge. The Berlin Republic's commitment to antifascist, democratic ideals translated into renewed efforts to establish commemorative monuments at sites that had been forgotten and to reinvigorate projects that had already begun.

Some of the postunification memorials to the Holocaust are small-scale, local installations that speak to a very specific dimension of the Holocaust. The Scheunenviertel, home of the New Synagogue, contains a large concentration of *Stolpersteine*, the brass inlaid cobblestones produced by the German artist Gunter Demnig. These "stumbling stones" commemorate the mostly Jewish residents who suffered persecution during the Nazi era and, in many cases, perished. The *Stolpersteine* go nearly undetected, often catching the viewer by surprise, but when visitors notice them, they are reminded that the Holocaust reached into the same urban spaces that present-day tourists comfortably survey. Rather than overwhelm tourists with inconceivable numbers, each stone remembers an individual caught up in the Nazi machinery of persecution. The *Stolpersteine*, though, are not confined to the Scheunenviertel, or to Berlin, or even to Germany. Demnig has placed stones in cities throughout Europe, in Denmark, Austria, Hungary, the Czech Republic, the Netherlands, Poland, and Italy.[42]

Similar to the *Stolpersteine*, but also more provocative, is the decentralized memorial entitled "Places of Remembrance" by the American artists Renata Stih and Frieder Schnock. Also using a strategy of camouflage, the memorial catches the viewer by surprise, blending into the urban landscape until it is noticed. Installed in 1993, it consists of eighty small signs placed on existing lampposts surrounding the Bayerischer Platz in the Schöneberg district, each showing a colorful image on one side and a brief text on the other. Each of the texts recalls one of the anti-Semitic provisions of the Nuremberg Laws and other anti-Semitic decrees promulgated during the 1930s and 1940s. For example, a colorful painting of a house cat lures the viewer to a text recalling a law forbidding Jewish citizens the right to own pets. Another depicts a park bench, with the law requiring Jews to sit only on designated benches in parks. When residents first noticed the signs, they alerted the police, fearing that anti-Semites had posted them.[43]

Just west of Potsdamer Platz, the Tiergartenstrasse is dominated by Hans Scharoun's Berliner Philharmoniker, part of the complex of museums and spaces called the Kulturforum, but in 1940 it designated the administrative headquarters of the Nazis' euthanasia program at Tiergartenstrasse 4, which went by the code name T4. Until recently,

Figure 4.1. One of the dozens of signs placed by Bayerischer Platz by Renata Stih and Frieder Schnock, August 2014. This sign explains that Jews may sit only on designated benches. Photo by the author.

only a large sculpture by Richard Serra, which the city purchased in 1988, commemorated the site, later augmented by an unassuming plaque laid into the sidewalk. At first look it is unclear whether Serra's sculpture was meant to adorn the Philharmonic or commemorate the victims of euthanasia. The plaque was installed in an apparent effort to address the sculpture's lack of specificity.[44] The near invisibility of the memorial text on a broad expanse of sidewalk between the Tiergarten park and the Kulturforum posed interesting questions about memorialization: Does the plaque represent an attempt to obscure rather than to acknowledge this chapter of Nazi atrocity? Or does it mark a shameful episode in history in an appropriately non-monumental fashion? The plaque, which begins "In Honor of the Forgotten Victims . . ." ("Ehre den vergessenen Opfern . . ."), seems almost to repeat that act of forgetting in its very form. Its late addition to the site suggests the emergence of a painful memory that had been repressed. Nevertheless, the discovery of the plaque in an area dedicated to high culture also surprises the viewer the same way the *Stolpersteine* and Stih and Schnock's signs do.

In September 2014, a new memorial design was unveiled in front of the Philharmonic, just meters away from the plaque and the Serra sculpture. The new memorial is part conceptual design and part education center, consisting of two dark granite half walls parallel to one another in a line running from the northeast to the southwest. The easternmost half wall can serve as a bench, while the westernmost structure is waist high with engraved information and video screens about the euthanasia operations in Germany, documenting the victims, the locations where the killings occurred, and the personnel involved in the killings, many of whom helped develop the techniques for the mass killing of Jews in the East. The granite walls run about forty-two meters in length and are separated by about twelve meters. In between them stands the centerpiece of the memorial, a taller wall of blue glass situated at a diagonal angle from the surrounding granite walls and about half their length. The blue wall is intended to signify the ascent from darkness into the heavens, perhaps also referencing the cremation of the victims' bodies.[45] Visitors will see a scene turned blue as they gaze through the wall, perhaps reflecting the memorial's intention to remember difference and to invite identification with those who were murdered for theirs. The wall's skewed angle compared to the surrounding parallel lines may also reinforce the idea of difference, now reimagined as redemptive, aesthetic beauty. There is a dimension of kitsch to this blue wall that seems out of place with the heartless murders conveyed through image and text in the nearby granite. It appears ornamental in relation to the Philharmonic building, repeating the gesture of Serra's sculpture but in an oddly cheerful manner. Tourists will likely have positive responses to any effort to memorialize the euthanasia program, although what they will make of the blue glass wall remains to be seen. Students with whom I traveled reacted more positively to the new memorial than I did and enjoyed the challenge of decoding the installation's significance. I wonder, though, whether the task of interpreting the artwork displaces the contemplation of the facts that the installation presents, if for no other reason than because the central artwork has an almost playful tone.

Monumental Countermonuments

While the 1990s saw the continued development of Holocaust memory dispersed throughout the city's reach, the primary development in the urban memorial landscape has been the establishment of three massive memorials in Berlin's center: The Topography of Terror, the Jewish Museum, and the Memorial to the Murdered Jews of Europe. Despite their far larger size, each of these memorials is notable as an instantiation of the so-called countermonument, a term that can also be applied to such memorials as disparate as the *Stolpersteine*, the Places of Remembrance, or even Christo's Wrapped Reichstag in 1994, all of which reject traditional monumental forms of commemoration. James E. Young, whose pioneering work on Holocaust memorials has provided tremendous insight on Germany's culture of remembrance, characterizes countermonuments as "memorial spaces conceived to challenge the very premise of the monument."[46] Whereas traditional monuments claim permanence in their efforts at remembrance, countermonuments incorporate flux, ambiguity, and self-negation, leaving the memory work to the viewer.[47] Countermonuments reject a traditional aesthetic mode that is too closely aligned with state-sponsored, often triumphalist gestures; instead, they raise memory as a question that each generation must address for itself.[48] In doing so, countermonuments also resist the sentimentality of traditonal monuments:

> For a new generation of German artists, the possibility that memory of events so grave might be reduced to exhibitions of public artistry or cheap pathos remains intolerable. They contemptuously reject the traditional forms and reasons for public memorial art, those spaces that either console viewers or redeem such tragic memory of a murdered people. Instead of searing memory into public conscoiusness, they fear, conventional memorials seal memory off from awareness altogether; instead of embodying memory, they find that memorials may only displace memory. These artists fear rightly that to the extent that we encourage monuments to do our memory-work for us, we become that much more forgetful. They believe, in effect, that the initial impulse to memorialize events like the Holocaust may actually spring from an opposite and equal desire to forget them.[49]

It is certainly the case that a new generation of memorials tried to find its own form of expression that distanced itself from the monumentality that became so closely associated with the Nazi state and its brand of nationalism. I wonder, though, whether that makes these new memorials any less "monumental."

While the *Stolpersteine* or the easily overlooked signs by Stih and Schnock at Bayerischer Platz seem decidedly countermonumental in both scale and self-presentation, the components of Berlin's memory district have reverted to some aspects of the traditional monument: large, conspicuous locales of official remembrance that make gestures toward permanence in their form. The Topography of Terror fulfills the criteria of the countermonument in its presentation of negative space, here in the form of archeological pits, but the construction of a new building next to the Martin-Gropius-Bau museum at the same location returns the site to a more recognizable form of permanence. The Documentation Center may claim to be an ancillary feature of the Topography, but tourists will regard it as a gateway to the terrain and accept the instruction they receive there. Furthermore, in insisting on the exposure

Figure 4.2. The Topography of Terror, with the Documentation Center to the right, August 2014. Tourists are exploring exhibits placed along the excavated rooms that once included Gestapo interrogation cells. To the left at street level is a fragment of the Berlin Wall that remains in central Berlin. Photo by the author.

of foundations of the Third Reich era buildings, the Topography depends on the permanence of brick and mortar architecture from the past. The presentation of these exposed basements speaks a traditional language of musealized structures that enshrine memory as permanent.

The architect Daniel Libeskind's design for the Jewish Museum of Berlin exemplifies a different strategy, refusing to fade into the urban background. Opened in 2001, it is one of reunified Berlin's most highly visited spots. Together with Norman Foster's restored Reichstag and the concentration of contemporary designs by the architects Renzo Piano, Richard Rogers, and Helmut Jahn at Potsdamer Platz, Libeskind's museum is part of a postmodern architectural triumvirate in the reunified city's center. The Jewish Museum's lightening-bolt shape and titanium-zinc exterior stand in stark contrast to the stately, baroque Collegienhaus that stands next to it and serves as the museum's main entry and exit, as well as its gift shop. Libeskind's building exemplifies a new Berlin, boldly departing from the old while at the same time partnering with it. At

the same time, it successfully embodies the impossibility of commemorating the former vitality of Jewish culture in Berlin without also commemorating its loss. Upon entering the Collegienhaus, visitors proceed
down a dark passageway below street level before rising into the new
edifice housing the museum's exhibition space. Almost immediately, the
visitor is presented with several routes, referred to as "axes": the Axis of
Continuity, the Axis of Emigration, and the Axis of the Holocaust. "All
three underground axes intersect each other, just as the three realities
that characterize Jewish life in Germany are interconnected." ("Alle drei
unterirdischen Achsen kreuzen sich. So sind die drei Wirklichkeiten
miteinander verbunden, die jüdisches Leben in Deutschland charakte-
risieren.")[50] The Axis of the Holocaust leads to a dark tower, a cul-de-
sac signifying the termination of life for many of Germany's Jews. The
Axis of Emigration leads to a garden of trees on a slanted surface, a
simultaneously contemplative and disorienting space. The Axis of Continuity leads upstairs to the exhibition. Throughout, Libeskind's design
incorporates voids, negative spaces that transect the zigzag shape of
the building. Most of the voids are inaccessible, but they determine the
flow of tours through the exhibition and signify the irretrievable loss
of Jewish culture as an irreparable wound in Germany. While the exhibition focuses on the history of Jews in Berlin, daily life in the Jewish
community, Jewish religious practice, and the achievements of famous
Jewish individuals from Germany, its voids make continual reference
to the Holocaust. Visitors must enter a central void at one point to
reach the rest of the exhibition, but to do so they must walk across a
floor covered with metal disks that look like spent film canisters at first
glance. Upon closer inspection, the disks depict abstract faces signifying the multitude of the dead. The museum seems to be intentionally at
cross-purposes with itself, both celebrating the past and mourning its
irretrievability—certainly in keeping with the self-questioning nature of
the countermonument.

In contrast to the POLIN museum in Warsaw, which creates generous, unobtrusive internal spaces that allow the exhibits and displays
to shine, the exhibition of the Jewish Museum of Berlin pales in comparison to the impressive architecture of the structure that houses it.
Its audacious design draws about 700,000 visitors annually, more than
the number of visitors to the information center of Berlin's Memorial

to the Murdered Jews of Europe.[51] The museum directors are eager to represent Jewish culture in Germany not as a stale artifact but, rather, as a once-living presence. The inclusion of interactive stations throughout the museum, or public lectures about Jewish-German relations in the present or latter-day genocides such as those in Rwanda and Darfur, arise from this desire to make the museum relevant to the present, not simply a memorial to the dead. One museum staff member, Stefanie Hardick, insists, "We are not a Holocaust museum, but a house of life. . . . The basic idea, to create a museum that didn't only concern itself with German-Jewish themes but, rather, sees its task much more broadly and deals with problems of the present, is very successful." ("Wir sind kein Holocaust-Museum, sondern ein Haus des Lebens. . . . Die Grundidee, ein Museum zu machen, das sich nicht nur mit deutsch-jüdischen Themen befasst, sondern seine Aufgabe viel breiter sieht und sich mit Problemen der Gegenwart beschäftigt, ist sehr erfolgreich.")[52]

Despite such claims, the Jewish Museum is, at least in part, also a Holocaust museum. Tourists, for whom any reference to Jews in Germany will forever evoke the Holocaust, often come expecting to see some depiction of the Shoah. Despite the desire on the part of the museum to be seen as a "house of life," Libeskind's architectural voids fulfill tourists' expectations and render the Holocaust as the organizing principle around which tourist traffic flows. The building itself becomes a memorial, an architectural allegory that instantiates the loss of Berlin's Jewish past through the performance of tourism. But because the mazelike museum does not explicitly address the people, ideologies, and decisions that set genocide into motion, the building instead seems to exemplify the oft-repeated trope of the Holocaust as incomprehensible, inhuman, beyond the reach of human understanding. Certainly Libeskind's homage to the philosopher Jacques Derrida's notion of difference, as the inability of language to signify beyond itself, seems to champion a view that situates the Holocaust beyond *logos*, that is, beyond the ability to represent it or convey it in language.[53] The building's disorienting design reaffirms shock, confusion, even awe as responses to the genocide. It is worth asking if such reactions come at the expense of contemplation and understanding. Recalling the fear among some contemporary artists that monuments supplant memory, it is worth considering how the experience of the museum itself, however countermonumental its embrace of negative space may be, preempts certain kinds of memory work in favor of others. In insisting on absence as the central trope of remembrance, the museum certainly highlights the Holocaust as the negation of a people and the collapse of cherished Enlightenment ideals of humanity and civilization. In incorporating voids amid the traces of the past, the museum has framed the Holocaust as an ontological problem of presence and absence, but that theoretically countermonumental perspective may outshine the kind of memory work that the exhibition itself seems to desire: engagement with historical records, appreciation of cultural artifacts, and a commitment to prevention of future genocides.

Much the same can be said about the architect Peter Eisenmann's design for the Memorial to the Murdered Jews of Europe: It is equally bold in design and scale and yet equally at cross-purposes with its countermonumental ambitions. The massive commemorative structure and subterranean museum occupies nearly five acres between the Brandenburg Gate and Potsdamer Platz. The field of unmarked cement steles on an undulating pavement provides no text, thereby freeing the viewer from any interpretation prescribed on site. This would seem to fulfill that aspect of countermonuments that James E. Young describes as "brazen, painfully self-conscious memorial spaces conceived to challenge the very premises of their being."[54] Young, who also served on the commission that ultimately selected Eisenmann's design, describes the site as embodying questions, not answers, and that for him is its justification. Rather than signal Germany's attainment of *Normalität*, Young argues, Eisenmann's design continually generates debate by refusing to "draw a bottom line under this era so that a reunified Germany can move unencumbered into the future"[55]

The problem that the memorial faces—and that countermonuments in general face—is the problem that awaits all avant-garde movements: In trying to defy received notions of familiar art forms, the avant-garde succeeds in a momentary disruption, but it is ultimately assimilated into the repertoire of artistic expression and interpretation, subject to the same dictates of the art market that it sought to overturn, susceptible to the same emergence of codified readings circulated in guided tours, art history texts, and in museums themselves.[56] In the case of Eisenmann's memorial, the absence of a prescriptive text does not preclude the same kind of allegorization of the Holocaust that Libeskind's museum overtly enacts. Like the Jewish Museum, the Holocaust memorial's form is not a neutral, blank slate upon which viewers are free to project infinite readings; rather, it adds a new form to an already-functioning repertoire of Holocaust representations. Visitors to the memorial will bring that portion of the repertoire they have absorbed or rehearsed to their encounter with Eisenmann's structure. Inevitably, the steles may symbolize gravestones for the murdered millions to some tourists, while for others still they will represent a weight on the German conscience. The tourist who enters the memorial from any of its sides gravitates toward its center, where the ground is at its deepest and the steles at their highest. This experiential quality of the memorial is both part of its power and part of its representational dilemma. Either it represents nothing in particular, or the movement through the center and out again symbolizes something about the Holocaust. Perhaps it is the experience of the Nazis' victims, their isolation and sense of disorientation throughout their ordeal of deportation and extermination. And what does the visitor make of the fact that there is light at the end of the tunnel, that unlike the majority of deported Jews, the tourist rises again out of the memorial's isolating maze? Does the cheerful city into which the visitor emerges present itself as the new home of the perpetrators, or does it rather offer a redemptive moment to the tourist, a vision of a hopeful future for which the Holocaust was a destructive precursor? If one compares the oft-repeated trope of a descent into darkness and reemergence into light that one finds in so many Holocaust museums—the Jewish Museum of Berlin, the United States Holocaust Memorial Museum, Yad Vashem—then that redemptive moment itself dispels the countermonumental aspiration to remain antiredemptory and instead recalls the function of traditional monuments that promise the future as the reward for past sacrifices.

The perspective of tourism offers a cautionary note to the hopes placed in the countermonument as an antiredemptory, self-questioning gesture. The majority of visitors to Libeskind's museum, Eisenmann's memorial, or Wilms and Hallmann's Topography of Terror will be city tourists visiting Berlin. They will experience these sites often as part of a guided tour through the vibrant center of a reunified capital city, and they will see them as examples of what has become possible only since reunification. If these memorials testify to the horrific ways in which Germany's history has been aberrant, their monumentality reclaims the mantle of normality for the post-1989 present. They have become part of a memory district similar in appearance to the National Mall in Washington, DC, or Mount Herzl in Jerusalem, with the exception that Berlin's monuments commemorate the state's victims, not its victories.[57] As important as that distinction is, the concentration of massive, permanent edifices dedicated to a memory that should never be forgotten suggests that the monument is here to stay. Indeed, as Young himself has stated, "The countermonument paradoxically reinvigorates the very idea of the monument itself," and the degree to which these memorials attempt to incorporate certain features of other countermonuments suggests he is right.[58] But their simultaneous, contradictory embrace of monumentality suggests that it is time to question the sustainability of countermonuments as moments of resistance and instead acknowledge that they are likely to be assimilated into an authoritative idiom of commemoration.[59]

From the point of view of tourists to Berlin, the new memory district allows the Federal Republic to reclaim its past after forty years of division. Tourists will experience these new central memorials as contiguous with nearby monuments to the German past: the Brandenburg Gate, the Reichstag, the Berlin Cathedral, the Victory Column, and the royal façades on the Unter den Linden boulevard. The exposure to these disparate locales will coalesce into a composite experience of a city that both atones for its wrongs and celebrates its past glories. The centralization of sites of remembrance may actually remove some of the labor necessary to engage in a more exhaustive form of memory work through tourism. There remain those tourists whose itineraries through the city recall the dispersed nature of Holocaust commemoration in Berlin prior to the establishment of a "memory district." There are always tourists willing to venture from the prescribed path.

And there will always be tourists who upset general expectations of decorum and respect. Eisenmann's memorial in particular has become a lightening rod for criticism of badly behaved tourists (and natives) who see the space as a place to play hide-and-seek, to leap from stele to stele, or to attempt to inscribe graffiti. As Young writes, Eisenmann and the memorial anticipated this problem and made changes to the original design to inhibit such behavior, but it continues nonetheless.[60] One German-Jewish artist called attention to the disrespectful activity by superimposing images of tourists playing at the memorial onto scenes of atrocity at the death camps.[61] While it is clear that these tourists are not engaging in reflective remembrance, those who take it upon themselves to protect the memorial are fulfilling the site's aspirations for taking responsibility for memory. What is ironic (but not necessarily improper) in all of this is the way in which misbehavior gets associated with foreign tourists and moral indignation becomes a domestic quality. Here, again, Germany can act out a sense of normality.

Seen in the context of tourism, I doubt whether Berlin's new Holocaust memorials eschew any state-sponsored view of history or avoid privileging the voice of the German state over the silence of the Holocaust's victims. While that may be regrettable, it may also be inevitable. The interpretations of the site are not endless, and over time some readings are likely to establish themselves as dominant, while others will be forgotten. The Jewish Museum, the Topography of Terror, and the Memorial to the Murdered Jews of Europe have undeniably become de facto monuments through which a reunified Germany enunciates its aspirations to itself and its visitors. Whether they are loved or hated, debated or ignored, these new memorials are not the first to commemorate the Holocaust. Perhaps more than symbolizing a line drawn under a troubled past, as Young feared, the diversity of its monuments taken as a whole—some small, some massive; some central, some remote—testifies to the Berlin Republic's willingness to carry on the inquiry into its past. The Holocaust transpired not only in the extermination camps and the mass graves of Eastern Europe but also in villas and office buildings, in local rail stations and in quiet neighborhood streets, on buses and trams. If tourism to Berlin is to continue to inform visitors about the Final Solution, then it must look for Berlin's memory in the ordinary places that are perhaps less spectacular but no less powerful.

5

Jerusalem

The murder of six million Jews was a prime causative factor
in the creation of the state of Israel. This was in accordance
with an ancient and powerful dynamic of Jewish history: redemption through suffering.
—Paul Johnson, *A History of the Jews* (1987)

It is a sunny day as my spouse and I leave our hotel in Jerusalem. After
a ten-minute cab ride, our driver drops us off atop Har ha-Zikaron, the
Mount of Remembrance, a hill that feels like an island of tranquility just
beyond the city's otherwise busy, winding streets. We exit the taxi and
enter a brand new structure of white stone and glass that is the Visitor's
Center of Yad Vashem, Israel's central site for Holocaust commemoration since 1957. The setting is serene, and the quiet that envelops the
hill belies the disturbing images and narratives we know we are going
to encounter inside. I have had this experience before, the strange disjuncture between beautiful natural scenery on the one side and the ugly
artifacts of the Holocaust on the other. My first visit to Auschwitz was
equally sunny, and at Birkenau, the trees and fields enclosed industrialized mass murder in a bucolic frame. But at Yad Vashem the tranquility
suits a place of commemoration in a land that represents survival.

Although Yad Vashem was opened six decades ago, the first building
we see upon arrival looks brand new; in fact, Yad Vashem completed
a massive redevelopment in 2005, of which the new Visitor's Center is
clearly one part.[1] Inside a friendly woman at the counter rents us a self-
guided audio headset that will guide us through the next building in the
memorial complex, the new Holocaust History Museum (the museum is
otherwise free of charge). We reach the museum via a pedestrian bridge
over a gully from the Visitor's Center and enter the side of what appears
to be one end of an elongated, granite prism. Scanning the length of the
building before entering, we note that it bows downward into the ground

in the middle and reemerges upward on the other side of the hilltop.[2] As we enter at the southern end of the structure, our eyes take a minute to become accustomed to the dark interior. On the wall to the left, the interior of the prism's southern end, a grainy video shows people waving and smiling at the camera. Although clearly historical footage, the moving images render the figures life-size, and they seem to be waving effortlessly across time, as if to welcome us—the impression is that we are the curiosity to them, not the other way around. These grainy black-and-white movies depict Jewish life in Europe before 1933: family picnics in the woods, strolls in the park, walks around the yard. We are definitely tourists in their world, being admitted into a time and place that now exists only as a ghostly projection, yet it feels entirely simultaneous with our experience of the building. It's an illusion, but one that makes a point: This is what will be (has been) lost.

The waving figures make us self-conscious that we are tourists, but it feels like we are welcomed as such, not admonished for it. While we certainly expect to encounter an informative exhibition about the murder of six million Jews, it is this unapologetically affective quality of the moving pictures that makes the first impression inside the historical museum. I have developed a thick skin, but not an impervious one, and I feel disarmed by the poignancy of the projected figures who greet us. As an academic familiar with Holocaust representations in memorials, in the arts, and in historiography, I am conditioned to expect sober encounters with the facts of history that eschew sentimentality. Sadness and grief will not bring back the dead, and to indulge in those feelings as a privileged Western traveler who has never felt his life threatened would strike me as somehow self-serving, as though Yad Vashem (and, ergo, the Holocaust) were created to provide me and other tourists with an emotional adventure, not an educational encounter. I want to hold on to my intellectual agenda as armor, and I worry that my emotional responses will be somehow out of place, inappropriate, as if I came looking for a cathartic experience. My study of Berlin's countermonuments and their ambitions (if not their performances) has predisposed me to question cathartic promises of closure. After Yad Vashem, I am instead left wondering, Is there a meaningful role for sentiment in Holocaust memorialization after all? That question motivates this chapter, which explores Yad Vashem's decidedly redemptory narrative and tourists' receptivity to it.

As we enter the galleries, the emotionality of the display is more subdued, but it resurfaces at particular moments. The historical museums'
central corridor—the prism—is lined by two walls that lean inward,
topped with a glass roof running the entire length of the structure and
letting in sufficient daylight to mitigate the hallway's otherwise claustrophobic shape. The odd angles do not result in the disorientation that
Daniel Libeskind's Jewish Museum in Berlin enacts; rather, the linear
form offers numerous vantage points to see from one end to the other.
The building's prismatic form lets in light from above—a transcendental
metaphor that will be repeated. To either side of the central axis are the
galleries, aligned in distinct alcoves, each an exhibition space devoted
to a particular aspect of the Shoah as it unfolds over time and space:
Jewish life in Europe before 1933, the advent of the Third Reich and the
steadily intensified persecution of Jews throughout Europe, the implementation of the Final Solution and the deportations to the ghettos, the
mass shootings in the East, the camps, and the efforts at resistance. Near
the end of the galleries is the Hall of Names. It is Yad Vashem's mission
to record the name of every one of the six million Jewish men, women,
and children who died in the Holocaust and, if possible, to record a brief
biography for each one. That mission may never be fulfilled. At present,
the Hall has collected biographies on 2.7 million of the approximately
4.5 million identified victims, and it provides paperwork to visitors who
may be able to supply information about those not yet recorded.[3] The
hall is circular, with a domed ceiling adorned with photographic portraits of 600 victims, representing "a fraction of the murdered six million," funneling up to a bright sky at the top, as if ascending into heaven.[4]

That gesture of transcendence at the Hall of Names does not mark
the conclusion of the historical museum. There follows one more gallery
devoted to the establishment of the state of Israel. This gallery details the
first displaced persons camps in Europe, the efforts to identify survivors,
and the various destinations of exile for the many Jews who left Europe,
especially those who headed for the British Mandate of Palestine. The
exhibition documents the establishment of kibbutzim and the activism
of Zionist political and social movements, leading to the War of Independence and the Declaration of the State of Israel in 1948. The last video
shows the new state's first prime minister, David Ben-Gurion, speaking
to the Israeli Knesset's first assembly in Tel Aviv in 1949. From there the

Figure 5.1. The gateway to the Holocaust History Museum, whose southern entrance into the side of its massive prism lies across the "Bridge to a Vanished World," September 2013. Photo by the author.

visitor takes a few steps to exit the prism's northern terminus through a wide glass doorway that opens onto a shaded balcony. One walks out onto a stunning scene: a picturesque valley leading out into a sunlit scene of majestic hills covered with cypresses and cedars, a beautiful landscape out to the horizon, with developments visible in the distance.[5] At Yad Vashem, Israel presents itself as a promise fulfilled, a sanctuary from exile and persecution in diaspora and a restored future in an ancient land. Here is a response to the Holocaust that answers death with life, that embeds the memory of the dead in an almost mythic future.

There is much more to Yad Vashem than the Holocaust History Museum. The complex includes an art museum, a children's memorial, a synagogue, numerous outdoor memorials, performance and lecture spaces, and a substantial administrative and research complex. Tourists can choose their own path as they wander from site to site, and they can board a bus at several points that will ferry them back to the Visitor's Center or take them to nearby Mount Herzl, Israel's chief military cemetery and memorial site. But the Holocaust History Museum forms the core of the exhibition and is typically the conduit through which one enters the rest of the complex. The subsequent memorials offer moments to reflect on specific dimensions of the history about which visitors to the museum have just observed. By thus merging the historical exhibit with aesthetic reflections on its contents, the entire complex of Yad Vashem encourages a simultaneous sense of anguish and inspiration among its visitors, not just a numbing accumulation of information or an alienating array of isolated, abstract memorials. If the recent countermonuments of Berlin are intended to draw visitors into an intellectual, open-ended reflection on the past, Yad Vashem instead insists on a clear narrative that can leave only the most hardened soul immune to its emotional impact. Yad Vashem is walking a line as thin as the prismatic corridor of its museum, acknowledging the pain of the irreparable loss of six million while also presenting Israel as the redemption for Jewish suffering.

In its presentation of Israel's foundation as a modern state, there is much that the history museum does not address: the continuity of Jewish life in the territory of Israel for millennia, the history of Israel and Palestine from the Middle Ages through the Ottoman Empire, the decades of colonial rule by Great Britain, the long presence of Muslims and Christians in the same land, the wars that have responded to Israel's establishment, or the racial and ethnic diversity that has so long been a part of the region. Instead, Yad Vashem's museum presents a focused history of the Holocaust as a great rupture in Jewish history that demands redress and to which modern Israel itself is the necessary response. While the Zionist movement for the establishment of a Jewish state originated in Europe in the nineteenth century, well before the Shoah, the arrival of so many Jews who left Europe in the wake of genocide accelerated the realization of the Zionist aim. In 1948, fully half of all Israeli Jews were Holocaust survivors who could no longer believe in a secure life in diaspora.[6] Their role in establishing Israel was as critical as their eventual place in Israeli society's evolution and self-understanding. Yad Vashem in turn tells their story to its visitors, and like Warsaw and Berlin, the presentation of that story to tourists becomes part of a national narrative. This chapter explores the nexus between tourism and Israeli national identity as they intersect at the country's official site of Holocaust remembrance.

Intensely focused, the "ritualized journey" through of Yad Vashem's Museum of Holocaust History tells a singular story to its diverse population of visitors.[7] Tourists to Yad Vashem experience the linear narrative and its redemptive conclusion as a powerful argument for a Jewish state, one whose urgency in the immediate postwar era is hard to deny. Some who tour the museum may come already convinced of the redemptive narrative about Israel they will encounter; alternatively, others may be ignorant of it, and others still will be resistant to it.[8] Some who visit the museum are undertaking a pilgrimage to commemorate the dead, and for them the fallen are martyrs whose sacrifice made the state of Israel possible; for other visitors, no outcome can ease the pain of a loss that remains primarily a private, personal matter. Tour groups include domestic or international school groups with varying degrees of knowledge about, or interest in, the Holocaust. Other groups consists of travelers on guided tours of Jerusalem and Israel, with Yad Vashem but one stop on an expansive itinerary that may otherwise have a focus on Christianity or Islam, rather than Judaism. During our visit, we passed a large group of young conscripts from the Israeli Defense Forces, for whom a visit to Yad Vashem is a regular part of training, intended to remind them why they serve.[9] Regardless of their differences, visitors encounter a redemptive narrative about the land established by Jewish Europe's surviving remnant, precisely what makes Holocaust memorialization at Yad Vashem so distinct.

But as has been noted elsewhere, tourism is a cumulative experience, and tourists to Israel will incorporate their experience of Yad Vashem with their other impressions of Jerusalem or Israel. Very often, the same tourists go to the West Bank; hundreds of Christian pilgrims to Bethlehem cross the wall that divides Jerusalem from the Palestinian territories every day. Jerusalem itself presents a striking image of diversity, particularly in the Old City, where tourists stroll through ancient Jewish, Muslim, and Christian quarters. The fact that people of different ethnicities and faiths dwell in the city seem at odds with the consciousness of the unresolved conflicts between Israel and the Palestinians that dominates media representations of the region. Importing such awareness into Yad Vashem, tourists may struggle to resolve the tension between a redemptive story of Israel's founding and the present-day struggle of Arabs in the region, both Christian and Muslim, for independence. However tourists respond to the narrative of Yad Vashem, they will continue to encounter news of ongoing struggles in the region after the visit, which suggests that whatever sense of redemption the museum evokes is ephemeral in the framework of tourism.

The emphasis on redemption at Yad Vashem stands in stark opposition to the many admonitions in Holocaust studies against any representation of the genocide that appears redemptive.[10] One of those writers about the problem of redemption in Holocaust memory is James E. Young, whose work on German countermonuments forms an exploration of the "art of memory in an antiremdemptory age."[11] As we saw in the previous chapter, Germany's countermonuments are conceived to resist officially sanctioned readings or invite closure; instead, they call for ongoing reflection. Young champions such art as antiredemptory; however, rather than elaborate on the notion of redemption as a project with its own rationale, Young addresses its negation in the countermonument, so that any specification of redemption is at best implied. As the previous chapter outlined, Young regards countermonuments as exemplary for the way in which they "reject traditional forms and reasons for public memorial art, those spaces that either console viewers or redeem such tragic events, or indulge in a facile kind of *Wiedergutmachung* [reparation or compensation], or purport to mend the memory of a murdered people."[12] Furthermore, Young claims as antiredemptory those works that "refuse to assign singular, over-arching meaning to either events or our memory of them."[13] Young's opposition to redemptory representations (and he is by no means alone) can be traced to the earliest responses to the Holocaust articulated by Theodor Adorno. Other prominent scholars like Lawrence Langer, Alvin Rosenfeld, Eva Hoffman, and Geoffrey Hartman have all worried about art that exploits the Holocaust for artistic value.[14] But in recent years, some critics have begun to question the idea of redemption more closely, asking whether it is possible or even desirable to purge it from works of public memory. And as Yad Vashem demonstrates, the rejection of redemption is by no means a universal tenet of Holocaust memorialization.

The remainder of this chapter pursues the problem of redemption in Holocaust memorialization as it applies to tourism at Yad Vashem. First, I elaborate on the term's various meanings, which tend to remain underarticulated, by teasing out some of the different dimensions of the concept as it pertains Holocaust representation. Then I introduce yet another wrinkle to the fabric of redemption in Holocaust memory by recalling how tourism itself has been understood as a redemptive mode of travel, quite independently of the Holocaust. Tourists are in search of experiences that somehow make life more worthwhile, that offer experiences that connect them to other times and other places and thus affirm their place in the world. To link that general observation about tourism to Yad Vashem, I offer a brief history of Yad Vashem, charting how the various strands of redemptive narrative have developed and intertwined over time. By deconstructing the Yad Vashem's redemptive presentation of the Holocaust, it becomes possible to locate other memories that offer a critical foothold for tourists who want to exercise their own critical judgment. To conclude, I examine how Yad Vashem's current representations of the genocide intersect with tourists' search for meaning. How does the notion of tourism as inherently redemptory relate to the notions of redemption that circulate there? Given the overwhelming presence of redemptive narratives at Yad Vashem and within tourism itself, one might conclude that there is little chance for tourists to question the nature of redemption. But by looking at Yad Vashem as a place where different redemptive logics converge, I hope to show that, contrary to concerns about closure and totalizing narratives, the effort to advance a single authoritative, redemptory interpretation of the Holocaust may elude Yad Vashem. But first, what do we mean by redemption?

Unpacking Redemption

In order to better understand tourism and Holocaust memory at Yad Vashem, an effort to define redemption as it relates to Holocaust memory in clearer terms may help disentangle its multiple threads and show how it intersects with other modes of tourism in the region. Borrowing from the insights of other critics, I discern four distinct contexts in which the term "redemption" circulates in Holocaust memory, either as a goal or as a taboo, often without any clarification of how one context informs another: the aesthetic, the cognitive, the political, and the theological. It is the way in which the word "redemption" resonates simultaneously and even contradictorily across these four contexts that makes it both such an appealing, and yet worrisome, concept.

James E. Young's study of the countermonument as antiredemptory exemplifies the first sense of redemption at work in Holocaust memory, the aesthetic. Responding to Young, the philosopher Maeve Cooke summarizes the problem with redemptory art in terms similar to his: "First, it offers compensation for horrific suffering, for example through the pleasure evoked by way of the formal qualities of the work of art. Second, it produces closure by ascribing a singular, overarching meaning to historic events or to our memory of them."[15] Both Young and Cooke trace the argument against redemptive art to Theodor Adorno, who wrote that poetry after Auschwitz is barbaric, meaning that a retreat into the world of aesthetic practice was an unconscionable response to the Holocaust, since such art was itself part of the culture that produced the genocide.[16] After the orchestras at Auschwitz performed Mozart while fellow prisoners marched to their labor details, how can classical Western art absolve itself of its compatibility with genocide? But as both Cooke and Young acknowledge, Adorno did not condemn poetry or art per se; rather, he meant that the conventions of artistic practice would need to change in recognition of the barbarity that emerged in the midst of Western culture.[17] Typically, that agenda has resulted in a preference for artistically avant-garde, challenging works that eschew conventional notions of beauty in favor of austerity, even silence.[18]

While Cooke and Young both acknowledge the problems associated with aesthetic pleasure and master narratives, Cooke rightly points out that Young's aesthetic notion of redemption is underarticulated and, indeed, that much writing on post-Holocaust aesthetics insufficiently explains the term.[19] She calls for "a proper understanding of the idea of redemption [that] helps to avoid the dangers of instrumentalization [i.e., aesthetic pleasure in Holocaust representation] and authoritarianism [i.e., the imposition of a singular meaning on the Holocaust]."[20] Her own contribution to that discussion is to unpack Adorno's understanding of redemption in art, in which she makes very clear a distinction between redemption through aesthetic pleasure, on the one hand, and redemption as cognitive insight, on the other. She faults Young for ignoring the potential of art, including traditional art, to enable cognitive insight, a form of redemption against which Adorno has no objections.[21]

Cooke's view about redemption is shared by Jewish literature and visual culture scholar Brett Ashley Kaplan, whose work on the importance of beauty in Holocaust art offers a careful argument for the relevance of aesthetic pleasure in Holocaust representations. Kaplan's concern is that the doctrine against beauty—that is, aesthetic pleasure—leads to works that are at cross-purposes with themselves and "compromise the pedagogical and emotional aims of these texts, works, or spaces."[22] That is, if the aim of Holocaust memorial art is to teach and simultaneously to encourage sympathy with the victims, austere and self-negating works may instead alienate their audiences. (We saw this tension at work in Libeskind's Jewish Museum, whose deliberately disorienting architecture clashed with the informative intent of its displays.) Cooke concurs, arguing that aesthetically more accessible art invites ethical reflection, too, and that to deny its role in representing the Holocaust is itself a form of the very authoritarianism countermonumental art claims to reject.[23] What both Cooke and Kaplan point out is that aesthetic pleasure and consolation are, in fact, important accompaniments to ethical insight about the Holocaust. And as Cooke persuasively argues, ethical insight is a kind of redemption that Adorno would welcome.[24]

To summarize, Cooke and Kaplan propose that the second kind of redemption, cognitive insight, depends frequently on the possibility of the first—aesthetic pleasure. If one rejects aesthetic pleasure and insists only on cognitive appreciation of the Holocaust, then art is ruled out, leaving one to turn to more "scientific" approaches. Historiography, sociology, and anthropology offer portrayals of the Holocaust that prioritize delivering information over concerns for beauty. Of course, to do so would be to draw too bright a line between representational forms, and whatever the idiom, representation involves aesthetic considerations, even in works that do not announce themselves as art. This point is articulated by the renowned Holocaust historian Saul Friedländer, who survived the genocide while hiding in a Catholic school in France. Friedländer explores the problem of redemption as it affects Holocaust historiography as the historian's effort to "convincingly interpret the past."[25] Friedländer worries that subsuming the Holocaust into a purely rational explanation fails to account for those dimensions of the event that exceed rational comprehension, such as the horror and fear experienced by the victims:[26] "There lies the dilemma of the historian. On the one hand, he cannot but study the 'Final Solution' as any other past phenomenon. The reconstruction of the most detailed sequences of events related to the extermination of the Jews is progressing apace. On the other hand, for some historians at least, an opaqueness remains at the very core of the historical understanding and interpretation of what happened."[27] Opaqueness refers to that which exceeds the capacity of historiography to convey, and historians err, in Friedländer's view, when they fail to acknowledge its presence. By pointing to that which remains unaccounted for in Holocaust historiography, Friedländer hopes to avoid the production of totalizing accounts that explain everything too neatly and invite closure on the event. He rejects the kind of cognition that satisfies itself with factual knowledge while still arguing for the necessity of such knowledge as part of a more holistic, but never completed, engagement with the event.[28] Friedländer embraces the role of aesthetic practice in conveying the Holocaust's troubling affective attributes and sees it as a necessary accompaniment to cognition. He hopes that neither misunderstands itself as ultimately redemptive in the sense of closing off further inquiry.

While Friedländer understandably worries about the redemptive potential inherent in both cognitive and aesthetic representations of the Holocaust, other historians see a place for history as redemptive in that it can *initiate* inquiry. In fact, the case of another historian who wrote from within the event suggests that historiography has an important redemptive role to play in Holocaust memory, both as a source of information and as a persuasive account that moves future generations to learn from the catastrophe. As discussed in chapter 3 on Warsaw, Emanuel Ringelblum and his collective at the Oyneg Shabes archive worked tirelessly throughout the Nazi occupation of Poland to document the history of Jewish life in Poland and its eventual destruction. Watching helplessly as the Germans murdered 400,000 Jews in the Warsaw Ghetto and knowing his own chances for survival were bleak, Ringelblum was motivated to document history because it offered the only promise available to him of achieving some kind of redemption, however partial. To write and preserve the history of his people meant that his death would not be in vain. Determined that lessons should be learned from the calamity befalling his people, Ringelblum viewed history as a necessary teacher that would promote better understanding among peoples; furthermore, as the historian Samuel D. Kassow has so thoroughly documented in his important book on the Oyneg Shabes, it was Ringelblum's hope that the historical record he and his team generated would help bring those who were responsible for the Holocaust to justice.[29] The explanatory capacity of historiography was the vehicle for cognitive insight, but it was not only knowledge for its own sake that Ringelblum sought to preserve. Ultimately, he hoped knowledge and empathy could lead one day to a better politics, one that rejected the kind of prejudice and isolation that had led to the murder of his own people. Redemption would come, not in the form of a totalizing explanation of the event, but in an account that led to a better human society in the future.

In Ringelblum's fusion of redemption as knowledge and subsequent ethical action, he points us to the third sense of redemption: political redemption, understood as restitution, justice, and human rights guaranteed by states. In this political sense, redemption surfaces as the moral compass that drives the pursuit of justice through legal and political means. Political intonations of redemption circulate in the realm of legislation and jurisprudence, manifesting themselves in legal code and case law. Juridical responses to the Holocaust also form a founding principle of the postwar international order that led to the establishment in 1948 of Israel. The young state's trial of Adolf Eichmann in 1961 was not just the trial of one perpetrator and the testimony of dozens of survivors; rather, it was the assertion to the world by Israel of its right to punish the Holocaust's perpetrators in the name of the Jewish victims, to whom Israel had granted posthumous citizenship. Critics may reject redemptory gestures in works of art or in overly rational historical explanations of the Holocaust, but in doing so they are not automatically repudiating the necessity of legal justice. It remains necessary to indemnify survivors and to punish the guilty—although the question of what constitutes a just punishment remains contentious.

Never far from the notion of redemption as the dispensation of justice is the fourth, theological sense of the term. In the wake of the Holocaust, theologians have pondered the implications for how one understands the genocide in relation to ideas about God and justice, wondering how the existence of God can be squared with the perpetration of such evil. Furthermore, how does a post-Holocaust theodicy— that is, "a defence of God in light of evil [sic]"—regard the genocide in the Judaic tradition of a covenant between God and the Jewish people?[30] Some theologians describe the Holocaust as the third *Hurban*, or disaster, in the long course of the history of the Jewish people, preceded by the Babylonian and Roman destructions of the Temple in Jerusalem in 586 B.C.E. and 70 C.E., respectively.[31] Each disaster was incorporated into the perception of Jewish suffering as ultimately re-deemed through the covenant and the memory of future generations. The Judaic tradition of redemption through suffering has led some to frame the Holocaust as the covenantal obligation of the Jewish nation to protect itself from future destruction.[32] Although Zionism began as a largely secular movement responding to political realities of life in diaspora, the theological interpretation of the Holocaust extends a sa-cred obligation to both secular and religious forms of Zionism, making Holocaust memory part of what James E. Young and the Germanist and Holocaust studies scholar Jennifer Hansen-Glucklich describe as a "civil religion," a rite of the state. Yad Vashem is the central institution in which that civil religion is preserved and fostered, entwining politi-cal and theological senses of redemption with the museum's aesthetic and cognitive underpinnings.[33]

At Yad Vashem, tourists encounter all four dimensions of redemp-tion that I have outlined, with the entire complex evoking redemp-tion through aesthetic form, historical knowledge, political response, and transcendental possibility. The history museum's skylights, its con-cluding vista at the end of the central corridor, and nearby, the deporta-tion memorial's train car seemingly destined for the heavens, all suggest the possibility of transcendence amid destruction. The history museum's linear narrative, reinforced by its tunnel-like form, fuses aesthetic form with the fulfillment of its cognitive mission to inform and results in a narrative that leads teleologically from the murder of six million to the establishment of Israel. Aesthetics also merge with political redemption through Yad Vashem's use of landscape and architecture. The memo-rial complex incorporates the natural environment most explicitly in the Garden of the Righteous among Gentiles and along the Path of Re-membrance and Reflection, so that the land and the built structures of the memorial complex form a coherent whole. With its use of the bright limestone and concrete that typifies modern Jerusalem, Yad Vashem's new architecture renders the Holocaust an organic part of the natural and built environments of present-day Israel, even though it commem-orates events that happened far away.[34] Meanwhile, the architectural metaphors of transcendence subsume the Holocaust into a divine order, with implications for how Jews conceive of their covenant with God in the post-Holocaust era. The Holocaust History Museum's concluding exhibition about the establishment of the Israeli state easily blends with a theological view that sees the state as the practical fulfillment of the divine imperative to survive and even to thrive. The location of Yad Vashem adjacent to Israel's primary military cemetery and memorial on Mount Herzl further underscores the fusion between art, historiography, religion, and politics as redemptive projects and suggests that one mode of redemption legitimates all the others.

Figure 5.2. The view of the hills of Jerusalem from the northern end of the Holocaust History Museum, September 2013. Photo by the author.

I have highlighted the multiple connotations inherent in the concept of redemption because they open up a useful avenue for understanding the tourist's experience at Yad Vashem. The awareness of redemption as complex and multifarious is vital for retaining a critical perspective when visiting Yad Vashem, if for no other reason than because the museum presents an overwhelming, uninterrupted vision of redemption to its visitors that appears to resolve any ambiguity among its multiple valences.[35] Rather than highlight the differences between a political notion of redemption and an aesthetic, epistemological, or theological one, the museum synthesizes them into a cohesive, seamless unity. Any recognition by tourists of redemption as a complex notion that might include contradictions has to come from other sources, whether from other sites in Israel, or through one's own reading and study prior to the tour, or even through one's attitude toward participation in a guided tour. Tourism is an exchange, even if it is managed by agencies that try to position visitors as passive receivers of a managed experience. But tourists actively construct their experiences and adapt them to their own agendas. Tourists at Yad Vashem will inevitably negotiate the redemptive narratives of the museum with their own expectations and experiences. No matter how compelling the redemptive narrative of Yad Vashem may seem, it remains subject to challenges, revisions, even misunderstandings by tourists. What's more, tourism possesses its own redemptive logic quite separate from any concerns about Judaism, the Holocaust, or Israel, and the experiences visitors construct may or may not conform to the vision of redemption on display at Yad Vashem or anywhere else.

Tourism as Redemptive Journey

An easy way to make the argument that tourism is inherently redemptive would be to characterize all of its variations as pilgrimage or education, each of which has its own fairly transparent redemptive logic and each of which informs the history of tourism. In the first case, travel promises the renewal of one's faith, while in the second case travel emancipates its participants from the bonds of ignorance. But a stronger argument for tourism's inherently redemptive capacity would also include travel framed as pleasure: 3S tourism ("sea, sand, and sun"), urban sightseeing, camping, and so forth. That line of argument has been a mainstay of tourism studies, articulated by the anthropologists Dean MacCannell, Nelson Graburn, Malcolm Crick, and others who see tourism as a response to the disenchantment of everyday life in the modern era. In a post-Enlightenment world in which religion is no longer the central organizing principle of society, more secularly oriented forms of travel, even for pleasure, offer a substitute to religious pilgrimage.[36] Indeed, rest and fun become urgent ways to redeem a sense of self in an increasingly industrialized, global world that regards individuals as replaceable employees or anonymous members of mass society.[37] Tourists are in search for something extraordinary, if not explicitly transcendental, that points to life's meaning beyond the everyday routine.

When the Grand Tour emerged in the seventeenth century, the educational value of tourism was articulated in the West as the cultural maturation of the bourgeois, usually male traveler, who perfected his mastery of foreign languages, appreciated works of art and architecture, and impressed upon his hosts his own civilized bearing. Tourism's promises of redemption through education have never been innocent of its colonizing tendencies, and even contemporary forms of travel that frame themselves in terms of sustainability or humanitarian aide are caught up in debates about their own complicity with global capitalism and cultural hegemony.[38] Nevertheless, tourism continues to draw participants who believe in a shared humanity across all its diversity and see in travel an antidote to the ignorance that fuels violence and bloodshed.[39] The recurrence of genocide around the world after the Holocaust may make such dreams appear naïve and self-serving, especially to tourism's skeptics, but the fact remains that individuals still value travel as a transformative experience that helps bring the world closer together.[40] For example, Jackie Feldman's study of Israeli tour groups to Poland consistently reveals the belief of participants that they have undergone a transformative experience, measurable in part in a stronger sense of national identity, and even have an increasing willingness to serve in the Israeli military in order to secure peace and stability for Israel and its neighbors.[41]

More recently, the theory of "dark tourism" has offered a somewhat different account of the redemptive rationale for travel, especially as it pertains to sites of disaster. The dark tourism scholars Malcolm Foley and J. John Lennon argue that travel to places of calamity allows tourists to reconcile everyday life with pervasive representations of a chaotic world in the media.[42] Developing their theory in part by looking at sites of Holocaust perpetration, Foley and Lennon argue that dark tourism lures travelers who hope to resolve the tension between media representations of deadly events and their own sense of reality. While recognizing the redemptive motivations behind "dark tourists," the theory of dark tourism is rather skeptical about the fulfillment of such expectations, ultimately suggesting that the tourism industry is too susceptible to inauthenticity to offer any meaningful reconciliation with disaster.[43]

The skepticism concerning Holocaust-themed travel to Poland expressed by Feldman in chapter 3, and by Foley and Lennon about Holocaust tourism more generally, is an important reminder to distinguish between tourism's promise of redemptive experience, on the one hand, and its fulfillment, on the other. Although Feldman takes travelers seriously when they describe transformational experiences, he carefully argues that the structure of the tour may lead to foregone conclusions rather than to critical reflection.[44] Foley and Lennon tend to position tourists as uninformed travelers who are prone to believe in inauthentic representations of events that the tourism industry produces.[45] Tourists are too diverse to portray in such reductive terms, but it is nevertheless worthwhile to wonder whether tourists to Yad Vashem are not particularly susceptible to its Zionist narrative of redemption, given the appetite for redemption that motivates many of its visitors, and to ask about the critical potential of tourism at a place whose redemptive logic is so pervasive.

Dark tourism's contention that tourist sites embrace inauthenticity has little value in characterizing Yad Vashem. The memorial site's documentary displays, its archival and educational resources, and its commemorative events are indispensible sources of knowledge about the Holocaust, and they form one of the pillars of global Holocaust awareness. The museum presents a perspective on the Holocaust that is fundamental to Israel's raison d'être, providing a valuable lesson to visitors from abroad about the way in which the Holocaust informs present-day national identity in Israel. Certainly visitors to Yad Vashem have the opportunity to deepen their knowledge about the Holocaust, to consider some explanations as to how or why it occurred, and to encounter an Israeli national perspective on the event. The risk I would highlight is that the very authenticity of Yad Vashem may convince tourists to adopt its redemptive narrative wholesale and without question. If the problem with redemptory memorials stems from the concern that they will do the memory work for us, then the same concern must apply to Yad Vashem. Compared to those countermonuments in Berlin that aim to pose questions about the history they represent, Yad Vashem is not countermonumental. It embeds the Holocaust in an authoritative national framework to advance a clear message about the genocide and its aftermath. But such monumentality does not undermine the worth of a visit there; rather, it serves as a reminder that redemptive narratives play a critical role in Holocaust remembrance in Israel and elsewhere that grew out of particular historical circumstances. The evolution of Yad Vashem reveals a complicated history behind today's redemptory installation, a history that sheds light on the motivations and decisions that led to the redemptory experience that is its hallmark today.

History of Yad Vashem

The complicated history of Yad Vashem shows how the memorial site has developed in tandem with the modern state of Israel, reflecting the growing pains of the new state. By analyzing the history of Yad Vashem along with Israel's own formation, several writers have shown how the memorial has contextualized the Holocaust in different ways at different times, revealing tensions that have been inherent in Israeli Holocaust remembrance since the state's founding. Holocaust memory has not always been the cornerstone of an Israeli identity, nor has its reception by the public ever been uniform.[46] Israeli identity, like identity elsewhere, is hardly monolithic or static, and the history of Yad Vashem reveals the dynamic nature of Holocaust memory within Israel. As Israel has wrestled with how to incorporate the trauma of genocide into its collective identity, the foregrounding of suffering during the Holocaust and its redemption in modern Israel emerges only later at Yad Vashem.

Even though nearly half of all Israeli Jews in 1948 were Holocaust survivors, their story was greeted with ambivalence in public discourse during the country's founding years.[47] For a new state that had fought a war to establish itself, the memory of victimization in Europe during the Holocaust seemed less conducive to forging a positive new national identity than the heroic return to the land of Israel after two millennia of dias-pora.[48] The memory of the Holocaust in public discourse was subdued for decades, for the survivors who came to Israel were too traumatized about their experiences to speak or too focused on beginning a new life to dwell on the past.[49] Awareness of the trauma was never far beneath the surface, but it was spoken of in private, and survivors were frequently silent about their ordeals even with family members.[50] For the broader public, Holocaust memory evoked a sense of shame—why was there not more resistance like the Warsaw Ghetto Uprising of 1943? Why did Jews in the camps not fight back against their vastly outnumbered captors? Why did Jews in other parts of the world fail to provide more help? Such questions were uncomfortable reminders of diaspora and disunity at a time when Israel was consciously forging a collective future.

As Hansen-Glucklich documents, the idea for establishing a memo-rial in Jerusalem to the suffering of Europe's Jews had been conceived as early as 1942—the same year of the Wannsee Conference and the first mass deportations from the Warsaw Ghetto to the Operation Reinhard extermination camps.[51] News of the destruction of Jewish life in Europe had by then reached the Jews in Palestine and elsewhere around the world, who actively sought in vain to engage allies in putting an end to the destruction. Like Emanuel Ringelblum and the Oyneg Shabes in Warsaw, Jews in Palestine recognized the need to record the suffering in Europe for posterity. After the defeat of Germany in 1945, Jewish organi-zations could pursue their efforts to commemorate the genocide within the British Mandate more openly, since the threat of a Nazi invasion of Palestine had been crushed. Despite interruptions of the planning efforts during Israel's 1948 War of Independence, the planning commission en-trusted with developing a proposal continued its work, culminating in the 1953 law proclaiming the establishment of Yad Vashem. Ten years after the Warsaw Ghetto Uprising and five years after the founding of Israel, the law called for the establishment of an expansive facility that included a museum and an archive for collecting, preserving, and pre-senting information about the murdered Jews. It also conceived of the site as a place of education, of pilgrimage, and of artistic expression. A cornerstone-laying ceremony was held the following year.[52]

Even in these early founding years, public commemoration of the Holocaust, to the degree that it occurred, was cast in heroic terms.

Holocaust memory emphasized acts of resistance and cast the victims as martyrs whose bloodshed would be honored by Israel, not as power-less victims who died in the most abject of conditions. We can hear the insistence on heroism in the words of Mordecai Shenhavi, a Galician Jew who had emigrated to Palestine in 1920 and was one of the early propo-nents of the Yad Vashem memorial:[53]

> The power of our martyred brothers' and sisters' heroism arises and bursts forth from the [scene of the] crime and the devastation. The heroism of the Jewish mother, the steadfastness of the ghetto fighters, our people's participation in the underground armies in all the occupied countries— can it be that they will remain just an oral legend? Or shall we erect a monument to Jewish heroism, one that will symbolize our people's will to live and fight and will underscore its ability to endure the most severe and bitter trials that human history has ever decreed upon a nation?[54]

Even the 1953 law itself emphasizes heroism in its full name, "The Holocaust Remembrance and Heroism Law—Yad Vashem, 5713–1953." The desire to present the victims as heroes ran counter to the perception of many in Israel, particularly young Jews, that the six million victims had gone to their deaths "like sheep to the slaughter."[55]

Indeed, the incarnation of Yad Vashem that opened to the public in 1957 spoke in expressly heroic terms. It "focused on Jewish resistance in the Warsaw ghetto, the uprisings in Sobibór and Treblinka extermination camps, and the struggle of the survivors to get to Palestine. The first les-son has been that the Holocaust is the primary reason Israel must exist, the second that modern Jews are not like those who went so unresisting into the gas chambers."[56] The historian Tim Cole describes the way the former Holocaust history museum guided its visitors along a distinctly heroic narrative pathway.[57] The tour began at the memorial to the heroes of the Warsaw Ghetto Uprising of 1943, featuring duplicates of Nathan Rapoport's relief sculptures that appear on his memorial in the Warsaw Ghetto (the Warsaw Ghetto Square and Wall of Remembrance remain in place today). Cole affirms the observations of Young, who noted in 1993 that the early memorial's "official route for visitors begins with the 'Avenue of the Righteous Gentiles,' a promenade lined with trees planted by non-Jews to honor their rescue of survivors during the war. The end of the walk is crowned with a very small, fragile-looking rowboat used by Danish fishermen to ferry some six hundred Jews out of . . . Nazi-occupied Denmark on the eve of their roundup. Just beyond the boat, the memory path leads up a short flight of steps, from Gentile to Jewish heroism, into the Warsaw Ghetto Square."[58] The emphasis on heroism, even that of Gentiles, overshadowed the massacre of Jewish victims.

The Israeli public's attitude about Holocaust memory began to change in the 1960s. As in West Germany, where prominent trials of SS perpetrators brought the suppressed knowledge of the Holocaust back into the public arena in 1963, it was the 1961 trial of Adolf Eichmann that marked a shift in Holocaust memory in Israel, where survivors told their stories in a highly public way and brought attention to the immense suffering and the relative pointlessness of heroism as a way to understand the fate of most victims. With the Eichmann trial, which captured worldwide attention, Israel's pursuit of justice in the name of the murdered six million allowed the narrative of Jewish suffering to emerge alongside the national rhetoric of strength and resistance. As the theologian Mark H. Ellis argues, the surprising and decisive victory of Israeli forces over neighboring Arab aggressors during the Six-Day War in 1967 allowed for more space for the recognition of Jewish suffering during the Holocaust, which was now answered by modern Israel's military superiority and its demonstrated ability to safeguard the Jewish people as a sovereign nation. The juxtaposition of the Eichmann trial and Israel's military successes drew a bright line between victims in the Holocaust and victors in the Sinai, both of which were now very publicly in view.[59]

The sense that Israel had survived attempted annihilation in the Six-Day War made it possible to address the Holocaust in a way that had not been conceivable before. After the 1973 Yom Kippur War, which saw many more Israeli casualties, Yad Vashem itself marked this shift. As Tim Cole puts it, "The war in 1973 had a profound impact upon Israeli national consciousness, with high losses—more than 2,500 dead in one month—leading to a questioning of traditional images of national heroism."[60] The insistence on heroism began to waiver, Cole argues, and the recognition of martyrdom stepped increasingly into its place. In 1973, twenty years after the law establishing the memorial and the same year as the Yom Kippur War, Yad Vashem finally opened a museum that housed a permanent exhibit on the history of the Holocaust.

As we have seen in the previous chapters, worldwide interest in the Holocaust only grew stronger, beginning in the 1960s and picking up considerable speed by the early 1980s. Yad Vashem kept pace with that development, as Hansen-Glucklich writes:

> In 1973 a museum containing a more permanent exhibition was inaugurated. Increasingly over the years, Yad Vashem's complex of Holocaust museum and memorials has expanded substantially across its forty-five-acre site. The grounds of Yad Vashem now contain a number of memorials and monuments dedicated to particular groups of victims and heroes, including the *Pillar of Heroism*, the *Monument to Soldiers, Ghetto Fighters, and Partisans*; the *Valley of the Communities*; the *Memorial to the Deportees*; a memorial to Janusz Korczak and the children of the Warsaw Ghetto; and the *Children's Memorial*. By the beginning of the 1990 it became clear that the main exhibition building was inadequate and outdated, and on March 15, 2005, the new Holocaust History Museum was dedicated, designed by Moshe Safdie and Associates and occupying four times the size of the former Yad Vashem.[61]

Several of the newer memorials Hansen-Glucklich mentions are explicitly focused on the suffering of the victims. The memorial to the deportees is a boxcar on a rail bridge that suddenly ends over a ravine, suggesting simultaneous doom and transcendence, as the boxcar stands poised either to fall or to ascend into the sky. The Children's Memorial and the memorial to Janusz Korczak (the Jewish educator from Warsaw who elected to accompany Jewish children to their deaths at Treblinka) are heartbreaking sites that mourn lives barely lived. Young sees in the memorialization of children in particular an important shift in the emphasis on victimhood as opposed to heroism: "For in their innocence, their unrealized potential, and as symbols of the next, never-to-be-born generation, children continue to represent the victim-ideal."[62] Children who were denied future citizenship in Israel became appealing symbols for grounding the legitimacy of Israel in victimization, while avoiding the sense of shame that the early emphasis on heroism at Yad Vashem appeared to resist.

In their historical overviews of Yad Vashem, Hansen-Glucklich, Young, Cole, and others make clear that the today's redemptive narrative, whereby the victims of the Holocaust become martyrs for the new state of Israel *avant la lettre*, has been anything but straightforward. I am skeptical, though, that visitors touring the site have the opportunity to develop that same historical awareness in the framework of the tour. Hansen-Glucklich suggests that Yad Vashem cannot help but recall its own history through its geographical placement in Jerusalem, a city that is itself saturated with historical awareness. She notes that the architect Moshe Safdie's new Visitor's Center at Yad Vashem, although very modern, reiterates the architectural idiom of the rest of the city in its use of Jerusalem limestone, thereby evoking Jerusalem's own layered history.[63] The predominance of off-white stone in Jerusalem is the result of careful planning by urban developers and constitutes one of the city's most stunning features, allowing the old and the new to converge architecturally into a unified whole.[64] Jerusalem itself, Hansen-Glucklich argues, is a palimpsest—that is, a "layered topography" that builds new structures upon older, preexisting ones.[65] She acknowledges that "many cities have been metaphorically described as palimpsests," and indeed, Berlin and Warsaw provide further examples of layered topographies. But, she argues, "In the case of Jerusalem it is an especially fitting image, calling forth as it does the image of a city displaying a paradoxical temporality."[66] The notion of a paradoxical temporality refers to the ways in which various features of the built environment harken to different eras in Jerusalem's past, recalling its history under Jewish, Roman, Christian, and Muslim kingdoms and empires over the centuries. Still, it is a tall order for the architecture of the Visitor's Center and other new structures to invoke history as paradoxical temporality. While it may resonate with Jerusalem's rich past, the awareness of paradox and discord is, I would argue, elided at Yad Vashem by a fusion of old and new, of the built and the natural environments, that seems to blend paradox into harmony. To reveal a more complex view of the past to the tourists who visit the memorial and museum, the vague impression of historicity imparted by Yad Vashem's architecture would require the accompaniment of a consciously crafted historical narrative that engages tourists in the specificities of Holocaust remembrance in Israel over the last six decades. Such an understanding of Yad Vashem's process of development and its reflection of Israel's complex history would offer a potent corrective to the otherwise unrelenting narrative of national redemption that tourists encounter there.

By obscuring its own story of becoming, Yad Vashem diminishes the potential for tourists to appreciate the rich past that writers about the memorial complex have so successfully conveyed to their readers. Instead of unsettling their assumptions, tourists may leave with an oversimplified view of the Holocaust as a collective trauma adequately answered by the founding of Israel, despite the intentions of the museum to keep memory work alive. Most tourists will only engage with the site for a few brief hours, so any perception of the site's historical layers largely depends on the degree to which they will have informed themselves about the history of Holocaust remembrance in Israel. Materials at Yad Vashem's bookstore and website certainly make such information readily available, but the guided tour itself focuses on the details of Holocaust history rather than on the history of its remembrance in Israel. The fused narratives of Holocaust remembrance and the modern state's founding make the ability to question the redemptory messaging at Yad Vashem more difficult.[67] There is little space—literally—for the tourist to step outside the redemptive narrative, to question it, and to appreciate the complexities inherent in the concept of redemption and how the past is mobilized for the present.

While I would like to see more of its own history on display, I and other tourists are not solely dependent on Yad Vashem to learn about the site. Some will have been to Yad Vashem before and seen its earlier incarnations; others will have read about it or may feel inspired to do so after visiting. All of which is to reiterate that tourists do not experience particular sites as hermetically sealed containers of experience; rather, they weave them into broader impressions of the city they visit, placing one site in dialogue with other, and in the process reaching conclusions that may or may not conform to any given site's apparent message. To conclude this chapter, I explore the ways tourists may produce their own meanings of Yad Vashem.

Challenging Redemption in Tourism

Another way to phrase my concern is to compare Yad Vashem's redemptive narrative with the nature of memory at the Auschwitz-Birkenau Memorial and Museum and with the antiredemptive intentions of the countermonuments in Berlin. As noted in the first chapter, the memorial at Auschwitz-Birkenau lays bare its own history to tourists, almost by necessity. As a site of perpetration, camp memorials necessarily alter the space they are in charge of remembering, and the transparency by which the Auschwitz-Birkenau Memorial and Museum undergoes a continual process of restoration and incorporates images and narratives about its past helps tourists acquire a sense of authenticity in their visit in spite of the changes since liberation. Archeology is both a metaphor and a reality of memory at Auschwitz, recovering layers of evidence in an ongoing process of unearthing the past. Of course, Yad Vashem is not a site of perpetration, so the terrain does not present itself as an artifact of the Holocaust; rather, it signifies its aftermath. As we have seen, that aftermath has been shaped by shifting needs of public memory over time, not only in Israel but also in Germany, Poland, and, as we will see in the next chapter, the United States. If the geography of Yad Vashem itself is not answerable to an archeological mission of discovery, it nevertheless embeds knowledge of the Holocaust in a narrative that did not emerge instantaneously and that has its own metaphorical depths, despite the appearance of an almost seamless integration into modern Israel's landscape. By linking these two different sites, Holocaust tourism engages Yad Vashem and Auschwitz in a process of dialogue, which is in fact carried out both by the partnerships their administrations pursue and by the comparisons inevitably made by those who visit both.[68]

Berlin offers another point of contrast to the redemptive logic of Yad Vashem, and in considering both places, tourists may reach their own conclusions about which they prefer. While Yad Vashem's embrace of redemption has everything to do with Israel as the home of the victims of the Holocaust, German memorials speak from the opposite perspective. As memorializations from the nation that perpetrated the Holocaust, countermonuments make sense as efforts to avoid redemptory interpretations of the past. Instead, Berlin's countermonuments aim to evoke the complexity of memory by calling attention to their own status as aesthetic responses to historical trauma. The artists who conceptualize them try to avoid the authoritative gesture of traditional monuments that redeem the past within a collective narrative, in part by acknowledging and resisting art's own redemption of trauma through aesthetic practice. Whether they are ultimately successful in escaping a redemptive interpretation is questionable, but the manner in which countermonuments invite questions certainly offers critical space for the viewer to challenge whatever narrative they see on display. Compared to Gunter Demnig's *Stolpersteine* or Renate Stih and Frieder Schnock's installation on the Nuremberg Laws in Berlin's Bayerischer Platz, the undaunted embrace of an official, redemptive narrative at Yad Vashem stands boldly in the more classic monumental tradition. If, as proponents of the counter-monument have claimed, the problem of traditional monuments is their tendency toward redemption as historical closure, then it is fair to ask why that same tendency is tolerated at Yad Vashem. If the event itself is to be understood by future generations as ultimately irredeemable, then they must see in Yad Vashem a violation of that principle. If, however, redemption is ultimately unavoidable in trying to understand the Holocaust, then countermonuments are susceptible to the same pitfalls they self-consciously try to avoid. Perhaps even the taboo against redemptory representations in Germany is worth questioning, to the degree that Germany's search for normality, itself a search for redemption, can incorporate ongoing engagement with its past.[69]

The contested nature of redemption in Holocaust representation points to a tension between two admirable goals that are add odds with one another. On the one hand, one wishes for non-redemptive representations as a way to avoid closure and continue the work of collective memory. On the other hand, one wishes for redemption in the form of sympathy and historical understanding as ways to prevent future suffering. As Maeve Cooke and Brett Ashley Kaplan have suggested, perhaps the dichotomy is overstated and the real challenge is to find a way to make room for the redemptive tendencies of art and historical knowledge without closing off the inquiry that produces them. Yad Vashem illustrates the power redemptive narratives have to shape Holocaust remembrance. Were it to incorporate more self-reflective moments in its own displays, Yad Vashem could enact that tension between redemptory and antiredemptory representations in a way that would certainly enhance its visitors' engagement, if for no other reason than it would increase the range of narratives to which visitors might respond.

While I am skeptical that the powerfully redemptive narrative at Yad Vashem affords tourists much insight into the complicated history of Holocaust remembrance in Israel, there are always ways in which tourism preserves a space for questioning. Even when the experience of the guided tour can seem like an overpowering sensory experience of images and sounds, tourists are not automatons empty of agency. The audio tour, for example, is self-guided, and the individual tourist may choose which explanations to listen to and which to omit. The prescribed route through Yad Vashem may be mapped out, but tourists do not necessarily follow that path, whether by choice or by error; furthermore, they elect which displays they will study more closely and which they will encounter more cursorily. Tourists may follow a guide certified by Yad Vashem or arrive with a guide they have hired on their own who may supplement the tour with an account of changing Israeli perspectives on the Holocaust's memory. The notion of the "reverse gaze," explored in chapter 2, indicates that tourists are also always watching one another, with their attention never solely on the exhibition but, rather, refracted through an ongoing negotiation of the space populated with other tourists. The result can be a multiplicity of interpretations that exceed, and even undermine, the Israeli national framework.

In his thorough study of Holocaust memorialization, the Israeli anthropologist Jackie Feldman describes how the company of other tourists may lead visitors to multiple understandings, some of which may differ dramatically from those the site intends. "The understandings of Yad Vashem are, of course, not determined solely by the shaping of its space. The social context of the visit (school, group of survivors, military unit, new immigrants, diplomats, tourists, etc.), the narration of the guide, and the previous experience of the visitors generate different interpretations of the site."[70] A deeper appreciation of the ways in which the tourism is an ongoing process of multi-lateral negotiations reminds us that no monument is in complete control of its interpretation—including, as I argued in the previous chapter, the countermonument.

When the tourist is reintroduced into the equation, the formal qualities inherent in a memorial space surrender their semiotic autonomy to the meaning making ambitions of travelers. Yad Vashem's redemptive narrative may provide a ready-made memory of Holocaust history for tourists to take home, but that memory will be colored by the personal redemptive expectations tourists already bring to the site, some of which may not advance the same understanding about the Holocaust that Yad Vashem promotes. For example, a significant portion of tourists at Yad Vashem are Christians on a pilgrimage to the Holy Land. As the Jewish theology and museum studies scholar Avril Alba has elaborated, a Christian understanding of redemption is not necessarily troubled by Yad Vashem, whose own invocations of redemption Alba sees rooted in Judaic theology. Alba documents the ways in which Judaic and Christian traditions of redemption share important similarities and origins, but history reminds us that those similarities did not prevent the centuries-long persecution of Jews by Christians. Given the expansiveness and transportability of the notion of redemption, Yad Vashem is vulnerable to interpretations that universalize the suffering of the Holocaust in ways that exceed a specifically Jewish or Israeli narrative. Redemption as the search for understanding one's own place in the world may be an unavoidable element of museum going and site seeing, even if institutions set out to challenge any closure tourists may seek. Perhaps it would be better to combine Yad Vashem's narrative of the Holocaust as redeemed by the establishment of Israel with more frank questions about the difficult nature of redemption itself or a presentation showing how Israel has wrestled with its own memory of the Nazi genocide. Left too untroubled, some tourists will inevitably find redemption on their own terms and move on.

The search for redemption and its encouragement by Yad Vashem points to the important struggle between understanding the Holocaust as a specific, unique event that victimized the Jewish people and a universal challenge to notions of humanity. If a balance must be struck between the accommodation of redemption in Holocaust representation and the resistance to cheaply cathartic or totalizing accounts, then perhaps that replicates the balance that is so hard to strike between particular and universal understandings of the Holocaust. I suspect that, like the problem of redemption, that balance is an unattainable ideal that nevertheless keeps Holocaust remembrance alive. There can be no resolution to those dilemmas that banish either redemption or universalism without rendering the Holocaust as beyond comprehension, an event that offers no opportunities for imagining a better future. Yad Vashem refuses that kind of nihilism, even as its visitors test its redemptive narrative with their own interpretations.

6

Washington, DC

This museum is not an answer. It is a question mark. If there
is a response, it is a response in responsibility.
—Elie Wiesel, speaking at the dedication of the United
States Holocaust Memorial Museum, April 22, 1993

I paid my first visit to the United States Holocaust Memorial Museum
(USHMM) in 1994, one year after it had opened to the public. As a grad-
uate student of German literature, I viewed going to the museum as both
a personal and a disciplinary obligation, which somehow separated me
from the crowds of tourists I expected to share the space with (or so I
thought at the time). I made a point of arriving early to beat the multitude of expected visitors and soon found myself in a large, generous
space that was far from packed with tourists. I was standing in the Hall
of Witnesses, a space that was several stories tall and illuminated by skylights far above. The building's postmodern design evoked a historical
nod to the nineteenth-century and early twentieth-century industrial
era, when brick, steel, and glass were the new vocabulary in architecture
but were now arranged in a somewhat disorienting way that separated
form from function. The expansive room was reminiscent of rail stations
and factories, and shapes cut into the walls looked like train cars or trol-
leys in silhouette.

While the reference to the machinery of death at the Nazi concentra-
tions camps was obvious, I appreciated that the museum had chosen to
acknowledge its distance from actual sites of killing by referring to them
suggestively rather than replicating them.[1] At the same time, I found
the Hall of Witnesses something of an indulgence, feeling surprised
that a museum dedicated to the Holocaust was not saturated with exhibition materials from the outset. I both admired and was put off by
the postmodern ornamentation of the space, which seemed to convert
images from the concentration camps into aesthetic flourishes. I found

Figure 6.1. The Hall of Witnesses at the United States Holocaust Memorial Museum, with its steel girders and brick walls, as seen from the exhibition level, August 2015. Photo by the author.

myself thinking much more about the building than about the Holocaust; I even felt a sense of relief that I could ponder architecture rather than mass murder. The fact that the space was not overly crowded enhanced my initial sense of being spared from the instantly claustrophobic experience I had been expecting.

The next space in the museum's path revealed the Hall of Witnesses to have been a transitional space, a conceptual "air lock" that brought me in from the outside of touristy Washington, DC, and introduced me to a new atmosphere before letting me proceed. With other visitors, I rode to the third floor of the museum in a large elevator, where a speaker transmitted a voice recording of an American soldier describing a scene he encountered in Germany in 1945. The camp was Ohrdruf, a sub-camp of Buchenwald that was famously inspected by General Dwight D. Eisenhower in the company of journalists. Dread replaced relief as the elevator doors opened onto the main exhibition space, which was darker than the Hall of Witnesses, with more narrow display spaces and visitors in closer proximity to one another. Here began the kind of confrontation with history that I was both dreading and, obviously, seeking.

Among the lasting impressions I have of my first visit is the recollection of the museum as a place that demanded a lot of reading from me. Yes, there were plenty of images and video displays throughout, often at awkward angles over half-walls to obscure them from small children who perhaps should not be in the museum in the first place.[2] The difficulty of comfortably seeing the images redirected my attention to the text that accompanied them. Instead of staring at something that I could only respond to in horror, I resorted to the explanatory texts, hoping to read some satisfactory description of what I saw, something that would make the senselessness shown to me more sensible. At the very least, the words grounded the atrocious scenes within a historical framework, and I could begin to associate the images with a familiar narrative of Nazi brutality.[3] But the explanations were never adequate or commensurate to the scenes—and somehow I felt that was the point.

Other spaces followed: the section devoted to Jewish life in Europe, particularly the *shtetl*, and the Tower of Faces, a room whose walls displayed photographs of individuals from the town of Eisiskes in Lithuania, whose Jewish population was murdered by one of the Einsatzgruppen in 1941. Their faces demanded to be remembered as individuals, but their display en masse served to recall the far larger number of victims whose faces and stories are lost to history. (I was later to see a similar display at Yad Vashem's Hall of Names, although the photos there were couched in the redemptive symbolism of transcendence, winding gently

Figure 6.2. The Tower of Faces in the United States Holocaust Memorial Museum, August 2015, showing the Jewish residents of the town of Eisiskes, Lithuania, who were murdered in 1941. Photo by the author.

upward toward brightness overhead; the USHMM's Tower of Faces, by contrast, was square and narrow and seemed like the interior of a large chimney—surely by design.) Later came the cattle car on the second floor, through which one could walk quite by oneself, in contrast to the cruelly packed transports that the deportees had to endure. Finally, near the end of the exhibition on the first floor, visitors sat and listened to filmed testimony by survivors before entering the open space of the Hall of Remembrance, a hexagonal room that felt like sacred space, devoid of any documentation, with an eternal flame and places to sit and reflect. As I entered this sanctuary, I welcomed the opportunity to think about what I had just seen and read and to compare my expectations of the museum with the informative and, I thought, sensitive character of the exhibition I had just experienced.

Although some aspects of the exhibit struck me as too staged, I came away from the visit with a largely positive response to the exhibit, and my subsequent visits have reaffirmed my positive assessment, mirroring the views of many visitors today. The website TripAdvisor includes over 6,600 rated reviews of the museum, with 80 percent of the reviews calling the museum "excellent" and 14 percent "very good." Only 1.7 percent of visitors report that the museum was either "poor" or "terrible"; of the negative reviews, most address issues of access to the popular museum—the difficulty of obtaining tickets or the necessity of passing through security checkpoints.[4] Some laud the museum but complain about fellow tourists—a phenomenon one can almost guarantee at any tourist site, but that takes on sharper contours in the context of Holocaust tourism, as discussed in chapter 2. The positive reviews, in the vast majority, praise the care taken by the museum in crafting a presentation of the Holocaust that promoted reflection. While many visitors record their emotional responses to their visit ("depressing," "horrific," "very moving"), they usually see affect as a bridge toward deeper thought and an appreciation of difference. The comments of tourists suggest that they take heed of the museum's words displayed at the exit: "Think about What You Saw."

Perhaps the museum's final admonition to its visitors seems trite, intoning what should be a self-evident task to any museumgoer, let alone a visitor to a Holocaust museum. But beyond stating the obvious, the USHMM's parting words strike me as a conscious effort to resist the fleeting attention span often associated with tourism, which may encourage some visitors to engage with the Holocaust only for the duration of the tour, leaving reflection behind at the exit as they leave. To resist such a tendency, the museum's final admonition invokes the Jewish tradition of memory as the intergenerational bond that has allowed Judaism to survive for millennia in diaspora, reiterated since the Holocaust in the

Figure 6.3. The parting words of the United States Holocaust Memorial Museum to visitors exiting the building, August 2015. Photo by the author.

entreaty to "never forget." Would the experience of the museum have been different without these parting words? Their placement at the museum's exit betrays a fear that some visitors will not think about what they have seen. After all, the next steps will lead tourists out of the museum onto the streets, parks, and vistas of Washington, DC, perhaps to the flowering cherry trees around the nearby Tidal Basin, or to one of the Smithsonian museums, or to have a hot dog on the Mall. In any case, the next steps outside the doors will surely situate the USHMM firmly within a context that links it with other sites of tourism in the nation's capital.[5] And that, for many of the museum's critics, is only part of the problem.

There is no denying that the USHMM is firmly embedded in Washington's tourism industry, which otherwise focuses on America's founding beliefs, institutions, people, and the events that have shaped the canon of American history. The United States Holocaust Memorial Museum is one of Washington's most heavily visited attractions, with nearly two million visitors annually, outnumbering many of the Smithsonian museums on the Mall and making it as popular with tourists as the National Zoo.[6] The Holocaust museum benefits from its close proximity to the National Mall, just a few minutes walk from the Smithsonian Metro station and the Washington Monument.[7] As a part of capital city tourism, the museum is imbued with an official quality that speaks to the aspirations of American identity. Although independently managed, the museum has relied on the participation of prominent political figures, both past and present, who loom large in American life. The entrance to the Museum is adorned with engravings of statements by Presidents George Washington and Dwight D. Eisenhower; President Jimmy Carter established the President's Commission in 1978 that authorized the report recommending the establishment of the USHMM; President Ronald Reagan spoke at the cornerstone-laying ceremony in 1985; and President Bill Clinton spoke at the museum's official inauguration in his first year in office. Despite its independent status, the museum functions as a public, state institution. Always intended to be the national memorial to the Holocaust, its location on the Mall struck many on the commission as essential.[8]

For the museum's critics, the notion of a Holocaust memorial in the nation's capital is deeply problematic. The reality that visitors to the USHMM are, by and large, American tourists signifies to its detractors that the site misappropriates the Holocaust to serve American identity, not to foster memory of the Jewish victims of the Holocaust. The alleged misappropriation, critics argue, ignores the fact that the Holocaust was a European phenomenon and that its incorporation into American collective memory really serves to overemphasize the United States as liberator at the expense of other memories: the suffering of the victims, the failure of the United States to act more swiftly or decisively to intervene, or even American unwillingness to examine its own atrocities closer to home, quite apart from the Holocaust. Moreover, critics seem to take it for granted that tourists are unequal to the task of questioning those self-serving tendencies.[9] While these debates have been—and continue to be—explored by critics and scholars since before the museum opened, this chapter highlights a different aspect of the discourse of Americanization as it relates to Holocaust memory and the USHMM, and that is the degree to which Americanization and tourism are synonymous. Although tourism is not usually the central concern raised by the museum's critics and defenders, it is often invoked to advance a larger point about the problematic nature of an Americanized collective memory of the Holocaust. The concerns about presenting the Holocaust to throngs of tourists in the U.S. capital point toward a broader global phenomenon that is less American than some would insist: anxiety about the future of Holocaust remembrance.

Americanization of Holocaust Memory

What exactly do critics mean when they claim that the Holocaust's memory has become "Americanized"? The term is rather expansive, covering not only where the memory is situated but also who is remembering, for what purpose, and in what manner. It is certainly true that there has been a memory boom in the United States centered on the Holocaust, noticeable in a growing numbers of films, novels, testimonials, and documentaries in recent decades. In addition, the number of Holocaust memorials and museums dedicated around the United States in recent years has grown steadily, with new memorials on the state capitol grounds in Iowa and Ohio being some of the latest additions.[10] But claims about Americanization tend to focus not only on the quantity and location of Holocaust memorials, but also on the (often presumed) *manner* of representation, suggesting the emergence of an aesthetics of memorialization that is somehow idiosyncratically American. Such claims about the manner of memorialization are more complicated, and the label "American" can seem more like a convenient shorthand for what is, in fact, not uniquely American.[11] One can find aspects of both senses of Americanization—as a matter of geography and as a matter of aesthetics—in critiques of the USHMM, which typically present its location as determinative of both its aesthetic practice and the necessary critical response. In many cases, these critiques fail to notice how some practices presumed to be American have international origins that precede their appearance on American soil.

Among those global practices that are often subsumed under the label "American" is tourism. I was reminded of the link between tourism and clichés of American culture at a recent conference on the Holocaust in London, where a participant responded with dismay at the prospect of Holocaust memorials in Europe drawing "thousands of American tourists." In his comments, the stereotype of the noisome tourist was naturalized—and nationalized—as "American." Furthermore, his comments reflected puzzlement that U.S. travelers would be so keen to appropriate what he perceived as a "European" event. While the stereotype of the ugly American tourist is sometimes hard to refute, the almost automatic association of tourism with Americans points to a more complicated phenomenon in which American tourists become a synecdoche for the continuing internationalization of Holocaust memory. The specter of American tourists crowding Holocaust memorials in Europe seems to point at a future where there are no living witnesses and survivors to lend an authentic, living voice to resist some of tourism's worst tendencies. "American" becomes a shorthand way of referring to the evolving nature of Holocaust memory as that future nears.

To get at some of the tacit ways Americanization and tourism implicate each other in the discourse of Holocaust remembrance, it is worth taking a closer look at each of them separately. The following sections continue the discussion of the Americanization of the Holocaust as both a geographic and an aesthetic issue. Of course, the separation between the two dimensions of the term is artificial, since they usually go hand in hand. The growing frequency of Holocaust representations and memorialization in American culture raises its own unique concerns that are primarily matters of politics rather than aesthetics, but there is a sense in which the Americanization of Holocaust remembrance identifies a process that links the local with the global in a three-part process. First, Holocaust memorialization in America expands. Second, this leads to the transformation of Holocaust memory into something "American"— that is, a practice of collective memory that takes on forms that are presumably unlike traditions of Holocaust remembrance found elsewhere.

And third, these new forms of remembrance get exported, transforming Holocaust memory internationally because of American culture's global dominance. In the end, the concerns about a pervasive American aesthetic are also political, reflecting concern about the ownership of Holocaust memory.[12] After lending some specificity to the rather overburdened use of "American" as a modifier for Holocaust memory, I want to turn back to the issue of tourism and how it, too, gets constructed as American when it is linked to the Holocaust—a tendency illustrated above by my British colleague. After reflecting on the American/tourism nexus, I return to the United States Holocaust Memorial Museum as the site that gathers all of these discourses under one roof. I would like to clarify what underlies the frequent invocation of the museum's purported American-ness, which is inevitably presented as a fault. Ultimately, I want to suggest that the fears named by "Americanization" and "tourism" position the USHMM as a site for many critics to register anxieties about future Holocaust memory in a postsurvivor world, often at the expense of an appreciation of the memorial museum's specific contributions to Holocaust remembrance.[13]

The starting point for the memory boom in America, and the concerns about Americanization that follow, may well be the airing of NBC's miniseries *Holocaust* in 1978. Although there were important American contributions to the remembrance of the Holocaust before that date, such as the 1955 play *The Diary of Anne Frank*, the film of the same title in 1959, or Sidney Lumet's film *The Pawnbroker* in 1964, there had been no sustained representation of the genocide itself. While the term "Holocaust" had entered the American lexicon by the 1960s, its origin was the coverage of the Eichmann trial in Israel.[14] The presentation of the Holocaust as television drama in 1978 is a turning point, often credited for awakening interest in the Holocaust among millions of people internationally for whom the topic was barely on the horizon.[15] Despite its huge viewership, the broadcast drew a powerful condemnation from Elie Wiesel, who expressed outrage at the rendering of the Shoah as melodrama and characterized the story as false and cheap.[16] Both positive and negative responses to the miniseries speak to the twofold sense of "Americanization": On the one hand, the production was indicative of the sudden popularization of Holocaust representation within American culture. On the other hand, its broadcast abroad illustrated the growing influence of an American aesthetic, associated with Hollywood and mass media, in international Holocaust memory. That aesthetic was apparent in the way in which the miniseries evinced an American propensity for redemptory narratives. The final episode of *Holocaust* concludes with a group of liberated Jewish youths preparing to leave Europe for a new life in Palestine, aided by their American rescuers.

One consequence of the criticism of *Holocaust* as redemptory in a typically American way is that a certain slippage is introduced into the concept of redemption that has international implications, allowing for even foreign productions of Holocaust remembrance to be perceived as "American" if they partake in any of the stereotypically restorative aesthetics ascribed to U.S. culture. That slippage allows the popularity of Anne Frank's diary or foreign films like *Life Is Beautiful* to be seen as part of the Americanization of the Holocaust, even though both originate from European sources.[17] To the extent that international representations of the Holocaust employ manners of representation easily stereotyped as American, they enable critics to characterize the globalization of Holocaust memory as American without accounting for a more multi-lateral exchange of influences.

The first sense of Americanization—that the Holocaust has become suddenly very prominent in the American collective consciousness—is the topic of the historian Peter Novick's 1999 book, *The Holocaust in American Life*. In asking why the Holocaust suddenly became a topic of so much interest in the United States, despite its having occurred years ago in a place far away, Novick outlines the history of events that generated an accumulation of interest in the genocide first among American Jews and subsequently in American public discourse more broadly. He begins with the Eichmann trial, the Six-Day War, and the 1973 Yom Kippur War to show how events in Israel galvanized Jewish identity in the United States around a sense of existential threat. Israel's survival and the perception that anti-Semitism in the United States was on the rise raised fears of persecution that entered popular discourse in terms shaped by the Holocaust.[18] Jewish interests in the United States, Novick argues, turned the Holocaust into a rallying cry, with "Never Again" a ready response to any perceived threat to Jews around the world. The turn toward broader American interest beyond the Jewish community, Novick argues, came with the broadcast of *Holocaust* in 1978; that moment marks the beginning of a sustained effort to incorporate the Holocaust into American collective memory that has lasted for decades.[19] It is also the same year that President Jimmy Carter empowered a commission, led by Elie Wiesel, to draft plans for a national Holocaust memorial. As Novick states, "Since the 1970s, the Holocaust has come to be presented—come to be thought of—as not just a Jewish memory but an American memory."[20]

As Novick charts the development of Holocaust memory in the United States from one that was suppressed or limited primarily to Jewish survivors and their families to one that has found resonance among many Americans, he voices profound skepticism about the value of Americanizing the Holocaust.[21] One of his chief concerns is that survivors and victims groups in the United States have reformulated Jewish identity increasingly around the Holocaust, which informs a kind of "identity politics" around victimization. "I ask about our centering of the Holocaust in how we understand ourselves and how we invite others to understand us: 'Is it good for the Jews?'"[22] Seen thus, Jewish identity shares in a trend he sees in American culture more broadly, in which Americans increasingly invoke ethnicity or race to assert self-interests.[23] The underlying problem Novick has with the way the Holocaust gets invoked in recent American discourse is what he sees as a competition for suffering among various identity groups, whereby American Jewish groups vie for "primacy."[24] In such a framework, the invocation of the Holocaust as the focal point of Jewish identity can only be seen as a delayed instrumentalization of the catastrophe for ultimately political ends, rather than a genuine engagement that honors the historical and geographical specificity of the crime and its victims.

Describing the increasing role of the Holocaust as a "civil religion," especially among American Jews who increasingly placed it at the center of the Jewish identity, Novick takes note of the ritualized nature of Holocaust memory:

> One of the things I find most striking about much of recent Jewish Holocaust commemoration is how "un-Jewish"—how *Christian*—it is. I am thinking of the ritual of reverently following the structured pathways of the Holocaust in the major museums, which resembles nothing so much as the Stations of the Cross on the Via Dolorosa; the fetishized objects on

display like so many fragments of the True Cross or shin bones of saints;
the symbolic representations of the Holocaust—notably in the climax of
Elie Wiesel's *Night*—that employ crucifixion imagery.[25]

This last observation about the ritualized approach to the Holocaust
performed at museums might more accurately be characterized as
a concern about tourism as one of the vehicles for the increasing
universalization, or de-judaization, of the Holocaust.[26] That process of de-
specification would only intensify after 1978.

As the Holocaust broadened its claim on American collective consciousness with the broadcast of *Holocaust* and the beginnings of what
would become the United States Holocaust Memorial Museum, the concern about the growth of Holocaust representations in the United States
increasingly gave way to the fear that the Holocaust was becoming an
event that was no longer defined in terms of the victims' Jewishness. The
historical and geographic particularity of the event gave way to a universalist interpretation of "man's inhumanity to man."[27] As both Novick
and the historian Edward T. Linenthal document, the early discussions of
the Presidential Commission on the Holocaust struggled extensively on
whether and how to refer to the fact that, in addition to six million Jews,
the Nazis targeted other groups for murder: Sinti and Roma, Soviet prisoners of war, Communists and other political foes, Jehovah's Witnesses,
homosexuals, and anyone seen as aiding the enemy. While Wiesel insisted
on the centrality of Jewish suffering as the defining characteristic of the
Holocaust, other national groups demanded inclusion in the memorial's
planning, including Poles and Ukrainians, despite the fact that members
of both nations had participated in the murder of Jews.[28] Others on the
commission disagreed and saw the gesture of inclusivity as both politically
necessary and morally justified. If the museum's goal was to educate the
public about the Holocaust, the value in the lesson had to lie in drawing
universal conclusions from the particular details. Eventually, the commission settled on a formula for acknowledging the Nazis' many victims while
still retaining the centrality of Jewish suffering.[29]

Because Novick focuses his attention on the Holocaust as remembered
in American life, his critique tends to understate the global nature of many
of the phenomena he discusses. The invocation of the Holocaust in response to the perception of increasing anti-Semitism in the United States,

a phenomenon Novick treats with some skepticism, cannot be divorced from events occurring elsewhere around the globe. The murder of eleven athletes from the Israeli Olympic Team by members of the Black September Organization of Palestinians during the 1972 Olympic Games in Munich was certainly as important as the wars in Israel in shaping Jewish perceptions in America that anti-Semitism was on the rise, leading some to ask if the Holocaust might reoccur.[30] In Germany, the Red Army Faction, despite its professed antifascism, became increasingly anti-Semitic in its condemnations of Israeli policy toward Palestinians in the occupied territories, deliberately targeting Jewish organizations in some of its most notorious attacks.[31] In France, Charles de Gaulle's government became increasingly critical of Israel, as the New Left expressed increasing sympathy for Palestinians with increasingly vitriolic attacks against Jewish interests.[32] And Eastern Europe had its resurgences of anti-Semitism, such as Poland's 1968 purge of Jewish members from the Communist Party and the general campaign of "anti-Zionism" in the Eastern Bloc.[33]

If the new anti-Semitism of the post-Holocaust era was international in its expression, the effort to commemorate the Holocaust in the United States also found counterpart movements abroad. In Germany, organizations such as Aktion Sühnezeichen, a Christian antifascist youth league, and socialist youth movements in Eastern Europe built their antifascist identities increasingly around the commemoration of the Holocaust (see chapter 1).[34] In West Germany, intellectuals, authors, and activists were increasingly recalling the Nazi era in a program of *Aufarbeitung der Vergangenheit*, "working through the past," or, less felicitously, *Vergangenheitsbewältigung*, "mastery of the past." Both terms describe the efforts by some Germans to confront the Nazi past in literature, political discourse, and memorialization, often as a challenge to the West German government's perceived reluctance to acknowledge continuities with the past. We have seen how Israel increasingly made Holocaust memorialization a feature of its identity, beginning with an emphasis on heroic resistance and later stressing the experience of victimization (see chapter 5). And, of course, tourism to Holocaust sites in Europe was ever evolving, as Holocaust memory became an increasingly global affair. While Americans were gaining awareness about the Holocaust, so, too, were other parts of the world, and not simply in response to American examples. Yad Vashem had been open for twenty-one years before the

Carter commission convened, and the camp memorials in Poland had been designated as memorials as early as 1944.[35] Tourism to these sites was in place long before the USHMM opened its doors in 1993.

Yet there is no denying the impact of some American remembrances of the Holocaust in the global arena, and this addresses the second meaning of "Americanization" that circulates among critics who see Holocaust memory around the globe as increasingly dominated by American modes of representation, particularly in its reliance on popular culture and mass media. In this view, the concern lies with the export of American culture as a mode of representing the Holocaust to the rest of the world, leading to a homogenization of Holocaust memory that ignores local specificity. This view of Americanization tends to associate any element of kitsch or mass appeal, regardless of the memorial's location, as evidence of American cultural influence. Tim Cole's critique of the Auschwitz-Birkenau Memorial and Museum as "Auschwitz-land," discussed in chapter 1, is emblematic of that latter tendency. Andreas Huyssen, professor of German and comparative literature at Columbia University, has shown how debates about architecture in reunified Berlin often recirculated anti-American fears of Las Vegas–style kitsch and corporatism.[36]

The clearest critique of Americanization as bad taste comes from Alvin Rosenfeld, professor of Jewish Studies and English at Indiana University Bloomington and a prominent scholar of the Holocaust as represented in literature and the arts. Rosenfeld addresses the phenomenon of the Americanization of the Holocaust in a lecture delivered in 1995, where he links the USHMM, then open for two years, to other forms of mass culture, including film, and admits that such means of cultural production may have a greater reach on the public than scholarly histories or archival research. Rosenfeld laments the tendency he sees in popular culture to relativize the Holocaust into a story that universalizes at the expense of historical particulars.[37] Anticipating Peter Novick's study, he sees a tendency to appropriate the Holocaust as a way of advancing "a politics of identity based on victim status and the grievances that come with such status."[38] But while Novick situates identity politics in the rise of the Holocaust in American Jewish identity, Rosenfeld is concerned about a more generalized public, one that partakes in tourism to the USHMM. He worries that the museum caters to the visitors' self-indulgent tendency to see themselves as oppressed, to align themselves with the victims and their liberators rather than perpetrators, and to generalize the specific history of the Holocaust into a universalist narrative about humanity.

It is no coincidence that Rosenfeld's concern about American mass culture and the USHMM appears at a time when another landmark in Holocaust representation arrives, Steven Spielberg's *Schindler's List*, leading some media to dub 1993 "the Year of the Holocaust."[39] Rosenfeld maintains a tone of concerned skepticism with regard to the USHMM while still acknowledging its importance as a place of learning: "Its aim is to educate the American public about an historical experience of an excruciatingly painful kind, so much so that it would be the rare visitor who would emerge from this place unmoved. Just what it is that people will take away with them and will retain, however, we do not know."[40] Like Novick, Rosenfeld raises the concerns about universalizing history to serve an American culture of identity politics, but he acknowledges that, since the museum had been open only two years, it is too soon to judge. However, by situating his analysis of the USHMM in the context of Americanization, by which he chiefly means mass culture, the outcome cannot appear promising. Mass culture offerings—like Spielberg's *Schindler's List*, Anne Frank's diary, or novels like William Styron's *Sophie's Choice*—do not provide the same depth as academic studies, and Rosenfeld detects even in the best-intentioned popular works a superficiality that leads to falsely redemptive stories and to universalized readings of the Holocaust. Anne Frank's diary is popular because it offers a message of hope for humanity, not a story of her own doom and the destruction of European Jewry. *Schindler's List* presents a story of survival and remembrance rather than extermination. And *Sophie's Choice* replaces the Jewish victims with a Catholic Pole.[41] Seen in such company, one wonders how the USHMM can escape the same problems of redemption and universalization.

Of course, Rosenfeld has chosen American examples to illustrate the Americanization of the Holocaust. The presence of similar trends abroad does not enter the analysis, so that Poland's historical tendency to blur the distinction between Catholics and Jews at Auschwitz or Yad Vashem's insistence on a redemptive narrative that merges Judaic traditions with the Shoah as a civil religion informing Israeli politics do not come under the same scrutiny. There are sound objections to these tendencies abroad as well, but are we to understand the international appearance of redemptory, universalist interpretations of the Holocaust as Americanized, regardless of when or where they emerge?[42]

The aspect of the USHMM that is often cited as typically American is the way it shapes the visit not just as a presentation of facts and stories but also as an experience. Visitors to the museum are encouraged to take a small, passport-sized booklet that contains, in four paragraphs, the abbreviated biography of a person caught up in the Holocaust. Visitors follow the person's story as they move through the exhibition space of the exhibition space, so that by the end of the tour, the visitor has "gone through" the Holocaust through the eyes of an individual who was there. As James E. Young documents, the museum originally assigned these ID cards to visitors based on age, gender, and profession, although that is no longer the case.[43] Computer stations at various points in the museum updated the cardholder on various moments in that person's experience of the Holocaust. For Young, the ID cards, at least as originally implemented, go beyond individualizing the victims of the Holocaust and instead invite the visitor to confuse their visit to the museum with the individual's experience of the Holocaust.[44] One result is that non-Jewish visitors will claim the Holocaust as their own, at the expense of the victims' Jewish identity.

The experiential mode of tourism encouraged by the ID cards and certain elements of the exhibition is further reinforced by the building's architecture and layout. James Ingo Freed, the building's chief architect, has fashioned a space that evokes the materials and machinery of the camps, with the heavy use of bricks and steel in an effort to remove visitors from the memorial landscape of Washington, DC, and relocate them in an entirely different space. Instead of the emblems of democracy and civil liberties that the city champions just outside the museum, Freed's building evokes the materials, hues, and shapes of the camps. For Jennifer Hansen-Glucklich, Freed's design for the USHMM embodies the "architecture of experience," in contrast to Yad Vashem's "architecture of redemption." That dichotomy, however, overlooks both the experiential aspects of Yad Vashem and the redemptory features of the USHMM. In fact, it obscures the way redemption is figured as experience in both museums. At Yad Vashem, the pathway through the exhibit spaces feel intentionally claustrophobic and mazelike, suggestive of the inescapability of suffering in the Holocaust. The life-size images in videos at the Holocaust

History Museum's entrance, or in the display about the Warsaw Ghetto, further relocate the tourist in the world of Jews before and during the Holocaust in Poland. The highly redemptory Hall of Names, with the faces rising into a brightly lit sky, and the exit onto a balcony overlooking the hills of Jerusalem, all form part of the experience of redemption that Yad Vashem imparts to its visitors, who emerge from the visit into a typically sunny and tranquil landscape. At the USHMM, redemption is no less experiential, with visitors undertaking a journey through a dark history and emerging with the sense that their experience will help prevent future genocides. The experiential mode is especially apparent as visitors walk through a boxcar identical to those used in deportations or when they stand in a partially reconstructed barracks from Birkenau. One visitor even chides the museum for its elevator ride to the beginning of the upstairs exhibition, which he sees as a coy simulation of the experience of entering the gas chambers.[45] And yet much of the material on display in Washington, DC, is replicated from exhibits at Auschwitz-Birkenau, Yad Vashem, or numerous other Holocaust museums and memorials that opened long before the USHMM. The examples of anti-Semitic propaganda, the mounds of shoes, the canisters of Zyklon B are part of a shared idiom of Holocaust remembrance that predates the USHMM. Their presentation in a space designed to evoke the universe of the Holocaust gives rise to an experience from which visitors emerge, unlike the millions of dead, and they are encouraged to believe that they have undertaken the important task of bearing witness.[46] Visitors come to embody the redemptory promise of the USHMM as stewards of a collective memory, although how they will act on that responsibility is hard to say. What is certain, however, is that the experiential mode of the visit simulates a redemptory narrative in which the Holocaust becomes the catalyst for a better future. That is certainly the claim most tourists who comment on the museum make.

As Rosenfeld observes, that redemptory experience bridges the interior of the museum with the return to the commemorative terrain of Washington, DC, where tourists perceive the reassertion of democracy as a powerful response to their "experience" of fascism and the Holocaust. Rosenfeld worries that such a response leads to complacency, but I would suggest that it is just as possible that visitors will emerge with a more critical relationship to ideals symbolized on the Mall, especially given the museum's frank portrayal of U.S. failures to intervene and save more lives.[47] In any case, Freed's design seems to take into account a dynamic relationship between the museum and its surroundings that allow readers to engage in a plurality of interpretations. It is worth recalling in this context that the Mall in Washington has never been a static space with a singular, monumental significance. The installation of artist Maya Lin's Vietnam Veterans Memorial in 1982 and the more recent additions to the Mall of the National Museum of African American History and Culture, the National Museum of the American Indian, and the nearby Martin Luther King, Jr., Memorial demonstrate the inclusion of critical perspectives in the capital's memory district that evoke a far more complex relationship between the places of Washington, DC, and its many diverse visitors.[48] While critics rightfully question the degree to which the experiential mode of tourism gives way to inauthentic or inappropriately sentimental representations of the Holocaust, the problem is that such criticisms are not leveled as consistently or with as much vehemence at other places as they are toward the USHMM. Somehow representing the Holocaust in Washington, DC, through an experiential mode of tourism is presumed to be more problematic than it is elsewhere, which ultimately reinforces a stereotype of both Americans and tourism as fixed, superficial, and unreflective.

To summarize, "Americanization" is invoked both as a concern for the location as well as for the form of Holocaust memory. The fact that tourism, the world's largest industry, resurfaces in both articulations of Americanization suggests to me, at least, that the label refers to what is actually a global phenomenon with origins in multiple places. The use of the term, which in its aesthetic sense has particularly negative associations with mass culture, underscores the sense of anxiety that surrounds global Holocaust memory. At a time when living memory of the Nazi atrocities is disappearing, technologies of reproducing and disseminating historical knowledge are expanding at a pace that seems beyond control, a process in which tourism participates both through the relative ease of modern travel and the incorporation of digital social media into the experience of tourism. Questions of representation, mobility, and place—who promotes and manages memorial spaces, who has access to them—take on greater significance. The location of the USHMM in Washington, DC, highlights these urgent issues and brings the stakes in promoting tourism as a means of engagement with the Holocaust to the forefront. To the degree that tourism is understood as an American practice, its placement in Washington, DC, far from the events of the Holocaust, puts the USHMM at the center of concerns about the future of Holocaust remembrance.

USHMM Tourism and the Americanization of Holocaust Memory

Among its many implications, the "Americanization of the Holocaust" describes the ascendancy of Holocaust tourism as an international phenomenon. While the origins of Holocaust tourism are by no means exclusively American, modern-day tourism is often equated with a way of engaging with the world that is stereotypical of the American traveler: fleeting, lacking in seriousness, more concerned with affect than insight, commercial, and ignorant of cultural difference. The attention paid by skeptics to the USHMM's distance from the actual events of the Holocaust underscores the suspicion that tourism is an insincere or inauthentic medium for encountering a traumatic history. The linkage between tourism and Americanization is often more implicit than explicit, but the frequency with which tourism is invoked in criticisms of the USHMM is telling. In most cases, tourists lurk at the periphery of such critiques, often figured as passive consumers reacting to the museum's agenda. While the focus of such critiques is directed at the museum's representation of the Holocaust through its architecture, its contents, and its location, the very marginality of tourism as an element of these critiques is symptomatic of the prevalent bias against tourism. It is as if one need merely invoke tourists to prove the validity of the criticisms about the USHMM's representation of the Holocaust.

A particularly negative response to the USHMM that illustrates this point comes from the journalist and author Philip Gourevitch, who wrote about the newly opened USHMM for *Harper's Magazine* in 1993. Gourevitch finds many faults with the new museum adjacent to Washington's Mall, chief among them its assertion of American values to comprehend the Holocaust. He objects to the way in which the museum's location next to the National Mall appears to have co-opted Holocaust memory for national pride. He situates these elements of

Americanization alongside his critique of the displays and the people who look at them, attacking the USHMM as a venue that promotes mass voyeurism. His dismissive treatment of tourists renders them as prurient onlookers, leading Gourevitch to the inescapable conclusion that the museum itself is obscene. When, for example, Gourevitch discusses the gigantic photo of American troops standing around a mound of bodies at the Ohrdruf camp at the beginning of the main exhibition, he sees it as the first instance of the museum's relentless, near-pornographic re-exposure of victims, many of them naked, many dead, many about to be killed. In his unforgiving conclusion about the museum, Gourevitch bemoans the spectacle of tourists as voyeurs of murder:

> One way history is doomed to repetition at the Holocaust museum is that day in and day out, year after year, the videos of the Einsatzgruppen murders will play over and over. There, just off the National Mall in Washington, the victims of Nazism will be on view for the American public, stripped, herded into ditches, shot, buried, and then the tape will repeat and they will be herded into the ditches again, shot again, buried again. I cannot comprehend how anyone can enthusiastically present this constant recycling of slaughter, either as a memorial to those whose deaths are exposed or as an edifying spectacle for the millions of visitors a year who will be exposed to them. Didn't these people suffer enough the first time their lives were taken from them?[49]

The museum's partially obscured display of photographs and films, mentioned above, strikes Gourevitch as an especially lurid way of presenting images:

> This is what I wrote in my notebook: "Peep-show format. Snuff films. Naked women led to execution. People are being shot. Into the ditch, shot, spasms, collapse, dirt thrown in over. Crowds of naked people. Naked people standing about to be killed, naked people lying down dead. Close-up of a woman's face and throat as a knife is plunged into her breast—blood all over. Someone holds a severed head in his hand. Mass graves of thousands. Naked. Naked corpses. Naked corpses. Street beatings. The gun, the smoke, a figure crumbles. Naked corpses. Naked women dragged to death. Shooting. Screaming. Blackout. The film begins again."[50]

The film—the museum's use of that medium is no doubt part of Gourevitch's discomfort, rendering the museum a production that he wants to distinguish entirely from the event it represents. He underscores the implied artificiality of the museum by referring to the release in the same year of Spielberg's *Schindler's List*:

> It is not the Holocaust that is suddenly such a huge popular draw, but the Holocaust Museum and the Holocaust movie, "Schindler's List." The creators of these artifacts, and many who celebrate them, tend to indulge in vainglorious rhetoric, claiming that an affirmative public response to representations of the Holocaust places today's secondhand witnesses firmly on the right side in the struggle of good against evil.[51]

Gourevitch objects to the idea that these horrific images are repeated so far removed from their geographic origins. The association of the museum with one of the most famous Hollywood films about the Holocaust implies guilt by association, as if the USHMM's use of documentary film footage is made less authentic or more commercial by its simultaneity with Spielberg's feature film. What's more, the placement of the museum in the United States, instead of the actual sites of perpetration, suggests that tourists are less sincere in their motivations, seeking an easy path to self-righteousness instead of undertaking a more serious engagement—although what that more legitimate form of engagement would entail remains entirely unexplained. While it is possible that the museum gratifies a desire that Gary Weissman has called a "fantasy of witnessing," Gourevitch cannot find any merit in the motivation to bear even secondary witness to the genocide of Jews through necessarily mediated forms of representation.

Gourevitch's attack on the imagery displayed at the USHMM might well be applied to any number of Holocaust memorials and museums that rely on explicit images of Nazi atrocity, including the camp memorials and museums. Tourists to those sites can see identical photos at the Auschwitz-Birkenau Memorial and Museum, at Yad Vashem, at the House of the Wannsee Conference, and numerous other memorial locations. Despite the ubiquity of such photos, Gourevitch's outrage seems to be especially pointed in the case of the USHMM because of its location in Washington, DC, a place far removed from the events that the museum depicts, embedded in a landscape already crowded with tourists.[52] Like Cole's "Auschwitz-land," the USHMM is for Gourevitch a theme park, a term he uses in the subtitle of his review. The foregone conclusion is that tourists, filmgoers, and thrill seekers converge at the USHMM to engage in a particularly American exercise: that of transforming harsh realities into palatable forms of entertainment that offer escape into an ersatz reality.

Tim Cole also refers to the confluence of the USHMM's opening and the appearance of *Schindler's List* to drive home his contention that the Holocaust has become thoroughly American. His introduction to his volume *Selling the Holocaust* includes this assessment, rich with scare quotes, of American interest in the Nazis' murder of Europe's Jews:

> With the opening of the United States Holocaust Memorial Museum and first screening of Spielberg's Schindler's List, it seemed that the "Holocaust" had become as American as apple pie. The "Holocaust" was now both on the Mall in Washington, DC, just a few hundred feet away from the Washington Monument, as well as being filmed by Hollywood's most successful producer.[53]

Again we encounter a critic's fusion of concerns about location and aesthetic practices, with tourism lurking in the background. The museum's placement within walking distance of the Washington Monument coincides with the film's presentation at the nearest movie theater. The consumers of such venues are implicitly identical.

The charges made by Gourevitch, Cole, and to a somewhat more measured degree by Rosenfeld about the USHMM and its Americanization of the Holocaust may veer into hyperbole, but they address an undeniable reality, the stakes of which are considerable. It is a truism that Holocaust representation will reach wider audiences through mass cultural forms of representation, such as tourism and cinema, than through more elite or inaccessible modes. It is also right to consider how such representations risk trivializing or relativizing the Holocaust—although such an outcome should not be assumed guaranteed. Collective memory, with all its imperfections, is inevitable as personal memory vanishes, and such a prospect understandably produces a certain cultural anguish that history may become unmoored from access to experience.

The question Gourevitch, Cole, Rosenfeld, and others really seem to be asking is whether there is any value to be had in memorializing the Holocaust collectively, since it can never equal the personal memories of those who were there.

Put another way, one might ask, What lessons do tourists at the USHMM learn? The educational mission of the museum lies at its core and prompts the parting exhortation to "think about what you saw." One might survey the statements of visitors to the museum, who overwhelmingly express appreciation for the visit. Gourevitch, in any case, does not see any redemptory potential in his visit:

> The problem was simply that I could not make out the value in going through this. The Holocaust happened—it should be remembered and it should be found repellent. But I felt the way I did when I was a child waking from my nightmare: I know that this is hell and I know that it is true, but the ethical dilemmas and the political choices that I face in my life are not those of the Holocaust; nor are the crises of America those shown in this museum.[54]

Ironically, Gourevitch would go on to write powerful testimony about the Rwandan genocide, only a few years after asserting his distance from the ethical dilemmas and political choices raised by the Holocaust.[55]

Gourevitch casts doubt on the project of Americanization of the Holocaust as framed by the museum's project director, Michael Berenbaum, for whom the term "Americanization" referred to the effort to relay the history of the Holocaust "in such as way that it would resonate not only with the survivor in New York and his children in Houston or San Francisco, but with a black leader from Atlanta, with a midwestern farmer, or a northeastern industrialist."[56] Berenbaum argues that each society imprints its stamp on history, but that process can be honorable, provided it is faithful to the historical record. In the case of the USHMM, Berenbaum was insistent that the American public needed to confront the problem of bystanders and the failure of the U.S. government to intercede.[57] Furthermore, Berenbaum suggested that "the question of audience should not be confused with content. The Holocaust is only 'Americanized' insofar as it is explained to Americans and related to their history with ramifications for future policy."[58]

Key in Berenbaum's defense of the USHMM's inevitably American perspective is the recognition that there is nothing monolithic about either American history or American audiences. Indeed, that leads most critics to express worries that the museum insists on an overly universalist approach to the Holocaust. Novick and Rosenfeld, for example, both voice concerns about the "identity politics" that will invite audiences of any ethnic or national minority to lay claim to the status of victim and invoke the Holocaust as a point of comparison. It is true that the words "holocaust" and "genocide" have been claimed in problematic ways to describe other events, and that a pluralist approach can give way to a sense of competition among different victim groups. But this struggle between universalism and particularism as the right way to relate to the genocide of Europe's Jews is ultimately an unavoidable part of American culture, which struggles continuously to embrace plurality. That may partially explain the success of the USHMM in drawing a diverse domestic and international touring public.

Does this mean that the Holocaust, instead of being perceived as unique, will become just another historical event? Its representation will certainly come to resemble other events the more it is remembered through commercial mass media; through films, novels, and other genres associated with entertainment; and through tourism (all implicated in the term "Americanization"). Since the Holocaust has for so long been emphasized for its uniqueness, its unrepresentability, and its capacity to exceed the limits of comprehension, the notion that the Holocaust is also a part of history, not an exception to it, represents a fundamental shift in its place in collective memory. Coupled with the awareness that lived memory of the Holocaust must recede, the fear is that Holocaust memory will be rendered in presumably inadequate forms that employ increasingly identical strategies of representation.

The historian Thomas Laqueur laments that "this museum stands as an almost pathetic bulwark against the inevitable passing of the present into the past."[59] He finds the museum unequal to the task of memorializing the event. The question I have is whether the fault lies in the event or in the USHMM's act of memorialization? As Novick has stated plainly, the Holocaust is, of course, an event like any other in some sense.[60] It occurred in history; it has been documented through images and testimony; it has been portrayed on stage, screen, and page; and its traces are accessible to researchers, pilgrims, and other tourists. None of those commonalities can engage the ways in which the Holocaust was un-precedented. But museums are unlike texts and films in their placement in physical space, and the monumentality of the museum's location in Washington, DC, offers an antidote to the ephemerality of other forms of popular culture, especially in the digital age. Rather than markers of a collective memory that fades into the background of historical catastrophe, the continuing presence of tourists at the USHMM, and the debates that surround them, suggest that future generations may still generate a relationship to the Holocaust that remains anchored in the presentation of its artifacts and testimony and thereby puts universalizing impulses in contact with particular pieces of history. The burden does not fall on the museum's curators and directors alone to strike a balance between the universal and particular meanings of the Holocaust. Tourists share that responsibility.

Conclusion

Throughout this volume I have offered an account of how tourism has emerged as a dynamic force in the evolution of our collective memory about the Holocaust. Tourism does not merely receive the evolving memory, but participates in making it. To keep pace with the evolving interest of travelers, the core sites of Holocaust remembrance undertake continual efforts at preservation, restoration, and redesign. They must reflect new discoveries about the Nazi genocide that continue to emerge and about which some portion of the touring public will be informed.

As an example of the ongoing discoveries about the Shoah, the historian Dan Plesch took advantage of newly unsealed archival material from the United Nations War Crimes Commission, material that guided the Allies' prosecution of Nazi criminals. Plesch has recently published his book, *Human Rights after Hitler*, which reopens the question of what the Allies knew about the Holocaust—and when they knew it.[1] Museums that address the Allies' failure to save more Jewish lives during the Holocaust will need to incorporate Plesch's findings, perhaps reflecting more skepticism about any narrative that overly emphasizes liberation over inaction. Each new historical discovery has the potential to affect tourism, leading exhibitors to update or correct their displays and supplying travelers with critical information by which to measure the reliability of the places they visit. It is hard to imagine a time in the foreseeable future when the Holocaust will be deemed "finished" as a topic of inquiry by historians or by Holocaust tourists.

The foundations for Holocaust tourism were laid before the end of World War II, as survivors and liberators committed themselves to preserving evidence for the world to see. The early years of tourism to sites of Holocaust memory were very much defined by the politics of the Cold War, and tourism's movements were fairly restricted, at least for the majority of the traveling public. Over the last three decades, however, Holocaust tourism has emerged with impressive force, owing in large part to the accessibility of places that for many years lay beyond reach because of Cold War politics. But this growth in tourism also suggests something about the nature of travel and the flow of information in an era of globalization, the Internet, and the relative ease of modern travel. Another factor that has sparked the growth of Holocaust tourism is the awareness that the last eyewitnesses are passing away, no doubt fueling a sense of urgency that further explains the "memory boom," of which Holocaust tourism forms an integral part. When the last survivors have left us, I suspect that tourism to sites of atrocity will maintain its prominence, answering a need to understand how such monstrosity can unfold in our world. As eyewitnesses depart, place will become a proxy for living memory.

The Value of Being There

Place offers a sense of immediacy that compensates for the growing temporal distance to the genocide of Europe's Jews and the inevitable loss of lived memory. Even though sites change over time, there is something about inhabiting the coordinates of the calamity that promises a connection. Even if tourists have a false perception of place as unchanging, it remains a powerful motivation for those who seek an authentic portrayal of an event so often deemed beyond comprehension. The search for authenticity in Holocaust tourism may appear at first glance to be in tension with the reality that sites are mediated by their caretakers and by the tourism industry. The more apparent the act of memorialization, which is always an act of interpretation, the more it can potentially obscure aspects of the event being remembered. But tourists are more sophisticated than their critics usually presume, and they bring their own awareness of the tourism industry's practices to their encounters with place. What tourists often seek, especially in the case of Holocaust tourism, is not so much a moment frozen in time but, rather, an acknowledgment of how a past moment has transformed the world and their own place in it. Some memorial designs reflect on their own evolution, a case made most apparent at Auschwitz and some of the other camp memorials. Others offer a statement of remembrance that seems intent on overwriting the shortcomings of past representations. While the knowledge generated through tourism needs to be as accurate as possible, I prefer sites that incorporate not only the past of the Holocaust but also the imperfect past of Holocaust remembrance. The uses of Holocaust memory after the war incorporated intentional acts of amnesia to promote particular worldviews, and those gaps in memory can expose the ideologies through which the present views the past.

I have argued throughout this volume that those places of Holocaust memory that are relatively undeveloped have the power to impart a greater impact on their visitors than meets the eye. Among the sites this book has investigated, only a few remain comparatively undeveloped for tourism, and it is here, I argue, where the sense of connection to history can be most profound. Sobibór and Chełmno Village are sites of perpetration that have been left much as the SS intended, in a state of ruin and reclaimed by natural growth. Birkenau, too, is largely in a state of carefully maintained ruin, with the rows of barracks indicated only by their brick chimneys. Tourism plays a complicated role in the recuperation of such sites for public memory, both drawn by their sense of authenticity and yet fueling the economics of restoration that are resulting in their further development. The memorial at Bełżec and the stalled plans for Sobibór illustrate the dynamics of public memory played out in the tourist market, with all the attendant ambiguity that attends to the results. Bełżec's pre-2004 condition as a forlorn mass grave was a powerful testimony to the clandestine designs of Operation Reinhard and also to Poland's desire to distance postwar national identity from the fate of its Jewish compatriots. If the new memorial at Sobibór is installed in a way that displaces the isolation and abandonment to nature that currently mark the site, then a new idiom of public memory, however sincere its intentions, will overwrite a history of suppression that also must remain part of the story.

But even if I express skepticism about large-scale concrete memorials that displace the problematic memorial landscapes of the last seventy years, in the end representation is all we will have left to produce acts of remembrance. What matters is the critical capacity of tourism to engage with representation (or its apparent absence) in responsible ways. I am confident that tourism engages travelers who see past the newest installation and bring increasingly sophisticated perspectives on memorial culture. While some tourists will take exhibits at face value, others will continue to do the work of challenging sites of remembrance to demonstrate their faithfulness to the event they represent. The emergence of social media with extensive reach gives thoughtful tourists a medium of expression to which destinations must be increasingly responsive. They assure that, whatever the scale and apparent permanence, no memorial has the final word on the collective memory to which it contributes. While traditionally representational memorial spaces—ranging from Nathan Rapoport's Monument to the Heroes of the Warsaw Ghetto to the redemptive memorials spaces in Yad Vashem and the United States Holocaust Memorial Museum—attempt to authorize a particular kind of memory (the past seen as heroic or as suffering that can only be redeemed by a better future), tourism also accesses spaces that offer alternative narratives. Countermonuments—from the large-scale Berlin Memorial to the Murdered Jews of Europe to the small-scale *Stolpersteine*, or "stumbling stones," that dot city sidewalks throughout much of Europe—claim as their virtue their receptivity to the interpretations their viewers produce and thus seem to welcome the very inquisitiveness and critical reflection that, I argue, is already inherent in Holocaust tourism. In fact, even countermonuments are not insulated from the agency of tourists to produce meanings their designers reject. Tourists actually resist the intentions of countermonuments to eschew a state-sanctioned narrative of the past and instead resituate them within a framework their designers have tried to escape. The countermonumental idiom has become the predominant mode of Holocaust memorials in Germany, and tourists are likely to see such monuments as typically or officially German, even if such interpretations are "wrong" in the eyes of these who champion countermonuments for shunning authoritative, national narratives. The point is not to condemn countermonuments, but to acknowledge that it is only through their placement within tourism that their multiple and even inherently contradictory meanings come to light.

By highlighting the merits of Holocaust tourism in terms of its potential for casting a critical, even skeptical view toward memorials, I do not mean to suggest that memorials are inherently problems that tourists must overcome. For one thing, both traditional and more countermonumental installations spur tourists into undertaking the work of memory. Furthermore, memorials may help to recall a specific dimension of Holocaust history at a site that has been forgotten and thus reinsert memory at a particular place. As we have seen, at the more developed camp museums and memorials, commemorative installations need not come at the expense of authenticity. The memorial at Treblinka, for example, makes only the most abstract efforts to recall the terrain of the extermination camp. Rather than creating a facsimile of the death camp, its field of stone memorials surrounding the central cenotaph invites the tourist to imagine the destruction visited upon Poland's Jews, with thousands of communities extinguished. The photographic placards that document Treblinka's deadly operation serve as unobtrusive pictorial links to the history the memorial denotes. Rather than inviting a false sense of sharing the experience of the camp with the victims, they insert a screen between the tourist/viewer and the past they depict. Through a variety of strategies, Holocaust memorials and museums work to balance the tourist's desire to know the past as it was experienced with the only commendable alternative: to reflect and learn about that which cannot be experienced again. Gary Weissman's notion that tourists indulge in a "fantasy of witnessing" is not a condemnation but, rather, an acknowledgment of productive desires, in tourism and in other forms of representation, that generate knowledge.

The theme of witnessing informs a great deal of tourism to Holocaust memorials and museums, often in the form of an appeal sites make to those who visit them. But as Weissman and others suggest, the ability to answer the call to bear witness is hindered by the fact that the Holocaust transpired over seventy years ago. Given that obvious hurdle, it is striking that tourism still calls upon its participants to bear witness, from the frequent invocations of the phrase "Never Forget" to the placard outside the USHMM, "Think about what you saw." A skeptical view of Holocaust tourism might see the call to bear witness as another version of David Brown's formula, "They are tourists, I am not"—the disavowal of the tourist in favor of a more respectable identity. But tourism encompasses a range of identities and practices, including that of the pilgrim, the student, the teacher, the business traveler, and the vacationer, so why not also the witness? If we consider witnessing a communicative act involving the enunciation of testimony and its reception by a listener, then the case for Holocaust tourism as an act of witnessing becomes more plausible, despite the temporal divide. Museums do not only rely on the presentation of eyewitness accounts; their installations themselves are attempts to allow artifacts to "testify" to the events of the past.

Tourists can provide the audience for that testimony to complete the act of witnessing. But tourists are also eyewitnesses in their own right, if not to the Holocaust in a direct sense, then to its memory.

In my discussions with colleagues and friends about the phenomenon of Holocaust tourism, the response is often to think of tourism in its worst incarnations. Indeed, tourism includes a lot of problematic behaviors that apply to sites of Holocaust remembrance as much as anywhere else, despite the solemnity of the subject matter. I have seen tourists at concentration camps take photos where they are not permitted, smoke on grounds where smoking is prohibited, or laugh at places where laughter seems wholly inappropriate. Each time I have noticed not only my reaction but also the reactions of others nearby who find ways to express disapproval. This dynamic raises conundrums about the idea of policing behavior at a place where authority had the ability to murder others with impunity. The problematic aspects of tourism are part of the experience that can also generate a consideration of the ethics of one's role as a tourist at a site of atrocity. Alex Gillespie's notion of the reverse gaze is one way of characterizing the dynamic of tourists' interactions that, at least for some, will result in self-reflection.

Since the rise of the ubiquitous digital camera, one touristic practice seems to have garnered particular attention for its apparent inappropriateness. I refer to the "selfie," the insertion of one's own face into the frame and into—even over—the scene. In the context of Holocaust tourism, the foregrounding of one's self over the site of atrocity seems the worst kind of self-absorption, suggesting a lack of attention to the memory of the Holocaust and more attention paid to the present adventure of tourism. Selfies, it would seem, are the latest incarnation of touristic souvenirs that postcards from Auschwitz also exemplify, perhaps without any of the mediating qualities of the postcard's invitation for commentary.

From Postcards to Selfies: The Evolving Character of Holocaust Tourism

I chose postcards as the emblem for tourism because they are accoutrements of the tourist gaze, intertwining consumerism with the desire to share the unfamiliar with friends and family. The images on them may be artful or hackneyed, as can the messages tourists inscribe on the back. As simple as postcards appear, they, like tourism itself, can reveal a great deal about the tourist's search for meaningful experience. As David Prochaska and Jordana Mendelson, scholars in the emerging field of "postcard studies," write, "Postcards provoke scholars to examine complex relations among subject, producers, sender, and receiver, and to bring into question notions of authority, originality, class, gender, and power."[2] Postcards also give travelers bragging rights and can be seen as markers of privilege. They certify the making of the journey and affirm that one has seen the place depicted. In the case of photographic postcards, the image may be enhanced with exaggerated color or depict idealized weather, but the note on the back to the addressee pulls the fantasy of travel into the real. The tourist's signature is, in a sense, the authentication that the image is to be read referentially, that is, as an emanation of the real. When tourists knowingly send kitschy postcards, the reality tourists refer to is tourism itself, at least in one of its incarnations.

Tourists buy postcards at Auschwitz and the other sites discussed in this volume for many of the same reasons as they would at famous landmarks: to prove that they were there, to verify that an iconic image in fact relates to an actual place, and that the place is part of their shared world. But in the context of Holocaust tourism, postcards purchased at a camp memorial or Holocaust museum demand a different kind of reading from postcards of the Eiffel Tower or a sunny beach. Postcards from Auschwitz offer testimony and constitute acts of bearing witness to the memory of the Holocaust. They can serve as invitations to the recipient to undertake the same journey. Or they can be keepsakes that never get mailed, personal souvenirs that authenticate a journey, something tangible one can take away from a place that so often deals in abstract questions about history, humanity, and progress.

The postcards I have seen from Auschwitz have a particular aesthetic. They are usually in color, but the palette is subdued. The images often incorporate fog and appear to have been taken either early in the morning or at night. Some are winter scenes with the memorial grounds blanketed in snow. People are never in the frame. One image includes a crow in silhouette, perched on a lamp above the barbed wired fence enclosing part of Birkenau—the only creature I've seen on a postcard from Auschwitz. Some postcards are landscapes that incorporate structures of the camps, especially the Gate of Death at Birkenau. The general sense is one of haunting, the fog lending a ghostly presence to an otherwise de-populated scene. They show the camps emptied of the presence of others, conveying the places as tourists do not experience them while also assisting tourists in their own disavowal of tourism. Some postcards use a different strategy, focusing on what Barbie Zelizer refers to as "the accoutrements of atrocity" that were typical of early press coverage of the liberated camps: dented canisters of Zyklon B, an empty boxcar, the ruins of the gas chambers in Birkenau or the furnaces of the crematorium at Auschwitz I.[3] The absence of people reinforces the knowledge that these places and objects are linked to murder.

Postcards are profane, material objects. To purchase them at camp memorials challenges the assumption that these places are sacred and that they require respect for the dead whose ashes lie scattered throughout the grounds. That assumption of a tension is facile, however. First, there are few sites of avowed religious significance that do not themselves sell postcards and souvenirs, ranging from the Church of the Nativity in Bethlehem, where one can buy such items in the naves of the church itself; to Mecca in Saudi Arabia, where they are sold to participants in the Haj; to visitors to the Wailing Wall in Jerusalem, Judaism's most sacred site. Second, and perhaps more important, the tendency of tourism to merge the sacred with the profane, a dynamic that troubles its detractors, also sets in motion the kind of self-reflection that is typical of the tourists who are attuned to the ambivalence of their journeys. Of course, the image was procured, purchased on site from a vendor, and it ultimately testifies to the conversion of the camp into a memorial, its transposition from a place of atrocity into a place of learning and reflection, and, simultaneously, a place of exchange embedded within the tourism industry. Postcards are the reminder of the inseparability between commerce and contemplation in tourism generally. In the context of Holocaust tourism, their ambiguity is intense.

Enter the selfie. Postcards seem downright traditional, even quaint by comparison. If postcards from Auschwitz display an authorized aesthetic devoid of people, the selfie reinserts the subjectivity of the tourist into the enterprise of Holocaust tourism in a startling way. The comparatively recent phenomenon of selfies has typically been greeted by reactions ranging from puzzlement to condemnation, often by members of older generations who worry about the values exhibited by younger ones. The media studies scholar Alice Marwick observes that "this explosion in selfies has been explained, variously, either as evidence of an epidemic of narcissism among the young or as an empowering new self-presentation medium. . . . But the major shift in photography is not simply from film to digital but from the limited audiences that existed for family snapshots to the networked, potentially enormous audiences for all types of digital content."[4] In the age of social media, selfies have the ability to grant their authors "Instafame" and "microcelebrity."[5]

The capacity to reach large audiences is certainly one aspect of selfies that can result in fame, but it also produces its opposite: notoriety. Selfies at Auschwitz show how social media can invite unwelcome attention, despite the aims of the photographer. We have discussed the website created by the Berlin satirist Shahak Shapira, "Yolocaust," which effectively shamed tourists who took inappropriate selfies and other playful shots at the city's Memorial to the Murdered Jews of Europe. In 2014, an American teenager calling herself "Princess Breanna" posted a photo of herself smiling broadly in front of barracks in Auschwitz, garnering herself international condemnation in the media, and even receiving death threats.[6] Both cases received intense coverage and offered a platform for indignation at a new medium seen as calling attention to the person in the frame instead of the victims of the genocide.

But scholars are beginning to take a closer look at selfies, just as they are at postcards, seeing in them a new medium that addresses some of the same issues that Prochaska and Mendelson locate in their more established counterpart.[7] Perhaps there is more to the phenomenon than a search for instant celebrity, at least in some cases. Some selfies clearly center the subject in the frame and present him or her in an eroticized or embellished manner, but others show earnest expressions and decentered faces that let the background emerge more fully. As the form evolves, identifiable genres within the category of selfies will no doubt emerge, and critics will make distinctions between those that invoke good taste and those that are objectionable.

In the case of selfies at Auschwitz, it is worth considering the act of placing oneself in the frame at such a site. If official postcards erase the tourist, selfies reclaim the visitor's presence at the memorial. There is an act of agency, of immediacy to a place that has for so many decades been heavily mediated by others, often experts who exercise considerable influence over acceptable ways to represent the Holocaust. The assertion of the non-expert into the representation of Holocaust memory is a logical outcome of tourism in an age of mass travel and increased opportunities for self-representation through modern technology. Given the Third Reich's denial of individual identity to its victims, the claiming of that space in such an individualized manner through today's form of self-portrait is worth considering more fully as an act of defiance, perhaps against the authority of those who would limit the scope of legitimate representations of the genocide.

Selfies, postcards—as emblems of tourism's ostensibly more commercial side, they reinforce a tendency to react to Holocaust tourism with suspicion. Skepticism is salutary if it is embedded in an honest, unbiased consideration of the phenomenon that is ready to acknowledge its benefits as well as its pitfalls. This volume has argued for the possibilities for tourism to produce ongoing engagement with the past and for tourists' agency in creating knowledge from their experiences. Tourism promises its participants a degree of insight about oneself in relation to others, past and present, and tourists hold the industry accountable through the degree and nature of their participation in it. As Holocaust memorials emerge in distant places around the globe, far from the events they commemorate, the opportunities for engaging in it are reaching more people in a world that continues to see violence as a practical response to difference. Some Holocaust tourists may answer the call to heed the lessons they perceive about racism, religious intolerance, and the need to share this planet peacefully and sustainably; others may disappoint by returning to their routines, perhaps trying to forget what they saw, and resuming their prejudices. At a time when the future of Holocaust memory is uncertain, tourism continues to evolve in ways both beneficial and problematic, searching for ways to understand the destruction of Europe's Jews, the past's obligations on the present, and how to draw lessons without doing violence to the memory of the victims. Ultimately, as Holocaust tourism increasingly reaches everywhere, its evolution becomes our shared responsibility. As the emergence of selfies at Auschwitz shows, tourism remains a vital forum for contesting and defining the nature of Holocaust remembrance, whose future does not end when the last survivor has passed away.

NOTES

1 In years prior to 1990, the average rate of attendance was around 500,000 per year. See "Attendance" (n.d.) and "1990–1999" (n.d.).

2 "News" (n.d.).

3 The relationship between tourism and authenticity has been a mainstay of tourism studies. The social psychologist Gianna Moscardo offers a succinct and insightful summation of the "the authenticity debate" in tourism studies (Moscardo 2001: 6–10).

4 The voyeuristic aspects of Holocaust tourism certainly locate it within the repertoire of representational strategies that some find problematic, to say the least. The historian Carolyn Dean has written extensively on the notion of "pornography" that often gets invoked in critiques of Holocaust portrayals, especially regarding their depiction of the suffering of victims. Dean's (2003) analysis challenges the impulse to discount portrayals with a term as derogatory as "pornographic," asking her readers to think beyond the reflexive pessimism that it indicates. Her insights into the representation of victims more generally, including those of the Holocaust, are further elaborated in Dean (2004, 2010).

5 See Snow (2010: 43).

6 See Alba's chapter on the Sydney Jewish Museum (Alba 2015b: 135–185). The Shanghai Jewish Refugees Museum opened in 2007 and commemorates the 20,000 Jewish refugees from Europe who found asylum there during World War II.

7 United States Holocaust Memorial Museum (2016: 24).

8 "Anzahl der Besucher" (n.d.).

9 UNESCO (2003).

10 I develop this discussion further in chapter 1, specifically in reference to work by Cole (1999); Foley and Lennon (2000, 2007); and Pollock (2003). The term "Holocaust tourism" itself is used with considerable skepticism in works by Pollock, Cole, and Foley and Lennon, as well as by Kugelmass (1992, 1995); Struk (2004); and Ashworth (2010). Others—such as Stier (2003); A. Gross (2006); Feldman (2008); and Lehrer (2013, 2014)—approach the topic with more appreciation of its complexities and possibilities.

11 As the anthropologist Dean MacCannell wrote in 1976, when the field of tourism studies was in its nascence, "It is intellectually chic nowadays to deride tourists" (MacCannell 2013: 9). He went on to quote expressions of derision by the anthropologists Daniel Boorstin and Claude Lévi-Strauss as examples. Gianna

Moscardo suggests that such derision may be motivated by the desire of research-ers to distinguish their travels from that of tourists, whom they often portray as "passive, powerless, ignorant and easily duped" (Moscardo 2001: 8).

12 See Nash (1996: 2).

13 I refer here to the historian Tim Cole's characterization of the Auschwitz-Birkenau Memorial and Museum as "Auschwitz-land" (Cole 1999: 111).

14 Nash (1996: 1, 4–5); Smith (1989: ix–x).

15 Foley and Lennon (2000).

16 The anthropologist Valene L. Smith offers a succinct definition of tourism: "The motivations for individuals to travel are many and varied, but the foun-dation of tourism rests on three key elements (all must be operative) which form an equation: Tourism = leisure time + discretionary income + positive local sanctions (1)."

Smith goes on to list ethnic tourism, cultural tourism, historical tourism, environmental tourism, and recreational tourism as broad categories for leisure travel (Smith 1989: 4–5).

The sociologist John Urry's foundational work on the tourist gaze defines tourism as leisure travel to destinations that are distinguished from home or work and whose sites are anticipated by travelers through their encounters with images circulated by tourism professionals (Urry 1990: 2–3). Urry is especially interested in the advent of mass tourism in the modern age.

While Smith and Urry, along with Graburn (1989) and MacCannell (2013), emphasize the leisure aspect of tourism in their works, a historical look at tourism suggests closer linkages between business travel and tourism. The World Trade Organization, a chief source of data about tourism, explicitly includes business travelers who stay at least twenty-four hours in a destination in its statistics about tourism (Vellas and Bécherel 1995: 5–7; Hall and Paige 2006: 75–77). The inclusion of business travelers strikes me as critical, since the distinction between research and tourism is often couched in terms of "profes-sional travel" versus "leisure travel," and it overlooks how the two modes may be indistinguishable in terms of goods and services consumed, insights gained, photographs taken, leisure activities pursued, and so on.

Other scholars point out that even the distinction between "resident" and "tourist" is problematic, at least in cities that are common tourist destinations. "Residents consume the city in ways that are similar to tourists," while "many visitors to cities are now experienced users of cities who want to move beyond traditional tourism precincts" (Maitland and Ritchie 2009: 8, 9).

17 As the anthropologist Dennison Nash argues, the concern for authenticity has been a foundational topic in tourism studies, most commonly associated with Dean MacCannell's work on the subject. Tourism, in MacCannell's framework, is the search for authenticity beyond the alienation of the "social conditions in which they [i.e., tourists] live" (Nash 1996: 66). Daniel Boorstin, in contrast, insists on a portrayal of tourists as "drawn to pseudo-experiences," as opposed

to "travelers," a term he reserves for more sophisticated itinerants who seek "real experience" (as cited by Nash 66: 142).

18 See Aitchison (2001, 2005).

19 See Oppermann (1999).

20 For a relatively recent reassertion of the need for Marxist analyses of tourism, see Bianchi (2009).

21 See Lawton and Weaver (2000); and Weaver (2000).

22 See Moscardo, Faulkner, and Laws (2001: xxii–xxiv).

23 For a thorough history of the Grand Tour and its various incarnations since its inception in the eighteenth century, see Hibbert (1969); and Zuelow (2015).

24 Nash (1996: 2–4).

25 Nash addresses the self-reflexive aspect of tourism studies, acknowledging that both tourists and anthropological field researchers act as observers and participate in the portrayal of others (Nash 1996: 83).

26 Nash (1996: 3). See also Moscardo (2001: 8).

27 Nash (1996: 2–3).

28 See Erving Goffman, whose *Presentation of Self in Everyday Life* has been a touchstone for anthropologists and sociologists since its appearance in 1959. In particular, Goffman makes a distinction between sincere versus cynical performances of self. This distinction is separate from MacCannell's concern about authenticity and inauthenticity in tourism. According to Goffman, all presentations of self to others are "performances." The degree to which the performer believes in that performance may vary in degrees of sincerity or cynicism, but the artifice of selfhood remains in play. Authenticity, in contrast, speaks typically to the Western tourist's search for foreign cultures that remain somehow untouched by the forces of development and capitalism. Given the encounter between the native and the foreign at the heart of tourism studies, the notion that selfhood is performed according to different rules in different settings applies not only to the tourist's perceptions of the native, but vice versa, and also among tourists (Goffman 1959: 17–76).

29 The phrase refers to the title of the late historian George L. Mosse's groundbreaking publication from 1966. As the cultural historian Steven Aschheim has noted, "For many readers, schooled in older conceptions of the idea of 'high' culture, the title itself must have seemed shocking. Was not the very notion 'Nazi Culture' an oxymoron, a contradiction in terms? Who had not heard of Goebbels' perhaps apocryphal (but nevertheless famous) declaration that 'every time I hear the word "culture" I reach for my revolver'?" (Aschheim 1999: 296).

30 The attention to the destruction of culture informs the UN Convention on the Prevention and Punishment of the Crime of Genocide, which defines genocide not only as the murder of individual members of a group but also as any effort to eradicate a group's distinct culture. It extends to the eradication of groups by other means—forced sterilization, the inflicting of mental harm, or also the forcible relocation of children from the targeted group to another group. See Hinton (2002: 30–31, 43–44).

31 Nash (1996: 6–25). Nash's vision of interdisciplinarity extends only to other fields within the social sciences and leaves little space for the humanities to contribute to tourism studies. Summarizing the humanities as an "interpretivist approach," Nash seems to believe that the humanities are speculative and "can only contribute informed hypotheses to anthropological work, which has to be, in the end, scientific" (25).

32 In his groundbreaking work *The Interpretation of Cultures* (1973), the late anthropologist Clifford Geertz defines culture as follows: "It denotes an historically transmitted pattern of meanings embodied in symbols, a system of inherited conceptions expressed in symbolic forms by knowledge about and attitudes toward life" (Geertz 1973: 89). In similarly semiotic terms, Nash succinctly summarizes the term "culture" as developed in anthropology, emphasizing that it is a system of signifying practices: "Anthropologists have used the term culture to refer to various activities of human groups or societies. Such activities as tourism do not take place in a vacuum, nor are they unrelated, but rather comprise more or less integrated systems laden with the associative and dissociative tendencies that mark all social life" (Nash 1996: 5).

33 In an essay from 1984 entitled "Anti Anti-relativism," Geertz defends the value of relativist thinking in anthropology as having been largely misunderstood or mischaracterized by "anti-relativists." Part of the blame, Geertz argues, lies in the fact that the notion of relativism has been "grandly ill-defined" (264). Relativism emerges by necessity in the act of comparison by one culturally situated subject analyzing another. Geertz states that concerns about relativism are overblown. He insists that value judgments remain possible from within culture and do not require an extracultural, universalized position from which to make them.

34 See Bernstein (2001: 87).

35 The "emancipation from ignorance" refers to Immanuel Kant's famous answer to the question, "What is Enlightenment?" (Was ist Aufklärung?): "Enlightenment is the departure of the human being from his self-imposed dependency. Dependency is the inability to use one's own intelligence without the guidance of another." (Aufklärung ist der Ausgang des Menschen aus seiner selbst-verschuldeten Unmündigkeit. Unmündigkeit ist das Unvermögen, sich seines Verstandes ohne Leitung eines anderen zu bedienen.) See Kant (1974: 9).

36 See Bernstein (2001: 83–85 passim).

37 See Horkheimer and Adorno (1988). First published in 1944, when the crematoria at Auschwitz-Birkenau were burning ferociously, *Dialektik der Aufklärung* has proven foundational in framing Holocaust studies in its assertion that the existence of Auschwitz proves the collapse of the Western project of the Enlightenment. If the Enlightenment had been the dominant metanarrative of Western modernity, how, they ask, did the championing of reason lead to such unprecedented death on an industrial scale and through industrialized means? More important, if the Enlightenment's values of rational thought and democratic principles failed to prevent Auschwitz, what hope is there that these same values

can prevent Auschwitz from reoccurring in the future? For a satisfying analysis of *Dialektik der Aufklärung* and Adorno's subsequent development of a "negative dialectics," see Bernstein (2001: 84–92).

38 Nor does anthropology claim to account for the totality of the phenomena it studies. For example, Clifford Geertz's anthropological critique of science is explicitly not a rejection of the knowledge science produces; rather, it is a critique of the idea that such knowledge can emerge from beyond any cultural context. In situating knowledge within cultural contexts, Geertz opens himself to the criticism that he and other anthropologists are relativists, an objection Geertz finds overstated (Geertz 1984: 268).

39 On this point, see the work of the noted historian Saul Friedländer, which examines the limits of Holocaust representation within historiography, specifically, and within narrative discourse, more generally (Friedländer 2000: 10–11). See also Friedländer's edited anthology *Probing the Limits of Representation*, especially the introduction (Friedländer 1992).

40 See Trezise (2013: 36).

41 Studies on tourism and visuality include *Visual Culture and Tourism*, edited by the historian David Crouch and the media studies scholar Nina Lübbren (2003). See also the anthology *Theories and Concepts*, vol. 1 of *Tourism and Visual Culture*, edited by P. Burns, Palmer, and Lester (2010), who describe tourism as "a sensual undertaking dominated by visual imagery" (xvi). A recent discussion of the visuality of tourism in the era of digital technology comes from Robinson and Picard (2009), *The Framed World: Tourism, Tourists, and Photography*. Finally, Urry's important book *The Tourist Gaze: Leisure and Travel in Contemporary Societies* (Urry 1990) has been updated in an expanded third edition, in collaboration with Jonas Larsen, to address photography and digital technology as *The Tourist Gaze 3.0* (Urry and Larsen 2011).

Shenker's chapter on the United States Holocaust Memorial Museum also addresses the tension between the use of testimony for acquiring knowledge and its potential for voyeurism, arguing that the museum ultimately succeeds at promoting the former over the latter (Shenker 2015a: 70, 111).

42 The question of emplotment in historical representation of the Holocaust (and all events) is the subject of the historian Hayden White's essay, "Historical Emplotment and the Problem of Truth" (1992). White argues that narrative language is essential in the representation of history, but that narration always entails some degree of subjectivity.

43 Trezise (2013) address the ethics of listening to and representing testimony in his provocative volume, *Witnessing Witnessing: On the Reception of Holocaust Survivor Testimony*.

44 Levy and Sznaider address the distinction between personal/lived memory and collective memory in a way that mirrors the philosopher and sociologist Maurice Halbwachs's distinction between "social memory"—that which a collective or its members have directly experienced—and "historical memory"—that which is

"remembered" through institutions and recorded expressly for the benefit of those who have no direct memory of the event. See Halbwachs (1980); and Levy and Sznaider (2006: 30).

45 The globalization of Holocaust memory is the topic of Levy and Sznaider's important study, *The Holocaust and Memory in the Global Age* (2006). But the point for Levy and Sznaider is not to suggest that the global has replaced local, the regional, or the national; rather, it has produced "cosmopolitan memory," whereby local or national memory exists in relation with memory from other parts of the world. The memory of the Holocaust is "de-territorialized" in the global age, so sites of national remembrance are participants in a global network of memory. See Levy and Sznaider (2006: esp. 23–38).

46 Levy and Sznaider ask, "Who does the Holocaust 'belong' to in the global age? Can it belong only to the Jewish victims of the German perpetrators? How, for example, do immigrants to Germany remember the Holocaust? Or does the Holocaust belong to all who want to define themselves as victims?" (2006: 12). These questions illustrate the tension between universalist (the Holocaust as a crime against all humanity) and particularist (the Holocaust as the murder of European Jewry) approaches to Holocaust remembrance. Levy and Sznaider locate the universalist tendency within the context of the so-called Americanization of Holocaust memory, which they (and I) see as an alternative way to signal concerns about the globalization of Holocaust memory (Levy and Sznaider 2006: 131–135).

47 Urry argues that present-day tourism in particular has become a mass-cultural phenomenon, and he contrasts it with earlier centuries in which tourism was reserved for the elite. He is suspicious of such modern manifestations of mass tourism as "heritage tourism," which bears some affinity with Holocaust tourism for many participants, and which Urry and others see as a dubious appropriation of history as commodity (Urry 1990: 3–5, 109–112).

As Levy and Sznaider point out, the old Adornian presumption of mass culture's guilt by association with fascism (a politics of mass mobilization) needs to be reevaluated in the global age (Levy and Sznaider 2006: 134–138).

48 There are too many cases to cite here, but here is a short set of examples: Rosenfeld includes a strong attack on William Styron's *Sophie's Choice* (159–166) as a "Southern Gothic Novel" set in Auschwitz, whose fictional elements include some counterfactual representations of history (Rosenfeld 1980: 159–166). Cole offers a sustained critique of Steven Spielberg's *Schindler's List* and the "Schindler tourism" that now thrives in Kraków (Cole 1999: 73–94). Langer has a very thoughtful reflection on the problematic position of Anne Frank's story in Holocaust memory and of Roberto Benigni's unduly comedic film *Life Is Beautiful* (Langer 2006a: 16–29; 2006b: 30–47).

49 In its obituary of Wiesel, *The New York Times* characterized him as "the Auschwitz survivor who became an eloquent witness for the six million Jews slaughtered in World War II and who, more than anyone else, seared the memory of the Holocaust on the world's conscience" (Berger 2016).

50 Wiesel (1970), quoted in Diamond (1983: 231).

51 Wiesel (1978).

52 Wiesel (1989) writes:

> The Holocaust has become a fashionable subject, so film and theater produc-
> ers and television networks have set out to exploit it, often in the most vulgar
> sense of the word. "The Night Porter," "Seven Beauties," the docudrama
> "Holocaust," "Sophie's Choice," "War and Remembrance" (I speak of the film,
> not the book, which is both shattering and sensitive), "Murderers Among
> Us," the recent "Ghetto" that played on Broadway for several weeks and
> previously, to great acclaim, in Germany—these are only some of the most
> familiar examples over the years.

Instead, he urges his readers:

> Study the texts—such as the diaries of Emanuel Ringelblum and Chaim
> Kaplan; the works by the historians Raul Hilberg, Lucy Davidowicz, Martin
> Gilbert, Michael Marrus. Watch the documentaries—such as Alain Resnais's
> "Night and Fog," Claude Lanzmann's "Shoah" and Haim Gouri's "81st Blow."
> Listen to the survivors and respect their wounded sensibility. Open your-
> selves to their scarred memory, and mingle your tears with theirs.
>   And stop insulting the dead.

As the Jewish studies professor Jeffrey Shandler documents, Wiesel had plenty
of company in his dismissal of television as an appropriate medium, including
critics like Jean Beaudrillard and Claude Lanzmann (Shandler 1999: 166–175).

53 Kaes (1990: 114).

54 Dreisbach (2009: 92–95).

55 Cory (1980: 444–445).

56 Goodrich and Hackett (1984); Frank (1998).

57 Langer (2006a: 18–19).

58 *2014 Inbound Tourism Survey* (2015: 51). As the Anne Frank House reports, "In
2014 a record number of visitors [to the Anne Frank House] was received for the
fifth consecutive year; a total of 1,227,462 visitors. That is 32,006 more than the
previous record year of 2013. . . . The majority of the visitors came from outside of
the Netherlands, and around 140,000 were Dutch" (Anne Frank House 2015: 9).

59 Cohen describes as "phenomenology" his understanding of tourists as travelers who move through socially constructed notions of space and who construct
cultural meanings around notions of centers and peripheries as experienced by
individual travelers with varying interests and motivations (Cohen 1979: 183).

The cultural memory scholar Jessica Rapson emphasizes that the individual's
experience of space, whether that of nature or of a landmark, is also subject to
historically determined ideas about geography and nature (Rapson 2012: 165).

The sociologist Marie-Françoise Lanfant understands phenomenology as
"the rigorous description of the lived experience of the subject in the world
of things and others before any form of speculation on human nature and the
'laws' governing the social and physical environments in which it is evolving"

(Lanfant 2009: 243). In other words, phenomenology prioritizes subjective experience independent of universal axioms about social behavior or laws of physics, thus allowing for a variety of experiences regarding the same phenomenon. This variability is key in characterizing tourists' responses to the sites they visit.

The archeological theorist Christopher Tilley (1994) explains that the point of phenomenology "is the manner in which people experience and understand the world. Phenomenology involves the understanding and description of things as they are experienced by a subject" (12). More important, it is by an embodied subject whereby "the body [is] the privileged vantage point from which the world is apprehended" (13). Tilley's treatment of the phenomenology of space helps us understand how expectations are integral to the experience of space or, more precisely, of place, which is a space imbued with a particular cultural or personal significance, often bearing a name. "Place is both 'internal' and 'external' to the human subject, a personally embedded centre of meanings and a physical locus for action" (18).

60 What I am calling "phenomenological" overlaps to a considerable degree with what the anthropologist Edward M. Bruner (2005) describes as a performative theory of tourism. The idea behind his performative theory is that tourism is less a visit to a waiting place or culture than it is a co-production between travelers and their hosts that "generates new experiences and new stories" (24). The phenomenological aspect of performance surfaces in Bruner's observation that "the work of the tour is to transform a preexisting tourist tale from an abstract text into an embodied narrative, a somatic experience" (24). Bruner elaborates further that "a site may be generative and may construct meaning not as a silent text, but in action, in social practice, by the responses of the visitors to its physicality" (25).

61 In this sense, I am agreeing with Nash's characterization of the role of humanities-based inquiry into tourism studies, although the distinction he draws between the ideal of a science and the hypothetical contributions of humanities strikes me as overstated (Nash 1996). The hypotheticals engaged with here are based on empirical observation, not speculation.

62 Foley and Lennon (2000: 58).

63 Foley and Lennon (2000: 62).

64 The literary theorist Naomi Mandel offers a thoughtful critique on the idea of the incommensurability of the Holocaust with forms of representation. She concludes that, if the Holocaust "is to continue to function as an object of study, if its presence in the past is to continue to inflect and infect the present, the notion—however limited—of its incommensurability needs to be critically addressed. Such critique may well be the work that ethics after Auschwitz ought to undertake" (Mandel 2003: 518).

65 Bernstein (2001: 386–387).

66 These squads included not only the Einsatzgruppen of the SS but also other police and regular army troops. Concerning the involvement of police and other

paramilitary units who, unlike the four Einsatzgruppen, were not under the direct supervision of the SS, see especially *Ordinary Men* by the noted historian Christopher Browning (1992). His study describes the actions and choices of members of Germany's Reserve Police Battalion 101, which had been militarized during the war and deployed to Polish villages to participate in mass shootings of Jewish civilians.

CHAPTER 1. LISTENING TO AUSCHWITZ

1 For more about Konstanty Gebert, see Lebor (1999). The population figures come from an article by the syndicated columnist Allan C. Brownfield (2008), written for the American Council for Judaism. Brownfield explains: "Though community leaders are reluctant to provide estimates, they guess there are at least 20,000—perhaps 30–40,000—Poles who identify themselves as Jews. About 2,000 are active members of the Union of Jewish Religious Communities in Poland, an umbrella group founded in 1993 that today has chapters in Warsaw, Krakow, Lodz, and five other cities." Prior to 1939, Warsaw was home to nearly 400,000 Jewish residents, the largest population of Jews in any city in the world. Chapter 3 will discuss the state of Jewish life and its commemoration in Warsaw today in greater depth.

2 Pollock (2003: 175).

3 Pollock (2003: 189).

4 Pollock (2003: 175).

5 Pollock (2003: 179).

6 Pollock's formulation here is important, since she does not presume that all Jewish visitors fall into the category of "pilgrim": "As grandchildren of survivors or refugees, *some of these visitors might be counted as pilgrims*, painfully visiting the horrific unmarked and airy graves of forebears they never knew" (Pollock 2003: 179; my emphasis).

7 Pollock (2003: 188).

8 This trope also appears in *The Texture of Memory*, James E. Young's influential study of Holocaust memorials, where he articulates a similar fear of the conflation between the past and its representation. Young worries that tourists will mistake the presentation of artifacts at Auschwitz for the event itself, thinking they are directly witnessing the Holocaust. Tourists, in Young's words, may "lose sight of the fact that they [the artifacts] are framed for us by curators in particular times and places" and instead appear to tourists as "parts of a seemingly 'natural order'" (Young 1993: 128).

9 See Brown (1996: 38–39). Malcolm Crick makes a very similar observation. "Why do so many tourists claim that they are not tourists themselves and that they dislike and avoid other tourists? Is this some modern cultural form of self-loathing?" (Crick 1989: 307). Crick cites Dean MacCannell, who similarly observes, "The touristic critique of tourism is based on a desire to go beyond the other 'mere' tourists to a more profound appreciation of society and culture, and it is by no

means limited to intellectual statements. All tourists desire this deeper involvement with society and culture to some degree; it is a basic component of the motivation to travel" (MacCannell 2013: 10).

10 To the list one could add "medical tourism" (travel to places for more readily available surgeries, treatments, and pharmaceuticals); volunteer tourism, or "voluntourism" (where people donate time and labor to in areas hit by hardship); and "woofing" (derived from World Wide Opportunities on Organic Farms, a loose network that helps people travel to foreign countries to work on organic farms and perhaps learn another language).

11 John Urry's book, *The Tourist Gaze*, along with its updated version co-authored with Jonas Larsen, *The Tourist Gaze 3.0*, are probably the key texts in discussing the visuality of tourism.

12 Bruner's observations about the importance of narrative in the production of meaning in performances of tourism is relevant here, and they suggest ways of thinking about witnessing as a performance that follows a particular protocol of communication (Bruner 2005: 19–27). Shenker's *Reframing Holocaust Testimony* offers a sustained study of the protocols of testimony, which he also understands through the lens of performance (2015b: 11–17).

13 This evolution is best documented by Jonathan Huener in his important book, *Auschwitz, Poland, and The Politics of Commemoration* (2003).

14 Cole (1999: 98–99).

15 See Mintz (2001: 62). The performance theorist Vivian M. Patraka also refers to Auschwitz as a "monumental metonymy for the Holocaust, for all anti-Semitism(s), and for the consequences of intolerance." For Patraka, this metonymic usage of "Auschwitz" obscures historical and ideological distinctions and situates genocide too neatly in a Eurocentric framework (Patraka 1999: 120).

16 Chief among these has been James E. Young's groundbreaking book, *The Texture of Memory*, which appeared in 1993 and offers readers a careful reading of the site as a memorial. Of similar value to scholars of the camp's past and future is *Auschwitz: 1270 to the Present* by the historians Debórah Dwork and Robert Jan van Pelt (1996), who provide a study of the locale that reads its Nazi manifestation against the backdrop of a much longer past in Germany's cultural landscape, a past that modern day Germany has seemed eager to disavow. Taken together, both of these studies lay the groundwork for understanding what the site has become today, twenty years after the end of the Cold War, and what tasks lay ahead for those interested in the work of Holocaust memory.

17 Herein lies one of the chief contributions of Huener's book, which is, as he writes, "the first study of its kind to analyze the largely untapped postwar archival collections of the State Museum at Auschwitz, including its administrative documents, press archive, and collections of exhibition plans" (Huener 2003: 1–2).

18 The Operation Reinhard camps (Bełżec, Sobibór, and Treblinka, the extermination camps established to kill all the Jews in the General Government) murdered deportees using carbon monoxide fumes. Majdanek made use of

both carbon monoxide and Zyklon B (hydrogen cyanide) to murder Jews in gas chambers. See Hayes (2004: 272).

19 "Investigation of War Crimes" (n.d.).

20 See the historian Alexander Victor Prusin on the use of evidence from Nazi atrocities in war crimes trials from December 1945 through July 1946 (Prusin 2003). As Huener has noted, the idea of memorialization at Auschwitz was a priority of some prisoners during their internment (Huener 2003: 59).

21 "History of the Memorial" (n.d.).

22 See Huener (2003: 61–64). See also Auschwitz-Birkenau Memorial and Museum (n.d.).

23 "History of the Memorial" (n.d.).

24 Prusin has commented on the propaganda value these trials held for the imposition of a Soviet postwar order both within the Soviet Union and in Eastern Europe (Prusin 2003: 3, 12).

25 Huener (2003: 79–107).

26 As Huener makes clear, this relationship between the communist Polish leadership and their Soviet overlords was never without tension (Huener 2003: 83–86).

27 The historian Timothy Snyder discusses the Stalinist era's suppression of national and ethnic expression in Eastern Europe, as well as the persistence of anti-Semitism after the war. See Snyder (2010: 335–346).

28 Speaking of the Jewish victims in particular, Huener writes, "The State Museum at Auschwitz, it must be emphasized, never denied or effaced the Jewish genocide from its exhibitions. It did, however, marginalize this history or subsume it within the broader treatment of the 'Extermination of Millions,' as the title of the exhibit in Block 4 suggested" (Huener 2003: 75–76).

29 Huener (2003: 93–94).

30 "Overall Numbers by Ethnicity or Category of Deportee" (n.d.).

31 Charlesworth (1994: 580–581). According to the renowned Holocaust historian Raul Hilberg, over 50,000 Jews were murdered at Majdanek (Hilberg 2003: 958). The State Museum at Majdanek puts the number at ca. 60,000, or about 75 percent of the 80,000 prisoners who were murdered there. See "Extermination" (n.d.).

32 On the impact of the Holocaust on journalism, see the media scholar Barbie Zelizer's book, *Remembering to Forget* (1998).

33 Perhaps best known among these is Anne Frank, who was transported from Auschwitz to Bergen-Belsen, where she died shortly before the camp was liberated by the British.

34 See "Displaced Persons" (n.d.).

35 Huener documents the transition of Auschwitz from national memorial to Polish suffering to an international memorial acknowledging all victims but increasingly emphasizing the Jews as the vast majority (Huener 2003: 145–184). Young provides a rich description the evolution of the Auschwitz-Birkenau Memorial

and Museum nicely in his book, *The Texture of Memory* (1993: 128–154), where he accounts for the contested nature of remembrance at the site over time.

36 Medlik (1990: 95–96).

37 Huener refers to many of the commemorative events that have taken place at Auschwitz over the years as "political tourism," highlighting the way in which state officials make their visits known to the public for a particular agenda (Huener 2001: 513–515, 526).

38 Cole (1999: 99).

39 Young (1993: 133). See also "History of the Memorial" (n.d.).

40 Young (1993: 141).

41 Young (1993: 141).

42 Huener (2001: 514–515). See also Medlik (1990: 95–96).

43 "History of the Memorial" (n.d.)

44 "About the March" (n.d.).

45 Huener (2001: 515–516).

46 See Adorno's 1959 essay, "Was bedeutet: Aufarbeitung der Vergangenheit" (Adorno 2003b), which reflects critically on the impulse to both remember and forget the Nazi past in postwar Germany. This phrase, along with the common term *Vergangenheitsbewältigung* ("overcoming the past"), refers to efforts to acknowledge Germany's role in the perpetration of the Holocaust. The notion was further problematized by Jürgen Habermas in his intervention into the so-called *Historikerstreit*, or historians' debate, that was waged in West Germany in the 1980s. See his essay, "Vom öffentlichen Gebrauch der Historie" (Habermas 1987). For a thorough discussion of the historians' debate, see Charles Maier's book *The Unmasterable Past* (1987).

47 The ongoing presence of young Germans at Auschwitz is portrayed in Robert Thalheim's 2007 film, *Am Ende kommen Touristen*, which focuses on a young German carrying out his civil service obligation by assisting the staff at the Auschwitz-Birkenau Memorial and Museum.

48 "March of the Living: Western Region" (n.d.).

49 "Mission of the March" (n.d.).

50 Stier (2003: 179–183).

51 Kugelmass (1992: 397–400).

52 Kugelmass (1992: 400).

53 Feldman (2008: 257).

54 Feldman (2008: 266).

55 Huener (2001: 513–514). Huener's article also mentions the group Sozialistische Jugend, which conceives of its travel as part of establishing an international network of socialistically minded youths who hope to foster collaboration based on social values across national borders (516–520).

56 The sociologist Geneviève Zubrzycki's *Crosses of Auschwitz* (2009) offers a superb book-length study of the 1998 controversy surrounding Polish-nationalist expressions of Catholicism at Auschwitz.

On the topic of post–Cold War Catholicism and anti-Semitism in Poland, see also Huener (2003: 237); Reuters (2010); and Young's discussion of the Carmelite convent, and Cardinal Józef Glemp's role in the controversy, in *The Texture of Memory* (1993: 142–150).

57 Young (1993: 132).

58 Young points out how the process of arriving at a coherent message amid contested claims for memorialization at Auschwitz "reminded all that no memorial is ever-lasting: each is shaped and understood in the context of its time and place, its meanings contingent on evolving political realities. The wisest course, therefore, might be to build into the memorial at Auschwitz a capacity for change in new times and circumstances, to make explicit the meanings the site holds for us now, even as we make room for the new meanings it will surely engender in the next generation" (Young 1993: 154).

59 See Nash (1996: 39–57) for a good summary of this topic. In a chapter by the tourism scholars Renata Tomljenovic and Bill Faulkner in the anthology *Tourism in the 21st Century*, the link between tourism and deeper understanding across cultures is shown to correlate closely both with the degree of preparation prior to tourism and the degree and quality of contact with the hosts upon arrival (Tomljenovic and Faulkner 2001: 18–33).

60 MacCannell calls visitors to the Louvre or Eiffel Tower "pilgrims" in his discussion of sightseeing as modern ritual (MacCannell 2013: 42–43). Graburn refers to tourism as "The Sacred Journey" and positions tourism in modern society, where religion has receded in defining daily life, as the sacred alternative to the profane realm of work. Graburn characterizes tourism as "but one of a range of choices, or styles, of vacation or recreation—those structurally necessary, ritualized breaks in routine that define and relieve the ordinary" (Graburn 1989: 24–27, 23).

In a heavily cited contribution to the field of tourism studies by the late anthropologist Malcolm Crick, the distinction between tourists and pilgrims comes under close scrutiny. Crick suggests that tourism may be the name we give to "a contemporary form of an activity that occurs in all societies at all times," which in a prior era may have been labeled "pilgrimage" (Crick 1989: 313). In other words, the terms "tourist" and "pilgrim" may point to an even more fundamental characteristic of human society that involves travel, ritual, and play.

61 Several national soccer teams made a much-publicized visit to the camps during the 2012 Union of European Football Associations soccer championship co-hosted by Poland and the Ukraine. Interestingly the site banned all visitors from wearing soccer-related attire that might invoke nationalist sentiments, and the teams dressed in regular attire. When only three members of Germany's national team visited the site, Dieter Graumann, president of the Central Council of Jews in Germany, scolded the absent team members for missing an important opportunity to reach a wide audience (Dann 2012).

62 There are other ways to invoke the formula, however: the tourist versus the student (Pollock 2003), the tourist versus the sophisticated traveler (Boorstin 1992), and the tourist versus the anthropologist (Nash 1996).

63 Crick (1989: 335).

64 "As Chaucer's *Canterbury Tales* suggest, these religious pilgrimages evolved into more than just the pursuit of religious fulfillment. Pilgrim hostels en route to religious attractions were replaced by inns which provided opportunities for entertainment, social gatherings, matchmaking, gambling and illicit activities" (Pearce 2001: 112). See also Crick (1989: 335).

65 See "I Will Survive" (1978); "Dancing Auschwitz" (2010); and Spritzer (2010).

66 Crick (1989: 333).

67 "In 2016, 2,053,000 people from all over the world visited the sites of the former Auschwitz and Auschwitz II-Birkenau camp, which are under the care of the Museum. It is a record in the almost 70-year history of the Museum." ("Report, 2016" 2017: 32).

68 This has given rise to the discussion of a "Holocaust industry," a term that serves as the title for Norman Finkelstein's extremely problematic book on the Holocaust in culture and in politics (2000).

69 *Schindler's List* (1993); Cole (1999: 82–83).

70 Cole (1999: 23), original emphasis. As mentioned in the introduction, for a very thoughtful critique of the place of Anne Frank in Holocaust memory, see Langer (2006a: 16–29). See also Rosenfeld (2011a: 95–139; 2011b: 140–162).

71 "I like to think that I went to Auschwitz with the loftier intentions of the 'pilgrim'" (Cole 1999: 114–115).

72 Cole (1999: 111).

73 Alan Steinweis offers a critique of Cole's book, which he finds a valuable study diminished by its reliance on "many passages seemingly formulated for shock value" (Steinwas 2009: 304). Like Cole, Young sounds a similar but more nuanced warning when he discusses the use of Birkenau in films such as *War and Remembrance* and *Triumph of the Spirit*, which involved the temporary construction of set façades, which to Young "seemed to infect the rest of the ruins, to corrupt them with its fiction. The props threatened to turn all of Birkenau into a movie set, a theme park" (Young 1993: 144).

74 For a closer analysis of such reenactments, see the noted Jewish studies scholar Barbara Kirshenblatt-Gimblett's analysis of Plimoth Plantation (1998). Kirshenblatt-Gimblett describes a symbiotic relationship between the archeological fragments presented in the site's museum and the virtual reality the plantation reenactment generates on the basis of those fragments. The absence of reenactment at Auschwitz-Birkenau is obvious; in fact, it is actively denied to tourists, who neither see nor experience a simulation of selection, forced labor, gassing, cremation, or any of the horrors perpetrated at the camp.

See also Edward Bruner's discussions of New Salem, Illinois, where Lincoln spent six years before moving to Springfield to practice law. Local residents are hired as actors and wear period costume at the site, usually foregrounding scenes of domesticity (Bruner 2005: 127–144). Bruner places tourism in a pivotal position between historical knowledge and folklore at such sites, and while he suggests that tourists come to consume the folklore more than to correct the record, he contends that they do so with some self-awareness.

Kirshenblatt-Gimblett identifies the origin of such sites in Artur Hazelius's open-air museum of Scandinavan life in Skansen, Sweden, which opened in 1891 (Kirshenblatt-Gimblett 1998: 40–41). In Poland, the word *skansen* has become a generic term for such open-air ethnographic tourist destinations, although reenactment in the manner of living history sites in the United States is not an essential feature.

75 For a longer discussion of the relationship between Holocaust tourism and authenticity, see Reynolds (2016).

76 A perusal of the responses on the websites *VirtualTourist* (www.virtualtourist .com) and *TripAdvisor* (www.tripadvisor.com) will certainly verify that those who take the time to write about their experiences have thoughtful responses to the visit. On *TripAdvisor*, there are roughly 3,400 reviews of "Excellent," compared to 16 reviews of "Terrible," a factor of 200:1, and the comments insist on the trip's importance for the reviewers. See "Things to Do, Oswiecim" (n.d.); and "Auschwitz-Birkenau State Museum" (n.d.).

77 Shenker affirms this observation, noting that "it is crucial to remember that the work of testimony originates in a primary interpersonal encounter and not only as a media by-product" (2015b: 192). In other words, as much as one should pay attention to the institutional structures that bear on the production and presentation of survivor testimony, the intersubjective, affective dimensions of the person-to-person conversation cannot be overlooked.

78 Thomas Trezise's volume, *Witnessing Witnessing*, emphasizes the centrality of a listener, reader, or viewer to receive testimony. As his title makes clear, Trezise is interested not only in how we listen to testimony, but also in how we can witness the interpretation of testimony. Witnessing is relevant "both to the situation of address wherein a survivor bears witness to a listener, reader, or viewer and the position one may take as a witness to their interaction" (Trezise 2013: 2).

Noah Shenker's *Reframing Holocaust Testimony* (2015b) makes a similar case but also pays attention to the institutional dynamics of scholars, museum curators, and tourists who are also part of the performance and production of testimony.

Gary Weissman similarly emphasizes the intersubjective quality of witnessing, even as he proposes the term "nonwitness" to describe readers and listeners of testimony. His point is not to deny any value in reading or listening but to insist that "in none of these cases are [we] witnessing the actual events of the Holocaust. Rather, we are experiencing representations of the Holocaust, all of them created or preserved in its aftermath" (Weissman 2004: 20). Weissman aims to understand the desire so many have to witness a past that is no longer directly accessible. In proposing the term "nonwitnesses," he appears to downplay the ways we can witness "representations of the Holocaust," which is in fact the focus of his book. While I appreciate his concern for the over-broadening of the term "witness" to describe those who were not there, I would prefer to account for the act of witnessing as always involving two subjects, an enunciator and a receiver.

79 See Bruner, who notes that "the site itself has agency" (2005: 24).

80 Wiesel (1979: 9), as cited in Felman (1992: 5–6). See also the sociologist Annette Wieviorka's work, *The Era of the Witness*, which she marks as beginning with the Eichmann trial of 1961 (Wieviorka 2006: 57).

81 Friedländer (2000) addresses the distinction between the affective possibilities of literature (specifically "tragedy") and the facticity of historiography. Weissman (2004) sees the distinction between factual knowledge of what he calls the "nonwitness" and the affective experience of the survivor or victim as the crucial gap that motivates "fantasies of witnessing" in the present.

82 Shenker's *Reframing Holocaust Testimony* discusses the importance of the video archives that have emerged to preserve survivor testimony and persuasively argues for the importance of the context for producing and viewing such videos, pointing out how attention to administrative dimensions of training interviewers or recording and editing conversations allows for a more critical engagement with such works that allows us to observe the "intersecting narrative structures" (Shenker 2015b: 8) that link history, memory, and witnessing in complex ways.

83 This attention to the affective performance of sharing testimony by survivor is a key aspect of Laub's approach to testimony and trauma through the lens of psychoanalytic therapy. Trezise claims to have a similar concern, which leads him to accuse Laub of having failed to listen adequately to the testimony of a survivor whom Laub recorded for the Fortunoff Video Archive for Holocaust Testimonies at Yale. Trezise singles out Laub, himself a Holocaust survivor, in an especially sharp rebuke of the way in which some scholars have responded to the testimony of others, which leads one to wonder whether Trezise has adequately listened to Laub. See Trezise (2008) for his objection to Laub's quality of listening, and see Laub (2009) for his response.

84 Levi (1996: 9–10).

85 Wiesel (2006: viii).

86 Wiesel (2006: viii–ix).

87 Wiesel (2006: ix).

88 As Wieviorka points out, early witnesses to the Holocaust found their accounts of horror often went unheeded, as the world around them concentrated on recovery after the war. "The rare efforts to bring memory to public attention were largely in vain" (2006: 54). Wieviorka argues throughout her volume that the reception of testimony depends on the political or social conditions in which the testimony is heard. Shenker (2015b) reinforces that notion by calling attention to the institutional structures that procure and present testimony.

89 See Laub (1992a, 1992b). Laub (1992a) comes in for harsh criticism by Trezise (2013), and Laub (1992b) from Agamben (1999).

90 Laub (1992b: 80), original emphasis.

91 Weissman (2004: 94).

92 Weissman (2004: 92).

93 Weissman (2004: 17).

94 Weissman (2004: 101). Trezise opens his book, *Witnessing Witnessing*, with a similar caution about the motivations behind the desire to write and read survivor testimony, which he sees as arising from an anxiety about the loss of direct, lived memory in the near future (Trezise 2013: 1).

95 Weissman (2004: 5).

96 Weissman points out that children of survivors are not necessarily better informed about the Holocaust than anyone else. The experience of growing up with a survivor parent does not inevitably translate into the kind of historical knowledge Weissman distinguishes from experience. "The Holocaust recognized by a survivor's child is not the Holocaust that others learn about through reading and viewing texts and visiting museums and memorial sites." See Weissman (2004: 19, 18).

97 Weissman (2004: 5).

98 In 2007 I was able to participate in a tour led by Bernard Offen of the Podgórze district of Kraków, which the Nazis designated as the Jewish ghetto, and the nearby Płaszów concentration camp. Offen is a survivor of Płaszów, Mauthausen, Auschwitz, and Dachau. He has written about his childhood memories of his neighborhood's life before 1939, its destruction, and the murder of his father in Auschwitz and his mother and sister in Bełżec in his book, *My Hometown Concentration Camp* (Offen 2008). At the United States Holocaust Memorial Museum, survivors sometimes occupy a desk near the main gathering point outside the permanent exhibition to answer questions by visitors.

99 An earlier version of Agamben's discussion and his thoughts on witnessing Auschwitz is in my article "Tourism, the Holocaust, and the Humanities" (Reynolds 2011).

100 Agamben (1999: 33).

101 Since the dead cannot speak, Agamben insists that a new ethics is necessary, one that demands witnessing on behalf of the dead.

102 Agamben (1999: 12).

103 Trezise (2013) and La Capra (2004) fault Agamben for an overly abstracted representation of Auschwitz that universalizes the category of the *Muselmann* (one who was near death) and obscures the diverse experiences of victims and survivors. Trezise faults Agamben for singling out the *Muselmann* as the exemplar for the witness of the concentration camp experience.

   La Capra, a noted scholar of European intellectual history, sees in Agamben's writing a desire "to raise the stakes and 'up the ante' (which is already astronomically high) in theoretically daring, jarringly disconcerting claims"

designed to secure his reputation as a theorist. He also shares the objection to
Agamben's treatment of the *Muselmann* as universalizing and producing an
"overly homogenous view of Auschwitz." See La Capra (2004: 156, 161).

A thoughtful reading of Agamben comes from the art historian Nicholas
Chare, who takes Agamben's theoretical impulses more seriously than La Capra
does but seconds the critique that Agamben bases his theory of witnessing too
exclusively—and unnecessarily—on the *Muselmann* (2006: 44, 66n4).

104 See Agamben's discussion of Foucault in *Homo Sacer* (1998: 3–7, 19) and of
Schmitt, in the same volume (1998: 8–42).

105 Chare writes that the "concentration camp is the materialization of this state,"
referring to the state of exception in which those deemed outside the law are
placed within a zone of exclusion (2006: 44). Agamben himself further elaborates
on this notion in his volume, *State of Exception* (2005).

106 Agamben (1999: 15–24).

107 John Demjanjuk was convicted in 2011 in Germany as an accessory to murder for
his participation as a guard at the Sobibór death camp. In 2014, former SS guard
Oscar Groening was tried on the same charges for his having been in the SS at
Auschwitz. In 2016, Reinhold Hanning was also convicted for being an accessory to murder at Auschwitz. Demjanjuk died while awaiting an appeal to his
verdict; Groening received a sentence of four years at the age of ninety-three; and
Hanning was sentenced to five years in prison at the age of ninety-four.

108 See the historian Rebecca Wittman's book *Beyond Justice* (2005). For a German-
language account of the Auschwitz trials and their import on Holocaust remembrance in Germany, see "Ein Volk von Gehilfen: Der Auschwitz-Prozess, 1963–65,"
by the German historians Thomas Flemming and Bernd Ulrich (2005).

109 Agamben (1998: 7).

110 Agamben (1998: 169).

111 As an example of the enforcement of this policy, visitors in June 2012 were forbidden entry if they wore soccer clothing or other articles that could stoke rivalry
among visitors.

112 Dwork and van Pelt (1996) point out that the visitor has already entered the
"camp" without knowing it, since many of the buildings that appear to lie outside
the memorial complex were, in fact, part of the camp system.

113 The museum complex also includes eleven national exhibitions located in other
blocks at Auschwitz I. Visitors must view these on their own, for they are not
part of the guided tour. A twelfth national exhibition created by Italy in 1980
was closed in 2011 because, as the museum administration explains, it was "not
educational in any way, [and] it failed to meet the basic requirements for national
exhibitions as set by the International Auschwitz Council, which have been in
force since the 1990s." See "News" (n.d.).

114 Bruner characterizes four kinds of authenticity as operative in tourism. The first
is the degree to which a site convinces its visitors that it is true to the historical
record; the second is the degree to which the site would conform to the historical

record and lived experiences of contemporaries; the third is the degree to which a site is original, rather than a copy; and the final sense describes authenticity as the expression of an authority as to the veracity of the site. I concur with his observation that "the problem with the term authenticity, in the literature an in fieldwork, is that one never knows except by analysis of the context which meaning is salient in any given instance" (Bruner 2005: 149–150, 151). I would add a fifth term, and that is "transparency." I argue that Auschwitz is authentic in all senses Bruner articulates except the second—it makes no attempt to replicate the site as prisoners and perpetrators would have experienced it. But the way in which Auschwitz does not claim to be a reenactment and is transparent about what is original and what is reproduction only reinforces the experience of authenticity in tourism.

CHAPTER 2. PICTURING THE CAMPS

1 The photos Sontag (1973) describes as "unreal" are family portraits, which she characterizes as idealized representations. She does not deny the reality of the objects in the photo; rather, she denies the embellished depiction of families that the objects are intended to project.

2 The relationship between tourist photography and ritual is a recurring motif in tourism studies. MacCannell speaks of photography as "sacralizing" its sites (2013: 45). The noted Australian cultural critic Donald Home calls tourists "pilgrims with cameras" (Home 1984: 11, quoted in Harjes and Nusser 1999: 254). Urry and Larsen characterize photography as a "ritual of quotation," which has important implications for the conclusion of this chapter (2011: 8). Robinson and Picard expand the notion of ritual as it pertains to photography to the "full range" of photographic practice "before, during, and after the trip" (2009: 2). And Desmond links photography to the construction of the "ethnographic gaze" (1999: 37–40), which tends to primitivize the object in the lens.

3 Sontag writes, "The activity of taking pictures is soothing, and assuages general feelings of disorientation that are likely to be exacerbated by travel" (1973: 9).

4 The anthropologists Mike Robinson and David Picard write about the importance of tourism as a means for recording the world and sharing it with the "vast majority of populations who essentially remained 'at home.' Here was the educational function of travel as mediated through the texts and images produced 'in situ' and brought back for conspicuous display" (2009: 2).

5 Culler (1990: 2). Culler also writes that tourists are "interested in everything as a sign of itself. . . . All over the world the unsung armies of semioticians, the tourists, are fanning out in search of the signs of Frenchness, typical Italian behaviour, exemplary Oriental scenes, typical American thruways, traditional English pubs" (Culler 1990: 127, quoted in Urry and Larsen 2011: 5).

6 The social psychologist Alex Gillespie examines such behavior in greater depth in developing his notion of the "the reverse gaze." See esp. Gillespie (2006: 344–347).

7 Sontag takes aim at the omnipresence of photography, which takes anything and anyone as its object. "Taking photographs has set up a chronic voyeuristic relation

to the world which levels the meaning of all events" (Sontag 1973, 11). Despite her misgivings about the potentially voyeuristic nature of photography, Sontag steps back from this rather harsh condemnation of photography in her later book, *Regarding the Pain of Others* (2003).

8 Urry and Larsen (2011: 14). To critics who have suggested that he reduces tourism to visual experience, Urry responds by acknowledging the importance of other sensory aspects of tourists' experiences but insists on the "tourist gaze" as an indispensable feature of tourism. The tourist gaze is a concept that describes not so much a privileging of one sense over all others but an articulation of power in a Foucauldian sense, allowing us to describe "power relations between gazer and gazee within tourism performances, different forms of photographic surveillance and the changing climates that the global tourist gaze seems to generate" (15).

9 Brink's study on Holocaust photography is careful not to suggest that viewing such photos is reducible to voyeurism, but she does offer a careful account of how the concerns over voyeurism have led Holocaust memorials to change the nature of their photographic displays over time (Brink 1998: 204–220).

10 In an incisive essay on the problem of dismissing tourism as voyeuristic, Lisle argues that

> making negative judgments about the voyeurism of disaster tourists is too simple. Arguing that voyeurism is wrong not only fails to acknowledge the totalizing reach of both tourism and spectacle, it also fails to account for why people feel the need to gaze upon sites of tragedy *in person*. People are not just repulsed by sites of horror—they are also attracted to them as possible containers of authenticity and reality. And it is this *desire* to visit and gaze upon sites of atrocity that presents a much more complex political problem—one that cannot be dismissed with clean moral judgments. Rather, voyeurism must be understood as a powerful discourse that regulates our consumption of catastrophe, disaster and violence through *both* desire and repulsion. (Lisle 2004: 16–17, original emphasis).

11 As Young has written, "Indeed, of all the dilemmas facing post-Holocaust writers and artists, perhaps none is more difficult, or more paralyzing, than the potential for redemption in any representation of the Holocaust" (Young 2000b: 5–6). I discuss the notion of redemption as it relates to Holocaust tourism at greater length in chapter 5.

12 I am sympathetic to Gary Weissman's sustained critique of scholars who dismiss popular efforts to comprehend the Holocaust while claiming legitimacy under the aegis of scholarship for their own efforts to do so. For example, in reference to criticisms about visitors to the United States Holocaust Memorial Museum, Weissman observes, "By blaming the popular audience, however, we obscure the degree to which this desire for a Holocaust experience of one's own, and for a consequent understanding of the Holocaust that is less historical than 'immediate' and 'personal,' underlies much work done by scholars in the field of Holocaust

studies. What bearing might this desire to know 'what it was like' have on how scholars understand the Holocaust and how this understanding is presented in their scholarship?" (2004: 96).

13 Lisle (2004: 19).

14 As Barbie Zelizer, Cornelia Brink, Janina Struk, and Daniel H. Magilow discuss in separate works, the narrative impulse in assembling sequences of photos applies to pictures taken by Nazis and liberating armies. For Zelizer, a renowned professor of media and communications, the photos taken by the Allies who liberated Buchenwald, Dachau, and other western camps were instrumental in the production of a postwar narrative of collective guilt on the part of Germans (Zelizer 1998: 136–138). Both Zelizer and Brink have argued how the campaign did not produce the desired effect and instead led to a desire to forget, both in Germany and beyond (Brink 1998: 84–92; Zelizer 1998: 162–163). A photographer and writer, Struk discusses how the perpetrator photos taken in ghettos and camps were often assembled into photo albums intended to preserve a soldier's personal memory, but they eventually were published and recontextualized as acts of bearing witness (Struk 2004: 94–98). Magilow, a historian of the Holocaust and of photography, discusses such a series of pictures taken by Heinrich Jöst, a soldier of the Reichswehr with a camera in the Warsaw Ghetto, which have been variously interpreted as complicity with oppression and sympathy for the victims (2008: 38–61).

15 Zelizer (1998: 194–197); Hirsch (2012: 106–107). Struk comments on the recirculation of the same images and concludes, "It seems time to call a halt to the repetitive and frequently reckless use of these photographs out of respect for those who died" (2004: 215)—while reproducing those very images in her own study.

16 Brink discusses the changing relationship between viewers and exhibitors of photos over time, taking into account not only evolving understandings about ethical and historical imperatives but also the changing relationship between viewers and images in an increasingly media-saturated world (1998: 182).

17 The term "prosthetic memory" is the title of the art historian Alison Landsberg's important study on the way historical memory of specific minorities is grafted onto a generalized American collective memory via mass culture. She discusses the Holocaust as prosthetic memory in her fourth chapter (2013: 111–139).

18 Hirsch (2012: 36).

19 Sontag (1973: 147).

20 Weissman's *Fantasies of Witnessing* (2004) probes this desire further and, while acknowledging a gap between expectation and experience, focuses more on what motivates people to seek opportunities for secondary witnessing.

21 The historian Patrick Montague discusses the various efforts to tally the number of dead from Chełmno and concludes that the number is probably higher than 152,000, but early estimates of over 300,000 were grossly inflated (2012: 183–188).

22 Chełmno is not directly accessible by train, although one may take a bus from the nearby town of Koło.

23 On my first visit in 2010, the doors were locked, and no one answered our knocks, despite the sign proclaiming the building open. In 2016, the office was staffed with friendly attendants who provided helpful tourist literature. The existing structures had received fresh coats of plaster and paint, the parking area had been paved with stones, and a new administrative building stood at the northern edge of the grounds.

24 Montague offers a detailed account of the killing operations at the mansion in his well-documented *Chełmno and the Holocaust* (2012: 55–58, 81–82).

25 Montague relays the written eyewitness testimonies of Szlama Winer and Michał Podchlebnik, who were assigned to the Rzuchów forest burial and cremation detail (2012: 96–114).

26 Grzegorczyk and Wąsowicz (2015: 43).

27 Montague (2012: 157–174).

28 Ulrich Baer develops the linkage between landscape photography and some of the more neglected camp memorials, including Sobibór, in his essay, "To Give Memory a Place: Holocaust Photography and the Landscape Tradition" (Baer 2000). His essay was written well before recent excavations that may lead to a more visible memorial.

29 Sontag (1973: 119).

30 Urry and Larsen describe the fulfillment of anticipation as one of the pleasures of the tourist gaze: "Tourists gaze upon places because there is anticipation, nurtured through daydreaming and fantasy, of intense pleasures from gathering experiences that differ from those customarily encountered. Such anticipation is constructed and sustained through a variety of non-tourist technologies, such as film, TV, literature magazines, CDs, DVDs and videos" (2011: 4).

31 See Urry and Larsen (2011: 179, 187).

32 See Urry and Larsen, who note that "tourists are not just written upon, they also enact and inscribe places with their own stories and can follow their own paths" (2011: 193).

33 Sontag (1973: 126–137); and K. Burns (1997: 23). While Benjamin situates skepticism about photography as art in its mechanical nature (1972: 22–26), Bourdieu locates its aesthetic mediocrity in its accessibility to the masses (1990: 129–149).

34 As Baer has also pointed out, though, these concerns about the Holocaust's resistance to representation "are, increasingly and incorrectly, viewed as mere academic concerns" (Baer 2005: 70).

35 See Sontag's discussion of the realization that photographs could be retouched and thus lose their presumed documentary reliability. The capacity for distortion apparently overcame people's hesitation at being photographed, once they realized they could use the camera to produce an idealized self-image. "The news that the camera could lie made getting photographed much more popular" (1973: 85).

36 My search of "Chelmno nad Nerem" on *Flickr* (www.flickr.com), of "Chełmno Concentration Camp Memorial" on *Google* (www.google.com), or of "things to

do" near "Chełmno, Poland" on *TripAdvisor* (www.tripadvisor.com) on December 16, 2016, yielded no such overtly stylized tourist images.

37 Sontag writes, "They [i.e., photographs] are a grammar and, even more importantly, an ethics of seeing" (1973: 3).

38 Brink discusses the shift away from *Leichenbergpädagogik*, or the pedagogy of mounds of corpses, to other kinds of images in museums and memorials dedicated to instructing visitors about the Holocaust (1998: 200–210).

39 Sontag (1973: 21).

40 See also Zelizer on the problem of habituation to atrocity photos (1998: 213–220).

41 "For photographs to accuse, and possibly to alter conduct, they must shock" (Sontag 2003: 81).

42 Sontag also came to this view in her later work: "Yet there are cases where repeated exposure to what shocks, saddens, appalls does not use up a full-hearted response. Habituation is not automatic." Sontag also insists on the importance of narrative to move beyond shock to understanding: "Harrowing photographs do not inevitably lose their power to shock. But they are not much help if the task is to understand. Narratives can make us understand" (Sontag 2003: 82, 89).

43 See Baer (2005: "Picturing Nothing," 73–75).

44 See the work of the historian and former director of Yad Vashem Yitzhak Arad, whose *Belzec, Sobibor, Treblinka: The Operation Reinhard Camps* provides a superb documentation of the personnel and procedures involved in the Operation Reinhard exterminations (Arad 1987).

45 Arad (1987: 286–298, 322–341).

46 Arad (1987: 390–391).

47 See Lebovic (2014).

48 For more on the controversies over the Sobibór memorial, see Jewish Telegraphic Agency (2015).

49 See the American studies scholar Catrin Gersdorf, who writes:

> I suggest that the landscape of the past two centuries is indicative of a culture's ecological imaginary; i.e., it indicates how a culture (that is, a national, regional, trans-regional community) imagines and then acts upon its imagined relationship with nature. In doing so, I presuppose a conceptual double-existence of landscape: on the one hand, a landscape is an image and idea projected on actual topographies, canvases, celluloid or the digital universe of zeros and ones; on the other hand, landscape is the material expression of images and ideas translated back into the actuality of physical aesthetically enhanced environments. (2004: 35)

50 Kaplan's notion of "unwanted beauty" as generative of a search for deeper understanding is relevant here (2007).

51 As Baer observes of Dirk Reinartz's picture of Sobibór and a similar picture by Mikael Levin of the Ohrdruf camp, "By casting the enormity of the Holocaust within the traditional genre of landscape photography, Reinartz and Levin emphasize that this question of the viewer's position, as belated witnesses to those

originally on the scene of the crime, touches upon all efforts to explain the past, to judge, to mourn, to remember, to learn, to understand" (2005: 68).

52 Tourists may witness, among other things, errors in the information presented to them, which range from incorrect numbers of victims to a failure to identify Jews as the primary group targeted for extermination. At Sobibór, the original memorial erected in 1965 referred incorrectly to 250,000 Soviet prisoners of war as the camp's victims, not Jewish civilians. "About the Museum" (n.d.-c). See also Young's discussion of the original monument plaque at Auschwitz-Birkenau, which misstated the number of victims murdered there as 4 million (1993: 141).

53 Bełżec was in one sense the deadliest camp—only five people are known to have escaped, of which only two survived the war, fewer than any of the other camps. All other deportees, including the death commandos, perished. Arad discusses the estimates of the numbers of victims murdered at Bełżec, concluding that 600,000 is the lowest possible number. He also discusses the five documented escapes from Bełżec (Arad 1987: 127, 264–265).

54 Arad (1987: 371).

55 Gilbert (1997: 209–210).

56 "About the Museum" (n.d.-a).

57 Rosenblatt (2000).

58 Upon seeing the newness of the memorial and museum complex at Bełżec, my travel companions and I wondered about the sources of funding and the site's relevance to Polish remembrance of the Holocaust. In fact, the new memorial resulted from a 1995 agreement between the United States Holocaust Memorial Museum and the Polish government, and "half of the costs related to the construction of the commemoration was incurred by donors from the United States whose names are enlisted on the wall of the Museum's main hall" ("About the Museum," n.d.-a).

59 My search for tourist photos taken of Bełżec after 2004—using "Belzec" on *Flickr* (www.flickr.com), "Bełżec Memorial" on *Google* (www.google.com), "Museum-Memorial at Bełżec" on *TripAdvisor* (www.tripadvisor.com), and "Travel Guide, Bełżec" on *VirtualTourist* (www.virtualtourist.com), all on December 17, 2016—show that the rubble field is the most common motif, while the museum's discrete exterior is rarely in the frame.

60 Zelizer's *Remembering to Forget* (1998) pays close attention to the important ways in which collective amnesia accompanies collective memory.

61 In *Photography: A Middle-Brow Art*, Bourdieu characterizes popular photography as an adherence to social conventions and rules, thereby discounting any subversive or aesthetic ambition. Referring to photography as an "imitation of art," Bourdieu goes on to fault the realism common in popular photography as a sign of its "conformity with rules which define its syntax within its social use, to the social definition of the objective vision of the world; in conferring upon photography a guarantee of realism, society is merely confirming itself in the tautological certainty that an image of the real which is true to its representation of objectivity

is really objective" (Bourdieu 1990: 73, 77). In short, popular photography rein-
scribes social conventions about what can be deemed "real."

62 See Arad (1987: 298, 341) on the numbers of escapees from Treblinka and Sobibór,
respectively.

63 Arad (1987: 298).

64 Works that feature images from Franz's album include scholarly products like
Arad's *Bełżec, Sobibór, Treblinka* (1987) and Sereny's *Into That Darkness* (1983) and
tourist literature like Kopówka's and Tołwiński's *Treblinka* (2007).

65 See Magilow (2008).

66 Gutman and Gutterman (2002: 75–76).

67 Gutman and Gutterman (2002: 74).

68 As Zelizer notes, "Most photographs of the concentration camps were made by
the most organized of documenters—the Nazis themselves (1998: 44).

69 The pictures of prisoners taken at Auschwitz I, showing them head-on, in profile,
and at an angle, are displayed in the exhibition space in Block 6. They were taken
by Wilhelm Brasse, a Polish prisoner at Auschwitz who died in October 2012. See
the obituary by Hevesi (2012).

70 Sontag (1973: 11).

71 Brink (1998: 209–210).

72 Brink suggests that the impossible pull between two opposing subjectivities in
atrocity photos reveals a trace of the Holocaust itself, experienced as an irreconcilable dilemma for the viewer. "Es scheint, als könne der Betrachter diese Bilder
sich nur für jeweils eine Seite entscheiden. Vielleicht liegt in dieser Bearbeitung
des historischen Geschehens, in der die Grenzen der Vermittlung zwischen
Lernenden und der "Sache" sichtbar werden, eine Spur des Geschehens selbst"
(It seems as though the viewer of these images can only pay attention to one aspect at a time. Perhaps this way of processing the historical event, which exposes
the limits of exchange between observers and their "subject matter," reveals a trace
of the event itself.) See Brink (1998: 210).

73 Benjamin, writing in 1931, describes aura as an emanation from a distant time and
place that imbues the classical work of art with its uniqueness; photographs of art
works, by contrast, lack the aura of the original work of art by virtue of their reproducibility: "What is aura? A peculiar web of space and time: the unique manifestation of a distance, however near it may be" (1972: 302). In "The work of Art in
the Age of its Mechanical Reproducibility," written in 1935, Benjamin characterizes the aura as that which seems to emanate from the work of art understood as a
unique object created at a particular historical place and time (1955: 437–438).

   Without conflating the concepts, it is possible to link the loss of aura, which
Walter Benjamin associates with the ability to reproduce original works of art
through photos, and the loss of impact, feared by Sontag and others when we
become too accustomed to viewing the same images.

74 Discussing the repetition of the same iconic images of the Holocaust across
numerous publications, Hirsch sees a sign of traumatic fixation rather than a

working-through of the past. Rather than sensitize viewers to the shock of their horrific images, Hirsch argues that "their repetition in books and exhibitions can be seen as a refusal to confront the trauma of the past. . . . In my reading, repetition is not a homeopathic protective shield that screens out the black hole; it is not an anesthetic, but a traumatic fixation" (Hirsch 2012: 121).

75 See Gutman and Gutterman (2002: 75–76).

76 See Magilow (2008: 38–45).

77 The number of victims at Majdanek, as with the other camps, is hard to discern, but recent research suggests the number may be higher. The Majdanek Memorial lists the number of dead as nearly 80,000, of whom approximately 60,000 were Jewish. See "Extermination" (n.d.).

The United States Holocaust Memorial Museum lists the number of dead at between 80,000 and 110,000 at the main camp alone, with up 130,000 if the subcamps are included, with a total of 89,000–100,000 Jewish victims. See "Lublin/Majdanek Concentration Camp" (n.d.)

78 Arad (1987: 365–369).

79 See Olesiuk and Kokowica (2009).

80 Zelizer (1998: 50).

81 Zelizer (1998: 51).

82 Zelizer (1998: 49).

83 Zelizer (1998: 53).

84 Zelizer (1998: 100).

85 Zelizer (1998: 129).

86 Zelizer (1998: 69–71).

87 One wonders if the insistence on bearing witness played a compensatory role for journalists, who were confronted with atrocity they could not prevent. Zelizer also draws this conclusion, although for her the compensatory role of journalism lay in restoring "some perspective to the horror"—that is, regaining some sense of control over that which was so overwhelming (Zelizer 1998: 71). I would suggest that it also restored a sense of agency in the face of a collective failure to act in time to avert the atrocities.

88 Zelizer (1998: 57, 160–162, 188–189).

89 Urry (1990: 194).

90 Urry argues that tourism is always constructed in relation to other modes of experience. "[Tourism in] any historical period is constructed in relation to its opposite, to non-tourist forms of social experience and consciousness. What makes a particular tourist gaze depends upon what it is contrasted with; what the forms of non-tourist experience happen to be" (Urry 1990: 2).

91 Hirsch develops this traumatic reading of repetition in Holocaust photography in her work on "postmemory," relating it to the role played by family photos among Holocaust survivors and their children. Rather than inure viewers to images of the violence, "repetition connects the second generation to the first, in its capacity to produce rather than screen the effect of trauma that was lived so much more

directly as compulsive repetition by survivors and contemporary witnesses"
(Hirsch 2012: 108).

92 Gillespie (2006: 360).

93 Gillespie (2006: 344).

94 Gillespie (2006: 347).

95 In an insightful article written for the *New Yorker*, Timothy Ryback discusses
the difficulty preserving the hair of victims and the controversial but undeniably
powerful role these human remains play as a form of Holocaust testimony:
> Since then, the human hair has continued to bear witness: on the second floor
> of Block IV, a former Auschwitz barrack, it lies in heaps inside a row of large
> display cases. In the dim light, individual braids, tight knots, and occasional
> elegant waves can be distinguished in the dull, tangled mass. A faint scent of
> naphthalene—the chemical used in mothballs—permeates the still air. As visi-
> tors file into the room and stand before the windows, some shake their heads,
> some look away, some are moved to mutterings of disbelief. Most stand for a
> moment or two in silence, then turn and leave the room. (Ryback 1993: 69)

96 See Gillespie (2006: 354–357).

97 Sontag (2003: 18).

98 Sontag (2003: 82).

99 Sontag (2003: 102).

CHAPTER 3. WARSAW

1 Davies (1982: 2:428).

2 Prior to the establishment of the sealed ghetto, Jews and Poles lived among each
other in Warsaw, as they did in the many *shtetlekh* throughout Poland, encountering one another in public spaces and through economic exchange. However,
it would be inaccurate to speak of a thoroughly assimilated Jewish population
in Warsaw. The philosopher and Holocaust researcher Barbara Engelking-Boni
writes, "Notwithstanding the many assimilated, upper-middle-class, and professional Jews in Warsaw, Poles and Jews generally made up two different communities, and social barriers were hard to overcome. They created feelings of alienation
and remoteness on both sides. The growing anti-Semitism, aggressive publications in the press, anti-Jewish squads, and excesses at universities contributed to
the growing popularity of Zionist and socialist ideas in the Jewish community. . . .
Despite the goodwill of many people on both sides, the gap between the two communities widened and conflicts became sharper in the 1930s" (Engelking-Boni
2003: 47). Part of the prewar divide between Poles and Jews stemmed from the
fact that many of the city's Jews spoke little or no Polish but rather conversed in
Yiddish.

3 The writer Eva Hoffmann provides a concise history of Jews in Poland since
before the eleventh century in her book *Shtetl* (Hoffman 1997: 25–28). The POLIN
museum of Jewish history in Poland also speaks of the "thousand year history of
Polish Jews" ("About the Museum," n.d.-b).

4 Vinecour (1977: 2–5); Johnson (1987: 250–252); Hoffman (1997: 31–35); and Kassow (2007: 19–20).

5 Vinecour (1977: 1–18 and passim); and Webber (2009: 44–45, 141).

6 As the anthropologist Jack Kugelmass points out, the history of other minorities in Poland can also be invoked to obscure the special place of Jews in Poland as "a nearly ubiquitous other at the very core of Polish economic, social, and cultural life" (Kugelmass 1995: 297). Hoffman (1997) portrays the long history of the shared history of Jews and Poles by focusing on the history of Brańsk, a town in the eastern province of Podlaskie near the border to Belarus.

7 Kassow (2007: 18–19).

8 Todd M. Endelman, professor of modern Jewish history, points out that conversion did not necessarily mean a complete rejection of one's Jewish heritage. Ultimately, the Nazis reclassified roughly 2,000 converts in Warsaw as Jews based on their ancestry and sent them to the ghetto (Endelman 1997: 28, 53n1).

9 Kassow provides a superb history of the rise of Yiddishist movements in Poland, which encompassed political organizations such as the General Jewish Labor Bund (called simply "the Bund") and the LPZ (the Left Zionist Party). In contrast, the Judenrat in the Warsaw Ghetto was dominated by Polish-speaking Jews who, at least in Ringelblum's opinion, looked with disdain upon the Yiddish-speaking masses (Kassow 2007: 22–30, 111, 117 and passim).

10 Kassow (2007: 19–21).

11 On the knowledge within the Warsaw Ghetto of the death camps, see Kassow (2007: 285–299); and Johnson (1987: 508).

12 The coalition included the ZOB (the Jewish Combat Organization) and the ZZW (the Jewish Military Union). See Gutman (1982: 236–243, 293–297); and Snyder (2010: 282–292).

13 Judt (2005: 804). Similar numbers are reported by the Jewish Community of Warsaw ("What Is Community?" 2011); the World Jewish Congress ("Poland," n.d.); and the United States Holocaust Memorial Museum ("Warsaw," n.d.).

14 Gutman (1982: 400).

15 See Bruner, whose idea of tourism as performative emphasizes the importance of movement. Writing about Lincoln-themed tourism in Illinois, Bruner writes, "The meanings of New Salem Historic site for tourists are constructed in the performance of the site, as visitors move through the village and as they interact with the interpreters" (2005: 164). Even in places like Warsaw that are not historic reenactments with guides in character, tourists negotiate their pathways, interact with locals, and encounter narratives of the city in guidebooks, guided tours, placards, etc.

16 The main representative body of Jews living in Germany today is the Zentralrat der Juden in Deutschland, or the Central Council of Jews in Germany.

17 Poland today has one of the lowest percentages of foreign-born residents of any country in the European Union, according to Eurostat, the statistical office of the European Union, at about 612,000 out of a population of 38 million in

2015, or 1.6 percent, significantly lower than its Eastern European neighbors the Czech Republic (3.9 percent), Slovakia (9 percent), and Hungary (5 percent). In neighboring Germany, 12.5 percent of the resident population is foreign-born (see "Population [Demography, Migration, and Projections]," n.d.). Poland has numerous ethnic minorities that are Polish-born, including minority Slavic peoples and Jews, but they remain a small percentage of Poland's present-day population, less than 5 percent according to the 2011 Polish census (Główny Urząd Statystyczny 2012: 17).

18 Łysoń (2006: 183, and n.d.).

19 According to data from the World Bank, Poland has enjoyed a consistently positive rate of growth in its gross domestic product since the end of Communism, the only EU country to experience growth during the international financial crisis that began in 2008. See "GDP Growth (Annual %)" (n.d.).

20 Calel Perechodnik, a member of the hated Jewish Police in the ghetto, documents the fate of the nearby town of Otwock, about 23 kilometers southeast of Warsaw's center (Perechodnik 1996: 25–51 and passim). The historian Jan T. Gross's study of the Polish village of Jedwabne, about 140 kilometers northeast of Warsaw, shows that murderous actions against Jews by their Polish neighbors did not necessarily require the authorization of the German occupiers (J. Gross 2001: 80–84).

21 For the source of the epigraph and his detailed description of his experience of the Warsaw Ghetto, see Karski (2010: 312, 302–319). See also Wood and Jankowski (2014: 102–114) on Karski's role as witness to the Warsaw Ghetto on behalf of the Home Army and the leaders within the Jewish underground with whom it had connections.

22 For a detailed account of Karski's meeting with Roosevelt, see Wood and Jankowski (2014: 176–180). They point out that Karski did not offer a detailed account of the ghetto; rather, he discussed the plight of Jews in Poland more broadly, though no less convincingly (178–179). See also Maciej Kozłowski's 1987 interview with Karski, who describes Roosevelt's response to his presentation as polite but non-committal: "Apart from polite generalities, he [Roosevelt] said nothing important, either on Poland or on Jewish questions. He said only that Poland had a friend in the White House and that the Nazi criminals would be punished after the war" (Kozłowski 1990: 93).

23 For more about Jędruczszak, see the obituary published by the Virtual Shtetl, "News: Mieczysław Jędruszczak (1921–2016)" (n.d.).

24 *Shalom Foundation* (n.d.).

25 For more on today's remnant community and its resilience, see Gebert (2014).

26 Gawron et al. (2012: 24).

27 As Kassow notes, "From a postwar perspective, applying such terms as 'public sector' or 'space' to the Warsaw Ghetto might seem problematic and strange. As soon as the ghettos were established, their Jewish inmates had difficulty finding the right words to describe their new reality. Terms that made sense in a normal community took on an ironic connotation in this twilight world, where people

tried to live the semblance of a 'normal' life even as they stepped over corpses in the street" (Kassow 2007: 93).

28 See Young (1993: 172).

29 Despite the isolation, goods were frequently smuggled in and out of the ghetto. Some people managed to leave the ghetto secretly and seek shelter in "Aryan" Warsaw, but as Engelking-Boni reminds us, most inhabitants of the ghetto lacked the means to do so. She also stresses the psychological sense of isolation and abandonment that was only exacerbated by the knowledge that their Polish compatriots lived in better conditions just a few feet away (Engelking-Boni 2003: 50, 49). Tourism cannot replicate the experience of isolation or abandonment that Jews living in the ghetto endured; it can only hint at those experiences through momentary impressions.

30 Young (1993: 175–182).

31 Young (1993: 176).

32 Bruner's attention to folklore about Lincoln at New Salem, Illinois, or the Israeli legend at Masada offers a potent account of the tensions and co-existence in historically minded tourism between scholars and the general public. Rather than disparage lore to the benefit of historical scholarship, Bruner points out how both are constitutive of one another and part of tourism as a performative, dialogic process that is continually rewritten (Bruner 2005: 144, 166–168, 188).

33 "The Warsaw Rising: Was It All Worth It?" (2010).

34 "Concern as Controversial Rightist Party Wins Poland's Election" (2015). See also Diehl (2015).

35 See the volume *Contested Memories* (Zimmerman 2003a), which takes up the changing landscape around Polish memory of World War II generally and the Holocaust more specifically. See also Lehrer's *Jewish Poland Revisited* (2013), which explores the relationship between Holocaust tourism and Jewish heritage tourism and addresses the shifting understandings around Polish and Jewish identity and culture.

36 Rabbi and freelance writer Earl Vinecour provides numbers of Jewish survivors after the war, which decreased after pogroms in Kraków and Kielce in 1945 and 1946, respectively, and again after the 1968 purges (Vinecour 1977: 6). A philosopher, mathematician, and member of Poland's Jewish community, Stanisław Krajewski documents the problems in arriving at a reliable number for Jews in postwar Poland, in part because of the difficulty of defining who is a Jew: "Do we include marginally Jewish Jews? Do we include non-halachic Jews (children with only a Jewish father) and do we include Catholics of Jewish origin, or at least those among them who have some Jewish feelings? . . . On the basis of my experiences, I believe, as do quite a few of my friends, that in Poland today there are more marginal Jews than there are official members of the Jewish organizations" (Krajewski 2003: 292). Figures from the *Statistical Yearbook of the Republic of Poland 2016* (Rozkrut 2016) indicate that there are 2,320 registered members Jewish communities throughout Poland; the Jewish Community of Warsaw has over 600

registered members. But those numbers are far lower than the number of people who identify as Jewish and participate in the community, and some estimates range as high as 30,000 Jews in Poland (Gawron et al. 2012: 11).

37 The continued suffering and loss experienced by Poland's Jews after World War II is a tale that, until recently, has been hard to locate in Warsaw's tourist landscape. Now that the POLIN museum has opened, that story now occupies space in Warsaw's most prominent new tourist destination. The permanent core exhibit, opened in 2014, includes a section on postwar Jewish life and the Communist Party's anti-Semitism.

38 Kirshenblatt-Gimblett (2016), who led the team that curated the core exhibition of the POLIN museum, discusses the way she incorporates the Holocaust and its aftermath in the museum in her acceptance speech for the 2015 Marshall Sklare Award, "An Ethnographer in the Museum." See also *Shalom Foundation* (n.d.).

39 Similar monuments have been in stalled in Kielce and Łódź in Poland and in Tel Aviv, Israel. In Warsaw, the bench appears almost as a sofa, allowing for the installation of an audio system that plays segments of an interview with Karski in Polish. See "Warsaw Unveils New Karski Bench" (2013); and Wood and Jankowski (2014: 239).

40 Wood and Jankowski (2014: 32–34).

41 For a discussion of the "anti-Zionist" purges in Poland and its effects on Holocaust memorialization, see Huener (2003: 169–184).

42 "News: Mieczysław Jędruszczak (1921–2016)" (n.d.).

43 See Lehrer (2013: 12–17).

44 The late historian Teresa Prekerowa estimated the small percentage of Poles who actually helped Jews during the Nazi occupation at 1–2.5 percent (Prekerowa 1990: 74, cited in Zimmerman 2003b: 5).

45 This phenomenon is even more pronounced in Kraków's Kazimierz district, with its many restaurants in Szeroka Street featuring Jewish dishes alongside Polish standards.

46 "Private Tour: Warsaw's Jewish Heritage by Retro Fiat" (n.d.).

47 See Bedford et al. (2008: 186–189); and Lehrer (2013: 32–36, 134–137).

48 See Lehrer (2014: 23–24).

49 Lehrer has studied these figurines and other popular depictions of Jews extensively since the late 1990s. She has edited a collection of critical essays to accompany an exhibition of the figurines that she curated in Kraków in 2013 (Lehrer 2014), as well as a monograph on Jewish heritage tourism in Poland, especially in Kazimierz (Lehrer 2013). In both works, Lehrer pushes past the opposing assumptions that the *Żydki* are either anti-Semitic or innocently nostalgic. See also Kugelmass (1992: 390–392).

50 See Judt (2005: 822–823).

51 Bedford et al. (2008: 8).

52 Stallings (2007: 52–54).

53 Bedford et al. (2008: 83).

54 In contrast, Snyder writes, somewhat hyperbolically, that "Poles beyond the walls of the ghetto lived and laughed" while the remaining Jews in the Ghetto were fighting and dying in 1943 (2010: 290). Snyder quickly adds that some Poles, including members of the Polish resistance, aided the Warsaw Ghetto Uprising, and some even died; however, his main point—that the fate of Jews transpired quite distinctly from the fate of Poles—is hard to find echoed in many guidebooks that portrays both Polish and Jewish suffering as a twin aspects of Poland's victimization by the Nazis. By the time "Aryan" Warsaw rebelled in August 1944, most of Jewish Warsaw had already vanished into the crematoria of Treblinka.

See also the historian Yisrael Gutman, who goes into great detail on the issue of Poles' reactions to the Ghetto Uprising and, in particular, the degree of assistance by the Polish resistance to the Jews of the Warsaw Ghetto in 1943 (Y. Gutman 1982: 401–426).

55 Kugelmass writes, "But whereas Poles see the past as redemption of the present, for the Jews the Jewish past in Poland is unredeemed" (1995: 282). For Kugelmass, the unredeemed past is what motivates Jewish heritage tourism to Poland.

CHAPTER 4. BERLIN

1 Ladd estimates the number of Jews in Berlin in the 1920s as 170,000 (1997: 113). The United States Holocaust Memorial Museum states that 160,000 Jews lived in Berlin in 1925 and that more than 500,000 Jews lived in Germany by 1933 ("Germany: Jewish Population," n.d.).

2 The phrase comes from Arendt's *Eichmann in Jerusalem*, and it has been a point of contention among critics ever since its publication in 1963. Some see in the phrase a diminishment of Eichmann's guilt, as well as that of other functionaries involved in the planning and execution of the Final Solution. The historian Dan Diner (1997) finds in Arendt's phrase a tendency toward universalism, implying that evil can be found in everyone, and it therefore ameliorates Eichmann's guilt. Others, like the independent scholar Stephen Miller (1998) and the late Israeli journalist Amos Elon (2006/2007), defend Arendt and insist that "banality" doesn't mean insignificance; rather, it means the capacity of some individuals to incorporate mass murder as if it were a reasonable state function. I concur with Miller's and Elon's understanding of the phrase.

3 See the tours on offer by *Viator*, a subsidiary of the popular website *TripAdvisor*, e.g., "Berlin Cultural and Theme Tours" (n.d.).

4 Charles Meng's study *Shattered Spaces* (2011) provides a rich comparison of the efforts by Germany and Poland to rediscover and, in many cases, restore traces of Jewish history, both in their respective capitals and in other places where Jewish life once thrived.

5 This is the significance Ladd's title, *The Ghosts of Berlin* (1997), which explores the pivotal moments of Berlin's history through its architectural and memorial presence.

6 See Huyssen, who writes: "There is perhaps no other major Western city that bears the marks of twentieth-century history as intensely and self-consciously as Berlin. This city-text has been written, erased, and rewritten throughout this violent century, and its legibility relies as much on visible markers built of spaces as on images and memories repressed and ruptured by traumatic events" (Huyssen 1997: 59–60).

7 See the historian Rudy Koshar's *Germany's Transient Pasts* (1998a), for an extensive history of the built environment as memorial in Germany from the nineteenth century to the present day. A significant contribution of Koshar's book is that he embeds the discussion of memorialization of the Third Reich in a much longer and more international movement of memorialization without erasing the specificity of postwar German memories.

8 Till (2005: 7, 21–23, 53, 123, 149–150, 196–207, 223).

9 Huyssen's assertion that tourism to Berlin was on the decline after the early 1990s may have been true from the perspective of 1997, but twenty years after his article, "The Voids of Berlin," with many of the construction projects Huyssen documents completed, his contention has proven to be premature. See *VisitBerlin* (n.d.).

10 See Huyssen (1997); and Ladd (1997). The city of Berlin has developed an expansive website portal that provides a good overview of the city's tourist destinations and diversions. See Berlin (n.d.).

11 Some Berliners explicitly resent the presence of so many tourists, who are staying for longer periods of time and are blamed for rising rents in the city (Rogers 2015).

12 Habermas's *Die Normalität einer Berliner Republik* (1995) combines several important essays on the conflicting ideologies behind the desire for normality, insisting that such a notion for Germany must be based on a rejection of the nationalist elements of Germany's past and should instead embrace a multi-cultural European identity (Habermas 1995: 167–188). Koshar also takes up the notion of normality, revealing its persistence throughout the postwar era and endorsing Habermas's understanding of a politics that remembers the good and the bad from its past (Koshar 1998b: 339–340).

13 For a thorough discussion of the origins of the discourse of "normalization" in the Federal Republic of Germany and a review of some of the key episodes in recent history that have invoked it, see Olick (1998).

14 Levy and Sznaider (2006: 23–38 and passim).

15 See Sontag (1973: 110, 167); Seaton (2009: 75–85); and Urry and Larson (2011).

16 Of the nearly 80 million overnight stays booked by foreign visitors to Germany in 2015, most were from other European countries, although the United States is the third-highest source of hotel bookings. China ranks eleventh, and the numbers of travelers from Asia and Latin America have been growing ("2015. Facts. Figures. Destinations" 2016: 10, 23–24).

17 See Levy and Sznaider (2006: 151); and Olick, Vinitzky-Seroussi, and Levy (2011: 36). Huyssen rather disparagingly refers to "the general memory obsessions of the 1990s" (Huyssen 1997: 60).

18 Young (2000b: 7–8, 95–96).
19 Young (1993b: 27–48).
20 Till (2005: 83).
21 Ladd (1997: 96, 240).
22 Ladd (1997: 84).
23 The relationship between tourism and war that Lisle has identified is perfectly il-
    lustrated in Cold War Berlin. This was not some version of dark tourism, a theory
    that focuses on death as commodity. Instead, tourists were drawn to a version of
    life on the opposite side of a border that was portrayed as utterly distinct from
    their own. One could literally enter enemy territory and return (Lisle 2000: 92–97
    and passim).
24 See Huener (2001: 524–525).
25 There were other factors also: the trial of Adolf Eichmann in Jerusalem in 1961,
    as well as the generational challenges by young Germans of the so-called second
    generation to their elders in the late 1960s, particularly in the West, which formed
    part of the international antiwar movement among students in western Europe
    and the United States.
26 See the articles by Cory (1980) and Kaes (1990) on the impact of the television
    miniseries *Holocaust* in Germany. Shandler's *While America Watches*, a history
    of television's role in shaping Holocaust memory, also includes a chapter on the
    broadcast and its critics (Shandler 1999: 155–178).
27 Ladd (1997: 113–114).
28 Something of the same dynamic is at work in Berlin's Jewish Community today.
    See Connelly (2007).
29 A previous camp had operated in Oranienburg from 1933 to 1934 under Ernst
    Röhm's SA (Sturmabteilung); this prior camp was closed after the purge that mur-
    dered Röhm and many of his followers on the so-called Night of the Long Knives,
    which resulted in the subordination of the SA to the SS. See "1933–1934 Oranien-
    burg Concentration Camp" (n.d.).
30 Ladd (1997: 144–147).
31 Ladd (1997: 114). See also "Geschichte" (n.d.).
32 The Centrum Judaicum gives guided tours through the Scheunenviertel neigh-
    borhood. Sites on this walking tour include the foundations of the city's "Old Syn-
    agogue" and Berlin's oldest Jewish cemetery in the Große Hamburger Strasse, and
    the Rosenstrasse memorial. This latter memorial commemorates a demonstration
    by non-Jewish German women whose Jewish husbands had been detained by the
    Gestapo.
33 The Centrum Judaicum credits the chief of the local police precinct, Wilhelm
    Krützfeld, with the protection of the building from the destruction of Kristall-
    nacht. Despite *Gleichschaltung*, or "alignment," it is apparent in this example that
    different state and city entities could diverge in their support of Nazi ideology,
    often with no significant consequences. Krützfeld was transferred to another

post and forcibly retired in 1940, but he was not imprisoned or sent to the front. "Chronology of the History of the New Synagogue" (n.d.).

34 See Bill Rebiger's volume, *Jewish Berlin* (2014), which presents a convenient compendium of Jewish-themed sites in the city, calling attention both to Berlin's Jewish history and present-day manifestations of Jewish life.

35 See, e.g., "Kosher Food in Berlin" (n.d.).

36 "Jews in West Germany" (n.d.).

37 The controversies were covered closely in both the German and Israeli presses. An example of the German coverage of the circumcision debate can be found in an article by Barbara Hans (2013). For an example of the latter, see Ahren (2012); and Jewish Telegraphic Agency (2016), both in the *Times of Israel*.

38 See Ladd (1997: 142–144).

39 "Der historische Ort" (n.d.).

40 "Josef Wulf" (n.d.).

41 Till thoroughly documents the history of the Topographie des Terrors (Till 2005: 63–105).

42 "Timetable" (n.d.).

43 Young (2000b: 115).

44 Ladd (1997: 153).

45 According to the design concept by Ursula Wilms, Nikolaus Koliusis, and Heinz W. Hallmann, "The glass wall 'points from the dark ground into the direction of the sky' and represents the connection between the viewer and the people who, though physical murdered by the Nazi euthanasia program, live on in our not-forgetting and remembering." ("Die Glaswand, 'deutet die Richtung aus dem dunklem Grund zum Himmel hin an' und steht sinnbildlich für die Verbindung des Betrachters zu den durch die NS- 'Euthanasie' zwar physisch getöteten aber durch unser Nicht-Vergessen und Erinnern doch weiter lebenden Menschen." [*sic*]; my translation). See "Tiergartenstrasse 4 in Berlin" (n.d.).

46 Young (2000b: 96).

47 Young (1993: 29).

48 Young (2000a: 48).

49 Young (2000b: 96).

50 "Der Libeskind-Bau" (n.d.); my translation.

51 "Jahresbericht, 2013/2014" (2015: 27).

52 Meisner and Kessler (2011); my translation.

53 See Young (2000b: 178).

54 Young (2000b: 7).

55 Young (2000b: 194).

56 This characterization of the avant-garde recapitulates the line of argument by Peter Bürger in his book, *Theory of the Avant-Garde* (Bürger 1984).

57 See Till (2005: 202).

58 Young (1993: 48).

59 The American studies scholar Andrew S. Gross writes, "Indeed, and international recognizable memorial architecture seems to be emerging, one emphasizing gaps, voids, incongruities and the personal relation to what theorists and commentators have begun to call 'negative' or 'evil sublime'" (A. Gross 2006: 73).

60 Young (2000b: 210–213).

61 The artist, Shahak Shapira, maintains the website, although he has taken down the images for reasons he explains. See Shapira (2017); and Sommer (2017).

CHAPTER 5. JERUSALEM

1 The editors of one of museum's publications explain that, "as part of the Yad Vashem development plan that was launched in the early 1990s, a new museum complex has been built. The complex, tailored to the needs of the present and future generations, is meant to respond to the immense numbers of visitors to Yad Vashem. The complex includes a new Holocaust Historical Museum—where some 100 video screens accompany the exhibit with survivor's' testimonies and original film clips including cinematic diaries that recount the Holocaust narrative—a Holocaust art museum, a pavilion for changing exhibitions, a viewing center, and a study center" (Gutterman and Shalev 2008: 22–23).

2 The museum is a prism-shaped triangular building that pierces the mountain with both ends cantilevering out in to the open air. According to Moshe Safdie, the building's architect, "The triangular shape of the building was chosen in order to support the pressure of the soil over the prism while allowing daylight to enter through the glass room" (Gutterman and Shalev 2008: 25).

3 "What Are Pages of Testimony?" (n.d.).

4 "Hall of Names" (n.d.).

5 In her in-depth study of the museum, Hansen-Glucklich describes how the "healing properties surrounding the landscape, designed by landscape architect Shlomo Aronson, are evoked repeatedly throughout the Yad Vashem complex— for example, in the dramatic and affirmative exit from the museum overlooking the Jerusalem hills" (Hansen-Glucklich 2014: 62).

6 Young (1993: 213).

7 Hansen-Glucklich (2014: 67).

8 Germany's *Neon Magazine* reports a trip to Yad Vashem undertaken by a group nationalistic, xenophobic Germans who expressed doubt about the number of Jewish victims and Germany's degree of guilt in the Holocaust. See Maurer (2017).

9 For a lengthy discussion of the role Holocaust memorialization in the training and behavior of Israeli troops, see Feldman (2008: 202–203, 245–248).

10 In addition to the works of James E. Young, the admonition against redemptory representations finds a strong voice in the works of Alvin Rosenfeld, especially in his volumes *A Double Dying* (1980) and *The End of the Holocaust* (Rosenfeld 1980, 2011c). Another critic of redemptory representations is Lawrence Langer, especially in his books *Preempting the Holocaust* and *Using and Abusing the Holocaust*

(Langer 2000, 2006c). Weissman takes strong issue with Langer's critique of redemptory narratives, and he faults Langer for not acknowledging the sincere motivations for redemptory understanding (Weissman 2004: 96–132).

11 Young (2000a: 5).

12 Young (2000a: 480).

13 Young (2000a: 57).

14 In addition to the books by Rosenfeld (1980, 2011c) and Langer (2000, 2006c), see Hartman (1996); and Hoffman (1997).

15 Cooke (2006: 267).

16 Young (2000b: 6, 196). As a rebuttal to the antiaestheticist tendency in Holocaust studies, see Kaplan (2007), which is a sustained examination of the place of aesthetic experience in Holocaust-themed art and an argument for an acknowledgement of the importance of beauty (variously defined) as an affective dimension of Holocaust remembrance.

17 Young (2000b: 196); and Cooke (2006: 271).

18 See Kaplan (2007: 3–6 and passim).

19 Cooke faults Young for not sufficiently acknowledging the impossibility of purging art of redemption and insists that Adorno himself acknowledged that redemption could not be separated from art (Cooke 2006: 269). Young, however, acknowledges the impossibility of art that purges all of its recuperative capacity, but he highlights the way artworks can still enact the gesture of eschewing their own redemptory tendencies (Young 2000b: 5–6).

20 Cooke (2006: 271).

21 Cooke (2006: 269).

22 Kaplan (2007: 3).

23 Cooke (2006: 278).

24 Cooke (2006: 268–271).

25 Friedländer (1989: 61).

26 See Young (2000a: 44, 57).

27 Friedländer (1989: 61).

28 Friedländer cautions that an overreliance of rationality in historiography may lead to an "undue restraint and paralyzing caution" that fail to account for the emotional dimensions of the event (Friedländer 2000: 11).

29 Kassow (2007: 213, 372–383, 387).

30 Alba (2015a: 19).

31 Alba writes, "The Holocaust, while devastating in scope and reach, was still part of a familiar Jewish story—a story that reached back into ancient times, befitting the traditional Yiddish appellation *der dritter hurban*—the Third Destruction" (Alba 2015a: 95).

32 The theologian Mark H. Ellis develops this idea out of an analysis of the theological interpretations of the Holocaust advanced in the works of Elie Wiesel, the philosopher Emil Fackenheim, and Rabbi Irving Greenberg (Ellis 1990: 6–31). Ellis is attentive to the ways in which the theological justification for the

establishment of Israel depends heavily on understanding of the Holocaust as the result of Jewish powerlessnesss in the Diaspora (19).

33 Young (1993: 260); and Hansen-Glucklich (2014: 60). For more on the secular origins of Zionism and the tension between Zionism and (particularly Orthodox) Judaism, see Gilbert (2008: esp. 9–26, 275–278, 560).

34 Hansen-Glucklich (2014: 56–57).

35 Young offers this incisive comment on the erasure of ambiguity: "After substituting civil religious values like heroism, bravery, and courage for traditional values like faith and patience, the ministers of the civil religion would have all forget that such substitutions were made" (Young 1993: 260).

36 Crick (1989: 313); Graburn (1989: 23–27); and MacCannell (2013: 42–43).

37 MacCannell discusses the evolution of leisure as a cultural production that responds to industrialization, which banished the signifying practices of culture from work (MacCannell 2013: 29–37).

38 See MacKinnon (2009).

39 See Lisle (2000: 93–95).

40 See Tomljenovic and Faulkner (2000: 24–29). They conclude that the degree of enhanced cross-cultural understanding depends on the preparation undertaken by groups prior to travel and the degree and quality of contact with the host population during the journey.

41 Feldman (2008: 244 and passim).

42 Foley and Lennon (2000: 10, 16–21).

43 Foley and Lennon (2000: 62).

44 See Feldman's characterization of "Poland Voyages as National Pilgrimages" (Feldman 2008: 255–258).

45 For example, they regard the majority of "dark tourists" as "those who visit due to serendipity, the itinerary of tour companies or the merely curious who happen to be in the vicinity. " They continue, "To those, the importance of merchandising (and, possibly, personal or authoritative recommendations) to secure an 'impulse purchase' or visit becomes central to the product involved" (Foley and Lennon 2007: 23).

46 Feldman offers the most thorough overview of Holocaust memory in Israel and contextualizes Yad Vashem within that broader development (Feldman 2008: 30–55). Alba offers a very rich account of Holocaust memory in Israel, with attention to the role of Judaic theology (Alba 2015a: 89–134). See also Young (1993: 244–247); Cole (1999: 122–131); and Hansen-Glucklich (2014: 57–60).

47 Young (1993: 211–213); Cole (1999: 123–124); and Feldman (2008: 33–35).

48 As Hansen-Glucklich notes, "A rich literature exists on the instrumentalization of Holocaust memory in Israel for political reasons and on the shifting of memory practices over time. Scholars agree that Holocaust commemoration in Israel's immediate postwar years focused on heroic figures, including ghetto fighters, partisans, and Jewish soldiers" (Hansen-Glucklich 2014: 59).

49 See Wieviorka (2006: 72–73).

50 In her introduction to *The Generation of Postmemory*, Hirsch documents the silence around the Shoah in her own family (Hirsch 2012: 4–6). Art Spiegelman's influential comic *Maus* portrays his effort to record his father's testimony as a survivor (Spiegelman 1986, 1991).

51 Hansen-Glucklich (2014: 57–58). See also Brog (n.d.: 4).

52 Young (1993: 250).

53 Brog (n.d.: 4–5).

54 Mordecai Shenhavi, as quoted in Gutterman and Shalev (2008: 12); the interpolation in square brackets is from Gutterman and Shalev.

55 "Throughout its development, Yad Vashem reflected changes in Israeli conceptions of the Shoah and its relation to the State. In the early years of statehood, Israel saw itself as the antithesis to the Jewish victims who were seen as going as sheep to the slaughter, while it claimed to be the legitimate heir to Diaspora Jewry. This was reflected in the landscape by the proximity of Yad Vashem to the Mt. Herzl military cemetery, along with the separation by a wall, barrier, and circle of trees. These instruct us that we have entered a different world, the Europe of the Shoah, and that Yad Vashem is a foreign land within Israel" (Feldman 2008: 48).

56 McGreal (2005).

57 Cole's visit to Yad Vashem took place in the late 1990s, prior to the new design for the site that opened in 2005 (Cole 1999: 121–122).

58 Young (1993: 250–251).

59 Ellis (1990: 6–15).

60 Cole (1999: 129).

61 Hansen-Glucklich (2014: 58).

62 Young (1993: 258).

63 Young (1993: 53–56).

64 Hansen-Glucklich (2014: 54).

65 Hansen-Glucklich (2014: 53).

66 Hansen-Glucklich (2014: 55).

67 Young notes that, while the type of religiously inflected national narrative Yad Vashem advances is "the traditional prerogative of the state, critical visitors must also retain the right to remark the ways divine authority tends to accrue to a state's institutions" (Young 1993: 260).

68 The cooperative relationship of Yad Vashem, the Auschwitz-Birkenau Memorial and Museum, and the United States Holocaust Memorial Museum includes an apparent exchange of items for display at the various sites. The remote sites in Washington, DC, and Jerusalem exhibit artifacts provided by Auschwitz, and the learning centers exchange information from their archives and engage a common community of scholars as well as tourists.

69 This is ultimately the view expressed by Habermas, for whom "normality" must not come at the expense of collective amnesia (Habermas 1995: 167–188).

70 Feldman (2008: 49).

CHAPTER 6. WASHINGTON, DC

1 For many critics, even the indirect references are too much like a recreation. Thomas Laqueur faults the broadly "Holocaustal environment"—a phrase he attributes to the architect James Ingo Freed that I have been unable to confirm (Laqueur 1994: 30). Freed explained his intentions to avoid replication: "Ultimately I decided that the building itself had to have the flesh and blood of the Holocaust, to have its spirit running through, but somehow not be visible. Nothing reconstructed, nostalgia forbidden, overtly Holocaustal images could not go into it. I would have to develop an architecture that would necessarily be incomplete, caught between the denial of replication and the improbability of invention" (Freed 2012: 15). One wonders whether the architect, in placing his aims for the building squarely at the heart of an irresolvable paradox, invites a nostalgic relation to the event after all. Surely one must examine the architecture in relation the exhibit it houses, which serves to critique the era's faith in industrial technologies "to humanize and improve the world. Well no, not so. It is a normative vision gone sour" (21).

2 Laqueur (1994: 30).

3 As Novick points out, the museum makes recourse to narrative logic in order to historicize the Holocaust. Novick sees in historicity a source of resistance to what he claims are the oversimplifying tendencies of collective memory, which "sees events from a single, committed perspective" (Novick 1999: 4). As I argue below, one of the features of American collective memory has been its struggle to reflect plurality.

4 In February 2017, *TripAdvisor* hosted 6,684 rated reviews of the United States Holocaust Memorial Museum, with an additional 979 unrated reviews. The ratings for the museum were as follows: excellent: 5,356; very good: 982; average: 227; poor: 80; and terrible: 39. See "United States Holocaust Memorial Museum" (n.d.).

5 As Linenthal documents, the placement of the museum in Washington, DC, was not a foregone conclusion, and it remains a source of debate about the "Americanization" of the Holocaust (Linenthal 1995: 57–61).

6 Visitor statistics to Washington, DC's Smithsonian museums are obtainable online at "Visitor Statistics" (n.d.). The United States Holocaust Memorial Museum's annual reports include the number of visitors each year, with the most recent report for 2016 showing 1.6 million visitors (United States Holocaust Memorial Museum 2016).

7 President Jimmy Carter established the commission that recommended the establishment of the museum by executive order, and Congress subsequently donated the federally owned land to the museum commission; however, the museum commission was responsible for raising the funds to design and construct the memorial and to manage it (Linenthal 1995: x).

8 Linenthal explains that New York City was another strong contender for the location of the future museum, largely because the city was home to the country's largest Jewish community. Some members of the commission worried that the

museum's placement in New York City would have rendered it the memorial for American Jews, not for the country as a whole (Linenthal 1995: 57–58).

9 Among those critics who voice skepticism about tourists at the USHMM are Rosenfeld, Novick, and Cole. Rosenfeld acknowledges the educational value of the museum but suspects American visitors will inevitably make recourse to a universalist framework that loses the specificity of Jewish suffering in the event (Rosenfeld 1995: 13–18). Novick examines the tendency at the USHMM to encourage visitors to identify with victims, missing an important lesson about the potential to become a perpetrator and thereby undermining the museum's claim of educational value (Novick 1999: 13 and passim). Cole sees the museum as proof that "the 'Holocaust' is being made in America" (Cole 1999: 148).

10 Shefler (2013).

11 Alba argues that the USHMM actually borrows some of its narrative conception from the Beth Hatefutsoth museum in Tel Aviv (2015a: 32, 70). In general, Alba illustrates how the tendencies so often associated with the USHMM are part of a global system of representation of the Holocaust within "sacred secular space," which invokes metahistorical discourse that transcends any particular national historical narrative.

12 Cole describes a concern for rivalry between Yad Vashem and the USHMM (Cole 1999: 146–148); Novick describes how arguments over the inclusion of non-Jewish victims at the USHMM also raise the question of who "owns" Holocaust memory (Cole 1999: 214–222). See also Linenthal (1995: 52–56).

13 My critique of the use of "American" shares important similarities with Bruner's critique of postmodern theorists of American culture, especially Jean Beaudrillard and Umberto Eco (Bruner 2005: 145–168).

14 Novick (1999: 133).

15 See Kaes (1990: 114–117); and Novick (1999: 209–214).

16 Wiesel (1978). On the viewership numbers, Kaes (1990: 116) states that the broadcast was seen by "20 million West Germans (i.e., by every other adult) in the last week of January 1979." Cory (1980: 444) mentions that the series was viewed by 222 million people worldwide.

17 See Langer (2006a: 16–29; 2006b: 30–47).

18 Novick (1999: 170–181).

19 Novick (1999: 209).

20 Novick (1999: 207).

21 Novick sees a risk in the argument advanced by Michael Berenbaum, project director of the USHMM from 1988 to 1993, who insisted that making the Holocaust important for all Americans would make it more important for Jewish Americans and thus would preserve its memory and importance for Jewish identity (Novick 1999: 207–210).

22 Novick (1999: 11).

23 Novick (1999: 188–190); see also Linenthal (1995: 228–248).

24 Novick (1999: 9).

25 Novick (1999: 11).

26 Linenthal (1995: 44).

27 President Carter used this phrase at a White House Rose Garden ceremony on May 1, 1978, on the occasion of Israel's thirtieth anniversary (Linenthal 1995: 19).

28 Linenthal (1995: 38–41, 45).

29 Linenthal (1995: 49–56). As Linenthal makes clear, the commission's ultimate language did not resolve the matter to everyone's satisfaction. The debates over the definition of the Holocaust and who constituted its victims persisted.

30 Novick (1999: 175–181).

31 See Herf (2008: 11, 15, 20).

32 De Gaulle characterized Israel and the Jewish people as "domineering" at a press conference in November 1967, causing an international outcry (Jewish Telegraphic Agency 1967).

33 See Timm (1997: 49–72); and Huener (2003: 169–184) on anti-Zionism and anti-Semitism in Poland and East Germany, respectively.

34 Also see Huener (2001).

35 The first museum on the history of the Holocaust at Yad Vashem opened its doors in 1973, but other parts of the memorial opened in 1957.

36 Huyssen (1997: 67–72).

37 Rosenfeld (1995: 5, 15–17).

38 Rosenfeld (1995: 17).

39 Cole (1999: 13–14, 177); Weissman (2004: 10); and Hansen-Glucklich (2014: 73).

40 Rosenfeld (1995: 14).

41 Rosenfeld makes this latter point about Styron's *Sophie's Choice* in his book, *A Double Dying* (1980: 159–166).

42 The English professor Hilene Flanzbaum observes that the term is "under fire" because, for some (and here she names Rosenfeld), "it automatically signals America at its worst: crassness, vulgarization, and selling out" (Flanzbaum 1999: 5).

43 See Young (1999: 76–77).

44 Young (1999: 77).

45 "A guard urged us into a gray steel elevator. It, like much of the architecture and design detail, is (as the architect said) 'broadly holocaustal'—an oxymoron if ever there was one. Aggressively solid doors that shut with an ominous assertiveness, industrial-style rivets, the same cramped, claustrophobic quality that would characterize the galleries, whispered ever so coyly of the gas chamber" (Laqueur 1994: 30).

46 Nor is that belief without merit, whatever shortcomings one may find in the value of secondary witnessing. I concur here with Weissman's thesis in his book, *Fantasies of Witnessing* (Weissman 2004), which demands that scholars take more seriously the search by so many individuals worldwide for some authentic connection to the Holocaust.

47 As Young writes, this is the view of Berenbaum (Young 1999: 80). The noted Jewish theologian Alan Mintz acknowledges the museum's "forthright treatment of

America's reluctance to accept refugees and the insensitivity to the fate of Europe's Jews" (Mintz 2001: 32).

48 See Linenthal on the history of the Mall in Washington, DC (Linenthal 1995: 67–72).

49 Gourevitch (1993).

50 Gourevitch (1993).

51 Gourevitch (1995).

52 As observed in chapter 2, the recirculation of the same images from the Holocaust draws attention to addressing photography's role in depicting atrocity, from Sontag (1973), to Zelizer (1998), to Struk (2004), to Hirsch (2012).

53 Cole (1999: 13–14).

54 Gourevitch (1993).

55 Gourevitch (1998).

56 Berenbaum (1990: 20).

57 Berenbaum (1990: 21).

58 Berenbaum (1990: 22).

59 Laqueur (2004: 31).

60 Novick (1999: 9).

CONCLUSION

1 One of the core arguments of Plesch's book is that the Allied governments knew as early as December 1942 that the Nazis had begun exterminating European Jews using gas, earlier than commonly thought and raising important questions about the failure to rescue more Jews from Europe (Plesch 2017: 3, 6, 69–84).

2 Prochaska and Mendelson (2010: xi).

3 Zelizer (1998: 160–161).

4 Marwick (2015: 141–142).

5 Marwick (2015: 137–138).

6 See articles by Durando (2014); Margalit (2014); and Markus (2017).

7 For example, see recent books by Rettburg (2014); and Freitas (2017).

BIBLIOGRAPHY

"1990–1999." n.d. *Auschwitz-Birkenau Memorial and Museum*. http://auschwitz.org.

"1933–1934 Oranienburg Concentration Camp." n.d. "Gedenkstätte und Museum Sachsenhausen." Stiftung Brandenburgische Gedenkstätten. www.stiftung-bg.de.

2014 Inbound Tourism Survey. 2015. The Hague: NBTC Holland Marketing. PDF book. www.nbtc.nl.

"2015. Facts. Figures. Destinations." 2016. Frankfurt: German National Tourist Board. PDF booklet. www.germany.travel.

"About the March." n.d. International March of the Living. www.motl.org.

"About the Museum." n.d.-a. Bełżec Miejsce Pamięci i Muzeum, www.belzec.eu.

"About the Museum." n.d.-b. POLIN Museum of the History of Polish Jews. www .polin.pl.

"About the Museum." n.d.-c. Sobibór Miejsce Pamięci i Muzeum. www.sobibor -memorial.eu.

Adorno, Theodor. 2003a. "Kulturkritik und Gesellschaft." In: *Kulturkritik und Gesellschaft I* (1951). Gesammelte Schriften in 20 Bänden. Vol. 10.1:11–30. Frankfurt: Suhrkamp Taschenbuch Wissenschaft.

———. 2003b. "Was bedeutet: Aufarbeitung der Vergangenheit" (1959). In *Kulturkritik und Gesellschaft II*. Gesammelte Schriften in 20 Bänden. Vol. 10.2:555–572. Frankfurt: Suhrkamp Taschenbuch Wissenschaft.

Agamben, Giorgio. 1998. *Homo Sacer: Sovereign Power and Bare Life*. Translated by Daniel Heller-Roazen. Stanford, CA: Stanford University Press.

———. 1999. *Remnants of Auschwitz: The Witness and the Archive*. Translated by Daniel Heller-Roazen. Brooklyn, NY: Zone Books.

———. 2005. *State of Exception*. Translated by Kevin Attell. Chicago: University of Chicago Press.

Ahren, Raphael. 2012. "Three Months after Circumcision Ban, German Government to Legalize Rite." *Times of Israel*, 2 October. www.timesofisrael.com.

Aitchison, Cara. 2001. "Theorizing Other Discourses of Tourism, Gender and Culture: Can the Subaltern Speak (in Tourism)?" *Tourist Studies* 1, no. 2 (November): 133–147.

———. 2005. "Feminist and Gender Perspectives in Tourism Studies: The Social-Cultural Nexus of Critical and Cultural Theories." *Tourist Studies* 5, no. 3 (December): 207–224.

Alba, Avril. 2015a. *The Holocaust Memorial Museum: Sacred Secular Space*. The Holocaust and Its Contexts. New York: Palgrave Macmillan.

———. 2015b. "A Redeemer Cometh: The Survivor in the Space." In *The Holocaust Memorial Museum: Sacred Secular Space*, 135–185. New York: Palgrave Macmillan.

Am Ende kommen Touristen. 2007. Film, directed by Robert Thalheim. In German.

Anne Frank House. 2015. "Annual Report, 2014." Amsterdam: Anne Frank House.

"Anzahl der Besucher im Ort der Information, 2005–2016." n.d. Stiftung Denkmal für die Ermordeten Juden Europas. www.stiftung-denkmal.de.

Arad, Yitzhak. 1987. *Belzec, Sobibor, Treblinka: The Operation Reinhard Death Camps.* Bloomington: Indiana University Press.

Arendt, Hannah. 2006. *Eichmann in Jerusalem: A Report on the Banality of Evil* (1963). New York: Penguin Classics.

Aschheim, Steven E. 1999. "George Mosse at 80: A Critical Laudatio." *Journal of Contemporary History* 34 (April): 295–312.

Ashworth, Gregory J. 2010. "Holocaust Tourism: The Experience of Kraków-Kazimierz." *International Research in Geographical and Environmental Education* 11, no. 4:363–367.

"Attendance." n.d. Auschwitz-Birkenau Memorial and Museum. http://auschwitz.org.

Auschwitz-Birkenau Memorial and Museum. n.d. http://auschwitz.org.

"Auschwitz-Birkenau State Museum." *TripAdvisor.* www.tripadvisor.com.

Baer, Ulrich. 2000. "To Give Memory a Place: Holocaust Photography and the Landscape Tradition." *Representations* 69:38–62.

———. 2005. "To Give Memory a Place: Contemporary Holocaust Photography and the Landscape Tradition." In *Spectral Evidence: The Photography of Trauma*, 61–86. Cambridge, MA: MIT Press.

Barthes, Roland. 1981. *Camera Lucida: Reflections on Photography.* (1980). Translated by. Richard Howard. New York: Hill & Wang.

Bedford, Neal, Steve Fallon, Marika McAdam, and Tim Richards. 2008. *Poland.* 6th ed. Victoria: Lonely Planet.

Benjamin, Walter. 1955. "Das Kunstwerk im Zeitalter seiner technischen Reproduzierbarkeit." In *Schriften*, edited by Theodor W. Adorno, 1:366–405. Frankfurt: Suhrkamp.

———. 1972. *A Short History of Photography* (1931). Translated by Stanley Mitchell. Oxford: Oxford University Press.

Berenbaum, Michael. 1990. *After Tragedy and Triumph: Essays in Modern Jewish Thought and the American Experience.* Cambridge: Cambridge University Press.

Berger, Joseph. 2016. "Elie Wiesel, Auschwitz Survivor and Nobel Peace Prize Winner, Dies at 87." *New York Times*, 2 July. www.nytimes.com.

Berlin. n.d. "Tourism and Travel." *Berlin.de.* www.berlin.de.

"Berlin Cultural and Theme Tours." n.d. *Viator.* www.viator.com.

Bernstein, J. M. 2001. *Adorno: Disenchantment and Ethics.* Cambridge: Cambridge University Press.

Bianchi, Raoul V. 2009. "The 'Critical Turn' in Tourism Studies: A Radical Critique." *Tourism Geographies* 11, no. 4:484–504.

Boorstin, Daniel. 1992. *The Image: A Guide to Pseudo-events in America* (1962). New York: Vintage.

Bourdieu, Pierre. 1990. *Photography:A Middle-Brow Art* (1965). Translated by Shaun Whiteside. Stanford, CA: Stanford University Press.

Brink, Cornelia. 1998. *Ikonen der Vernichtung: Öffentlicher Gebrauch von Fotografien aus nationalsozialistischen Konzentrationslagern nach 1945.* Berlin: Akademie Verlag.

Brog, Mooli. n.d. "In Blessed Memory of a Dream: Mordechai Shenhavi and Initial Holocaust Commemoration Ideas in Palestine, 1942–1945." Yad Vashem—The World Holocaust Remembrance Center. PDF booklet. www.yadvashem.org.

Brown, David. 1996. "Genuine Fakes." *The Tourist Image: Myths and Myth Making in Tourism.* Edited by Tom Selwyn, 33–47. Chichester: Wiley.

Brown, Robert McAfee. 1983. *Elie Wiesel: Messenger to All Humanity.* Notre Dame, IN: University of Notre Dame Press.

Brownfield, Allan C. 2008. "Jewish Life Revives in Poland as Poles Confront Their Country's Complex History of Interaction with Judaism." Issues of the American Council for Judaism. Atlanta: American Council for Judaism. www.acjna.org.

Browning, Christopher. 1992. *Ordinary Men: Reserve Police Battalion 101 and the Final Solution in Poland.* New York: Harper Perennial.

Bruner, Edward M. 2005. *Culture on Tour: Ethnographies of Travel.* Chicago: University of Chicago Press.

Bürger, Peter. 1984. *Theory of the Avant-Garde.* Translated by Michael Shaw. Theory of History and Literature no. 4. Minneapolis: University of Minnesota Press.

Burns, Karen. 1997. "Topographies of Tourism: 'Documentary' Photography and 'The Stones of Venice.'" *Assemblage* 32 (April): 22–44.

Burns, Peter M., Cathy Palmer, and Jo-Anne Lester, eds. 2010. *Tourism and Visual Culture.* Vol. 1: *Theories and Concepts.* Wallingford: CAB International.

Chare, Nicholas. 2006. "The Gap in Context: Giorgio Agamben's *Remnants of Auschwitz.*" *Cultural Critique* 64 (Autumn): 40–68.

Charlesworth, Andrew. 1994. "Contesting Places of Memory: The Case of Auschwitz." *Environment and Planning D: Society and Space* 12 (July 14): 579–593.

"Chronology of the History of the New Synagogue." n.d. Centrum Judaicum. www .centrumjudaicum.de.

Cohen, Eric. 1979. "A Phenomenology of Tourist Experiences." *Sociology* 13 (May): 179–201.

Cole, Tim. 1999. *Selling the Holocaust: From Auschwitz to Schindler: How History Is Bought, Packaged, and Sold.* New York: Routledge.

"Concern as Controversial Rightist Party Wins Poland's Election." 2015. *Times of Israel,* 26 October. www.timesofisrael.com.

Connelly, Kate. 2007. "Berlin's Jews Face Split after Dispute over Russian Influx." *Guardian,* 16 April. www.theguardian.com.

Cooke, Maeve. 2006. "The Ethics of Post-Holocaust Art: Reflection on Redemption and Representation." *German Life and Letters* 59, no. 2 (April): 266–279.

Cory, Mark. 1980. "Some Reflections on NBC's Film *Holocaust*." *German Quarterly* 53, no. 4 (November): 444–451.

Crick, Malcolm. 1989. "Representations of International Tourism in the Social Sciences: Sun, Sex, Sights, Savings, and Servility." *Annual Review of Anthropology* 18:307–344.

Crouch, David, and Nina Lübbren, eds. 2003. *Visual Culture and Tourism*. New York: Berg.

Culler, Jonathan. 1990. "Semiotics of Tourism." *American Journal of Semiotics* 1, nos. 1/2:127–140.

"Dancing Auschwitz." 2010. Filmed by Jane Korman. 3 parts. Part 1: "I Will Survive Auschwitz." *YouTube*. Posted by recon1s14. https://www.youtube.com/watch?v=cFzNBzKTS4I.

Dann, Uzi. 2012. "Ahead of Euro in Poland, Top Teams Visit Auschwitz Death Camp." *Haaretz*, 5 June. www.haaretz.com.

Davies, Norman. 1982. *God's Playground: A History of Poland in Two Volumes*. New York: Columbia University Press.

Dean, Carolyn J. 2003. "Empathy, Pornography, and Suffering." *differences: A Journal of Feminist Cultural Studies* 14, no. 1:88–124.

———. 2004. *The Fragility of Empathy after the Holocaust*. Ithaca, NY: Cornell University Press.

———. 2010. *Aversion and Erasure: The Fate of the Victim after the Holocaust*. Ithaca, NY: Cornell University Press.

"Der historische Ort." n.d. Haus der Wannsee-Konferenz. www.ghwk.de.

"Der Libeskind-Bau." n.d. Jüdisches Museum Berlin. www.jmberlin.de.

Desmond, Jane C. 1999. *Staging Tourism: Bodies on Display from Waikiki to Sea World*. Chicago: University of Chicago Press.

Diamond, Denis. 1983. "Elie Wiesel: Reconciling the Irreconcilable." *World Literature Today* 57, no. 2:228–233.

The Diary of Anne Frank. 1959. Film, directed by George Stevens. Los Angeles: Twentieth Century Fox.

Diehl, Jackson. 2015. "Poland's Disturbing Shift to the Right." *Washington Post*, 29 November. www.washingtonpost.com.

Diner, Dan. 1997. "Hannah Arendt Reconsidered: On the Banal and the Evil in Her Holocaust Narrative." Translated by Rita Bashaw. *New German Critique* 71 (Spring/Summer): 177–190.

"Displaced Persons." n.d. United States Holocaust Memorial Museum. www.ushmm.org.

Döblin, Alfred. 1965. *Berlin Alexanderplatz: Die Geschichte von Franz Biberkopf* (1929). Berlin: Deutscher Taschenbuch Verlag.

Dreisbach, Tom. 2009. "Transatlantic Broadcasts: *Holocaust* in America and West Germany." *Penn History Review* 16, no. 2:76–97.

Durando, Jessica. 2014. "Auschwitz Selfie Girl Defends Actions." *USA Today*, 23 July. www.usatoday.com.

Dwork, Debórah, and Robert Jan van Pelt. 1996. *Auschwitz: 1270 to the Present*. New York: Norton.

Ellis, Marc H. 1990. *Beyond Innocence and Redemption: Confronting the Holocaust and Israeli Power*. New York: Harper & Row.

Elon, Amos. 2006/2007. "The Excommunication of Hannah Arendt." *World Policy Journal* 23, no. 4:93–102.

Endelman, Todd M. 1997. "Jewish Converts in Nineteenth-Century Warsaw: A Quantitative Analysis." *Jewish Social Studies*, n.s., 4:28–59.

Engelking-Boni, Barbara. 2003. "Psychological Distance between Poles and Jews in Nazi-Occupied Warsaw." In *Contested Memories: Poles and Jews during the Holocaust and Its Aftermath*, edited by Joshua D. Zimmerman, 47–53. New Brunswick, NJ: Rutgers University Press.

"Extermination." n.d. Majdanek Miejsce Pamięci i Muzeum. www.majdanek.eu.

Feldman, Jackie. 2008. *Above the Death Pits, Beneath the Flag: Youth Voyages to Poland and the Performance of Israeli National Identity*. New York: Berghahn Books.

Felman, Shoshana. 1992. "Education and Crisis, or the Vicissitudes of Teaching." In *Testimony: Crises of Witnessing in Literature, Psychoanalysis, and History*, by Shoshana Felman and Dori Laub, 1–56. New York: Routledge.

Finkelstein, Norman. 2000. *The Holocaust Industry: Reflections on the Exploitation of Jewish Suffering*. New York: Verso.

Flanzbaum, Hilene. 1999. "Introduction. " In *The Americanization of the Holocaust*, edited by Hilene Flanzbaum, 1–17. Baltimore: Johns Hopkins University Press.

Flemming, Thomas, and Bernd Ulrich. 2005. "Ein Volk von Gehilfen: Der Auschwitz-Prozess, 1963–65." In *Vor Gericht: Deutsche Prozesse in Ost und West nach 1945*, 110–129. Berlin: Be.bra-Verlag.

Foley, Malcolm, and J. John Lennon. 2000. *Dark Tourism: The Attraction of Death and Disaster*. New York: Continuum.

———. 2007. "JFK and Dark Tourism: A Fascination with Assassination." *International Journal of Heritage Studies* 2, no. 4:198–211.

Frank, Anne. 1998. *The Diary of a Young Girl*. Edited by Otto H. Frank and Mirjam Pressler (1947). New York: Penguin Books.

Freed, James Ingo. 2012. *An Architect's Journey: Designing the United States Holocaust Memorial Museum*. Edited by Janet Adams Strong. [Cranford, NJ]: Piloti Press.

Freitas, Donna. 2017. *The Happiness Effect. How Social Media Is Driving A Generation to Appear Perfect at Any Cost*. New York: Oxford University Press.

Friedberg, Anne. 1999. *The Virtual Window: From Alberti to Microsoft*. Cambridge, MA: MIT Press.

Friedländer, Saul. 1989. "The 'Final Solution': On the Unease in Historical Interpretation." *History and Memory* 1, no. 2:61–76.

———. 1992. "Introduction." In *Probing the Limits of Representation: Nazism and the "Final Solution,"* edited by Saul Friedländer, 1–21. Cambridge, MA: Harvard University Press.

———. 2000. "History, Memory and the Historian: Dilemmas and Responsibilities." *New German Critique* 80:3–15.

Der Führer schenkt den Juden eine Stadt. 1944. Short film, directed by Kurt Gerron. Prague, Nazi Germany: Aktualita.

Gawron, Edyta, et al., eds. 2012. *Field Guide to Jewish Warsaw and Kraków.* Warsaw: Taube Foundation for the Renewal of Jewish Life in Poland.

Gay, Peter. 2001. *Weimar Culture: The Outsider as Insider.* 1968. New York: Norton.

"GDP Growth (Annual %)." n.d. World Bank. www.worldbank.org.

Gebert, Konstanty. 2014. "How to Live When You Are Not the Last." In *Deep Roots and New Branches. Personal Essays on the Rebirth of Jewish Life in Poland since 1989,* edited by Shana Penn. Warsaw: Taube Foundation for Jewish Life and Culture.

Geertz, Clifford. 1973. *The Interpretation of Cultures: Selected Essays.* New York: Basic Books.

———. 1984. "Anti Anti-relativism." *American Anthropologist,* n.s., 86, no. 2 (June): 263–278.

"Germany: Jewish Population." n.d. United States Holocaust Memorial Museum. www .ushmm.org.

Gersdorf, Catrin. 2004. "History, Technology, Ecology: Conceptualizing the Cultural Function of Landscape." *Icon* 10:34–52.

"Geschichte." n.d. Centrum Judaicum. www.centrumjudaicum.de.

Gilbert, Martin. 1997. *Holocaust Journey: Travelling in Search of the Past.* New York: Columbia University Press.

———. 2008. *Israel: A History.* New York: Harper Perennial.

Gillespie, Alex. 2006. "Tourist Photography and the Reverse Gaze." *Ethos* 34, no. 3:343–366.

Główny Urząd Statystyczny. *Wyniki Narodowego Spisu Powszechnego Ludności i Mieszkań, 2011.* 2012. PDF book. http://stat.gov.pl.

Goffmann, Erving. 1959. *The Presentation of Self in Everyday Life.* New York: Doubleday.

Goodrich, Frances, and Albert Hackett, dramatists. 1984. *The Diary of Anne Frank.* Acting ed. New York: Dramatists Play Service.

Gourevitch, Philip. 1993. "Behold Now Behemoth: The Holocaust Memorial Museum: One More American Theme Park." *Harper's Magazine,* July. https://harpers.org.

———.1995. "What They Saw at the Holocaust Museum." *New York Times Magazine,* 12 February.

———. 1998. *We Wish to Inform You That Tomorrow We Will Be Killed with Our Families.* New York: Picador.

Graburn, Nelson H. H. 1989. "Tourism: The Sacred Journey." In *Hosts and Guests: The Anthropology of Tourism,* edited by Valene L. Smith, 21–36. Philadelphia: University of Pennsylvania Press.

Gross, Andrew S. 2006. "Holocaust Tourism in Berlin: Global Memory, Trauma and the 'Negative Sublime.'" *Journeys* 7, no. 2:73–100.

Gross, Jan T. 2001. *Neighbors: The Destruction of the Jewish Community in Jedwabne, Poland*. Princeton, NJ: Princeton University Press.

Grzegorczyk, Andrzej, and Piotr Wąsowicz. 2015. *Kulmhof: Death Camp in Chełmno-on-Ner: A Guide to a Place of Remembrance*. Translated by Anna Klimasara. Luboń: Martyr's Museum in Żabikow.

Gutman, Israel, and Bella Gutterman, eds. 2002. *The Auschwitz Album: The Story of a Transport*. Jerusalem and Oświęcim: Yad Vashem and Auschwitz-Birkenau Memorial and Museum.

Gutman, Yisrael. 1982. *The Jews of Warsaw, 1939–1945: Ghetto, Underground, Revolt*. Translated by Ina Friedman. Bloomington: Indiana University Press.

Gutterman, Bella, and Avner Shalev. 2008. *To Bear Witness: Holocaust Remembrance at Yad Vashem*. Jerusalem: Yad Vashem.

Habermas, Jürgen. 1986. "Eine Art Schadensabwicklung." *Die Zeit*, 11 July.

———. 1987. *Vom öffentlichen Gebrauch der Historie: Eine Art Schadenabwicklung: Kleine politische Schriften VI*. Frankfurt: Suhrkamp.

———. 1995. *Die Normalität einer Berliner Republik*. Frankfurt: Suhrkamp.

Halbwachs, Maurice. 1980. *The Collective Memory* (1950). Translated by Francis J. Ditter, Jr., and Vida Yazdi Ditter. New York: Harper & Row.

Hall, C. Michael, and Stephen J. Paige. 2006. *The Geography of Tourism and Recreation: Environment, Place and Space*. 3rd ed. New York: Routledge.

"Hall of Names." n.d. Yad Vashem. www.yadvashem.org.

Hans, Barbara. 2013. "Cutting Controversy." *Spiegel Online*, 23 September. www.spiegel.de.

Hansen-Glucklich, Jennifer. 2014. *Holocaust Memory Reframed: Museums and the Challenges of Representation*. New Brunswick, NJ: Rutgers University Press.

Harjes, Kirst, and Tanja Nusser. 1999. "An Authentic Experience of History: Tourism in Ulrike Ottinger's Exil Shanghai." *Women in German Yearbook* 15:247–263.

Hartman, Geoffrey. 1996. *The Longest Shadow*. Bloomington: Indiana University Press.

Hayes, Peter. 2004. *From Cooperation to Complicity: Degussa in the Third Reich*. New York: Cambridge University Press.

Herf, Jeffrey. 2008. "An Age of Murder: Ideology and Terror in Germany." *Telos* 144:8–37.

Hevesi, Dennis. 2012. "Wilhelm Brasse Dies at 94; Documented Nazis' Victims." *New York Times*, 25 October, Europe, A29.

Hibbert, Christopher. 1969. *The Grand Tour*. London: Weidenfeld Nicolson.

Hilberg, Raul. 2003. *The Destruction of the European Jews* (1961). New Haven, CT: Yale University Press.

Hinton, Alexander Laban, ed. 2002. *Genocide: An Anthropological Reader*. Oxford: Blackwell.

Hirsch, Marianne. 2001. "Surviving Images: Holocaust Memory and the Work of Postmemory." *Yale Journal of Criticism* 14:5–37.

———. 2012. *The Generation of Postmemory: Writing and Visual Culture after the Holocaust*. Gender and Culture Series. New York: Columbia University Press.

"History of the Memorial." n.d. Auschwitz-Birkenau Memorial and Museum. http://auschwitz.org.

Hoffman, Eva. 1997. *Shtetl: The Life and Death of a Small Town and the World of Polish Jews.* Boston: Houghton Mifflin.

Holocaust. 1978. Television miniseries, directed by Marvin J. Chomsky. New York: NBC.

Home, Donald. 1984. *The Great Museum.* London: Pluto Press.

Horkheimer, Max, and Theodor Adorno. 1988. *Dialektik der Aufklärung: Philosophische Fragmente* (1944). Frankfurt: Fischer Taschenbuch Verlag.

Huener, Jonathan. 2001. "Antifascist Pilgrimage and Rehabilitation at Auschwitz: The Political Tourism of Aktion Sühnezeichen and Sozialistische Jugend." *German Studies Review* 24, no. 3 (October): 513–532.

———. 2003. *Auschwitz, Poland, and the Politics of Commemoration, 1945–1979.* Athens: Ohio University Press.

Huyssen, Andreas. 1995. *Twilight Memories: Marking Time in a Culture of Amnesia.* New York: Routledge.

———. 1997. "The Voids of Berlin." *Critical Inquiry* 24:57–81.

"Integration." n.d. Jüdisches Gemeinde zu Berlin. www.jg-berlin.org.

"Investigation of War Crimes." n.d. Auschwitz-Birkenau Memorial and Museum. http://auschwitz.org.

"I Will Survive." 1978. Sung by Gloria Gaynor. Written by Freddie Perren and Dino Fekaris. On the album *Love Tracks.* Polydor.

"Jahresbericht, 2013/2014." 2015. Berlin: Stiftung Jüdisches Museum Berlin. PDF booklet. www.jmberlin.de.

Jelavich, Peter. 1993. *Berlin Cabaret.* Cambridge, MA: Harvard University Press.

Jewish Telegraphic Agency. 1967. "Criticism Mounts against De Gaulle in France for Attack on Israel, Jewish People." 1 December. www.jta.org.

———. 2015. "Sobibór Memorial Plans Suspended following Protests." *Times of Israel,* 4 June. www.timesofisrael.com.

———. 2016. "German Party Calls for End to Ritual Slaughter." *Times of Israel,* 26 April. www.timesofisrael.com.

"Jews in West Germany." n.d. Zentralrat der Juden in Deutschland. www.zentralratdjuden.de.

Johnson, Paul. 1987. *A History of the Jews.* New York: Harper Perennial.

"Josef Wulf." n.d. Haus der Wannsee Konferenz. www.ghwk.de.

Judt, Tony. 2005. *Postwar: A History of Europe since 1945.* London: Penguin.

Kaes, Anton. 1989. *From Hitler to Heimat: The Return of History as Film.* Cambridge, MA: Harvard University Press.

———. 1990. "History and Film: Public Memory in the Age of Electronic Dissemination. *History and Memory* 2, no. 1:111–129.

Kant, Immanuel. 1974. "Beantwortung der Frage: Was ist Aufklärung?" (1784). In *Was ist Aufklärung? Thesen und Definitionen: Kant, Erhard, Hamann, Herder, Lessing,*

Mendelssohn, Riem, Schiller, Wieland, edited by Ehrhard Bahr, 9–17. Stuttgart: Phillip Reclam.

Kaplan, Brett Ashley. 2007. *Unwanted Beauty: Aesthetic Pleasure in Holocaust Representation.* Urbana: University of Illinois Press.

Karski, Jan. 2010. *Story of a Secret State: My Report to the World.* Washington, DC: Georgetown University Press.

Kassow, Samuel D. 2007. *Who Will Write Our History? Rediscovering a Hidden Archive from the Warsaw Ghetto.* New York: Vintage.

Katz, Steven T. 2005. *The Impact of the Holocaust on Jewish Theology.* New York: New York University Press.

Kirshenblatt-Gimblett, Barbara. 1998. *Destination Culture: Tourism, Museums, and Heritage.* Berkeley: University of California Press.

———. 2016. "2015 Marshall Sklare Award Lecture—An Ethnographer in the Museum: Reflections from POLIN Museum of the History of Polish Jews." *Contemporary Jewry* 36:3–13.

Kopówka, Edward, and Piotr Tołwiński. 2007. *Treblinka: The Stones Are Silent.* Translated by Andrzej Dąbrowski. Siedlce: Muzeum Regionalne w Sieldcach.

Koser, David, and Roan Schmidt. 2009. *Hauptstadt des Holocaust: Orte nationalsozialistischer Rassenpolitik in Berlin.* Berlin: Stadtagentur.

Koshar, Rudy. 1998a. *Germany's Transient Pasts: Preservation and National Memory in the Twentieth Century.* Chapel Hill: University of North Carolina Press.

———. 1998b. "'What Ought to Be Seen': Tourists' Guidebooks and National Identities in Modern Germany and Europe." *Journal of Contemporary History* 33:323–340.

"Kosher Food in Berlin." n.d. *Jewish-Berlin.com.* www.jewish-berlin.com.

Kozłowski, Maciej. 1990. "The Mission That Failed: The Polish Courier Who Tried to Help the Jews." In *My Brother's Keeper: Recent Polish Debates on the Holocaust,* edited by Antony Polonsky, 81–97. London: Routledge.

Krajewski, Stanisław. 2003. "The Impact of the Shoah on the Thinking of Contemporary Polish Jewry: A Personal Account." In *Contested Memories: Poles and Jews during the Holocaust and Its Aftermath,* edited by Joshua D. Zimmerman, 291–303. New Brunswick, NJ: Rutgers University Press.

Kugelmass, Jack. 1992. "The Rites of the Tribe: American Jewish Tourism in Poland." In *Museums and Communities: The Politics of Public Culture,* edited by Ivan Karp, Christine Mullen Kreamer, and Steven Lavine, 382–427. Washington, DC: Smithsonian Institution Press.

———. 1995. "Bloody Memories: Encountering the Past in Contemporary Poland." *Cultural Anthropology* 10, no. 3:279–301.

La Capra, Dominic. 2004. *History in Transit: Experience, Identity, Critical Theory.* Ithaca, NY: Cornell University Ptess.

Ladd, Brian. 1997. *The Ghosts of Berlin: Confronting German History in the Urban Landscape.* Chicago: University of Chicago Press.

Landsberg, Alison. 2013. *Prosthetic Memory: The Transformation of American Remembrance in the Age of Mass Culture*. New York: Columbia University Press.

Lanfant, Marie-Françoise. 2009. "The Purloined Eye." In *The Framed World: Tourism, Tourists, and Photography*, edited by Mike Robinson and David Picard, 239–256. New Directions in Tourism Analysis. Farnham: Ashgate.

Langer, Lawrence L. 2000. *Preempting the Holocaust*. New Haven, CT: Yale University Press.

———. 2006a. "Anne Frank Revisited." In *Using and Abusing the Holocaust*, 16–29. Bloomington: Indiana University Press.

———. 2006b. "Life Is Not Beautiful." In *Using and Abusing the Holocaust*, 30–47. Bloomington: Indiana University Press.

———. 2006c. *Using and Abusing the Holocaust*. Bloomington: Indiana University Press.

Laqueur, Thomas. 1994. "The Holocaust Museum." *Threepenny Review* 56:30–32.

Laub, Dori. 1992a. "Bearing Witness, or the Vicissitudes of Listening." In *Testimony: Crises of Witnessing in Literature, Psychoanalysis, and History*, by Shoshana Felman and Dori Laub, 57–74. New York: Routledge.

———.1992b. "An Event without a Witness: Truth, Testimony and Survival." In *Testimony: Crises of Witnessing in Literature, Psychoanalysis, and History*, by Shoshana Felman and Dori Laub, 75–92. New York: Routledge.

———. 2009. "On Holocaust Testimony and Its 'Reception' within Its Own Frame, as a Process in Its Own Right: A Response to 'Between History and Psychoanalysis' by Thomas Trezise." *History and Memory* 21, no. 1 (Spring/Summer): 127–150.

Lawton, Laura, and David Weaver. 2001. "Nature-Based Tourism and Ecotourism." In *Tourism in the 21st Century: Reflections on Experience*, edited by Bill Faulkner, Gianna Moscardo, and Eric Laws, 34–48. New York: Continuum.

Lebor, Adam. 1999. "A Week in the Life of Konstanty Gebert." *Independent*, 19 June, 18.

Lebovic, Matt. 2014. "At Sobibór: Building in the Heart of a Death Camp." *Times of Israel*, 8 March. www.timesofisrael.com.

Lehrer, Erica. 2013. *Jewish Poland Revisited: Heritage Tourism in Unquiet Places*. Bloomington: Indiana University Press.

———, ed. 2014. *Lucky Jews: Poland's Jewish Figurines*. Kraków: Korporacja Halart.

Levi, Primo. 1996. *Survival in Auschwitz: The Nazi Assault on Humanity* (1958). Translated by Stuart Woolf. New York: Touchstone. Also published as *If This Is a Man*.

Levy, Daniel, and Natan Sznaider. 2006. *The Holocaust and Memory in the Global Age*. Translated by Assenka Oksiloff. Philadelphia: Temple University Press.

Life Is Beautiful. 1997. Film, directed by Roberto Benigni. Santa Monica, CA: Miramax Films.

Linenthal, Edward T. 1995. *Preserving Memory: The Struggle to Create America's Holocaust Museum*. New York: Penguin.

Lisle, Debbie. 2000. "Consuming Danger: Reimagining the War/Tourism Divide." *Alternatives: Global, Local, Political*, 25, no. 1:91–116.

———. 2004. "Gazing at Ground Zero: Tourism, Voyeurism, and Spectacle." *Journal for Cultural Research* 8, no. 1:3–21.

"Lublin/Majdanek Concentration Camp: Areas of Research." n.d. United States Holocaust Memorial Museum. www.ushmm.org.

Lupu, Noam. 2003. "Memory Vanished, Absent, and Confined: The Counter-memorial Project in 1980s and 1990s Germany." *History and Memory* 15, no. 2:130–164.

Łysoń, Piotr, ed. 2016. "Tourism in 2015: Statistical Information and Elaborations." Warsaw: Central Statistical Office. PDF booklet. http://warszawa.stat.gov.pl.

———, ed. n.d. "Tourism in the Capital City of Warsaw in 2015." Warsaw: Central Statistical Office. PDF file. warszawa.stat.gov.pl.

MacCannell, Dean. 2013. *The Tourist: A New Theory of the Leisure Class* (1976). Berkeley: University of California Press.

MacKinnon, J. B. 2009. "The Dark Side of Volunteer Tourism." *Utne Reader*, November–December. www.utne.com.

MacPhee, Graham. 2002. *The Architecture of the Visible: Technology and Urban Visual Culture*. London: Continuum.

Magilow, Daniel H. 2008. "The Interpreter's Dilemma: Heinrich Jöst's Warsaw Ghetto Photographs." In *Visualizing the Holocaust: Documents, Aesthetics, Memory*, edited by David Bathrick, Brad Prager, and Michael D. Robinson, 38–61. Rochester, NY: Camden House.

Maier, Charles. 1987. *The Unmasterable Past: History, Holocaust, and German National Identity*. Cambridge, MA: Harvard University Press.

Maitland, Robert, and Brent W. Ritchie. 2009. *City Tourism: National Capital Perspectives*. Wallingford: CAB International.

Mandel, Naomi. 2003. "Ethics after Auschwitz: The Holocaust in History and Representation." Review of *Beyond Auschwitz: Post-Holocaust Jewish Thought in America* by Michael L. Morgan, *Poetry after Auschwitz: Remembering What One Never Knew* by Susan Gubar, and *Holocaust Representation: Art within the Limits of History and Ethics* by Berel Lang. *Criticism* 45, no. 4:509–518.

"March of the Living: Western Region." n.d. https://motlthewest.org.

Margalit, Ruth. 2014. "Should Auschwitz be a Site for Selfies?" *New Yorker*, 26 June. www.newyorker.com.

Markus, Lilit. 2017. "Holocaust Selfies Are Inevitable If You Turn Solemn Sites into Tourist Traps." *Guardian*, 9 October. www.theguardian.com.

Marwick, Alice E. 2015. "Instafame: Luxury Selfies in the Attention Economy." *Public Culture* 27, no. 1:137–160.

Maurer, Marco. 2017. "Undercover-Reise mit Rassisten. *Neon*, 11 January. www.stern.de.

McGreal, Chris. 2005. "This Is Ours and Ours Alone." *Guardian*, 15 March. www.theguardian.com.

Medlik, S. 1990. "Focus on Eastern Europe." *Tourism Management* 11, no. 2:95–98.

Meisner, Judith, and Judith Kessler. 2011. "Wir sind kein Holocaust-Museum." *Jüdisches Berlin*, 29 September 29. www.jg-berlin.org.

Meng, Michael. 2011. *Shattered Spaces: Encountering Jewish Ruins in Postwar Germany and Poland*. Cambridge, MA: Harvard University Press.

Miller, Stephen. 1998. "A Note on the Banality of Evil." *Wilson Quarterly* 22, no. 4:54–59.

Mills, Stephen F. 2003. "Open Air Museums and the Tourist Gaze." In *Visual Culture and Tourism*, edited by David Crouch and Nina Lübbren, 75–90. New York: Berg.

Mintz, Alan. 2001. *Popular Culture and the Shaping of Holocaust Memory in America*. Seattle: University of Washington Press.

"Mission of the March." n.d. International March of the Living. www.motl.org.

Montague, Patrick. 2012. *Chełmno and the Holocaust: The History of Hitler's First Death Camp*. Chapel Hill: University of North Carolina Press.

Moscardo, Gianna. 2001. "Cultural and Heritage Tourism: The Great Debates." In *Tourism in the 21st Century: Reflections on Experience*, edited by Bill Faulkner, Gianna Moscardo, and Eric Laws, 3–17. New York: Continuum.

Moscardo, Gianna, Bill Faulkner, and Eric Laws. 2001. "Introduction: Moving Ahead and Looking Back." In *Tourism in the 21st Century: Reflections on Experience*, edited by Bill Faulkner, Gianna Moscardo and Eric Laws, xviii–xxxii. New York: Continuum.

Mosse, George L. 1966. *Nazi Culture: Intellectual, Cultural, and Social Life in the Third Reich*. New York: Grosset & Dunlap.

Nash, Dennison. 1996. *Anthropology of Tourism*. Tourism Social Science Series. Oxford: Elsevier Science.

"News." n.d. Auschwitz-Birkenau Memorial and Museum. http://auschwitz.org.

"News: Mieczysław Jędruszczak (1921–2016)." n.d. *Wirtualny Sztetl*. www.sztetl.org.pl.

Novick, Peter. 1999. *The Holocaust in American Life*. Boston: Houghton Mifflin.

Offen, Bernard. 2008. *My Hometown Concentration Camp: A Survivor's Account of Life in the Kraków Ghetto and Płaszów Concentration Camp*, with Norman G. Jacobs. Oxford: Vallentine & Mitchell.

Olesiuk, Danuta, and Krzysztof Kokowica. 2009. *If the People Fall Silent, Stones Will Shout . . .* (unpaginated). Lublin: Państowe Muzeum na Majdanku.

Olick, Jeffrey K. 1998. "What Does It Mean to Normalize the Past? Official Memory in German Politics since 1989." *Social Science History* 22, no. 4:547–571.

Olick, Jeffrey, Vered Vinitzky-Seroussi, and Daniel Levy, eds. 2011. *The Collective Memory Reader*. New York: Oxford University Press.

Oppermann, Martin. 1999. "Sex Tourism." *Annals of Tourism Research* 26, no. 2 (April): 251–266.

"Overall Numbers by Ethnicity or Category of Deportee." n.d. Auschwitz-Birkenau Memorial and Museum. http://auschwitz.org.

Patraka, Vivian M. 1999. *Spectacular Suffering: Theater, Fascism, and the Holocaust*. Bloomington: Indiana University Press.

The Pawnbroker. 1964. Film, directed by Sidney Lumet. Los Angeles: Allied Artists and American International Pictures.

Pearce, Philip. 2001. "Tourist Attractions: Evolution, Analysis and Prospects." In *Tourism in the 21st Century: Reflections on Experience*, edited by Bill Faulkner, Gianna Moscardo, and Eric Laws, 110–129. New York: Continuum.

Perechodnik, Calel. 1996. *Am I a Murderer? Testament of a Jewish Ghetto Policeman.* Edited and translated by Frank Fox. Boulder, CO: Westview Press.

The Pianist. 2002. Film, directed by Roman Polanski. Universal City, CA: Focus Features.

Plesch, Dan. 2017. *Human Rights after Hitler: The Lost History of Prosecuting Axis War Crimes.* Washington, DC: Georgetown University Press.

"Poland." n.d. World Jewish Congress. www.worldjewishcongress.org.

Pollock, Griselda. 2003. "Holocaust Tourism: Being There, Looking Back and the Ethics of Spatial Memory." *Visual Culture and Tourism.* Edited by David Crouch and Nina Lübbren, 175–189. New York: Berg.

"Population (Demography, Migration, and Projections)." n.d. Eurostat. ec.europa.eu.

Prekerowa, Teresa. 1990. "The 'Just' and the 'Passive.'" In *My Brother's Keeper: Recent Polish Debates on the Holocaust*, edited by Antony Polonsky, 72–80. London: Routledge.

"Private Tour: Warsaw's Jewish Heritage by Retro Fiat." n.d. *Viator.* www.viator.com.

Prochaska, David, and Jordana Mendelson. 2010. *Postcards: Ephemeral Histories of Modernity.* University Park: Pennsylvania State University Press.

Prusin, Alexander Victor. 2003. "'Fascist Criminals to the Gallows!': The Holocaust and Soviet War Crimes Trials, December 1945–February 1946." *Holocaust and Genocide Studies* 17, no. 1:1–30.

Rapson, Jessica. 2012. "Emotional Memory Formation at Former Nazi Concentration Camp Sites." In *Emotion in Motion*, edited by David Picard and Mike Robinson, 161–178. Farnham: Ashgate.

Rebiger, Bill. 2014. *Jewish Berlin: Culture, Religion, Daily Life Yesterday and Today.* Berlin: Jaron Verlag.

"Report, 2016." 2017. Auschwitz-Birkenau Memorial and Museum. Oświęcim: Państwowe Muzeum Auschwitz-Birkenau w Oświęcimiu. PDF file. http://auschwitz.org.

Rettburg, Jill Walker. 2014. *Seeing Ourselves through Technology: How We Use Selfies, Blogs, and Wearable Devices to See and Shape Ourselves.* New York: Palgrave MacMillan.

Reuters. 2010. "Polish Bishop Accuses Jews of Using Holocaust as Propaganda." *Haaretz*, 25 January. www.haaretz.com.

Reynolds, Daniel P. 2011. "Tourism, the Holocaust, and the Humanities." *International Journal of the Humanities* 9, no. 3:157–165.

———. 2016. "Consumers or Witnesses? Holocaust Tourists and the Problem of Authenticity." *Journal of Consumer Culture* 16, no. 2:334–353.

Robinson, Mike, and David Picard. 2009. *The Framed World: Tourism, Tourists, and Photography.* New Directions in Tourism Analysis. Farnham: Ashgate.

Rogers, Thomas. 2015. "Berlin is the Post-tourist Capital of Europe." *New York Magazine*, 17 March. http://nymag.com.

Rosenblatt, Shaul. 2000. "Bełżec: The Forgotten Camp."*AISH.com*, 9 August. www.aish.com.

Rosenfeld, Alvin. 1980. *A Double Dying: Reflections on Holocaust Literature*. Bloomington: Indiana University Press.

———. 1995. "The Americanization of the Holocaust." David W. Belin Lecture in American Jewish Affairs. Ann Arbor, MI: Jean and Samuel Frankel Center for Judaic Studies.

———. 2011a. "Anne Frank: The Posthumous Years." In *The End of the Holocaust*, 95–139. Bloomington: Indiana University Press.

———. 2011b. "The Anne Frank We Remember/The Anne Frank We Forget." In *The End of the Holocaust*, 140–162. Bloomington: Indiana University Press.

———. 2011c. *The End of the Holocaust*. Bloomington: Indiana University Press.

Rozkrut, Dominik, ed. 2016. *Statistical Yearbook of the Republic of Poland, 2016*. Warsaw: Central Statistical Office. PDF file. http://stat.gov.pl.

Ryback, Timothy W. 1993. "Evidence of Evil." *New Yorker*, 15 November, 68–81.

Schindler's List. 1993. Film, directed by Steven Spielberg. Universal City, CA: Universal Pictures.

Seaton, Tony. 2009. "Purposeful Otherness: Approaches to the Management of Thanatourism." In *The Darker Side of Travel: The Theory and Practice of Dark Tourism*, edited by Richard Sharpley and Philip R. Stone, 75–108. Aspects of Tourism. Bristol: Channel View Publications.

Sereny, Gitta. 1983. *Into That Darkness: An Examination of Conscience*. New York: Vintage.

Shalom Foundation. n.d. shalom.org.pl.

Shandler, Jeffrey. 1999. *While America Watches: Televising the Holocaust*. New York: Oxford University Press.

Shapira, Shahak. 2017. "Yolocaust." yolocaust.de.

Shefler, Gil. 2013. "Holocaust Memorials Proliferate in Towns Big and Small." *JWeekly*, 27 June. www.jweekly.com.

Shenker, Noah. 2015a. "The Centralization of Holocaust Testimony: The United States Holocaust Memorial Museum." In *Reframing Holocaust Testimony*, 56–111. Bloomington: Indiana University Press.

Shenker, Noah. 2015b. *Reframing Holocaust Testimony*. Bloomington: Indiana University Press.

Shirer, William. 2005. *Berlin Diary: The Journal of a Foreign Correspondent, 1934–1941* (1941). [New York]: Black Dog & Leventhal.

Shoah. 1985. Film, directed by Claude Lanzmann. New York: IFC Films.

Smith, Valene, ed. 1989. *Hosts and Guests: The Anthropology of Tourism* (1976). 2nd ed. Philadelphia: University of Pennsylvania Press.

Snow, Rachel. 2010. "Correspondence Here: Real Photo Postcards and the Snapshot Aesthetic." In *Postcards: Ephemeral Histories of Modernity*, edited by David

Prochaska and Jordana Mendelson, 42–53. University Park: Pennsylvania State University Press.

Snyder, Timothy. 2010. *Bloodlands: Europe between Hitler and Stalin*. New York: Basic Books.

Sommer, Alison Kaplan. 2017. "No More Shoah Selfies: Why the Controversial 'Yolocaust' Project Was Taken Down." *Haaretz*, 27 January. www.haaretz.com.

Sontag, Susan. 1973. *On Photography*. New York: Picador.

———. 2003. *Regarding the Pain of Others*. New York: Picador.

Spiegelman, Art. 1986. *Maus: A Survivor's Tale*. Vol. 1. New York: Pantheon.

———. 1991. *Maus: A Survivor's Tale*. Vol. 2. New York: Pantheon.

Spritzer, Bev. 2010. "'Dancing Auschwitz' Elicits Mixed Response." *Shalom Life*, 15 July. www.shalomlife.com.

Stallings, Douglas, ed. 2007. *Fodor's Poland*. New York: Fodor's Travel Publications.

Steinweis, Alan E. 2009. *Kristallnacht, 1938*. Cambridge, MA: Harvard University Press.

Stier, Oren Baruch. 2003. *Committed to Memory: Cultural Mediations of the Holocaust*. Amherst: University of Massachusetts Press.

Struk, Janina. 2004. *Photographing the Holocaust: Interpretations of the Evidence*. London: I. B. Tauris.

Styron, William. 1979. *Sophie's Choice*. New York: Random House.

"Things to Do, Oswiecim." *VirtualTourist*. www.virtualtourist.com.

"Tiergartenstraße 4 in Berlin: Gestaltungswettbewerb für Gedenk- und Informationsort entschieden." n.d. *Spurensuche*. www.sigrid-falkenstein.de.

Till, Karen. 2005. *The New Berlin: Memory, Politics, Place*. Minneapolis: University of Minnesota Press.

Tilley, Christopher. 1994. *A Phenomenology of Landscape: Places, Paths, and Monuments*. Oxford: Berg.

"Timetable." n.d. *Stolpersteine*. www.stolpersteine.eu.

Timm, Angelika. 1997. *Jewish Claims against East Germany: Moral Obligations and Pragmatic Policy*. Budapest: Central European University Press.

Tomljenovic, Renata, and Bill Faulkner. 2001. "Tourism and World Peace: A Conundrum for the Twenty-First Century." In *Tourism in the 21st Century: Reflections on Experience*, edited by Bill Faulkner, Gianna Moscardo, and Eric Laws, 18–33. New York: Continuum.

Trezise, Thomas. 2008. "Between History and Psychoanalysis: A Case Study in the Reception of Holocaust Survivor Testimony." *History and Memory* 20, no. 1 (Spring/Summer): 7–47.

———. 2013. *Witnessing Witnessing: On the Reception of Holocaust Survivor Testimony*. New York: Fordham University Press.

Triumph of the Spirit. 1989. Film, directed by Robert M. Young. Culver City, CA: Triumph Films/Sony Pictures.

Tuan, Yi-Fu. 1977. *Space and Place*. Minneapolis: University of Minnesota Press.

UNESCO. 2003. "Sustainable Development: Toward More Responsible Tourism." http://en.unesco.org.

United States Holocaust Memorial Museum. 2016. *Performance and Accountability Report, Fiscal Year 2016*. Washington, DC: United States Holocaust Memorial Museum. www.ushmm.org.

"United States Holocaust Memorial Museum." n.d. *TripAdvisor*. www.tripadvisor.com.

Urry, John. 1990. *The Tourist Gaze: Leisure and Travel in Contemporary Societies*. Theory, Culture, and Society. Thousand Oaks, CA: Sage.

Urry, John, and Jonas Larsen. 2011. *The Tourist Gaze 3.0*. Thousand Oaks, CA: Sage.

Vellas, François, and Lionel Bécherel. 1995. *International Tourism: An Economic Perspective*. New York: St. Martin's Press.

Vinecour, Earl. 1977. *Polish Jews: The Final Chapter*. New York: New York University Press.

VisitBerlin. n.d. "Berlin Welcomes Record Number of Tourists and Convention Participants in 2014: 28.7 Million Overnight Stays 25 Years after the Fall of the Wall." www.visitberlin.de.

"Visitor Statistics." n.d. "Newsdesk: Newsroom of the Smithsonian." Smithsonian. www.si.edu.

War and Remembrance. 1988–1989. Television miniseries, directed by Dan Curtis. New York: ABC.

Warf, Barney, and Santa Arias, eds. 2009. *The Spatial Turn: Interdisciplinary Perspectives*. Abingdon: Routledge.

"Warsaw." n.d. *Holocaust Encyclopedia of the USHMM*. United States Holocaust Memorial Museum. www.ushmm.org.

"The Warsaw Rising: Was It All Worth It?" 2010. *Economist*, 31 July. www.economist.com.

"Warsaw Unveils New Karski Bench." 2013. Jan Karski Educational Foundation. www.jankarski.net.

Weaver, David. 2001. "Sustainable Tourism: Is It Sustainable?" In *Tourism in the 21st Century: Reflections on Experience*, edited by Bill Faulkner, Gianna Moscardo, and Eric Laws, 300–311. New York: Continuum.

Webber, Jonathan. 2009. *Rediscovering Traces of Memory: The Jewish Heritage of Polish Galicia*. Bloomington: Indiana University Press.

Weissman, Gary. 2004. *Fantasies of Witnessing: Postwar Efforts to Experience the Holocaust*. Ithaca, NY: Cornell University Press.

"What Is Community?" 2011. Jewish Community of Warsaw. warszawa.jewish.org.pl.

"What Are Pages of Testimony?" n.d. Yad Vashem. www.yadvashem.org.

White, Hayden. 1992. "Historical Emplotment and the Problem of Truth." In *Probing the Limits of Representation: Nazism and the "Final Solution,"* edited by Saul Friedländer, 37–53. Cambridge, MA: Harvard University Press.

Wiesel, Eli. 1970. *A Beggar in Jerusalem: A Novel*. New York: Random House.

———. 1978. "Trivializing the Holocaust: Semi-fact and Semi-fiction." *New York Times*, 16 April. www.nytimes.com.

———. 1979. "The Holocaust as a Literary Inspiration." In *Dimensions of the Holocaust*, by Elie Wiesel, Lucy Dawidowicz, Dorothy Rabinowitz, and Robert McAfee Brown, 5–19. Evanston, IL: Northwestern University Press.

———. 1989. "Art and the Holocaust: Trivializing Memory." *New York Times*, 6 November. www.nytimes.com.

———. 1993. "Elie Wiesel's Remarks at the Dedication Ceremonies for the United States Holocaust Memorial Museum, April 22, 1993." Washington, DC: United States Holocaust Memorial Museum. www.ushmm.org.

———. 2006. *Night* (1960). Translated by Marion Wiesel. London: Penguin Classics.

Wieviorka, Annette. 2006. *The Era of the Witness*. Ithaca, NY: Cornell University Press.

Wittman, Rebecca. 2005. *Beyond Justice: The Auschwitz Trial*. Cambridge, MA: Harvard University Press.

Wolosky, Shira. 2001. "The Lyric, History, and the Avant-Garde: Theorizing Paul Celan." *Poetics Today* 22, no. 3:651–668.

Wood, E. Thomas, and Stanisław M. Jankowski. 2014. *Karski: How One Man Tried to Stop the Holocaust*. Rev. ed. Lubbock: Texas Tech University Press; East Stroudsburg, PA: Gihon River Press.

Young, James E. 1993. *The Texture of Memory: Holocaust Memorials and Meaning*. New Haven, CT: Yale University Press.

———. 1999. "America's Holocaust: Memory and the Politics of Identity." In *The Americanization of the Holocaust*, edited by Hilene Flanzbaum, 68–82. Baltimore: Johns Hopkins University Press.

———. 2000a. "Against Redemption: The Arts of Counter-Memory." In *Humanity at the Limits: The Impact of Holocaust Experience on Jews and Christians*, edited by Michael A. Signer, 44–59. Bloomington: Indiana University Press.

———. 2000b. *At Memory's Edge: After-Images of the Holocaust in Contemporary Art and Architecture*. New Haven, CT: Yale University Press.

Zelizer, Barbie. 1998. *Remembering to Forget: Holocaust Memory through the Camera's Eye*. Chicago: University of Chicago Press.

Zimmerman, Joshua D, ed. 2003a. *Contested Memories: Poles and Jews during the Holocaust and Its Aftermath*. New Brunswick, NJ: Rutgers University Press.

Zimmerman, Joshua D. 2003b. "Introduction: Changing Perception in the Historiography of Polish-Jewish Relations during the Second World War." In *Contested Memories: Poles and Jews during the Holocaust and Its Aftermath*, edited by Joshua D. Zimmerman, 1–16. New Brunswick, NJ: Rutgers University Press.

Zubrzycki, Geneviève. 2009. *The Crosses of Auschwitz: Nationalism and Religion in Post-Communist Poland*. Chicago: University of Chicago Press.

Zuelow, Eric G. E. 2015. *A History of Modern Tourism*. London: Palgrave.

INDEX

ABOUT THE AUTHOR

Daniel P. Reynolds is Seth Richards Professor in Modern Languages in the German Department at Grinnell College, Iowa. Since 2007, he has been researching tourism at Nazi extermination and concentration camps, deportation memorials, museums, and other commemorative sites of the Holocaust. His past publications include articles on modernist, postcolonial, and contemporary German literature and on Holocaust tourism.